THE POWER OF THE WORD

Elisabeth Schüssler Fiorenza

THE POWER OF THE WORD

Scripture
and the
Rhetoric of Empire

FORTRESS PRESS
Minneapolis

THE POWER OF THE WORD
Scripture and the Rhetoric of Empire

Cover design: Zan Ceeley
Book design: Christy J. P. Barker

Library of Congress Cataloging-in-Publication Data

Schüssler Fiorenza, Elisabeth, 1938–
  The power of the word : Scripture and the rhetoric of empire / Elisabeth Schüssler Fiorenza.
    p. cm.
  Includes bibliographical references and index.
  ISBN-13: 978–0–8006–3833–7 (alk. paper)
  ISBN-13: 978–0–8006–3834–4 (alk. paper)

  1. Bible—Influence. 2. Bible—Criticism, interpretation, etc.
  3. Bible—Feminist criticism. I. Title.
  BS538.7.S38 2007
  220.601—dc22
                                2007031009

Manufactured in the U.S.A.

Contents

To

María Pilar Aquino

Kwok Pui Lan

Fernando F. Segovia

R. S. Sugirtharajah

Vincent L. Wimbush

Colleagues and Friends in Transformative Struggles

Acknowledgments

The idea for this book was first conceived in response to the invitation of Rev. Prof Lung-kwong LO, Ph.D., Director of the Centre for Christian Studies, President of The Methodist Church, Hong Kong, and Director of the Divinity School of Chung Chi College at the Chinese University of Hong Kong. I am deeply grateful to him and the Divinity School of Chung Chi College for the invitation to the Chuen King Lectureship and especially for the wonderful time Francis and I had at the Chinese University of Hong Kong and China in January 2005.

Chapters one, four, and five in their beginning stages I presented as the Chuen King Lectures. I especially want to thank my two colleagues, Professors Kwan Shui-man and Wong Wai Ching Angela, for their careful response to my lectures. I hope they will see that I have learned and benefited greatly from their questions and sought to incorporate their suggestions not only in the further development of these chapters but also in that of the whole book.

I am not only grateful to the attentive audience in Hong Kong, but also to those who came to my lectures at St. Mark's Anglican Church in Niagara-on-the-Lake, Canada, at the Universities of Basel, Switzerland, Münster and Berlin, Germany, Claremont, San Diego, Phoenix, as well as Meredith College in Raleigh, North Carolina, and enthusiastically responded to my presentations on parts of this book with many questions and suggestions. My thanks also to the Immaculate Heart Community in Los Angeles, the Jesuit Alumni Association of Arizona, and the Arizona Foundation for Contemporary Theology for inviting me to lecture on the topic. People present at these lectures raised many perceptive questions which have helped to clarify my arguments and test them out in critical discussions. To all those who participated, my heartfelt thanks. I also have learned much from the enthusiasm and keen interest of my students in my course on *Religion and Politics in Early Christianity* at HDS.

The research and completion of this work has been made possible through a sabbatical from Harvard University Divinity School and a Luce Fellowship. I am grateful to the Association of Theological Schools for awarding me this fellowship and I want especially to thank Ms. Lynn Szwaja from the Henry Luce Foundation, Inc. for encouraging this project.

The edition of this text has greatly benefited from the work and suggestions of my research assistant Ms. Margot Stevenson, who took some time out from her dissertation research to polish my grammar and style, to standardize foot-noting, to proofread the whole manuscript, and to assemble the bibliography. I am especially grateful to my colleagues Melanie Johnson-DeBaufre and Joseph Marchal, who have made time in their very busy schedules to carefully read the manuscript. I very much appreciate their critical and constructive feedback which has greatly improved this work.

Thanks are first of all due to Michael West, Editor-in-Chief of Fortress Press, who has supported my work over the years and has encouraged me to conceptualize this volume as a companion volume to my book *Rhetoric and Ethic*. I am grateful to him for being always encouraging while patiently waiting for the manuscript as well as for expediting the publication of it. I also want to thank Ulrike Guthrie for copy editing the work and to Neil Elliot and Carolyn Banks for shepherding the book through the production process.

Finally, as always I am greatly indebted to Francis Schüssler Fiorenza for his love, encouragement, and support in all that I do and to Chris Miryam Schüssler-Fiorenza for the great times we have had together in Madison.

I dedicate this work to my colleagues and friends María Pilar Aquino, Kwok Pui-lan, Fernando F. Segovia, R. S. Sugirtharajah, and Vincent L. Wimbush in recognition for their decolonizing work and pioneering academic leadership. I hope they will accept this token of gratitude and I am looking forward to con-tinuing our collaboration for change in the years to come.

Chapter 1

The Rhetoric of Empire: Introduction[1]

In recent years, New Testament or Christian Testament (CT)[2] scholarship has rediscovered and re-emphasized as an important field of study the power of the Roman Empire and its shaping of early Christian life and literature. In the biblical academy, such studies of the Roman Empire have emerged at the same time as publications on contemporary forms of empire and its exploitations are being widely discussed, including that of the United States as the new empire and globalization[3] as an expression of American imperial political and cultural power. The intellectual context of such studies, moreover, has not just been the renewed popular and academic interest in empire[4] but also the arrival of postcolonial criticism in religious,[5] the*logical[6] and biblical studies.[7] Finally,

1. I have coined the neologism, kyriarchy/kyriocentrism [from Gk. *kyrios* = domination by the emperor, lord, slave-master, father, husband, elite propertied colonizing male], as a synonym of empire in antiquity and modernity.

2. I use the term "Christian Testament," instead of "New Testament," in order to avoid the supersessionist, anti-Jewish implications of the designations "Old" and "New Testament." Christian scriptures include *both* Testaments.

3. See the excellent article by María Pilar Aquino, "The Dynamics of Globalization and the University: Toward a Radical Democratic-Emancipatory Transformation," in *Toward a New Heaven and a New Earth: Essays in Honor of Elisabeth Schüssler Fiorenza*, ed. Fernando F. Segovia (Maryknoll, N.Y.: Orbis, 2003), 385–406.

4. See especially Michael Hardt and Antonio Negri, *Empire: A New Vision of Social Order* (Cambridge, Mass.: Harvard University Press, 2000), and its broad discussion.

5. See especially the work of Andrea Smith, *Conquest: Sexual Violence and American Indian Genocide* (Cambridge: South End Press, 2005).

6. In order to indicate the brokenness and inadequacy of human language to name the Divine, I have switched in my book *Jesus, Miriam's Child, Sophia's Prophet: Critical Issues in Feminist Christology* (New York: Continuum, 1994), from the orthodox Jewish writing of G-d, which I had adopted in *But She Said* and *Discipleship of Equals*, to the spelling of G*d with an asterisk, which seeks to avoid the conservative, malestream association which the writing of G-d has for Jewish feminists. Since the*logy means "speaking about G*d" or "G*d-talk," I write it in the same way.

7. See, e.g., Wes Avram, ed., *Anxious About Empire: Theological Essays About the New Global*

the growing political influence of biblical and other religious fundamentalisms around the world has sparked renewed interest in religion.

Empire Studies as a New Field in Biblical Studies

While the study of the Roman Empire has always been part and parcel of historical Christian Testament scholarship, such studies have often tended either to celebrate Rome's accomplishments as a great civilizing power in the Mediterranean world of the first century CE, or to focus narrowly on the persecution of Christians by the Roman authorities. For instance, in the 1980s a debate ensued in scholarship on the book of Revelation between liberationist scholars who read the book's symbolic language as anti-Roman and other scholars who denied that harassment and persecutions of Christians were at work at the time at all. The latter praised the benevolent cultural impact of imperial Rome for the citizens of Asia Minor, and read the anti-Roman symbolic language of the book as expressing the "resentment" of the author.[8]

The renewed focus of early Christian scholarship on the Roman Empire and its exercise of power has been invigorated by new approaches in the field of classics, such as the study of Roman imperialism[9] and cultural studies of

Realities (Grand Rapids, Mich.: Brazos, 2004); David Ray Griffin, John B. Cobb, Richard A. Falk, and Catherine Keller, *The American Empire and the Commonwealth of God* (Louisville, Ky.: Westminster John Knox, 2006); Richard A. Horsley, *Religion and Empire: People, Power and the Life of the Spirit* (Minneapolis, Minn.: Fortress Press, 2003).

8. For this debate, see, for instance, Elisabeth Schüssler Fiorenza, *The Book of Revelation: Justice and Judgment*, 2nd edition with a new epilogue (Minneapolis, Minn.: Fortress Press, 1998); see especially also the classic work of W. M. Ramsay, *The Letters to the Seven Churches*, updated edition by Mark W. Wilson (Peabody, Mass.: Hendrickson, 2001), which appeared first in 1904. For the more recent discussion see Steven J. Friesen, *Imperial Cults and the Apocalypse of John: Reading Revelation in the Ruins* (Oxford: Oxford University Press, 2001); Nelson Kraybill, *Imperial Cult and Commerce in John's Apocalypse* (Sheffield: Sheffield Academic, 1996); Leonard J. Thompson, however, in *The Book of Revelation: Apocalypse and Empire* (Oxford: Oxford University Press, 1990), argued for no persecution at all.

9. See, e.g., Paul Veyne, *The Roman Empire* (Cambridge, Mass.: Harvard University Press, 1987); D. J. Mattingly, ed., *Dialogues in Roman Imperialism: Power, Discourse and Discrepant Experience in the Roman Empire* (Portsmouth, R.I.: Oxbow, 1997); Susan E. Alcock, ed., *The Early Roman Empire in the East* (Oxford: Oxbow Monograph 95, 1997); Clifford Ando, *Imperial Ideology and Provincial Loyalty in the Roman Empire* (Berkeley, Calif.: University of California Press, 2000); Craige B. Champion, ed., *Roman Imperialism: Readings and Sources* (Malden, Mass.: Blackwell, 2004).

antiquity.[10] It has also benefited from the inspirations of postcolonial biblical studies, which have emerged at the same time in the biblical academy, and their forerunner, liberationist biblical studies.[11] However, like all malestream studies, this new scholarship has seldom engaged or learned from critical feminist studies.

This new research on empire has left its footprints in all areas of early Christian studies,[12] but has been less focused on Pauline studies. These have mostly centered on Paul as a great individual and his religious opponents rather than on Paul's sociopolitical context, the imperial power of Rome.[13] Pauline anti-imperial studies have highlighted the interplay of religion and politics in the emperor cult, identified the imperial cross-cultural patronage system, and elaborated Paul's counterimperial gospel, which is regarded as being patterned after but totally different from the gospel of Caesar.[14]

10. See, for instance, the essays in *Experience in Rome: Culture, Identity and Power in the Roman Empire*, ed. Janet Huskinson (New York: Routledge, 2000); Judith Evans Grubbs, *Women and the Law in the Roman Empire: A Sourcebook on Marriage, Divorce and Widowhood* (New York: Routledge, 2002).

11. See Fernando F. Segovia, "Liberation Hermeneutics: Revisiting the Foundations in Latin America," in *Toward a New Heaven and a New Earth*, ed. Segovia, 106–32.

12. See, e.g., Warren Carter, *Matthew and Empire: Initial Explorations* (Harrisburg, Pa.: Trinity International, 2001); Yong-Sung Ahn, *The Reign of God in Luke's Passion Narrative: An East Asian Global Perspective* (Leiden: Brill, 2006); Richard J. Cassidy, *Christians and Roman Rule in the New Testament* (New York: Crossroad, 2001); Tat-siong Benny Liew, *Politics of Parousia: Reading Mark Inter(con)textually* (Leiden: Brill, 1999); Christopher Bryan, *Render to Caesar: Jesus, the Early Church, and the Roman Superpower* (Oxford: Oxford University Press, 2005). For postcolonial studies of the Fourth Gospel, see: Musa W. Dube and J.L. Staley, eds., *John and Postcolonialism: Travel, Space and Power* (London: Sheffield Academic, 2002); Jean K. Kim, *Woman and Nation: An Intercontextual Reading of the Gospel of John from a Postcolonial Perspective* (Boston, Mass.: Brill, 2004); and for later times, Averil Cameron, *Christianity and the Rhetoric of Empire: The Development of Christian Discourse* (Berkeley, Calif.: University of California Press, 1991).

13. As far as I can see, it has been Dieter Georgi who has inaugurated this work, having been inspired by the conferences on the Theory of Religion and Political Theology, which were organized by the Jewish philosopher Jacob Taubes in the 1980s in Germany. See the Preface to Dieter Georgi, *Theocracy in Paul's Praxis and Theology* (Minneapolis, Minn.: Fortress Press, 1991), VII with reference to Jacob Taubes, ed., *Religionstheorie und politische Theologie. Vol 3: Theokratie* (Paderborn: Ferdinand Schöningh, 1987). For the lack of postcolonial work in Pauline Studies see Joseph A. Marchal, "Imperial Intersections and Initial Inquiries: Toward a Feminist, Postcolonial Analysis of Philippians," *JFSR* 22:2 (Fall 2006): 5–32.

14. For a succinct review see Richard A. Horsley, ed., *Paul and Empire: Religion and Power in Roman Imperial Society* (Harrisburg, Pa.: Trinity International, 1997), 1–9.

Pauline anti-imperial studies take up and seek to complete the "new perspective," which is associated with Krister Stendahl[15] and E. P. Sanders,[16] and which has deconstructed the primarily Lutheran understanding of Paul by arguing that Paul was not the first great Christian the*logian who converted from Judaism to Christianity. While affirming the "new perspective," the anti-imperial approach rightly argues that this perspective still views Paul too much in terms of religious categories and thus perpetuates the modern separation of religion from politics.

These new Christian Testament studies of the Roman Empire have often sought to rehabilitate Christian writings, rather than proceeding in a self-critical fashion.[17] Studies of the gospels, the Pauline literature, or other writings, which examine their attitude toward the Roman Empire, have tended to argue that these were critical of Roman imperial power and resisted its structures of domination because they were written by subordinate and marginalized people. However, such historical arguments overlook that even resistance literature will re-inscribe the structures of domination against which it seeks to argue. A historical reading, which places the Roman Empire and early Christian writings alongside each other, ends up using the Roman Empire and its power as a foil, in order to underscore the non-imperial meaning of the lordship of Christ and the rulership of G*d. By claiming that the gospel of Paul is counter-imperial, such a reading is no longer compelled to inquire as to how such inscribed imperial language functioned in the past, and still functions today, and what this type of language does to readers who submit to its world of vision.

---

15. See Krister Stendahl, "The Apostle Paul and the Introspective Conscience of the West," *HTR* 56 (1963): 199–215.

16. E. P. Sanders, *Paul and Palestinian Judaism: A Comparison of Patterns of Religion* (Philadelphia, Pa.: Fortress Press, 1977).

17. See, for instance, the extensive work of Richard Horsley who deserves credit for revitalizing Early Christian empire studies, but tends to frame his discussion of Paul and Jesus in a rehabilitative fashion, arguing that both were subalterns critical of Roman imperial power. See Horsley, *Jesus and Empire: The Kingdom of God and the New World Disorder* (Minneapolis, Minn.: Fortress Press, 2002); Horsley, "Feminist Scholarship and Postcolonial Criticism: Subverting Imperial Discourse and Reclaiming Submerged Histories," in *Walk in the Ways of Wisdom: Essays in Honor of Elisabeth Schüssler Fiorenza*, eds. Shelly Matthews, Cynthia Briggs Kittredge, Melanie Johnson-DeBaufre (Harrisburg: Trinity International, 2003), 297–317; Horsley, "Subverting Disciplines: The Possibilities and Limitations of Postcolonial Theory for New Testament Studies," in *Toward a New Heaven and a New Earth*, ed. Segovia (Maryknoll: Orbis, 2003), 90–105.

Hence, feminist critics have pointed out that the anti-imperial approach, like the "new perspective," still remains within the traditional Protestant paradigm, which uncritically accepts Paul's rhetorical self-construction and continues to celebrate Paul as an heroic individual[18] and great the*logian, but now no longer constructs him over and against Judaism but over and against the political domination and religious paganism of the Roman Empire.[19]

Moreover, in order to sustain this anti-imperial interpretation of Paul, scholars have to eliminate all Pauline statements to the contrary, such as Rom 13:1-7 or 1 Cor 11:2-16, as "secondary insertions" or as "strategic advice" to communities in jeopardy. However, by refusing to look critically at the rhetoric of domination, which uses imperial imagery, titles and names for G*d and Christ, or at the rhetoric of obedience and submission in the Pauline letters, anti-imperial biblical scholarship cannot grasp the imperial ideology at work in early Christian writings, such as in Paul's letters or the book of Revelation.

Writings like the book of Revelation, which uses imperial language as anti-language,[20] still re-inscribe the language of empire. Anti-languages are often used by those on the margins of society, who speak in code so that not everybody can understand them. Anti-language, according to Michael K. Halliday, is a replication and subversion of the grammar and vocabulary of the dominant speech community. Anti-language is used by outsiders for constructing a reality that is an alternative reality to that of the dominant society. Even though anti-language uses words of the dominant group in a different way, so that they can only be understood by "insiders," anti-language still re-inscribes language patterns of the dominant speech community.

Although language and anti-language stand in opposition to each other, both the dominant society and the subgroup share the same overarching system of meaning, since they are both part of the same imperial order. The Pauline and post-Pauline literature fosters imperial subordination, insofar as, for instance, it interprets the execution of Jesus as "dying for our sins"—sins that were ostensibly

---

18. See the excellent paper by Melanie Johnson-DeBaufre and Laura Nasrallah, "The Pauline Correspondence: Struggling Subjectivities under Empire," presented in the "Paul and Politics" Section at the SBL annual meeting in 2006.

19. See Chapter 2 for a fuller argument.

20. This term was created by the linguist Michael K. Halliday, *Language as Social Semiotic: The Social Interpretation of Language and Meaning* (Baltimore, Md.: University Park Press, 1978).

brought into the world by a woman—or as they legitimate in Christological and the*logical terms subordination to the emperor, the slave-master, the father, and the husband. Attempts by scholars to rescue early Christian scriptures as anti- or counter-imperial literature tend to overlook that the language of empire and its violence, which are encoded in them, have shaped Christian religious and cultural self-understanding and ethos throughout the centuries and still do so today. Such language of subordination and control is not outdated historical language. Rather, as belonging to sacred scripture, this language is performative language, which continues to determine Christian identity and praxis today. Consequently, such language needs not merely to be understood but also to be made conscious and be critically deconstructed.

If one does not deliberately deconstruct the language of imperial domination in which scriptural texts remain caught up, one cannot but valorize and re-inscribe it. If one has understood this problem, one cannot simply continue to engage in a purely historical reading. Rather, it becomes necessary to engage in a critical interpretation that seeks to investigate the impact of the discourses of empire on the language, imagery, and message of Christian scripture. Such a reading, which seeks to decolonize the religious imagination, has as its goal not to whitewash the Christian scriptures, nor to absolve Paul from the blame of having inscribed empire, but rather to make us conscious of such inscriptions.

Hence, in this work I intend to explore not only how the power of empire has shaped and affected Christian scriptures, but also how it still shapes our self-understandings today. For Christian scriptures and interpretations could and can be used in the service of empire, colonialist expansion, racist exploitation, and heterosexist discrimination, because they have been formulated in the context of Roman imperial power and therefore are determined by this rhetorical political imperial context. They advocate and instill the ethos of empire: submission, violence, and exclusion; they speak, as well, about G*d and Christ by analogy to imperial rulers, who are presumed to be male. Imperial rhetoric either eclipses wo/men[21] or uses them as figures to argue and "think with" (Claude Levi-Strauss).

---

21. In order to lift into consciousness the linguistic violence of so-called generic male-centered language, I write the term "wo/men" with a slash, in order to use the term "wo/men" and not "men" in an inclusive way. I suggest that whenever you read "wo/men," you need to understand it in the generic sense. Wo/man includes man, "s/he" includes "he," and "female" includes "male." Feminist studies of language have elaborated that Western, kyriocentric (that is, master,

My uneasiness here is not simply with the Roman Empire as the historical context of the emerging early Christian movements, but with the residu-
al, mostly unconscious, biblical inscriptions of empire and its subordinating
"power over." I am not primarily concerned with identifying these inscriptions
and cataloging them, because this would not be a book-length but a life-long
project. Rather, I am concerned to explore methods and approaches of conscientization, detoxification, and decolonization[22] that would allow wo/men to
critically name and adjudicate such imperial biblical inscriptions in the interest
of constructing a scriptural ethos of radical democracy, which provides an historical alternative to the language of empire.[23]

A Radical Democratic Ethos

Such an ethos of radical democracy cannot be imposed on religious people
but must be recognized by them as intrinsic to their religious vision and commitment. For instance, in his book *The Challenge of Fundamentalism: Political
Islam and the New World Disorder*, Bassam Tibi defines "religious fundamentalism not as a religious faith, but as a political ideology based on the politicizing
of religion for sociopolitical and economic goals in the pursuit of establishing

---

lord, father, male centered) language systems understand language as both generic and as gender-
specific. Wo/men always must think at least twice, if not three times, and adjudicate whether we
are meant or not by so-called generic terms, such as "men," "humans," "Americans," or "professors." To use "wo/men" as an inclusive generic term invites male readers to learn how to "think
twice" and to experience what it means *not* to be addressed explicitly. Since wo/men always must
arbitrate whether we are meant or not, I consider it a good spiritual exercise for men to acquire
the same sophistication and to learn how to engage in the same hermeneutical process of "thinking twice" and of asking whether they are meant when I speak of wo/men. According to Wittgenstein, the limits of our language are the limits of our world; hence, such a change of language
patterns is a very important step towards the realization of a new feminist consciousness.

22. I generally use the verb form "decolonizing" rather than the adjective "postcolonial" in
order to indicate an active continuing dynamic process rather than one already concluded. See
also Fernando Segovia, *Decolonizing Biblical Studies: A View from the Margins* (Maryknoll, N.Y.:
Orbis Press, 2000), XI who argues "that the discipline of biblical criticism has witnessed, over
the last quarter of a century, a process of decolonization and liberation . . ." which, I would add,
is still ongoing.

23. See also John W. De Gruchy, *Christianity and Democracy* (Cambridge: Cambridge University Press, 1995); Cornel West, *Democracy Matters* (New York: Penguin, 2004); Sharon D.
Welch, *After Empire: The Art and Ethos of Enduring Peace* (Minneapolis, Minn.: Fortress Press,
2004).

a divine order."[24] Like others, he diagnoses such religious fundamentalisms as responding to a deep crisis on the nation-state level and on the transnational level of economic globalization. He sees an urgent need "to shape new outlooks on cross-cultural grounds." We cannot continue to impose Western views of democracy and human rights, he argues, but must ask "how can people of different cultures and civilizations speak a common language of human rights and democracy in *their own tongues?*"[25]

Tibi argues that on an ethical level there are strong affinities between Islam and democracy[26] and that it is quite possible to derive a list of democratic rights and liberties from Islamic sources for a cross-cultural morality. Yet, "unless there is a rethinking of Islamic doctrines, no Islamic contribution to an international cross-cultural morality can be offered."[27]

What Tibi says about Islam equally applies to Christianity. In the interest of a cross-cultural morality and religious-spiritual vision it is necessary to rethink scripture and the*logical doctrines, which are deeply enmeshed with the power, violence, and language of empire used in naming and expressing the Divine. One needs to study how Christian faith and imagination speak of empire "in its own tongues," in order to find out whether and how Christian religion also can speak "in its own tongue" a language of human rights and democracy. In *Rhetoric and Ethic*, I argued that, to do this critical work, biblical scholarship must be re-conceptualized as a critical rhetoric and ethic of inquiry,[28] which approaches all intellectual perspectives and methodological turns with an ethical-religious reflexivity, a reflexivity that has been pioneered by feminist[29] and other "liberationist"[30] studies.

---

24. Bassam Tibi, *The Challenge of Fundamentalism: Political Islam and the New World Disorder* (Berkeley, Calif.: University of California Press, 1998), 20.

25. Tibi, *The Challenge of Fundamentalism*, 180.

26. See also Larry Diamond, Marc F. Plattner, and Philip J Costopoulos, *World Religions and Democracy* (Baltimore, Md.: The Johns Hopkins University Press, 2005).

27. Tibi, *The Challenge of Fundamentalism*, 190.

28. For the elaboration of such critical reflexivity in biblical interpretation, see Melanie Johnson-DeBaufre, *Jesus Among Her Children: Q, Eschatology and the Construction of Christian Origins* (Cambridge, Mass.: Harvard University Press, 2005), 11–17.

29. See for instance Denise Kimber Buell, *Why This New Race: Ethnic Reasoning in Early Christianity* (New York: Columbia University Press, 2005).

30. See, for instance, Brian K. Blount, *True to Our Native Land: An African American New Testament Commentary* (Minneapolis, Minn.: Fortress Press, 2007); Marrla Breetschneider, ed., *The Narrow Bridge: Jewish Views on Multiculturalism* (New Brunswick: Rutgers University Press, 1996);

To that end, biblical interpretation cannot only be deconstructive but must also search for traces of a scriptural rhetoric that can inspire the resistance to empire. This project is especially important for those religious people for whom the bible is key in understanding the world and G*d. Hence, scriptural and the*logical emancipative work always has to have two focal points: the Roman Empire as the context and social location of Christian scriptures, on the one hand, and contemporary forms of empire and global possibilities for resistance, on the other. To that end, it becomes necessary to re-conceptualize the sub-discipline of biblical the*logy not as a confessional dogmatic discipline, but as a rhetorical-emancipative inquiry into biblical and contemporary religious world-constructions and their political deployments today. Such a critical biblical the*logy is not only needed for intra-Christian discourses but also for cultural-political ones.

Rather than assuming that scriptural discourses are counter-empire, socio-critical[31] biblical studies would, for instance, need to:

- explicitly reflect on its sociopolitical religious location and ideological functions
- understand biblical discourses as inscriptions of struggle and reconstruct them as public debates of the ekklēsia[32]
- identify the languages of empire and its death-dealing ideologies inscribed in scriptures
- identify biblical visions and values that would contribute to a radical democratic understanding of society and religion
- foster an understanding of biblical authority that allows for the questioning of the text in a critical practice of the discernment of the Spirit

Donna Berman, ed., *The Coming of Lilith: Essays on Feminism, Judaism, and Sexual Ethics*, 1972–2003 (Boston: Beacon Press, 2005).

31. Since "critique" and "critical" are often understood in a negative, deconstructive, and cynical sense as "not approving," and "tending to find fault" with somebody or something, or with people and things, I need to point out that I use this term in its original sense of *crisis*. This expression is derived from the Greek word, *krinein/ krisis*, which means judging and judgment, evaluation and assessment. A critical approach is interested in weighing, evaluating, and judging texts and their contexts, in exploring *crisis* situations and seeking for their adjudications. Its goals and functions are opposite to those of a positivist approach of "pure" science or a literalist one of fundamentalisms.

32. *ekklēsia* (Gk. "assembly") is usually translated as a religious term, "church," but is primarily a political term of ancient democracy. See the discussion in this chapter below.

- create public discourses and debates that could intervene in the discourses of the religious right and other antidemocratic groups

These issues are some of those that need to be discussed. Such discussion needs to go hand in hand with a study of how Christian scriptures are impregnated not only with the language of empire but also with the logic of radical equality, because, for instance, *ekklēsia*, as a political term of ancient democracy, entails equality, inclusivity, citizenship, and decision-making power for all members of the Christian community. Such a transformation of biblical studies has as its goal to contribute to a critical political and religious culture of equality. Changing the ethos and praxis of the discipline in this way would mean to reposition it in the public space of the ekklēsia of wo/men, as the horizon and space of biblical and religious studies.[33]

Since *ekklēsia* is not primarily a religious but a political term,[34] such a change would position biblical scholarship in the public sphere of the *cosmo-polis* and transform it into a critical discourse that is dedicated to producing knowledge that will further the well-being of all the inhabitants of the planet today. Biblical studies, understood as such a critical discourse, could build rhetorically on the ancient Greek democratic notions of *polis* and *ekklēsia*, but would need to change them from signifying exclusion and privilege[35] to signifying radical democratic equality. If Biblical studies were positioned in the space of the ekklēsia, redefined in egalitarian inclusive terms, they could speak both to the publics of religious bodies, such as church, synagogue or mosque, and to the publics of civic society at large. Feminist theory and the*logy are an indispensable resource, I submit, for achieving such a transformation of biblical studies.

Yet the historical approach of imperial studies and the mostly literary character of postcolonial studies in biblical studies have paid little attention to a critical feminist analysis of language. This analysis has pointed to the obfuscating

33. See the very perceptive elaboration of my work, in terms of critical theory: Marsha Aileen Hewitt, "Dialectic of Hope: The Feminist Liberation Theology of Elisabeth Schüssler Fiorenza as a Feminist Critical Theory," in Segovia, *Toward a New Heaven and Earth*, 443–58.

34. K.L. Schmidt, "ekklēsia," in *Theological Dictionary of the New Testament*, vol. III, ed. Gerhard Kittel (Grand Rapids, Mich.: Eerdmans, 1964), 514–16; and especially the forthcoming dissertation of Anna C. Miller, *Democratic Discourse of the Ekklesia in 1 Corinthians* (Harvard University, 2006), which shows that the political ekklēsia-discourse was very much alive in the first century CE.

35. See Page duBois, *Torture and Truth* (New York: Routledge, 1990).

function of grammatically masculine language, which inscribes the elite male as the generic human being (man). Since anti-imperial and postcolonial studies, like liberation the*logy, have been developed to analyze imperial domination of the "generic" citizen, or the "generic" colonized and oppressed, they often have proceeded without paying much attention to a critical feminist analytics and the workings of gender in biblical texts. In consequence, the discussion of empire has generally not focused on wo/men but speaks in generic terms of citizens, the colonizer, or the Third World, or it deploys a dual systems analysis of patriarchy and imperialism, as though both were independent structures of domination.

Moreover, postcolonial biblical studies often distance themselves from liberation the*logy and understand themselves as cultural rather than as the*logical studies.[36] Hence, it is necessary to develop a critical feminist decolonizing approach to the problem of "scripture and empire" that is able not only to focus on wo/men's situation in imperial structures of domination but also on the power of biblical texts in wo/men's lives. Feminist biblical decolonizing studies[37] have not only the task to trace such kyriarchal inscriptions of empire in Christian

36. For a critical discussion of this question, see Fernando F. Segovia, "Liberation Hermeneutics: Revisiting the Foundations in Latin America," in *Toward a New Heaven and a New Earth*, ed. Segovia, 106–32 and R. S. Sugirtharajah, *Postcolonial Criticism and Biblical Interpretation* (Oxford: Oxford University Press, 2002), 103–123.

37. For the work of feminist biblical studies, see, e.g., Janice Capel Anderson, "Mapping Feminist Biblical Criticism," *Critical Review of Books in Religion* 2 (1991): 21–44; Elizabeth Castelli, "Heteroglossia, Hermeneutics and History: A Review Essay of Recent Feminist Studies of Early Christianity," *The Journal of Feminist Studies in Religion* 10/2 (1994): 73–78; see also, Silvia Schroer and Sophia Bietenhard, eds., *Feminist Interpretation of the Bible and the Hermeneutics of Liberation* (Sheffield: Sheffield Academic, 2003); Kathleen O'Brien Wicker, Althea Spencer Miller, Musa W. Dube, eds., *Feminist New Testament Studies: Global and Future Perspectives* (New York: Palgrave, 2005). For Jewish feminist interpretations, see the work of Esther Fuchs, Ilana Pardes, Adele Reinhartz, Tal Ilan, Amy Jill Levine, Cynthia Baker, or Alicia Suskin Ostriker and many others; see also Esther Fuchs, "Points of Resonance," in *On the Cutting Edge*, eds. Jane Schaberg, Alice Bach, and Esther Fuchs (New York: Continuum, 2004), 1–20. For Muslim feminist hermeneutics, see, e.g., Amina Wadud, *Qur'an and Woman: Rereading the Sacred Text from a Woman's Perspective* (Oxford: Oxford University Press, 1999); Barbara F. Stowasser, *Women in the Qur'an: Traditions and Interpretations* (New York: Oxford University Press, 1994); Asma Barlas, "Believing Women," in *Islam: Unreading Patriarchal Interpretations of the Qur'an* (Austin, Tex.: University of Texas Press, 2002). For the history of Christian feminist interpretation, see Patricia Demers, *Women As Interpreters of the Bible* (New York: Paulist, 1992); Marla Selvidge, *Notorious Voices: Feminist Biblical Interpretation, 1500–1920* (New York: Continuum, 1996); Gerda Lerner, *The Creation of Feminist Consciousness: From the Middle Ages to Eighteen-seventy* (New

scriptures but also need to search for traces of thorough-going egalitarian spiritual visions that would enable us to articulate a biblical ethos of radical democracy and human rights as an alternative to the imperial ethos of domination and subordination offered by Christian biblical fundamentalisms.

As always, I approach this task with the hermeneutical lenses of a critical feminist[38] hermeneutics of liberation.[39] Since the word feminism/feminist, in many scholarly and popular audiences, still evokes not only a complex array of emotions, negative reactions, and prejudices, but also a host of different understandings and meanings, it still calls for some clarification. Because the f-word *feminist* is still or again, in most of the world, a "dirty word" tainted by politics, I hasten to explain how I understand the f-word. My preferred definition of feminism is expressed by a well-known bumper sticker which, with tongue in cheek, asserts, "feminism is the radical notion that wo/men are people,"[40] which means they are fully entitled and responsible citizens. This definition alludes to the democratic assertion, "We, the people," and positions feminism within radical democratic discourses, which argue for the rights of all the people who are wo/men. It evokes memories of struggles for equal citizenship and decision making powers in society and religion. It requires that we look at empire from

---

York: Oxford University Press, 1993), and especially, also, the work of Elisabeth Gössmann. See also her biography, *Geburtsfehler weiblich. Lebenserinnerungen einer katholischen Theologin* (München: Iudicium Verlag, 2003).

38. I use "feminist" as an umbrella term which is not linked to any specific identity category, in order to signify an intellectual and social movement. Such a formal category needs to be contextually specified, with respect to, e.g., womanist, mujerista, Latina, queer, Western, global, critical, liberationist, etc., since there are numerous articulations of feminist theory and practice. Such a political use of "*feminism,*" as an umbrella term, seeks to avoid the fragmentation and splintering of feminist power, which makes it still marginal in societies and religions around the globe.

39. For an initial articulation of such a feminist the*logy of liberation, see my article "Feminist Theology as a Critical Theology of Liberation," *Theological Studies* 36/ 4 (December 1975): 606–36; see also my books *Discipleship of Equals: A Critical Feminist Ekklesia-logy of Liberation* (New York: Crossroad, 1993); *The Power of Naming: A Concilium Reader in Feminist Christian Theology* (Maryknoll, N.Y.: Orbis, 1996); *Grenzen überschreiten. Der theoretische Anspruch feministischer Theologie. Ausgewählte Aufsätze* (Münster: LIT Verlag, 2003). See also, Wanda Deifelt, "Feminist Theology: A Key for Women's Citizenship in the Church," in *Toward a New Heaven and Earth*, ed. Segovia, 237–48; Ivone Gebara, "A Feminist Theology of Liberation: A Latin American Perspective with a View Toward the Future," in *Toward a New Heaven and a New Earth*, ed. Segovia, 249–68; and Gustavo Gutiérrez, "The Theology of Liberation: Perspectives and Tasks," in *Toward a New Heaven and a New Earth*, ed. Segovia, 287–99.

40. This definition is generally attributed to Chris Kramarae and Paula Treichler but I could not find a source to substantiate this attribution.

the perspective of those wo/men who are suffering multiple dominations that exclude them from full citizenship.

This radical democratic definition accentuates that feminism is a revolutionary political concept and, at the same time, ironically underscores that at the beginning of the twenty-first century, feminism should be a common sense notion. According to this political definition of feminism, men can advocate feminism just as wo/men can be antifeminist. This radical democratic definition also implies that feminism is not just concerned about gender but also about race, class, imperialism, and other forms of domination which determine the lives of wo/men.

Feminism, as I understand it, cannot be concerned only with gender injustice and gender marginalization but must also address other forms of domination, such as racism, poverty, religious exclusion, heterosexism, and colonialism, all of which are inflected by gender and themselves inflect gender.[41] That the category *woman* is not just ambiguous and divided in itself but also inflected by race, class, and colonial relations is underscored by bell hooks:

> White feminists did not challenge the racist-sexist tendency to use the word "women" to refer solely to white women; they supported it. For them it served two purposes. First, it allowed them to proclaim white men world oppressors while making it appear linguistically that no alliance existed between white women and white men based on shared racial imperialism. Second, it made it possible for white women to act as if alliances did exist between themselves and non-white women. . . .[42]

In order to take into account not only the ever changing definitions of woman as a social-political category but also subaltern women's and men's experiences of domination by elite women and men, I write wo/men in a broken fashion, to destabilize this category *woman*. Moreover, rather than advocating a dual systems analysis—imperialism and feminism—as anti-imperial studies and feminist postcolonial studies seem to do, I have developed a complex

41. See also the excellent contribution of Ken Stone, "Biblical Interpretation as a Technology of the Self: Gay Men and the Ethics of Reading," in *Bible and Ethics of Reading*, eds. Danna Nolan Fewell and Gary A. Phillips, Semeia 77 (Atlanta, Ga.: Scholars, 1997), 139–55.

42. bell hooks, *Ain't I a Woman: Black Women and Feminism* (Boston, Mass.: South End, 198), 140.

analysis of interstructured and multiplicative dominations and have coined the neologisms *kyriarchy/kyriocentrism* (from Gk. *kyrios* = domination by the emperor, lord, master, father, husband, elite propertied male), as descriptive of the workings of empire.

These neologisms seek to express the intersecting structures of dominations and to replace the commonly used term, *patriarchy*, which is often understood in terms of binary gender dualism. As an analytic category, kyriarchy articulates a more comprehensive systemic analysis of empire, in order to underscore the complex inter-structuring of dominations, and to locate sexism and misogyny in the political matrix—or better, "patrix"—of a broader range of dominations.[43] Feminism, in this sense, is a critical theory and praxis that seeks to transform kyriarchal, i.e., emperor, lord, slave-master, father, elite male determined power relations of domination. Such a sociocritical analysis of the structures of domination, in terms of kyriarchy, frees wo/men from the compulsion to negotiate identity in essentialist gender terms. It allows one to understand gender not just as an ideological concept but as an ever-shifting position and social formation constituted by structures of domination and networks of power. In short, this analytics does not restrict itself to gender analysis but seeks to comprehend the complex multiplicative interstructuring of gender, race, class, age, national, and colonial dominations and their imbrication with each other. It seeks to expose the embeddedness of wo/men's oppression in the entire domain of Western society, culture, and religion and thereby to reveal that the subordination and exploitation of wo/men is crucial to the maintenance of kyriarchal or imperial cultures and religions.

The history of emancipation, in western societies and world religions, could be written as a history of struggles against the kyriarchal exclusions and exploitations of empire. These struggles seek to claim, for wo/men, the political power of ekklēsia, as well as the religious power of the "word." Feminist scholarship and theories are best conceptualized in terms of such political and rhetorical struggles[44] both for wo/men's full citizenship and wo/men's public speaking in the ekklēsia, the democratic assembly or congress of full citizens. Consequently,

43. See my books, *But She Said: Feminist Practices of Biblical Interpretation* (Boston, Mass.: Beacon, 1992) and *Sharing Her Word: Feminist Biblical Interpretation in Context* (Boston, Mass.: Beacon, 1998) as well as the introduction to *Searching the Scriptures* (New York: Crossroad, 1993–1994).

44. For the analysis of the Wo/men's Movement as rhetorical, see Karlyn Kohrs Campbell,

sociocritical feminist biblical studies explicitly need to adopt a theoretical framework that stresses the agency and authority of wo/men as political and intellectual religious subjects.

By moving to the center of its attention wo/men who struggle for survival at the lowest level of the kyriarchal pyramid, biblical studies of empire, I suggest, would be able to explore the political-public context of biblical texts and the values they advocate not by omitting or relegating the question of "wo/men" to the sidelines, but by taking such texts about wo/men as a critical measure of interpretation. What Eloise A. Buker has said about philosophy also holds true for critical biblical studies of empire:

> By beginning with the simple assumption that wo/men are as central to cultural [political and religious] life as [elite] men are, and by seeking to articulate just gender [race, class, ethnic, transnational] relationships, one modifies philosophical foundations such as liberalism, Marxism, psychoanalysis, existentialism and socialism [postcolonialism]. . . . In this sense, feminist theories perform a radical hermeneutics that appropriates [in an eclectic fashion] other philosophies in order to reflect on issues arising from women's confrontation with injustices.[45]

I have added several modifications in parentheses, in order to broaden and explicate Buker's statement, which holds even more true after these qualifications are taken into account. However, putting wo/men at the center of attention when reading biblical texts would mean adopting a rhetorical understanding of language. It would mean questioning the totalizing assumption of a postmodern understanding of language which insists that language does not refer to something outside the text but that words have meaning only in relation to other words. Nevertheless words and meaning are not free-floating but they form patterns of discourses which organize our understanding. "Woman," as the object of knowing and as the knowing subject, has been discursively constructed and is always already determined by its location in a phallogocentric

---

"The Rhetoric of Women's Liberation: An Oxymoron," in *Contemporary Rhetorical Theory: A Reader*, eds. John Louis Lucaites, Celeste Michelle Condit, Sally Caudill (New York: Guilford, 1999), 397–410.

45. Eloise A. Buker, "Feminist Social Theory and Hermeneutics: An Empowering Dialectic," *Social Epistemology* 4 (1990): 23–39.

symbolic order, "an order which is at the basis of binary, either/or thinking and which by the very nature of its 'phallic' discourse is unable to express the feminine."[46]

In short, a rhetorical understanding of language assumes that words are always addressed to someone, articulated for a certain purpose of communication, and shaped by particular sociohistorical contexts and situations. To qualify ekklēsia with "wo/men" means to understand wo/men in sociopolitical terms rather than in terms of philosophical essentialism or the symbolic phallocentric order that constitutes the feminine.

A Critical Political Feminist Hermeneutics

Let me stage a debate on the consequences that this understanding of kyriocentric language has for interpreting biblical texts and historical sources, either as a closed system of meaning or as rhetorical practices of meaning making. I will do so by first representing such a closed kyriocentric language system as we find it in the postmodern deconstruction of Jorunn Økland, and then by referencing my own work, which has developed a critical rhetorical understanding of language and text. Finally, I will stage this debate in the space of feminist theoretical imagination, as it has been mapped by Nancy Fraser.

First, in various publications Jorunn Økland has championed a deconstructivist reading that is indebted to the French philosopher Luce Irigaray, who discusses the great philosophers of Western culture and comes to the conclusion that in a phallogocentric paradigm, the feminine is not "not yet" represented but rather is "non-representable." Irigaray not only points to the omission of the feminine in Western philosophy but also to the oblivion of sexual difference altogether. Økland draws from this the conclusion

> that women do not have a history, and that the representation of "woman" in phallogocentric texts need not have anything in common with those embodied humans we define as "women" around us today. The word "woman" only functions in the discourse as an empty category with

46. Valerie Bryson, *Feminist Debates: Issues of Theory and Political Practice* (New York: NYU Press, 1999), 38.

changing content. . . . Following Irigaray, we have to ask, whether Paul had a view of women at all. What could he possibly see? At most, he could see, "women" as a category of otherness in relation to the male.[47]

Consequently, she argues throughout the dissertation that in 1 Corinthians 11–14 Paul was not speaking about women or their behavior but about the order of the community, and that he uses "woman" because the feminine stands for disorder, confusion, and disunity. In this understanding, Paul was not concerned about women but about creating peace and harmony in what he perceived to be a chaotic disorderly assembly.

> First Corinthians 11–14 displays a phallogocentric way of thinking: wo/men are seen as carriers of particularity, sex and gender; men's genderedness is hidden behind claims of representing the universal humanity and non-gender. To conclude, before modernity "male" and "female" were more like cosmic entities. When first the feminine as a transcendent or at least transhistorical *essence* was abandoned, and next the concept of woman was demonstrated to be historically contingent, it means that "woman" is a term with changing content, an instable category. "Woman" is nowhere a topic in its own right for Paul.[48]

While I would agree with Økland that Paul was not concerned to "define 'woman' in her own right" and that his discourse is thoroughly androcentric, or as I would say kyriocentric, this does not mean that his text was formulated without certain wo/men in the Corinthian community in mind. Neither the ideological construct of the space of the ekklēsia in ritualistic terms, nor the disagreement

47. Jorunn Økland, "Feminist Reception of the New Testament: A Critical Reception," in *The New Testament as Reception*, eds. Mogens Müller & Henrik Tronier (Sheffield: Sheffield Academic, 2002), 131–57, esp., 151.

48. Jorunn Økland, *Women in Their Place: Paul and the Corinthian Discourse of Gender and Sanctuary Space* (London: T. & T. Clark, 2005), 21f. Melanie Johnson-DeBaufre observes after reading this quotation: "What I notice about the work of Økland, I see a lot in discursive-deconstructive readings. She moves from rejecting any access to embodied wo/men and then moves to making a claim about (embodied) Paul and what he has in view. Thus a deconstructive argument *does* serve to construct an argument about things outside the text. And, predictably, it is to confirm that there were no wo/men there." For a similar objection see also Joseph A. Marchal, *JBL* 124/4 (2005): 771–75.

with the actions of wo/men in the community is exclusive of the other. Moreover, Økland, following Irigaray, does not take into account that in Roman antiquity we do not merely find a dual gender construction, as in modernity, but also, for instance, discursive constructions of three genders because the Roman gender system allowed for a third gender that was neither male nor female.[49]

Second, in order to sustain her reading in an Irigarayan framework,[50] Økland says that she does not distinguish between male/masculine and female/ feminine and she uses the English word *gender* like the Norwegian *kjønn*, which includes both sex and gender. She also does not distinguish between *sex* as a naturalizing designation (male/female), *gender* as an ideological practice (masculine/feminine), and *woman/man* as a socially/economically/politically and not just an ideologically constituted group. If she had done so, she would have recognized that Paul does distinguish between the two gender terms; in Gal 3:28 he uses "male/masculine and female/feminine" (*arsen kai thēly*), whereas in 1 Corinthians he speaks of woman (*gynē*). I point this out because Økland can only sustain her Irigarayan reading of Paul because she does not distinguish between the three designations *female, feminine,* and *woman.*

---

49. Dominic Montserrat, "Reading Gender in the Roman World," in Janet Huskinson, ed., *Experiencing Rome*, 153–82, esp., 157ff; for the hypothesis of a "one sex model" in antiquity see Thomas Laqueur, *Making Sex: Body and Gender from the Greeks to Freud* (Cambridge: Harvard University Press, 1990).

50. J'annine Jobling, *Feminist Biblical Interpretation in Theological Context: Restless Readings* (Burlington,Vt.: Ashgate, 2002), points out, in a careful and very perceptive reading of my work, that on the one hand Irigaray misreads my work when she claims that it "merely reproduces the phallogocentric economy by neutralizing sexuateness"(p. 48). On the other hand, Jobling argues that my "feminism is indeed a 'feminism without women'" because my definition of wo/men as a socio-political collective entity indicates not only the fracturedness of "wo/men" but also includes subordinated men and fails to think sexual difference outside of the logic of identity (p. 153). However, she overlooks that the writing of *wo/men* with a slash conceptualizes wo/men not only in socio-political but also in linguistic terms, insofar as I also use *wo/men* as an inclusive generic term (*wo/men* includes men). Hence the word *wo/men* signifies a sociological political group and, at one and the same time, functions as inclusive language by standing kyriocentric language on its head. Moreover, Jobling's objection holds true only if one remains within the Irigarayan/Lacanian framework. The basic difference, then, seems to be one of theoretical framework. Whereas Jobling believes that "the concepts and categories of 'women' and 'men' would, in all likelihood, persist even if the sexes could not be distinguished by their socio-political locations with respect to dis-tribution of power" (p. 154), I would argue that "the sexes" are constructed by such socio-political power-relations and cannot persist outside of them. For the difficulty of articulating racial, class, and "other than gender" differences in an Irigarayan framework, see the dissertation of Linda Jean Miller, *Divinity, Difference and Democracy: A Critical Materialist Reading of Luce Irigaray's Politics of Incarnation* (Harvard Divinity School, Th.D. thesis, 2006).

Because Økland claims that I do not "problematize the language categories themselves and how they work," she can argue that I read the New Testament as a "record." Because allegedly in my view "women are women, there are no problems in the relationship between the word and the character of the reality it denotes."[51] She bases her argument on a narrow reading of *In Memory of Her*, without taking chapters 2 and 3 into account where I explore the reading of androcentric language and the problem of historical reconstruction. She neglects that I have further developed and explicated—not restated as she claims—this theoretical framework in my books, *But She Said, Sharing Her Word,* and *Rhetoric and Ethic.* This elision is rather baffling[52] in such a theoretically sophisticated work, but understandable if one considers that such a recognition of my whole work would have required an acknowledgment that the difference between our approaches is theoretical and not exegetical-historical. Whereas Økland adopts Irigaray's ahistorical method of reading, in *Sharing Her Word*[53] I have argued with reference to the feminist philosopher Andrea Nye's work[54] that a purely deconstructive reading à la Derrida, Lacan, or Irigaray is able to crash, mimic, and parody the male/masculine text and tradition but cannot ultimately comprehend wo/men as speaking subjects and historical agents. As a method and theory of reading, deconstruction is very useful for tracing ideological inscriptions. Yet, because it cannot engage in reconstruction, this approach is not able to conceive of an alternative space of wo/men's presence, agency, and power within kyriarchal language systems.[55]

The obliterating power of kyriocentric texts and theories is well expressed in the *mythos* of Athena. Nevertheless, the myth also "reveals" an alternative space within kyriarchal power, but not as that of sexual difference. Athena, the patron

51. Økland, *Women in Their Place,* 149 ff.
52. See also the review of her book by Joseph A. Marchal, *JBL* 124/4 (2005): 771–75, who points to my way of writing "wo/men" in order to indicate "the instability and exclusionary function of the term" (174).
53. Schüssler Fiorenza, *Sharing her Word,* 88–104.
54. Andrea Nye, "The Hidden Host: Irigaray and Diotima at Plato's Symposium," *Hypatia* 3/3 (1989): 45–61.
55. See also Suzanne Dixon, *Reading Roman Women* (London: Duckworth, 2001), 25. "Given the complexities, is it expecting too much to try and extract 'real life,' or real Roman women from them? I think not. . . . If we do our homework about each type of source, we can afford to be brave and step outside 'our field.' After all, we have already revolutionized ideas of what history is all about and whose history is worthy of retrieving."

Goddess of the classic Athenian city-state, was not only the patron of the arts, technological and scientific knowledge, but also the Goddess of war. According to Hesiod, she came fully-grown and armored from the head of her father Zeus. However, Athena only appears to be motherless. Her real mother is the Goddess Metis, the "most wise woman among Gods and humans."[56]

According to the myth, Zeus, the father of the Gods, was in competition with Metis who appears in the bible as Chokma-Sophia-Wisdom. Zeus, the highest God in the divine kyriarchal pyramid, duped her when she was pregnant with Athena because he feared that Metis, Divine Wisdom, would bear a child who would surpass him in wisdom and power. Hence he changed her into a fly. But this was not enough! Zeus swallowed Metis, the fly, in order to have her always with him and to benefit from her wise counsel. This mythical story of Metis and Zeus reveals not only the father of the Gods' fear that the child of Wisdom would surpass him in knowledge, but it also lays open the obliterating effects of the kyriocentric ethos and the conditions under which wo/men, in kyriarchal cultures and religions, are able to produce knowledge.

Read with a hermeneutics of suspicion, the myth of Metis and Athena shows that kyriarchal systems of knowledge and power seek to objectify wo/men and to swallow them up in order to co-opt their wisdom and knowledge for their own kyriarchal interests of domination. However, the myth also invites us to re-member Metis. A feminist hermeneutics of remembering—or better "Metics"—therefore has to investigate critically kyriarchal myths, texts, traditions, and practices as to how much they marginalize, make invisible, or distort experience, tradition, language, knowledge, and wisdom, leading to women's elimination from cultural and religious consciousness and records. This feminist hermeneutics also has to show how the vision and work of Metis, although co-opted by the kyriarchal system, continues to work at undermining it. Hence, a critical feminist interpretation cannot limit its work to deconstruction but also needs to read the kyriocentric text "against the grain," in order to produce knowledge that recovers wo/men as historical agents of Metis within the space of "Zeus," the kyriarchal sacred power space of empire. To do so, we need to opt

56. See my article "Der 'Athenakomplex' in der theologischen Frauenforschung," in Dorothee Sölle, ed., *Für Gerechtigkeit streiten. Theologie im Alltag einer bedrohten Welt* (Gütersloh: Kaiser Verlag, 1994), 103–11.

for a theory of kyriocentric language and text that does not "naturalize" dualistic gender notions, as if they were closed in upon themselves, but recognizes the agency of the "mythologist" who has told the story of Zeus and Metis and why he has done so. We need to recognize the rhetoricity of kyriocentric language and text which does not merely reflect "reality" but rather constructs a symbolic universe that stands in relation to it.

Just as a deconstructivist postmodern understanding of language and text, so also a pragmatic rhetorical understanding of text focuses on the ambiguity and instability of grammatically gendered language, which constitute rhetorical language and texts. However, as distinct from an understanding of language and text as a closed system of internally related signs, a rhetorical theory of language neither subscribes to the logic of identity,[57] nor assumes linguistic determinism, nor operates within a dualistic gender framework, because a rhetorical theory of language does not understand language as a self-contained closed system. Rather, language and text are conceived as cultural conventions, or sociopolitical practices, that enable speakers and audiences, writers and readers to negotiate linguistic ambiguities and to create meaning in specific rhetorical contexts and sociopolitical locations.

In this rhetorical understanding, language is neither a gendered straitjacket into which our thoughts must be forced, nor is it a "naturalized," closed gendered linguistic system, but language is rather a medium that is shaped by its sociopolitical contexts and that changes in different sociopolitical locations. Such a rhetorical understanding of language underscores that grammatically androcentric language can function either as gender specific or as generic inclusive language. In their interaction with androcentric—or better, kyriocentric texts—readers/hearers decide how to give meaning to them from their own, specific sociopolitical rhetorical situations and cultural-religious "ideological" contexts. How meaning is constructed depends not only on how one reads the social, cultural, and religious markers inscribed in the text but also on the

---

57. For the notion of the "logic of identity," see, e.g., Teresa L. Ebert, "The 'Difference' of Post-modern Feminism," *College English* 53 (1991): 893: "any identity is always *divided within* by its other which is not opposed to it but rather 'supplementary.' However, the logic of identity banishes this 'difference within' the privileged term by projecting its 'otherness' onto a secondary term seen as outside, thus representing the 'difference within' as an external dichotomy. In doing so the phallogocentric logic is able to assert its primary (male) terms as seemingly coherent 'identities without differences,' as self-evident 'presences.'"

kinds of "intertexts," preconstructed "frames of meaning," common sense understandings, "aha-experiences," or "reading paradigms" one uses when interpreting kyriocentric linguistic markers and textualized symbols.

Situating the Argument of This Book

When placed within the broader frame of feminist political theory, the importance of this debate becomes apparent. For it consists of a deliberation between
two different feminist frameworks of interpretation and their significance for
reading scripture in the context of empire. In a constructive article entitled
"Mapping the Feminist Imagination," the political theorist Nancy Fraser[58] has
sought to correct the standard feminist narrative of progress, according to which
feminism has developed from an exclusionary white, middle-class, heterosexual
women-dominated movement to a broader movement that allows for the inclusion of the needs of wo/men of color, lesbians, working class, migrant, and
poor wo/men.

Fraser is not only critical of the standard feminist narrative because it is
modernist and progressivist, but also because it tells the story of feminist theory and movement as an internal development without making connections to
broader sociopolitical developments. Fraser, in turn, seeks to make such connections when she reconstructs three phases in the trajectory of second wave
feminism. Feminism, in its first phase, which Fraser characterizes as "redistribution," began its life as one of the New Left and Civil Rights social movements
that sought to engender the "socialist imaginary" and an "expanded idea of
social equality," arguing for justice and equal rights and presupposing the welfare state and social democracy. This phase sought for the social well-being of
wo/men.

The second phase, which Fraser terms "recognition," sought the acknowledgment of cultural differences. This phase, which coincided with post-communism
and post-colonialism, was dedicated to bringing about cultural change and

58. Nancy Fraser, "Mapping the Feminist Imagination: From Redistribution to Recognition to Representation," *Constellations* 12/3 (2005): 295–307. For a fuller development of her
argument see also Fraser's article "Identity, Exclusion, and Critique: A Response to Four Critics,"
European Journal of Political Theory 6/3 (2007): 305–338.

transformation. Cultural change and recognition were always an important project of feminism but were now decoupled from the project of distributive justice and political-economic transformation. In the context of the right-wing, political and mono-capitalist developments of the mid-1980s and 1990s,

> [t]he turn to recognition dovetailed all too neatly with a hegemonic neo-liberalism that wanted nothing more than to repress all memory of social egalitarianism. The result was a tragic historical irony. Instead of arriving at a broader, richer paradigm that could encompass both redistribution and recognition, we effectively traded one truncated paradigm for another—a truncated economism for a truncated culturalism.[59]

The third emerging phase of the feminist imaginary is that of a transnational politics of "representation,"[60] which seeks to link and integrate the economic politics of redistribution and the cultural politics of recognition within a transnational frame. Since transnational maldistribution, misrecognition, and misrepresentation cannot be adequately addressed in a state-territorial frame, transnational feminist theory has to reframe the problem of meta-injustice in a global context.

Fraser understands "representation" as "claims-making" in political terms, not only as ensuring equal political voice for wo/men in national communities but also, and most importantly, in the transnational arena. This requires

---

59. Fraser, "Mapping," 299. The narrative of progress has been widely critiqued in Postcolonial Studies see, e.g., Anne McClintock, *Imperial Leather: Race, Gender and Sexuality in the Colonial Contest* (London and New York: Routledge, 1995); Ann McClintock, Aamir Mufti, & Ella Shohat, eds., *Dangerous Liaisons: Gender, Nation & Postcolonial Perspectives* (Minneapolis, Minn.: University of Minnesota Press, 1997).

60. Since Fraser is concerned with political misrepresentation but not with linguistic representation as "representing" wo/men in writing and research, she does not refer to the intense discussions on the "politics of representation" of white western feminists, whose cultural studies writings "represent" Third-World wo/men as passive victims. For this discussion, see especially Gayatri Chakravorty Spivak, "Can the Subaltern Speak?" in *Marxism and the Interpretation of Culture*, eds. Cary Nelson and Lawrence Grossberg (Urbana, Ill.: University of Illinois Press, 1988), 271–97, and Chandra Talpade Mohanti, "Under Western Eyes," in *Third World Wo/men and the Politics of Feminism*, eds. Chandra Talpade Mohanti, Ann Russo, and Lourdes Torres (Bloomington, Ind.: Indiana University Press, 1991), 51–80. It is clear that Fraser's concern is with "challenging the state—territorial framing of political-claims making" (Fraser, "Mapping," 304). She also argues that the center of feminist action in this third phase is no longer the West, that is the USA and Europe, but wo/men's movements around the world.

a reframing of disputes about injustice, which seeks to change the framework from the national state-territorial frame to a transnational global one. Thus transnational feminism is in the process "of reconfiguring gender justice as a three-dimensional problem, in which redistribution, recognition, and representation must be integrated in a balanced way . . . so as to challenge the full range of gender injustices in a globalized world."[61] In the process of being reconfigured, the three successive, overlapping stages of feminist political struggles, and their theoretical deliberations, become three dimensions of the problem that transnational feminist theory and politics faces today.

The post-9/11 political situation in the United States, which has far-reaching implications for global capitalism, Fraser suggests, is characterized by the strategy of a "gender-coded politics of recognition" that is invoked to "hide a regressive politics of economic redistribution." Both in the rhetoric of the "war on terror" as well as in the so-called "family-values" campaign, especially with regard to abortion rights and gay marriage, the manipulation of gender has been, according to Fraser, "a crucial instrument of Bush's victory" in the 2004 election. This victory was achieved through the alliance of "free-marketeers with Christian fundamentalists." The capitalist politics of regressive economic redistribution manipulated immigration, race, and gender codes and used anti-feminist politics of recognition "to conceal an anti-working class politics of regressive redistribution,"[62]—a politics that creates the social "insecurity society" as a successor to the welfare society.

In a time when people experience real economic and social insecurities, religious fundamentalism in general and Christian Evangelicalism in particular address this pervasive insecurity. However, they do not actually give people security but provide means to manage such insecurity. With Foucault, Fraser understands Evangelicalism "as a care-of-self-technology that is especially suited to neo-liberalism, insofar as the latter is always generating insecurity." She concludes that many working-class wo/men "are deriving something significant from Evangelicalism, something that confers meaning on their lives."[63]

61. Fraser, "Mapping," 305 ff.

62. Ibid., 301 ff.

63. Ibid., "Mapping," 303. However, she concludes that feminists have not yet "figured out how to talk to them or what feminism can offer them in its place." This remark reveals not only ignorance by a leading feminist theorist of the feminist work done in religion and the*logy, but also the assumption that feminism can be substituted for religion.

Fraser's mapping of the "feminist imagination" also opens up a theoretical space for mapping transnational feminist biblical interpretation.[64] With Fraser I suggest that such a transnational decolonizing interpretation also needs to articulate three dimensions: historical *redistribution*, ideological *deconstruction* and ethical—political as well as religious—the*logical constructive *re-presentation*, which requires a reframing of biblical studies so that they can "challenge the full range of injustices in the world," while at the same time articulating "technologies of the care of self" (Foucault) that inspire wo/men to struggle for survival and transformation.

Whereas in the first mode feminist interpretation seeks to "write wo/men back into history" and into the sociopolitical Christian imagination, in the second mode it is laying bare the ideological mechanisms of the kyriocentric text, so that the danger exists that embodied historical wo/men are again pushed to the margins or "written out of history." The third mode in turn seeks to integrate redistribution and ideological recognition with re-presentation by reframing biblical studies so that it can speak to the "care of the self." Let me give you an example that may highlight what is at stake.

Elizabeth A. Clark, who has decisively determined the first two modes of inquiry, argues that scholars must move beyond the first stage, in which we rediscover another historical woman, to the second stage, where we examine "how wo/men and gender are constructed in these texts." She characterizes the third stage as the "'afterlife' of the Lady where she lives on by leaving traces embedded in a larger social-linguistic framework."[65] By speaking of "stages," Clark leaves the impression that she uses a modern progressist framework, where the last stage is determinative and the previous ones are left behind as outdated or outmoded. She ends her book, *History, Theory, Text: Historians and the Linguistic Turn* with the following:

> Have we then no "real" Macrina (the sister of Gregory of Nyssa) or Monica (the mother of Augustine) in these representations? We are reduced to this option only if we imagine that ancient treatises transparently "refer" to. . . .

---

64. See my article "The Power of the Word: Charting Critical Global Feminist Biblical Studies," in Kathleen O'Brien Wicker, Althea Spencer Miller and Musa W. Dube, eds., *Feminist New Testament Studies: Global and Future Perspectives* (New York: Palgrave MacMillan, 2005), 43–62.

65. Elizabeth A Clark, "The Lady Vanishes: Dilemmas of a Feminist Historian after the Linguistic Turn," *Church History* 67/1 (1998): 1–31.

But, if with literary theorists, we abandon that view, we still have "lives" of Macrina and Monica—but ones molded by literary conventions. Moreover, their textual representation hint at "life outside the text," namely, (male) Christian writer's desire to stress that Christianity is open to all.[66]

What we are left with is representation determined by literary convention and hints of "life outside the text," as formulated by "(male) Christian writers." At this point, Clark could have moved to the third mode of sociopolitical representation and inquired as to what kinds of questions need to be asked for the historian to be able to "represent" the interest and desire of those who are marginal in or "outside" of the kyriocentric text. She could have explored from where comes male writers' interest in stressing, in their sociohistorical contexts, that Christianity is open to all. Why did they use "woman" to make this point? Why the interest of writers to represent unschooled wo/men as Christian philosophers and theologians? Can we rule out the argumentative ability of actual wo/men because of their lack of schooling? Is it possible to reconstruct, out of the traces these wo/men have left in the writings of male Christians, a Christian imaginary that understands wo/men—not just the Lady—as equals? However, such questions can only be generated, in the third mode of representation, when feminist inquiry moves past the purely deconstructive mode and seeks to address the "injustices" engendered by kyriocentric texts and historiography.

To ask such questions is possible if biblical studies are no longer conceived of as positivist historical or literary studies in the manner of deconstruction, but rather in the transnational mode of "reframing representation." This mode generates sociohistorical questions of survival, justice, and well-being, not in order to get the answers from the bible in an uncritical fashion, but in order to study whether and how the bible shapes Christian history and imaginary[67] in terms of radical equality, justice, and well-being for all wo/men in the *cosmopolis*. Rather than just to rule out such questions on the*logical grounds as too fundamentalist and on historical grounds as too modern,[68] or to debunk them on literary

---

66. Elizabeth A. Clark, *History, Theory, Text: Historians and the Linguistic Turn* (Cambridge, Mass.: Harvard University Press, 2004), 181.

67. Jan Nederveen Pieterse and Bhikhu Parekh, "Shifting Imaginaries: Decolonization, Internal Decolonization, Postcoloniality," in *The Decolonization of Imagination: Culture, Knowledge and Power*, eds. Jan Nederveen Pieterse and Bhikhu Parekh (London: Zed, 1995), 1–20.

68. See especially the anti-equality campaign of John H. Elliott, "Jesus was not an Egalitarian:

deconstructive grounds as expressing the desire of elite men, we need to find ways to articulate them as a research program that integrates all three modes of inquiry—the historical, the literary, and the the*logical. Such inquiry would articulate a radical democratic religious imaginary that sustains wo/men, in transnational struggles against the injustices and devastations of global empire and for the survival and well-being of all. At the same time, this inquiry needs to evaluate critically academic research, religious rhetoric, and public discourses as to their function in maintaining global exploitation, injustice, and violence.

An excellent example of this third mode of research is Elizabeth A. Castelli's book, *Martyrdom and Memory: Early Christian Culture Making.*[69] Castelli begins by laying out her theoretical framework and approach and by showing how it connects with her own experience and social location. Then, she elucidates how the competing imperial Roman and emerging Christian interpretations of power, submission, resistance, and victory shaped the discursive memory of martyrdom from its beginnings. The following chapters explore the central role of persecution and martyrdom in the development of early Christian discourses as effective vehicles for transmitting ideas about gender, power, and sanctity. Most important, Castelli goes on to show how the legacy of early Christian martyrdom still shapes modern understandings of the martyr figure and she reflects on the ambivalent ethics of the discourse of martyrdom, which lionizes suffering in contemporary political situations.

Castelli's book thus illustrates what it means to operate in the third mode. While following Fraser's theoretical framework, we need to reframe biblical and early Christian studies in such a way that we can analyze not only the struggles of wo/men in the Roman Empire but also, and equally important, make

A Critique of an Anachronistic and Idealist Theory," *Biblical Theology Bulletin* 32 (2002): 75–91; Idem, "The Jesus Movement was not Egalitarian but Family-Oriented," *Biblical Interpretation* 11 (2003): 173–210; see also Kathleen E. Corley, "The Egalitarian Jesus: A Christian Myth of Origins," *Forum* n.s. 1-2 (1998): 291–325; John Jefferson Davis, "Some Reflections on Galatians 3:28, Sexual Roles, and Biblical Hermeneutics," *JETS* 19 (1976): 201–8; Kathleen E. Corley, *Women and the Historical Jesus: Feminist Myths of Christian Origins* (Santa Rosa, Calif.: Polebridge, 2002); Corley, "Feminist Myths of Christian Origins," in *Reimagining Christian Origins: A Colloquium Honoring Burton L. Mack,* eds. Elizabeth A. Castelli and Hal Taussig (Valley Forge, Pa.: Trinity International, 1996), 51–67. For a critical discussion of these and other anti-egalitarian works, see especially Mary Ann Beavis, "Christian Origins, Egalitarianism and Utopia," *The Journal of Feminist Studies in Religion* 23/2 (2007), forthcoming.
69. Elizabeth A. Castelli, *Martyrdom and Memory: Early Christian Culture Making* (New York: Columbia University Press, 2004).

political-religious connections to the struggles, interests, and aspirations of wo/ men for survival and justice today, in a global empire that makes life increasingly poorer and more insecure for the majority of people. We can do so, I suggest, by carefully analyzing and reframing the workings of power, in the imperial discourses of the past and those of the present, as well as by constructing an imaginative space for articulating an alternative radical egalitarian discourse.

In short, the chapters of this book seek again to contribute towards a critical transformation of biblical studies and attempt to do so in the third feminist mode of reframing representation. The chapters circle around the question of how one can adequately deal with the rhetoric of empire, which is inscribed in scripture, and make conscious how its workings of "power over" continue to shape not only Christian discourses but also cultural-political discourses today. Each of the following chapters explores important aspects of existing approaches to the problematic, "empire and scripture."

Whenever I explore here this problem by staging a critical debate between my own approach and those of other readings, I do so not in order to prove the others wrong but in order to ferret out the hermeneutical implications of different ways to approach the problem. For instance, while I have learned much from the studies of the Roman Empire as a context of early Christian communities and writings, I believe that their critique often does not go far enough. Moreover, although I appreciate the important work done in postcolonial[70] and feminist postcolonial biblical studies,[71] I nevertheless raise the critical question as to whether a dual-systems analysis which understands imperialism and patriarchy as two independent social systems is able to comprehend the intersecting, multiplicative kyriarchal structures of domination, and whether a dual-systems analytic privileges one system over the other.

Finally, I recognize the important tools which postmodern deconstruction has given us, in order to interrogate the forms of knowledge that reproduce stereotyping forms of power and pervasive ideologies of kyriarchal domination in language, which colonizes the imagination. However, I disagree with the totalizing deployment of this approach, which tells us that there is no way to escape either the self-referential system of language or the structures of domination

---

70. See especially the work of Fernando F. Segovia and R.S. Sugirtharajah.

71. For pioneering work in feminist postcolonial studies see especially the work of Musa W. Dube, Laura Donaldson, and Kwok Pui-lan. See my discussion in Chapter 4.

in order to produce knowledge that is transformative.[72] Hence, I insist that we need not only methods of deconstruction but methods of re-construction and re-visioning for de-kyriarchalizing the imagination, de-imperializing scripture, and de-colonizing the Divine.

Historically, it is the political language of democracy articulated in different cultural "tongues" that provides an alternative space to kyriarchal imperialism. Although democracy has different shades of meaning in different historical contexts that are not always liberating, "democracy through the times, has been and still is the discourse that sets the terms for critique of current affairs and institutional orders and creates the basis for their change."[73] Radical democracy, which I have called the ekklēsia of wo/men, offers the language and space for the imagination to develop a public religious discourse "wherein justice, participation, difference, freedom, equality and solidarity set the ethical conditions."[74]

The challenge then seems to be today as to whether we can, in and through the deconstruction of kyriarchal inscriptions of biblical discourses, articulate an alternative biblical language and imagination different from that of the imperial imaginary. The crucial question is: since Christian fundamentalisms draw on the kyriarchal language of empire inscribed in the bible, is it also possible to draw on scripture for reconstructing a radical democratic egalitarian vision which is also inscribed in Christian scriptures? This is not just a problem for Christian and other religious biblical scholars but for all those who seek transformative practices of interpretation which are able to articulate radical democratic discourses inspired by the sacred scriptures of world religions. At the time as I am finishing this book, the Pax Americana of kyriarchal democracy displays more and more fascistic elements which are sanctioned by Christian language, the Israeli-Palestinian conflict worsens, and war with Iran looms on the horizon. Hence, this question becomes more and more pressing.

The following chapters approach this problem from different angles and directions and argue, in different ways, for the transformation of biblical studies

72. See also Leela Fernandes, *Transforming Feminist Practice: Non-Violence, Social Justice and the Possibility of a Spiritualized Feminism* (San Francisco, Calif.: Aunt Lute, 2003). While I agree with her critique of secularized feminism, and her attempt to reclaim the sacred for feminism, I do not think this can be or should be accomplished by spiritualizing feminism.

73. Adriana Hernández, *Pedagogy, Democracy, and Feminism: Rethinking the Public Sphere* (New York: SUNY, 1997), 31.

74. Adriana Hernández, *Pedagogy, Democracy, and Feminism*, 32.

in the horizon of the ekklēsia of wo/men. After this introduction, I explore how to understand and read scripture in the context of global empire. In chapter 2, I discuss the contemporary context of our reading of scripture and argue that a feminist decolonizing reading is called for, rather than a reading that interprets the inscriptions of empire as anti-imperial language.

If one takes seriously the power of imperial biblical inscriptions, the transformation of our understanding of scripture is necessary. Hence, I go on to examine the rhetorical power ascribed to scripture and propose a the*logical model of scriptural interpretation that redefines biblical authority as "power for liberation and well-being." Such an understanding of biblical authority requires critical engagement and calls for an ethics of interpretation. Rather than insisting on the imperial practices of submission and obedience as scriptural, we need to claim our spiritual authority to assess and reject them.

Chapter 3 seeks to display how such a critical reading and assessment of scripture is undertaken in the horizon of the ekklēsia of wo/men. It elaborates, first, the notion of the ekklēsia of wo/men as a radical democratic notion, which constitutes the hermeneutical space for a critical feminist reading of the inscriptions of empire. In a second step, I position the debate on "Paul and empire" in the hermeneutical space of the ekklēsia of wo/men in order to adjudicate the different reconstructions of Paul's rhetoric.

I compare a feminist critical and a postcolonial reading in chapter 4. To that end, I analyze the inscription of empire with the feminine figuration of Rome in the book of Revelation. I seek to show that a dual systems analysis, in terms of gender/patriarchy and imperialism, tends to "naturalize" and essentialize gender on the one hand and on the other to de-genderize imperialist domination, in its dualistic construction of "the West and the Rest" of the world. Rather than using such a dualistic epistemology, I propose an intersectional kyriarchal analysis that can decode the complex power of domination inscribed in biblical texts. Biblical texts shaped by the rhetoric of empire, I argue, must be detoxified in a critical process of decolonizing interpretation.

Chapter 5 explores the inscriptions of the ethos of kyriarchy and it does so with reference to the First Epistle of Peter on the historical level as well as on the contemporary level of interpretation. It is not accidental that the anti-feminist Christian Right has made the family, sexuality, and the citizen rights of wo/men the central cornerstone of its political rhetoric.[75] The bible is insistently invoked because it allegedly teaches the divinely ordained subordination of wo/men and the creational differences between the sexes as well as rejecting the "abomination" of homosexuality. As the 2004 presidential election has shown, this right-wing political rhetoric is effective because it defends the American family in the name of biblical Christianity.

Since every "faithful" reading internalizes this kyriarchal or imperial ethos which, in the process of "making sense," resonates with contemporary systems of domination and subordination, a complex method of detoxification or conscientization is called for. Such a complex critical rhetorical model and method for the process of detoxification and conscientization[76] consists in the following seven hermeneutical strategies of interpretation which I have called in *Wisdom Ways* the "dance of interpretation."[77] These moves are a hermeneutics of *experience*, of *domination*, of *suspicion*, of critical *evaluation*, of *memory and remembering*, of *imagination,* and of *transformation*.

Chapter 6 explores how the religious rhetoric of empire has determined not only Christian ethics but also Christian imagination and especially our speaking about G*d. The question of how to speak about the Divine is at the heart of Christian the*logy which literally means G*d-talk. How to imagine and speak about the Divine has become the central the*logical question in modernity and post-modernity.

In order to address this question, I first sketch how feminists address the problem of androcentric, or male-centered, G*d language. While feminist analysis, in general, emphasizes the issue of gendered language and discusses the question of the Goddess, liberationist and postcolonial feminist studies, as I

75. See Shirley Rogers Radl, *The Invisible Woman: Target of the Religious new Right* (New York: Dell Publishing Company, 1981); Sara Diamond, *Spiritual Warfare: The Politics of the Christian Right* (Boston, Mass.: South End Press, 1989); Hans Küng and Jürgen Moltmann, *Fundamentalism as an Ecumenical Challenge* (London: Concilium/SCM Press, 1992); "Fundamentalismen," *Beiträge zur feministischen Theorie und Praxis* 32 (1992); Courtney W. Howland, ed., *Religious Fundamentalisms and the Human Rights of Women* (New York: Palgrave, 1999); Carol Mason, *Killing for Life: The Apocalyptic Narrative of Pro-Life Politics* (New York: Cornell University Press, 2002).

76. For this expression, see Paulo Freire, *Pedagogy of the Oppressed* (New York: Harper & Row, 1971), *Education for Critical Consciousness* (New York: Seabury, 1973), *The Politics of Education* 9 (South Haley, Mass.: Bergin & Garvey, 1985).

77. Elisabeth Schüssler Fiorenza, *Wisdom Ways: Introducing Feminist Biblical Interpretation* (Maryknoll, N.Y.: Orbis, 2001), 165–205.

show in a second step, underscore that G*d-language is not just androcentric but kyriocentric (i.e., centered on the emperor, lord, master, father, husband, and elite male),[78] and that in Revelation, it functions as anti-language. In a third step, I approach the problem from a different angle, and review the scholarly discussion on monotheism, in order to show how this debate is determined by an ontological theoretical model that opposes the constructs *Monotheism—Polytheism* in a dualistic way.

This dualistic model, which was constructed in the interests of colonialism, obscures the fact that both monotheism and polytheism have sanctioned imperial power. Finally, I will propose three strategies for a decolonizing feminist speaking about the divine. The first is to identify biblical G*d language that does not re-inscribe the kyriocentric language of empire whereas the second engages the method of *reflective mythology*.[79] To overcome the dualism of monotheism-polytheism, I introduce thirdly the Wisdom figure Kannon/Kuan Yin that draws on Asian traditions. Finally, I suggest the four traditional hermeneutic moves—the *via negativa, analogica, eminentiae,* and *practica*—of traditional the*logy for destabilizing, and keeping in motion, any speaking about the Divine.

In the seventh and last chapter I argue that the critical explorations of the preceding chapters are only possible within a new paradigm of biblical studies. They require a complete transformation of the discipline to include not just interpretations of scriptural texts but also the practices of interpretation today. The chapter proposes a rhetorical emancipatory educational paradigm and explores its possibilities for the professional education of biblical scholars. I start by charting the impact of the change in populations, the impact of electronic communication, and the impact of the multiplicity of methodological approaches on the ethos and practices of biblical studies. Since both college and seminary teachers are shaped in and through their doctoral studies, one must pay special attention to doctoral education. Advanced biblical education needs to cultivate

78. See now the comprehensive translation of the bible in German, *Die Bibel in gerechter Sprache,* Ulrike Bail, Frank Crüsemann, Marlene Crüsemann, Erhard Domay, Jürgen Ebach, Claudia Janssen, Hanne Köhler, Helga Kuhlmann, Martin Leutzsch, and Luise Schottroff, eds. (Gütersloh: Gütersloher Verlagshaus, 2006).

79. For this concept, see Hans Conzelmann, "The Mother of Wisdom," in James M. Robinson, ed., *The Future of Our Religious Past,* Festschrift R. Bultmann (New York:1971); and my article "Wisdom Mythology and the Christological Hymns of the New Testament," in *Aspects of Wisdom in Judaism and Early Christianity,* ed. Robert L. Wilken (Notre Dame, Ind: Notre Dame, 1975), 17–42, which introduced this notion into feminist the*logical discussion.

transformative intellectuals who are not only at home in the academy but also can critically intervene in public discourses and uses of the bible, in religious communities, democratic public spaces, or global inter-religious relations.

Like the other chapters, this chapter also is able only to articulate pointers in the direction we need to go. The arguments of this chapter and the whole book are framed toward nurturing scholars, preachers, and Christian readers who are able to identify the rhetoric of empire inscribed in scripture and to make the connections between the rhetoric of scripture and contemporary global struggles for justice and well-being. Through this work I seek to contribute towards articulating a biblical emancipative imaginary that can envision alternatives to those of all kinds of fundamentalisms, as well as encourage and empower wo/men today for living well in the daily insecurity and violence of global empire.

Chapter 2

The Power of Scripture and the Rhetoric of Empire

In chapter 1, I articulated a theoretical space for mapping a critical trans-national feminist biblical interpretation. I suggested that such a decolonizing imaginary is necessary in order to articulate for biblical studies the three dimensions of trans-national feminist work, which are delineated by the political theorist Nancy Fraser. These are historical-redistribution, ideological deconstruction, and religious-the*logical[1] representation. They require a re-framing of biblical studies in the radical democratic space of the ekklēsia[2] of wo/men[3], so that these three feminist operations can "challenge the full range of injustices in the world," while at the same time articulating a radical democratic imaginary that can inspire wo/men to struggle for survival and transformation.

To address adequately the problem of "Scripture and Empire," one needs not only to use the postmodern method of deconstruction but also to develop a program of emancipative re-construction and re-imagination. At the same time, one needs to put these two methods to work tracing the scriptural articulations of empire not only in the past but also in the present. For empire is not only a force of the past but its power of domination and violence are very much operative today.

---

1. See footnote 6, Chapter 1: Introduction.
2. *ekklēsia* (Gr. "assembly") is usually translated as a religious term, "church," but is primarily a political term of ancient democracy—see the discussion in Chapter 1: Introduction and Chapter 2.
3. See footnote 21, Chapter 1: Introduction.

Empire as the Context of Scripture Today

In the past few years, a stream of books which conceptualize globalization in terms of empire has appeared. Some of these books discuss the rise and fall of the American empire. Others argue that China will be the next empire in the global market. Again others elaborate the moral and economic price to be paid for being an empire. While the American people fervently believe that the United States is a democracy, historians argue that it has always been an empire. The present American expansion of capitalist globalization, critical analysts point out, is secured by the military-industrial complex and justified also in Christian religious terms.

Globalization and Religion
In *Madang*, the *Journal of Contextual Theology in East Asia*, Kim Yong-Bok sums up this imperial situatedness of the*logy and biblical studies worldwide:

> The emergence of the Global Empire provides the new global context of theology. This context is ecumenical and universal. No theological reflection can avoid this context. All faiths and religions are bound to deal with this context. There may be different starting points, depending on the locus of the faith community. Whether one is at the seat and center of the empire or at its periphery, one is not outside of the empire.[4]

Insofar as many of the functions of the nation-state are taken over by multinational corporations, Michael Hardt and Antonio Negri have argued that nation states are no longer in control of globalization.[5] The danger of this shift from nation state to international corporation is that democratic government is being manipulated by lobbyists of trans-national corporations, and the system of global capitalism is not being held democratically accountable. Against Hardt and Negri's thesis of the demise of the nation-state, Ellen Meiksins Wood argues that global capital requires many nation-states in order to enforce and administer the global economy. As the only remaining superpower, the United States uses its military power

---

4. Kim Yong-Bok, "Asian Quest for Jesus in the Global Empire," *Madang* 1 / 2 (2004): 2.
5. Michael Hardt and Antonio Negri, *Empire: A New Vision of Social Order* (Cambridge: Harvard University Press, 2000).

to shape the political environment throughout the global system of multiple states. It does this not only directly, by forcing the restructuring of the regimes that are its targets, but also indirectly—not least, by forging coalitions and alliances in which it remains the dominant power—to organize relations among states as well as political alignments within them.[6]

Suzanne Pharr further elaborates the workings of such kyriarchal[7] power of domination in the context of capitalist globalization within the United States She argues that the neo-capitalist globalization of the economy, which keeps profits high by out-sourcing and reducing labor costs, has engendered a redistribution of wealth from the middle and working classes into the hands of the top 10 percent of the population. This redistribution could be accomplished because in the United States

> domination politics are founded on the belief that the rich are superior to the poor, men superior to women, white people to people of color, Christians to Jews and other religious minorities, heterosexuals to lesbians and gay men, able bodied people to people with disabilities.[8]

Such domination consists of both oppression, which exerts controlling power through discrimination, scapegoating, and violence and results in the denial of civil and human rights, and economic exploitation, which uses wo/men's labor and national natural resources in the interest of the top one percent of the world's population and without regard for the environment. The tools of the politics of domination are the ideology of entitlement of the elite; stereotyping of groups of people according to race, class, sexual identity, religion, age, nation; and scapegoating, which shifts our attention away from those in power, who are the source of the problem, toward a stereotyped group of people; and blaming the victim—meaning that the targets of injustice are blamed for having caused the injustice.

---

6. Ellen Meiksins Wood, "A Manifesto for Global Capital?" in *Debating Empire,* ed. Gopal Balakrishnan (London: Verso, 2003), 60–82, esp., 71.

7. The neologism kyriarchy/kyriocentrism (from Gk. *kyrios* = domination by the emperor, lord, master, father, husband, elite propertied male) refers to a regime of power which is subject to a critical mode of systemic analysis—see discussion in Chapter 1: Introduction.

8. Suzanne Pharr, *In the Time of the Right: Reflections on Liberation* (Berkeley, Calif.: Chardon, 2001), 12.

The effects of such a politics of domination on vilified groups are internalized oppression, which cannot be reduced to low self-esteem of individuals but creates a public mentality that accepts such negative labeling and practices of injustice as "naturally given" and "common sense." It often results in horizontal violence, contempt and internal conflict among the minoritized[9] and oppressed. It persuades them to act against their own interests and to search for individual solutions rather than to name systemic domination.

In light of the politics of domination and exploitation, the "new world order" of U.S. empire, spanning the globe, is aptly dubbed the Pax Americana, by analogy to the Pax Romana, because it lives by the principle: "Build a strong military force, as well as maximize financial returns and profits as much as possible, and everything will turn out fine." The predictable results of the neo-liberal militaristic economic model are socially unjust, politically destabilizing, culturally destructive, and ecologically unsustainable. Economic globalization[10] has been created with the specific goal of giving primacy to corporate profits and of installing and codifying such market values globally. Globalization works to amalgamate and merge all economic activities around the world within a single model of a global monoculture.

Social political theorists have warned that the American empire's declaration of permanent war against terrorism undermines democracy and human rights not only around the globe but also within the United States. For instance, the essayist and novelist Arundhati Roy has pointed out:

> [Neo—liberal capitalists] have mastered the technique of infiltrating the instruments of democracy—the "independent" judiciary, the "free" press, the parliament—and molding them to their purpose. The project of corporate globalization has cracked the core. Free elections, a free press, and an independent judiciary mean little when the free market has reduced them to commodities available to the highest bidder.[11]

9. I owe this expression to Fernando Segovia who introduced this term in his paper for the conference on "Race and Ethnicity in the New Testament and Early Christianity" at Harvard University Divinity School in March 2007.

10. See Jan Nederveen Pieterse, ed., *Christianity and Hegemony* (Oxford: Berg, 1992), 11–31; see also Paul E. Sigmund, "Christian Democracy, Liberation Theology: the Catholic Right and Democracy in Latin America," in *Christianity and Democracy in Global Context*, ed. John Witte, Jr., (Boulder, CO: Westview, 1993), 187–207.

11. Arundhati Roy, *An Ordinary Person's Guide to Empire* (Cambridge: South End, 2004), 3.

In many respects, wo/men are suffering most both from the globalization of market capitalism and from the sexual exploitation instigated by it. The systemic inequality, abuse, violence, discrimination, starvation, poverty, neglect, and denial of wo/men's rights that afflict the lives of wo/men around the globe is extensively documented.[12] A glance at statistical data on wo/men's situations around the world can easily document that wo/men as a group are disadvantaged worldwide in and through the processes of globalization. Wo/men still earn only two-thirds of what men in similar situations earn; the majority of people living in poverty are wo/men. Violence against wo/men and gynecide, that is, the killing of wo/men, is on the increase. War time rape, sexual trafficking, attacks against gay and lesbians, various forms of forced labor, illiteracy, migration, and refugee camps spell out globally wo/men's increasing exploitation. Rose Wu sums up this situation:

> The borderless societies that the global economy promotes continue to exploit women by selling them as "wives," forcing them into prostitution or engaging them in other kinds of exploitative work, such as working in sweatshops or working as domestic labour. . . . Women displaced from farms and collapsed domestic industries because of trade liberalization have been forced to seek survival by migrating to foreign lands where they often suffer abuse and harsh treatment at the hands of their recruiters and/or employers. Many become victims of sex trafficking.[13]

Moreover, the economic-ecological impact of globalization and its attendant exploitation and misery have engendered the ascendancy of the Religious Right and of global cultural and religious fundamentalisms,[14] which claim the power to define the true nature and essence of religion.[15] In past decades right-wing religious

---

12. See Christa Wichterich, *The Globalized Woman: Reports from a Future of Inequality* (New York: Zed, 2000); Ann-Cathrin Jarl, *In Justice: Women and Global Economics* (Minneapolis, Minn.: Fortress Press, 2003); Marjori Agosin, *Women, Gender, and Human Rights: A Global Perspective* (New Brunswick, N.J.: Rutgers University Press, 2001); and Beverly Wildung Harrison, *Justice in the Making: Feminist Social Ethics* (Louisville, Ky.: Westmintser John Knox, 2004).

13. Rose Wu, "Poverty, AIDS and the Struggle of Women to Live," *In God's Image* 24/3 (2005): 11, 12.

14. See, however, Gerd Theissen, *The Bible and Contemporary Culture* (Minneapolis, Minn.: Fortress Press, 2007), 75–150, who from a European perspective situates the bible and biblical studies in dialogue with a pluralistic world and contemporary secular culture.

15. See, for instance, the important study of Margaret Lamberts Bendroth, *Fundamentalism*

movements around the globe have insisted on the figuration of emancipated
wo/men as signifiers of Western decadence and modern atheistic secularism; they
have also presented masculine power as the expression of divine power.[16] Hence,
the interconnection between religious antidemocratic arguments and the debate
with regard to wo/men's place and role is not accidental or of merely intra-religious
significance. Wo/men's struggles for survival and well-being must therefore remain
at the heart of the discussions of global empire and its death-dealing violence.

Such religious fundamentalisms fulfill the need for certainty created by
global capitalism which "generates anxiety and fear as its normal concomi-
tants." Such fear and feelings of danger and vulnerability create "intensified
levels of anxiety, expressed as hostility towards foreigners, enemies, migrants,
differences of all kinds."[17] Religion that stresses dependency and submission to
an all-powerful G*d intensifies this insecurity wrought by global capitalism, by
promising certainty to those who are obedient to His will and punishment to
those who are not. Hostility to outsiders, homosexuals, feminists, pacifists, immigrants, and "terrorists" is religiously legitimated.

The Political and Religious Right in the U.S.A.

Suzanne Pharr sees the Religious Right as part of the political Right in the
United States, which she defines as a "confederacy of groups that promote an
agenda that limits access to social and economic equality and justice."[18] Right-
wing, well financed religious think tanks are supported by reactionary political

---

and Gender: 1875 to the Present (New Haven, Conn.: Yale University Press, 1993); on fundamentalism in America, as well as variegated contributions, see Hans Küng and Jürgen Moltmann,
eds., Fundamentalism as an Ecumenical Challenge (Concilium: London: SCM, 1992); see also
Bassam Tibi, The Challenge of Fundamentalism: Political Islam and the New World Disorder (Berkeley, Calif.: University of California Press, 1998).

16. See especially the declaration of the Division for the Advancement of Women on "International Standards of Equality and Religious Freedom: Implications for the Status of Women," in
Identity Politics & Women: Cultural Reassertions and Feminisms in International Perspective, ed. Val-
entine M. Moghadam (Boulder, Colo.: Westview, 1994), 425–38; Rebecca E. Klatch, "Women
of the New Right in the United States: Family, Feminism, and Politics," in Identity Politics &
Women, 367–88; most of the contributions in Identity Politics & Women are about women and
Islam in different parts of the world. However, see Sucheta Mazumdar, "Moving Away from a
Secular Vision? Women, Nation, and the Cultural Construction of Hindu India," 243–73, and
Radha Kumar, "Identity Politics and the Contemporary Indian Feminist Movement," 274–92.

17. Michael Rustin, "Empire: A Postmodern Theory of Revolution," in Debating Empire,
ed. Gopal Balakrishnan (London: Verso, 2003), 1–18, esp., 15.

18. Pharr, In the Time of the Right, 39.

THE POWER OF SCRIPTURE AND THE RHETORIC OF EMPIRE / 41

and financial institutions that seek to defend kyriarchal capitalism.[19] Hence, the politics of the religious Right has sought to erode the tax base for public services and to give public lands into the hands of private ownership. It is obvious that the white-supremacist far-Right's politics, with its often violent anti-gay, racist, anti-Semitic and anti-Muslim agenda, supports this politics of domination.

The second pillar of the political Right in the United States is the religious or theocratic Right. Since people feel insecure and threatened by globalization, the religious Right is called on to shift attention away from exploitation and militarism to moral-sexual issues, such as abortion, teenage pregnancy, family values, and to groups, such as illegal immigrants and homosexuals, who are struggling for civil and economic rights. The leaders of the Religious Right were recruited in the 1970s to support a racist backlash against the Civil Rights Movement, with its key elements of affirmative action and school busing.

> The theocratic Right could move masses of people because it could strate-
> gically exploit people's religious faith to advance their right-wing secular
> political agenda. . . . For example as the public school system was strug-
> gling to meet the challenges of racial integration, the theocratic Right
> launched a series of campaigns against "secular humanism" and sex edu-
> cation curricula, and in favor of prayer in the schools and "school choice."
> . . . Both . . . the overtly racist Right and the theocratic Right have created
> scapegoats for national social and economic problems.[20]

As a result of the successes of the Religious Right, publications and dis-cussions on religion and politics also have increased immensely in the United States and around the world. Theories of secularization, which presume the decline and erosion of religion in nations that have undergone modernization, have been seriously undermined since religion has proven to have a strong hold

---

19. For an excellent critical analysis of the involvement of religion in this global struggle, see especially the work of the late Penny Lernoux, *Cry of the People* (New York: Penguin, 1982); idem, *In Banks We Trust* (New York: Penguin, 1986); and her last book before her untimely death, *People of God: The Struggle for World Catholicism* (New York: Penguin, 1989); Robert B. Reich, *The Work of Nations* (New York: Vintage, 1992); Joan Smith, "The Creation of the World We Know: The World-Economy and the Re-creation of Gendered Identities," in *Identity Politics & Women*, 27–41.

20. Pharr, *In the Time of the Right*, 42.

on the public mind and great influence on public life and political actions. This
tenacious influence of religion, in the rhetoric of the public sphere, has become
politically articulated and organized by the Moral Majority in the 1970s, the
Christian New Right in the 1980s and 1990s, and the Republican party in the
2000s.[21] Kenneth D. Wald and Allison Calhoun-Brown affirm this revival of
religion in the socio-political sphere in their social-scientific survey of Religion
and Politics in the United States

> We have gone to such length to stress the staying power of religion for a
> reason. Religious conflict in politics is commonly treated as a throwback,
> an interesting diversion from the "real" issues of the modern era. But if
> religion remains a vital force in this day and age, then one cannot claim
> to understand the contemporary era without appreciating the role played
> by religion, especially in the realm of politics.[22]

However, as Pharr points out, the re-emergence of religion in the American
public sphere is not as positive as it seems. Rather, the re-emergence of religion
in politics serves the imperial interests of the United States and global capitalism.[23] Biblical rhetoric has been used by American presidents to articulate the
imperial mission of the United States. In his book *American Empire*, Andrew
Bacevich, a former military officer, points out for instance that

> Bill Clinton interpreted the end of the Cold War as signifying the "full-
> ness of time"—a scriptural allusion to the moment when God chose to
> transform history. . . . As the bloody twentieth century drew to a close,

21. The literature is extensive. See, for instance, Walter H. Capps, *The New Religious Right: Piety, Patriotism and Politics* (Columbia, S.C.: University of South Carolina Press, 1990); Law-rence Grossberg, *We Gotta Get Out of This Place: Popular Conservatism and Postmodern Culture* (New York: Routledge, 1992); Sara Diamond, *Spiritual Warfare: the Politics of the Christian Right* (Boston, Mass.: South End, 1989); James Hunter, *Culture Wars: The Struggle to Define America* (New York: Basic, 1991); Michael Barkun, *Religion and the Racist Right: The Origins of the Chris-tian Identity Movement* (Chapel Hill, N.C.: University of North Carolina Press, 1994); *The Emer-gence of David Duke and the Politics of Race,* ed. David Rose (Chapel Hill, N.C.: University of North Carolina Press, 1992).
22. Kenneth D. Wald and Allison Calhoun-Brown, *Religion and Politics in the United States* (Lanham, Md.: Rowman and Littlefield, 2007), 25.
23. See, e.g., Susanne Scholz, "The Christian Right's Discourse on Gender and the Bible," *Journal of Feminist Studies in Religion* 21:1 (2005) 81–100.

God's promise of peace on earth remained unfulfilled; it was now incumbent upon the United States, having ascended to the status of sole superpower, to complete God's work—or as members of a largely secularized elite preferred it, to guide history toward its intended destination.[24]

Kevin Phillips, a former Republican strategist, in turn has argued forcefully that the long American tradition of sectarian religion has attained unprecedented political influence under the presidency of George W. Bush.[25] For instance, at the first anniversary of 9/11 in 2002, president Bush addressed the nation from Ellis Island standing before the brilliantly illuminated statue of liberty. He concluded his address to the nation with the following words:

> Our country is strong. And our cause is even larger than our country. Ours is the cause of human dignity; freedom guided by conscience, and guarded by peace. This ideal of America is the hope of all mankind. [sic] That hope drew millions to this harbor. That hope still lights our way. And the light shines in the darkness. And the darkness will not overcome it. May God bless America.[26]

In the presidential elections of 2004, the Christian Right and Republican election strategists targeted bible-believing Protestants and pro-life Catholics with such great success that after the election the liberal "blue states" were ironically pictured as joining their northern neighbors to form the "United States of Canada," whereas the "red states" were said to form a union of religious conservatives, called "Jesusland," which outlaws wo/men's right to choose and same sex

---

24. Andrew J. Bacevich, *American Empire: The Realities & Consequences of American Diplomacy* (Cambridge, Mass.: Harvard University Press, 2002), 1–7.

25. For an analysis of the surge of fundamentalist and evangelical religion as well as its impact on the Republican party, see Kevin Phillips, *American Theocracy: The Peril and Politics of Radical Religion, Oil and Borrowed Money in the 21st Century* (New York: Viking, 2006).

26. http://www.whitehouse.gov/news/releases/2002/09/20020911-3.html#; see Stephen B. Chapman, "Imperial Exegesis: When Caesar Interprets Scripture," in Wes Avram, ed., *Anxious About Empire: Theological Essays on the New Global Realities* (Grand Rapids, Mich: Brazos, 2004), 91–102; Elizabeth A. Castelli, "Globalization, Transnational Feminisms and the Future of Biblical Critique," in Kathleen O'Brien Wicker, Althea Spencer Miller, Musa W. Dube, *Feminist New Testament Studies Global and Future Perspectives* (New York: Palgrave, 2005), 73–75.

marriage.[27] Messianic proclamations of President Bush, and his religiously inflected rhetoric of the all-encompassing American mission and its unending "war on terror," are correctly seen as attempts to engage religious language in the interest of empire. This missionary messianic rhetoric has been indicted by critical the*logians and biblical scholars[28] in the United States and around the world.

Christian religion and scriptures have been used consistently for legitimating Western expansionism and military rule as well as for inculcating the mentality of obedience and submission to the powers of empire. Just as the ideal of the "Pax Romana"[29] was sustained by military power and religious legitimization, so also the "Pax Americana" is maintained by military force and Christian rhetoric. The bible and biblical studies are clearly implicated since they are associated with Western colonialism. This complicity is aptly expressed in the pithy saying, which is ascribed to Bishop Tutu, among others: "When the missionaries arrived they had the bible and we had the land. Now we have the bible and they have the land."

Missionaries came to Asia or Africa not only in order to preach the gospel and to make converts but also in order to civilize and educate the heathens. As, for instance, the authors of *Sentimental Imperialists: The American Experience in East Asia* point out:

> Along with commerce a second persistent characterization of the American-East Asian relationship has been both evangelism bent on making converts and the export of Western culture and learning. Missionaries, however, were also conscious agents of cultural change. They came to Asia to do something to Asia and Asians, to reshape foreign societies.[30]

27. Kwok Pui-Lan, "Sexual Morality and National Politics: Reading Biblical 'Loose Women,'" in *Engaging the Bible: Critical Readings from Contemporary Women*, eds. Choi Hee An and Katheryn Pfisterer Darr (Minneapolis, Minn.: Fortress Press, 2006), 21–46, esp., 22.

28. See, e.g., Wes Avram, ed., *Anxious About Empire*; D. R. Griffin, J. B. Cobb, R. A. Falk, C. Keller, *The American Empire and the Commonwealth of God* (Louisville, Ky.: Westminster John Knox, 2006); Sharon D. Welch, *After Empire: The Art and Ethos of Enduring Peace* (Minneapolis, Minn.: Fortress Press, 2004); Vincent L. Wimbush, ed., *The Bible and the American Myth: A Symposium on the Bible and Constructions of Meaning* (Macon. Ga.:Mercer University Press, 1999).

29. For the importance of the concept of "Pax Romana" see Lorna Hardwick, "Concept of Peace," in Janet Huskinson, ed., *Experiencing Rome: Culture, Identity and Power in the Roman Empire* (New York: Routledge, 2000), 335–68.

30. James C. Thompson, Jr., Peter W. Stanley, and John Curtis Perry, *Sentimental Imperialists: The American Experience in East Asia* (New York: Harper Torchbooks, 1981), 44 ff.

Moreover, missionaries have played a crucial role in the shaping of American views of Asia. They provided "a model for later American governmental efforts to reshape developing societies on a world wide basis under secular auspices."[31] The form of biblical and religious legitimization most closely associated with colonialism has been hierarchical Catholicism and biblicist Protestantism, both of which are oriented toward the salvation of the soul and profess an individualistic the*logy, which preaches personal submission to the authority of scripture or to that of the Pope.

The Christian Right has singled out feminists as a major threat to empire. Antifeminist arguments are potent weapons in the defense of empire. This targeting of feminists comes to the fore, for instance, in the following quotation by a leader in the militant right-wing anti-abortion movement in the United States, who caricatured feminists as having "a very anti-male, lesbian-oriented, Marxist oriented, 'put-your-kids-in-day-care-and-go-out-and-pursue-a-career, pro-abortion mentality' that was nothing less than 'Satan's agenda.'"[32] At the same time as feminist discourse has been co-opted by the Bush administration,[33] in order to legitimate its militarism, its Christian right-wing social agenda, and its dismantling of hard-won civil liberties, feminist peace activists and scholars have been ridiculed because of their resistance to Bush's politics of domestic and global violence.[34]

Both because of the long and deep implication of the bible and Christianity in Western imperial dominations, and because of Christian fundamentalist rhetoric that equates feminism with godless humanism and Western decadence, it is indispensable to pursue a critical feminist analysis of empire that does not just focus on imperial ideologies but also on the intersecting structures of empire, i.e., kyriarchy. Such a critical decolonizing feminist inquiry places wo/men as a socio-political group at the center of attention; it does not just focus on gender but also on its intersections with race, class, age, nation, and culture in wo/men's lives.[35]

---

31. Ibid., 59.

32. Kenneth D. Wald and Allison Calhoun-Brown, *Religion and Politics in the United States* (Lanham, Md.: Rowman and Littlefield, 2007), 352.

33. See Laura Bush, "Radio Address by Laura Bush to the Nation," November 17, 2001. http:/www.whitehouse.gov/news/releases/20011117.html

34. Karen Beckman, "Feminism in the Time of Violence," in Elizabeth A. Castelli and Janet R. Jakobsen, eds., *Interventions: Activists and Academics Respond to Violence* (New York: Palgrave, 2004), 13–22, esp., 14. See also *Nothing Sacred: Women Respond to Religious Fundamentalism and Terror* (ed. Betsy Reed; intro. Katha Pollitt; New York: Thunder's Mouth Press, 2002).

35. Such feminist scholarly inquiry that is concerned with the ethics of interpretation,

Such a critical decolonizing feminist interpretation, however, does not just have a deconstructive but also a constructive task. For we do well not to overlook that globalization also presents possibilities for resistance and a more radical democratization in the United States and world-wide because "in a state of perpetual war, even the formal democracy of capitalist societies is under threat—in the so-called war against terrorism as it was in the Cold War."[36] As a consequence, radical democratic resistance is possible. Globalization also narrows geographical distances between people, fosters their growing interdependence, makes possible the interconnectedness of all being and engenders the possibility of communicating and organizing solidarity across national borders on the basis of human rights and justice for all. Through their critical and constructive analysis of biblical and the*logical inscriptions that are alternative to those of empire, feminist decolonizing religious and biblical studies can contribute to such emerging resistances to global empire.

A Political Definition of Feminist Studies in Religion

Hence, religious as well as democratic communities and feminist citizens face an ethical choice today: they can strengthen global capitalist dehumanization or they can support the growing interdependence of people; they can spiritually sustain the exploitation of capitalist globalization or they can engage the possibilities of radical democratization for greater freedom, justice, and solidarity which is also made possible by the technological market forces of globalization. World religions can inspire individuals and groups to support the forces of economic and cultural global dehumanization or they can abandon their exclusivist tendencies and together envision and work for a feminist spiritual ethos of global dimensions; they can either foster the fundamentalism, exclusivism,

---

however, is still labeled as strident "advocacy" scholarship. See, e.g., John J. Collins, *The Bible after Babel: Historical Criticism in a Postmodern Age* (Grand Rapids, Mich.: Eerdmans, 2005), 85: "Not all feminist scholarship is as fiercely engaged in advocacy as Schüssler Fiorenza. Mieke Bal . . . refuses to claim the bible to be either a feminist resource or a feminist manifesto." Yet, if one would apply to Collins' book Mieke Bal's terms, his book could be equally accused of "advocacy" because he discusses how biblical the*logy attributes "moral, religious or political authority to these texts." Nevertheless, he or his critics in the biblical academy would not label his work as "fierce advocacy" or his ethical criterion "love your neighbor as yourself" as "ideological" although scholars outside the biblical or theological academy would do so. If one sits in a glass house, one should be careful about throwing stones.

36. Ellen Meiksins Wood, "Manifesto for Global Capital?" 81.

and exploitation of a totalitarian global monoculture or they can advocate radical democratic spiritual values and visions that celebrate diversity, multiplicity,
tolerance, equality, justice, and well-being for all.[37] Such an ethical either-or
choice does not re-inscribe the dualisms created by structures of domination
but struggles to overcome and abolish them. It calls wo/men to decide between
supporting global struggles for domination or for greater justice, freedom, and
well-being.

Not only because of the diverse forms of wo/men's dehumanization by
capitalist globalization but also because of the variegated feminist struggles
around the globe for transforming the politics of domination, many divergent
and even contradictory articulations of feminism have emerged—including
womanism,[38] mujerista, latina, black, Asian, lesbian, queer, LGBT, postcolonial
or indigenous feminism—so that it is appropriate to speak of "feminisms" in
the plural.[39] Most agree, nevertheless, that contemporary feminism is not only
a political movement which is akin to other emancipative movements. It is also
an intellectual and religious methodology, both for investigating and theoriz-
ing the experiences and structures of wo/men's oppression and for articulating
norms of well-being and visions of change.

One hopes that the diverse theoretical articulations of feminism come together in their different critiques of the globalizing politics of domination and hold
that gender, like race, class, and nation are socially constructed rather than innate

37. For the role of the university in such struggles, see the very significant article by
María Pilar Aquino, "The Dynamics of Globalization and the University: Toward a Radical
Democratic-Emancipatory Transformation," in *Toward a New Heaven and a New Earth: Essays
in Honor of Elisabeth Schüssler Fiorenza*, ed. Fernando F. Segovia (Maryknoll, N.Y.: Orbis, 2003),
385–406.

38. See Stacey M. Floyd-Thomas, ed., *Deeper Shades of Purple: Womanism in Religion and
Society* (New York: New York University Press, 2006).

39. For such work, see, e.g., Musa W. Dube, ed., *Other Ways of Reading: African Women
and the Bible* (Atlanta, Ga.: SBL, 2001); María Pilar Aquino, Daisy L. Machado, and Jeanette
Rodríguez, eds., *A Reader in Latina Feminist Theology: Religion and Justice* (Austin, Tex.: University of Texas Press, 2002); Rosemary Radford Ruether, ed., *Gender, Ethnicity and Religion: Views
from the Other Side* (Minneapolis, Minn.: Fortress Press, 2002); and the articles by Vincent Wimbush, "In Search of a Usable Past: Reorienting Biblical Studies," and Ivone Gebara, "A Feminist
Theology of Liberation: A Latin American Perspective with a View toward the Future," in *Toward
a New Heaven and a New Earth: Essays in Honor of Elisabeth Schüssler Fiorenza*, ed. Fernando F.
Segovia (Maryknoll, N.Y.: Orbis, 2003), 179–98 and 249–69; see also the significant work edited
by Vincent Wimbush, *African Americans and the Bible: Sacred Texts and Social Textures* (New York:
Continuum, 2000).

or ordained by G*d. Feminist the*logies,[40] and studies in religion, thus have the goal not only fundamentally to alter the nature of malestream[41] knowledge about G*d, the self, and the world, but also to change institutionalized religions that have excluded wo/men from leadership positions throughout the centuries.

Consequently, feminists need to develop and engage in critical decolonizing practices of biblical interpretation in the context of contemporary capitalist market globalization, which can analyze the religious and scriptural rhetoric of empire at work in personal socialization and public discourses. Accordingly, feminist biblical the*logical inquiry has the task to focus on wo/men, when analyzing and critically evaluating the imperial power relations inscribed in scripture, which is understood the*logically as the Word of G*d and Divine revelation.

Thus, feminist studies in religion have to ask new the*logical questions and employ new religious ways of seeing in order to re-conceptualize the act of religious identity formation as a moment in the global praxis for liberation. The*logically, liberationist feminism understands all wo/men as the people of G*d created in Her image and hence it indicts the death-dealing powers of exclusion and oppression as structural sin and life-destroying evil. It asks for the transformation of the structures of domination, a transformation that is brought about by social movements for justice and change engendering a different self-understanding and vision of the world. Since the authority of the bible, as the "word of G*d," has been and still is used against such movements for change, it is necessary to investigate why scripture has been and still is used in support of domination.

Because of its religious-confessional, historical-positivist, or academic-postmodern ethos, however, biblical scholarship is ill-equipped to do this work of exploring the scriptural inscriptions of empire. Biblical studies need to adopt, rather than neglect, a critical feminist mode of inquiry in order to be able critically to displace the imperial ethos of scripture that is re-inscribed and internalized in the process of reading (or—as I would prefer—interpretation, since the majority of those who are illiterate and cannot read worldwide are wo/men).

40. See Ann Braude, ed., *Transforming the Faith of Our Fathers: Women Who Changed American Religion* (New York: Palgrave, 2004); Rosemary Radford Ruether, ed., *Feminist Theologies: Legacy and Prospect* (Minneapolis, Minn.: Fortress Press, 2007) which was published in celebration of the work of the now defunct Center for Women and Religion, Graduate Theological Union, Berkeley.

41. I have borrowed this term from feminist theorists and use it not in a pejorative way, but in order to signal that tradition, scripture, and language are elite male/masculine defined.

Both postcolonial and feminist studies therefore require a different ethos and practice of biblical studies.

Reshaping Biblical The*logical Studies

At first glance, critical biblical studies seem not to be aligned explicitly with Western colonialism and the ethos of empire because they allegedly are driven by scientific rationality and objectivity. Yet, anyone studying the history of biblical interpretation from the perspective of emancipative movements will recognize that biblical interpretation has been articulated for the most part not only by elite Western educated clergymen but also in the interest of imperial cultural and political benefits. In recent years, postcolonial biblical studies have amply documented this function of positivist biblical scholarship in the interest of empire, whereas feminist studies have shown that the majority of those who are dehumanized by global imperialism are wo/men and children who are dependent on wo/men. This is the case because like biblicist fundamentalism, so also positivist biblical studies seek to establish a single, one-dimensional meaning of the text.

Biblical Text and The*logy

In a perceptive essay "The Bible Teaches . . . Through a Glass Darkly,"[42] Wayne Meeks has sketched the genealogy of this situation.[43] He argues that language is not literal but cultural-contextual. We don't understand "it is raining cats and dogs" in a literalist sense, as animals actually falling from the sky, but instead know that the expression refers to a downpour of water; and we know this because of our cultural-historical meaning contexts. In a similar way, for most of Christian history, the "literal sense" of scripture has been its face value to a reader or hearer whose understanding was formed by her Christian faith and the tradition and practice of the church.

42. Wayne Meeks, "The Bible Teaches . . . Through a Glass Darkly," in Wayne Meeks, *Christ is The Question* (Louisville, Ky.: Westminster John Knox, 2006), 101–21.

43. See also Dale B. Martin, *Sex and the Single Savior: Gender and Sexuality in Biblical Interpretation* (Louisville, Ky.: Westminster John Knox, 2006), who polemicizes against the "myth of textual agency" which says that the Bible speaks and we have to listen submissively. However, as Joseph Marchal points out, he does not recognize the arguments about agency in the meaning making process which feminists have made for quite some time.

> In today's understanding of semantics the meaning, like all meaning, lived in the field between the text and the community that used it, between text and audience. Meaning was transactional but not consciously so. And it worked as the literal meaning precisely because the transactions were unconscious. The text meant what the text says.[44]

With the Protestant Reformation, which emphasized *sola scriptura* (scripture alone) and *claritas scriptura* (the clarity of scripture), this understanding of the plain sense, as defined by the common sense of the tradition, breaks down in the face of the unrestricted freedom of the interpreter guided by the Holy Spirit. This democratic emphasis of the Reformation has flourished in American Christianity with its populist conviction that everybody can understand the bible. Nathan Hatch has shown that different forms of American fundamentalism

> were grass-roots movements with democratic structure and spirit. All were extremely diverse coalitions, dominated by scores of self-appointed and independent-minded leaders. . . . They offered to tens of thousands the hope of understanding the Bible for themselves. A common Fundamentalist complaint about higher criticism of the Bible was that it removed "the word of God from the common people by assuming that only scholars can interpret it."[45]

Moreover, with the Enlightenment and its emphasis on reason and objective observation, a change took place in how texts were understood to have meaning. Now a text had meaning by referring to something outside itself, something in the "real" world of facts, events, and things. Now the question of whether a text or story about events and actions is true depends on the question of whether the events or actions told "really happened." The study of language and the bible becomes a historical discipline. Both professional and popular interpretations now share this understanding of "literal." When the literal sense becomes the historical sense, "literalism has become fundamentalism, its only alternative seems to be a knowing skepticism."[46]

---

44. Meeks, *Christ Is the Question,* 105.

45. Nathan O. Hatch, *The Democratization of American Christianity* (New Haven, Conn.: Yale University Press, 1989), 214, 215.

46. Meeks, *Christ Is the Question,* 107.

These two shifts in the understanding of the plain sense of scripture have engendered a steady professionalization of biblical interpretation, which means ever increasing specialization and control. Specialization fosters in biblical studies "a passionate devotion to the past" and makes possible sustained research that focuses on technical problems in the language of the insider. It separates scholars from those who want to understand what the bible meant not just in the past but what it teaches today. In the American context, this increasing specialization has led to subjectivism, pietism, and anti-intellectualism.

The biblical scholar is caught in between pious anti-intellectualism and the disrepute in the university that often sees her scholarship as a remnant of the dark ages or as ideological advocacy. The result is a "peculiar schizophrenia that makes popular discourse about religion so bizarre in the present day mass media." On the one end of the spectrum are the evangelicals, and the neoconservative political strategists, and on the other end "we find the democratization of nineteenth-century modernist historical criticism."[47] This social-religious location of biblical studies requires the revival of biblical-the*logical inquiry not as an historical or literary discipline but as ideology criticism and as a constructive-contextual democratic practice.

To address the problem as to whether and how to construct or articulate a biblical or scriptural the*logy, which can investigate and lift into consciousness both the inscriptions of empire in the text and the re-inscriptions of empire in the teaching of sacred scripture today, would require a re-conceptualization of biblical studies as a whole. The emergence of postmodern pluralism of methods in textual, historical, literary, psychological, or ideological criticism—a pluralism which is now generally accepted, at least in the North American academy—has challenged the sub-field of traditional biblical the*logy,[48] but it has not yet fashioned a new, commonly accepted understanding of the*logical inquiry.[49]

After the demise of the word-study approach, existential demythologization hermeneutics, and the salvation-history paradigm, the nature and rhetoric of biblical the*logy continues to be questioned. Traditionally, interpreters have separated hermeneutically the historical-critical approach as descriptive

---

47. Ibid., 113.

48. See the discussion in *Aufgabe und Durchführung einer Theologie des Neuen Testaments*, eds. Cilliers Breytenbach und Jörg Frey (Tübingen: Mohr Siebeck, 2007).

49. For a review of Old Testament the*logy, see John J. Collins, *The Bible after Babel: Historical Criticism in a Postmodern Age* (Grand Rapids, Mich.: Eerdmans, 2005), 131–61.

from the the*logical approach as normative. Since they have understood biblical the*logy as the re-statement of key doctrinal concepts, e.g., "G*d acting in history" or the "divinity of Christ," they have sought to locate these concepts in the text and to use biblical texts as proof-texts for dogmatic beliefs.

With the arrival of form and redaction-critical methods, scholars increasingly have attempted to synthesize individual biblical writings in the*logical terms.[50] Whole volumes—for example, on "the the*logy of Paul" or "the the*logy of Q"—have been published. More recently scholars have used narrative criticism to derive biblical the*logy from the textual articulation of the characters or the perspective of the narrator, whereas reader-response critics have located the*logical meaning in the interaction between reader and text. Social world studies, in turn, have taken over basic insights from the sociology of knowledge and assumed that the social arrangements portrayed by the text, and the symbolic arrangements inscribed in it, are correlated. Norman Petersen, for instance, distinguishes between symbolic universe and the*logy. Whereas the symbolic universe is the world of the text "as it is viewed," according to him, the*logy is the systematic reflection on that universe. The social roles in the "world as it is viewed" are correlated with the social roles in society.[51]

In a very perceptive article, A.K.M. Adam has explored the impact of modernity on the self-understanding of biblical studies, an impact which has led to the diagnosis of biblical the*logy as moribund and, in many cases, as in its demise. Adam argues that biblical scholars must abandon the modern attempt "to construct a biblical theology on a historical foundation."[52] Yet, Adam is careful to stress that this does not mean the passing away of historical analysis. Instead of constructing biblical the*logy on historical foundations and modern rationality, Adam proposes that

> a biblical theology will have to do with theology, with theological topics and concerns. Not the religion of Israel; not the religion of the first

50. See the by now classic work of Rudolf Bultmann, *Theology of the New Testament*, 2 Vols. (New York: Scribner's, 1951–55).

51. Norman R. Petersen, *Rediscovering Paul: Philemon and the Sociology of Paul's Narrative World* (Philadelphia, Pa.: Fortress Press, 1985), 29–30.

52. A.K.M. Adam, "Biblical Theology and the Problem of Modernity: Von Wredestrasse zu Sackgasse," *Horizons in Biblical Theology* 12 (1990): 1.

Christians; with theology as we know it and as we care about it (including topics like Creation, the Trinity, soteriology, ecclesiology and so on) which are usually excluded from biblical theology on the ground that they reflect the theologian's interest, rather than an interest which inheres to the text.[53]

What makes biblical the*logy the*logical, according to this view, is a traditional understanding of the*logy as dogmatic systematics. Proper "theological terms" are traditional dogmatic categories. Although Adam believes that the margins are a promising place to search for a biblical the*logy, he overlooks an important difference between the understanding of the*logy done in the margins and that practiced in the center, a difference that is significant for the understanding of biblical the*logy.

As Brian Blount[54] and Fernando Segovia[55] have pointed out, two fundamental differences distinguish the perspective of the margins from that of the Eurocentric center of biblical studies. The first is that the center stresses christology, and the question of *religious* salvation (soteriology), whereas the margins are concerned with social inequity and injustice. The second is that, whereas the center underscores the conceptual and formal issues of biblical texts as documents of the past and advocates their spiritual, purely religious, individualistic appropriation, the margins emphasize the interpersonal interaction between readers and text as well as the significance of social-religious location for biblical readings for today.

It is therefore instructive to note that Adam defines the difference in the understanding of biblical the*logy as one between center and margin, a difference that reflects the the*logian's interest, rather than an interest which inheres in the text. Hence, the difference between margin and center that Adam announces is not the difference which he actually inscribes as constitutive for biblical the*logy. Rather he falls back on the old difference that has plagued

53. Ibid., 12.

54. Brian K. Blount, *Cultural Interpretation: Reorienting New Testament Criticism* (Minneapolis, Minn.: Fortress Press, 1995), 1–23 and 175–94.

55. Fernando F. Segovia, "Introduction: Pedagogical Discourses and Practices in Biblical Criticism: Toward a Contextual Biblical Pedagogy," in *Teaching the Bible: The Discourses and Politics of Biblical Pedagogy*, eds. Fernando F. Segovia and Mary Ann Tolbert (Maryknoll, N.Y.: Orbis, 1998), 1–28.

the discussion of biblical the*logy at least since the famous address of Johann Gabler[56] in 1787, which is the difference between dogmatic and historical biblical studies.

In light of Wayne Meeks's diagnosis of the state of biblical scholarship, one needs to abandon the attempt to negotiate the Scylla of a purely rational-historical understanding of biblical the*logy and the Charybdis of dogmatic definition. Instead, one needs to re-conceptualize biblical the*logy as a critical the*-ethical rhetoric[57] that is conscious of its socio-political location. With liberation the*logians, I argue that the central the*logical question today is not the modern question of whether G*d exists but the ethical question of what kind of G*d religious communities and their scriptures proclaim. Is it a G*d legitimating the inequality, exploitation, and injustice of empire or is it a G*d inspiring liberation and well-being?

To that end, one needs to develop a multifaceted the*logical analysis, and engender a critical hermeneutical process, that is able to investigate the rhetoric of a text or tradition,[58] in its historical and contemporary contexts of empire, and adjudicate it in terms of an ethics of liberation—an approach which I will develop in the following chapters. One has to do so in order to be able to understand how biblical writings, which claim to be the word of G*d, actually speak about the Divine in the context of empire.[59] In the context of empire, such a

56. Johann P. Gabler, "An Oration on the Proper Distinction Between Biblical and Dogmatic Theology and the Specific Objectives of Each," in Ben C. Ollenburger, E. A. Martens and Gerhard F. Hasel, eds., *The Flowering of Old Testament Theology* (Winona Lake, Ind.: Eisenbrauns, 1992), 489–502.

57. For a perceptive overview and discussion see Johan S. Foss, "Theologie als Rhetorik," in *Aufgabe und Durchführung einer Theologie des Neuen Testaments*, eds. Cilliers Breytenbach und Jörg Frey (Tübingen: Mohr Siebeck, 2007), 247–271. See, however, the recent review article of Christian Testament The*logy by Frank Matera, "New Testament Theology: History, Method and Identity," *Catholic Biblical Quarterly* 67/1 (2005): 1–21, who seems either not to know or to disregard my proposal in *Rhetoric and Ethic*.

58. For a fuller development of a rhetorical approach see my books, *Revelation: Vision of a Just World* (Minneapolis, Minn.: Fortress Press, 1991); *Rhetoric and Ethic: The Politics of Biblical Studies* (Minneapolis, Minn.: Fortress Press, 1999); *Jesus and the Politics of Interpretation* (New York: Continuum, 2000). This approach seems to gain ground also in more recent research on Revelation. Compare, for instance, Robert M. Royalty Jr., "The Rhetoric of Revelation," *SBL 1997 Seminar Papers* (Atlanta, Ga.: Scholars, 1997), 596–617; Peter Antonysamy Abir, *The Cosmic Conflict of the Church* (Frankfurt: Peter Lang, 1995), 250–309; and David L. Barr, *The Reality of Apocalypse: Rhetoric and Politics in the Book of Revelation* (Atlanta, Ga.: Scholars, 2006).

59. Terence E. Fretheim, "Is the Biblical Portrayal of God Always Trustworthy?" in Terence

critical mapping and evaluation of biblical texts, their ethics and G*d-rhetoric, is able to explore and evaluate their the*logical values and visions as well as their internalizations in the process of reading.

The*logy,[60] in the original sense of the Greek word (*the*legein), means either "speaking about G*d" or "G*d speaking." *The*legein is a rhetorical activity or practice that is not restricted to the expert but is a radically democratic one. The subject, in the traditional understanding of the*logy, is "faith seeking understanding," whereas in a rhetorical understanding, the agent of biblical the*logy is the author and interpreter/reader of biblical texts. Consequently, biblical the*logy has the task of exploring critically all human speaking about G*d in its particular social-political contexts. "Doing the*logy," as the early feminist movement in religion has called it, calls for critical deliberation and accountability. In my view, the*logy is best understood, therefore, not as a system but as a rhetorical practice that does not conceive of language as clear transmission of meaning, but rather as a form of action and power that affects actual people and situations.[61]

If, however, the*logical language is best understood in the classical sense of rhetoric, as speech that constructs and shapes reality rather than as reflecting it, then an ethics of interpretation is called for.[62] Its task is to analyze and evaluate critically both how biblical scholars in general and biblical authors in particular speak about the Divine and what kind of ethical arguments they put forward. Biblical the*logy therefore must not be relegated to being just a confessional religious undertaking that is restricted to members of biblical communities. Rather, it is best understood as a social-political and cultural-political practice

---

E. Fretheim and Karlfried Fröhlich, *The Bible As Word of God In A Postmodern Age* (Minneapolis, Minn.: Fortress Press, 1998), 97–112.

60. In her discussion of the SBL Pauline Theology Group's work, Jouette M. Bassler points out that no agreement exists as to what is meant by the*logy and that the term is given a whole range of connotations. See "Paul's Theology: Whence and Whither?" in *Pauline Theology, Volume II: 1&2 Corinthians*, ed. David M. Hay (Minneapolis, Minn.: Fortress Press, 1991), 3–17. Rather than to understand the*logy in terms of system, core, or coherence, Bassler defines the*logy as "*activity.*" See also Steven J. Kraftchick, "Seeking a More Fluid Model: A Response to Jouette M. Bassler," *Pauline Theology*, 18–34.

61. See Jane P. Tompkins, "The Reader in History: The Changing Shape of Literary Response," in *Reader-Response Criticism: From Formalism to Poststructuralism* (Baltimore, Md.: The Johns Hopkins University Press, 1980), 201–32.

62. See my "The Ethics of Interpretation: Decentering Biblical Scholarship: SBL Presidential Address," *JBL* 107 (1988): 3–17, reprinted in *Rhetoric and Ethic*, as Chapter 1.

taking seriously its public responsibility, because the bible has shaped and still shapes not only the church but also the cultural-political self-understandings of the American imagination.

Scripture and Power

A discussion of Christian scriptures and empire, therefore, has always to have two reference points which constitute the context of our own readings and interpretations of scripture. These are contemporary forms of empire, on the one hand, and the Roman Empire as the context and social location of the Christian Testament, on the other. Both contexts need to be critically explored in an investigation of the power[63] and authority that is the*logically ascribed to scripture. If language is a form of power, and the power of scripture, as the sacred word of G*d, is used in the interest of domination, then it is necessary to assess and evaluate how its readings reproduce the power of empire inscribed in scripture.

To bring notions of scripture and empire together has an irritating, upsetting, and disturbing effect on our minds and jars Christian imagination and sensibilities. Whereas scripture is believed to be the authoritative, revealed, sacred word of G*d, empire evokes notions of domination, conquest, and subjugation. Insofar as it is claimed that scripture is the liberating word of a just and loving G*d, the rhetoric of scripture seems to be contradictory to and clashing with the rhetoric of empire, which advocates domination and submission. Hence, it is necessary to distinguish the sacred power of scripture from the power of empire that has shaped Christian scriptures. Imperial power is best understood as *potestas,* as the power of the emperor, lord, slave-master, father, in short of elite propertied colonizing men.

A critical feminist liberationist approach, therefore, needs to address the question of the power[64] of scripture and its authority. In order to do so, it

---

63. In her presidential Address to the Aristotelian Society, Dorothy Emmet enumerates five types of power: 1. Power as causal efficacy; 2. Power as creative energy; 3. Power as personal influence; 4. Ritual power; and 5. Legal power. In this interpretation the power of scripture would be a form of ritual power which consists in "performatory utterances." See "The Concept of Power," in *Proceedings of the Aristotelian Society,* New Series—Vol. LIV (London: Johnson Reprint, Co., 1954), 1–26, esp., 12.

64. For the scholarly discussion on power see Steven Lukes, ed., *Power: Readings in Social and Political Theory* (New York: New York University Press, 1986); Franco Crespi, *Social Action*

engages a "double" analysis of power. Imperial power can be conceptualized either as structural-pyramidal power, as kyriarchal relations of domination,[65] or it can be understood as operating horizontally as an ideological network of relations of domination.[66] Both modes of imperial power, the vertical and the horizontal, are at work in capitalist globalization. This kyriarchal (i.e., imperial) power-pyramid of domination is structured by race, gender, sexuality, class, empire, age, and religion, which are intersecting systems of "power over" that have multiplicative effects of dehumanizing exploitation and othering subordination.

In *Methodology of the Oppressed*, Chela Sandoval proposes a "double" analysis of oppressive power that can be metaphorized in two ways: the mobile interchange between power as sovereign, pyramidal, or—as I would say—kyriarchal that shapes differential identities of oppression, on the one hand, and power as a horizontal, circulating, continually regenerating, net-like performative, on the other hand. Under this new conceptualization of power as "circulating in a sort of electric pinball-game movement,"[67] new forms of hostility, antagonism, and violence become directed "horizontally," between and within social genders, classes, races, and peoples, which amounts to a "democratization of oppression." Whereas in the kyriarchal model of power the social location of every citizen-subject can be mapped, the lateral model of power "re-differentiates groups" differently:

---

and Power (Cambridge, Mass.: Blackwell, 1989); Michael Kelly, ed., *Critique and Power: Recasting the Foucault/Habermas Debate* (Cambridge, Mass.: MIT Press, 1995).

65. In two classic articles, Georg Simmel defines such "power over" as follows: "The group may assume the form of a pyramid. In this case the subordinates stand over against the superior not in an equalized mass, but in very nicely graded strata of power. These strata grow constantly smaller in extent but greater in significance. They lead up from the inferior mass to the head of a single ruler" (175). Against socialism and anarchism, he argues, "For so long in the future as prevision can reach, however, we may contest the possibility of a social constitution without superiority and inferiority, just as we may assert that the natural differences between human beings, which no common education can remove, will press for expression in external gradation of ranks, in differences of superordination and subordination" (400). See Georg Simmel, "Superiority and Subordination as Subject Matter of Sociology," *American Journal of Sociology* 2 (1896): 167–89, 392–415.

66. For the complex understanding of power in the work of Michel Foucault see, e.g., Alec McHoul and Wendy Grace, *A Foucault Primer: Discourse, Power and the Subject* (New York: New York University Press, 1997), 57–92.

67. Chela Sandoval, *Methodology of the Oppressed* (Minneapolis, Minn.: University of Minnesota Press, 2000), 72.

> Because they are horizontally located it appears as if such politicized identities . . . can equally access their own racial-, sexual-, national-, or gender-unique form of social power. Such conditions are then perceived as speaking democratically to and against each other in a lateral, horizontal—not pyramidal—exchange, although from *spatially* differing geographic, class, race, sex, or gender locations.[68]

This late-capitalist re-translation of difference allows hierarchical and material differences in power between people to be erased from consciousness, even while these same economic and social differences are bolstered. The growing metaphoric dominance of this newly conceived horizontal grid, networking the globe, generates a kind of double-reality and double-consciousness of power, with new and old formations at work all at once.[69]

But power must not be reduced to oppressive "power over," to the power of domination and rule, control and command, to *potestas*, the power of empire. Insofar as power circulates horizontally, it can also serve different ends. Power can also be understood as "power to," as capacity, energy and potential,[70] circulating as creative, energizing, enabling, and transformative power rather than as violent, antagonistic, and dominating power. "Power to" is best understood as ekklesial power, as *potentia*, as creative activity and strength.[71] Power can be wielded only by a few to dominate the many, or it can be seen as energizing everyone, as enriching, creative possibility for community and justice.[72] Power can be understood either as the "power over" of empire, as power of domination, or as radical democratic "power to," as power for liberation.[73]

68. Ibid., 73.

69. Ibid., 74.

70. Nancy Hartsock, *Money, Sex, and Power: Toward a Feminist Historical Materialism* (New York: Longman, 1983), 12.

71. For this distinction, see Hardt and Negri, *Empire*, who ascribe it to Spinoza.

72. Thomas E. Wartenberg, *The Forms of Power: From Domination to Transformation* (Philadelphia, Pa.: Temple University Press, 1990), 5.

73. Hannah Pitkin, *Wittgenstein and Justice* (Berkeley: University of California Press, 1972), 276–77, summarizes this dual understanding of power as follows: "It is important to distinguish between the expressions 'power to' and 'power over'. . . . One man [sic] may have power over another or others, and that sort of power is relational though it is not a relationship. But he [sic] may have power to do or accomplish something by himself [sic], and that power is not relational at all; it may involve other people if what he [sic] has power to do is a social or political action, but it need not." However, I do not agree with her contention that "power

If power always has this dual connotation, then we are able to adjudicate, in a process of evaluation and discernment, what kind of power each scriptural text espouses and authorizes, since Christian scriptures share in the rhetoric of "power over" and in that of the "power to." This observation compels us to raise the question as to whether a particular text of scripture espouses the power of empire, which as "power over" demands submission, subordination, and subjection, or whether it exhibits creative "power" which energizes and enables one to resist daily injustice and global exploitation.

In light of these two operations of power, scripture can be understood as "power over," in terms of the imperial "command-submission" structure, or it can be seen as enabling and energizing power. The power of the Word to exclude and to legitimate wo/men's second-class citizenship, and thereby to re-inscribe the "power over" of empire, is explicit, for instance, in the following Pauline and post-Pauline injunctions. At the same time, the imperative forms of these texts reveal the power of wo/men to speak in the ekklēsia or to have authority over men. It would not have been necessary to articulate such injunctions if wo/men would not have been participating in the debates of the ekklēsia or if they had not taught men.

> As in all the ekklēsiai of the saints,
> the women should keep silence in the ekklēsiai.
> For they are not permitted to speak,
> but should be subordinate, as even the law says. (1 Cor 14:33-34)

Or:

> Let a woman learn in silence with all submissiveness.
> I permit no woman to teach or to have authority over men;
> she is to keep silent.
> For Adam was formed first, then Eve; and Adam was not deceived,
> but the woman was deceived and became a transgressor.
> Yet woman will be saved through bearing children,
> if she continues in faith and love and holiness, with modesty.
> (1 Tim 2:11-15)

---

to" is not also relational power. Autonomy and relationality are not exclusive of each other but condition each other.

Not all scriptural texts are so obvious in promoting imperial power relations but all of them must be carefully analyzed and critically assessed as to what kind of power they advocate in particular situations. What kinds of values and mentality do the texts of scripture inculcate in readers who submit to their world of vision? What inspiration do they provide in the struggles against the global dehumanization of capitalist and militarist empire? The crucial question for interpretation is not so much what do these texts mean but what do *these* texts do to those who submit to their world of vision and power of imagination in various contexts that also determine the meaning of the text?

Yet, not only wo/men but also feminists have internalized that they do not have either the ecclesial or the academic authority and power of scriptural adjudication. Readers of biblical texts early on learn to develop strategies of textual valorization and validation rather than hermeneutical skills to interrogate critically and assess scriptural interpretations and texts, along with their visions, values, and prescriptions. If the literary canonization of texts, in general, places a work outside of any further need to establish its merits, the canonization of sacred scriptures, in particular, brings even more sympathy and uncritical acceptance. Canonization compels readers to offer increasingly ingenious interpretations, not only in order to establish "the truth of the text itself" or "a single sense" correct meaning of the text, but also in order to sustain affirmation of and submission to the authority of the bible, either as sacred scripture or as cultural classic.

Many students have expressed the anxiety which they have experienced in challenging and evaluating biblical texts in feminist terms. A widespread often unacknowledged fear exists that critical scrutiny of one's religious tradition will automatically engender a form of cultural relativism which believes that all religions are equally good and thereby would weaken allegiance to one's own religious community. Such anxiety is even greater when wo/men critically approach the bible. This unease is articulated in the following group reflection for one of my classes:

> This led to a discussion of how we feel a sense of great uneasiness at
> the thought of denying Scriptural authority altogether. For those of us
> from faith traditions, it was particularly difficult for us to go against what
> has been deeply ingrained in us. As a group we seemed to have much

problems with identifying a text as kyriarchal. But we had even more problems to re-envision the text. This seems to be an ongoing struggle for our group and its members. Giving ourselves the authority to go beyond critiquing, and actually rewriting the text, especially in the sense of re-imagining it without "historical facts" to support our ideas.[74]

This reflection indicates that these students felt they lacked either the the*logical or the scientific authority to work with biblical texts and therefore had difficulties claiming the power to interpret biblical texts. Hence, it is necessary in a concluding step to investigate critically the power of canonical scripture and to look at the the*logical understanding of the authority of scripture, which has been internalized as the "Word of G*d."

Many Christians have been taught that the words of scripture are divinely revealed and hence may not be approached with a hermeneutics of suspicion that seeks to ascertain what kind of power they promote. Their understanding of the power and authority of scripture is consciously, or not, shaped by the notion of power and authority "over" found in the book of Revelation.[75] The introduction to Revelation establishes a chain of revelatory authority which resides with G*d and is communicated through Christ or the angelic interpreter to John and through him to the audience. Strictly speaking, the words of the book do not represent John's discourse but rather claim to be divine discourse. The real author of Revelation is not John, but G*d, the risen Jesus, and the Spirit. The One in Human Likeness, and the Spirit, "speak" to the ekklēsiai and John merely transcribes their message (1:11, 19; 2:1—3:22).

The epilogue of Revelation reinforces this understanding. John not only blesses those who read, hear, and keep the words of prophecy (22:7; cf. 1:3)

---

74. Group Reflection, Womanist Theology Group, Harvard Divinity School, Fall Semester 1999.

75. See my books: *Priester für Gott: Studien zum Herrschafts- und Priestermotiv in der Apokalypse*, Neutestamentliche Abhandlungen n.s. 7. (Münster: Aschendorff, 1972); *The Apocalypse* (Chicago, Ill.: Franciscan Herald, 1976); *Hebrews, James, 1 and 2 Peter, Jude, Revelation*, with Reginald H. Fuller et al., Proclamation Commentaries (Philadelphia, Pa.: Fortress Press, 1977); *Invitation to the Book of Revelation: A Commentary on the Apocalypse, with Complete Text from the Jerusalem Bible* (New York: Doubleday, 1981); *The Book of Revelation: Justice and Judgment*, originally published 1985, second edition with a new epilogue (Minneapolis, Minn.: Fortress Press, 1998); *Revelation: Vision of a Just World*, Proclamation Commentaries (Minneapolis, Minn.: Fortress Press, 1991).

but also adds a curse at the end (22:18-19): anyone who would add something to the book he threatens with the terrible plagues that it forecasts. At the same time, he warns against subtracting anything. Such a powerful adjuration, however, also indicates that John is not sure how his work will be received and respected. Moreover, he seems to want to forestall the testing of his work, since it was a commonplace assumption, in Early Christianity, that prophecy required the discernment of the spirits and the testing of the prophets.

John's insistence on the divine authorship of Revelation has decisively influenced the*logical understandings of the power of scripture and of canonical authority. If one accepts his portrayal of the revelatory process, one comes to an understanding of scripture as the "dictated word of G*d," rather than as the inspired rhetorical response of biblical writers to specific the*-ethical problems arising in particular socio-rhetorical locations. The early Christian insight, that the Spirit must be discerned and the words and lifestyle of the prophets must be tested by the community, has been submerged in this understanding. Hence, it is too easily forgotten that readers of the Christian Testament are called to test the words of scripture and have the task to engage an ethics of interpretation for adjudicating the political and religious power of biblical texts.

Insofar as the power of the Word, and the authority of scripture as "power over," are considered to be divinely sanctioned, divine revelation has been understood by analogy to imperial power, which is exercised by a few and demands submission and obedience from the many. Biblical interpretation, therefore, cannot but re-inscribe the rhetoric of empire as divine rhetoric, if it understands scripture as the direct word of G*d.

The result of such an imperial understanding of revelation is a widespread biblicist literalism, or fundamentalism, and a lack of critical the*logical ability and spiritual practice to adjudicate scriptural texts. In order to foster the ability of spiritual discernment, biblical preaching, and the*logical education need to educate the people of G*d in a critical stance toward all human words, especially those that claim the unmediated power and authority of G*d.

Scriptural language symbolization and rhetoric call for critical feminist assessment, and the*-ethical evaluation in contemporary rhetorical situations of empire. Such a critical ideological evaluation is necessary because the symbolic world of scripture is not only a the*-ethical model *of* its own socio-political-religious world but also serves as a the*-ethical model *for* socio-political-religious life today. The scriptural language and metaphors we use shape our perception of the world in which we live. The uncritical fundamentalist or positivist re-inscriptions of the rhetoric of empire, as the word of G*d, do not simply misunderstand or misconstrue scripture. Rather, they are correct because the Roman Empire is the context of early Christian rhetoric and historically constitutive of it.

Nevertheless, as I have pointed out above, inscribed in scripture is not only the rhetoric of empire as "power over" and its demand for submission, suffering, obedience, and control; we can also still find traces of an alternative rhetoric of power which understands power as "power to," as creative liberating power for. Hence, all language of empire inscribed in scripture must be carefully explored and critically assessed in terms of what it does to those who submit to its sacred power of imagination: whether it advocates imperial "power over" or radical democratic "power to." What the Spirit says today to our own particular sociopolitical location, and our own rhetorical situation, must be assessed in a the*-ethical practice of rhetorical analysis and ideology critique that can trace G*d's power for justice and well-being, both in the bible and in today's political struggles against the domination of global empire.

The Authority of Scripture and the Authority of Women

Christian churches which continue to insist on the authority of the bible for Christian life and community face the the*logical problem of how such authority can be maintained in the face of critical biblical studies. These studies have underscored the bible's pluriformity, historicity, and linguisticality as well as proven its the*logical relativity and ideological function in the interest of relations of domination. A Christian dogmatic hermeneutic thus confronts a rhetorical situation that is determined by the the*logical problem of how to articulate revealed authority and authoritative truth in the face of critical biblical scholarship that intellectually rules out fundamentalist literalism and plenary inspiration.

At least since the nineteenth century, feminists have intensified this crisis of biblical authority insofar as they have pointed out that the bible has not only been written by human hands but by the hand of elite men. It is not only the product of past cultures but also has been, and still is, used to instill the dehumanizing violence of such cultures as "word of G*d." Particularly Protestant the*logical hermeneutics,[76] with its emphasis on "scripture alone" (*sola scriptura*

---

76. For this, see especially the work of Mary Ann Tolbert. See, e.g., her article, "Reading the Bible With Authority: Feminist Interrogation of the Canon," in Washington/Lochrie Graham/

and *claritas scriptura*), faces the additional problem of how to articulate the authority of scripture in the face of kyriocentric biblical texts.[77] If biblical norms and traditions are not only historically conditioned by empire but also ideologically determined, then one must ask what kind of authority the bible has for believing communities today, not only as a historically and the*logically limited book but also as one that inculcates the ethos and violence of empire.

Yet, this question is not just a problem for Protestantism. Although traditional Roman Catholic the*logy has insisted that the teaching authority of the church defines biblical norms and criteria, such an assertion does not provide a way out of the problem because the teaching authority of the hierarchy remains bound to the norms of scripture. Thus, both Protestant and Catholic the*logy have to develop a different approach to the problem raised by the insight into the historical, kyriocentric rhetoric of scripture.[78] Feminist approaches to the question of biblical authority also vary not only in terms of confessional dogmatics but also in terms of socio-political interests.

One widely known approach holds that scripture itself, or the canon as a whole, is the norm of truth. Texts that mandate the submission of slaves, for instance, are corrected by texts that stress the dignity of people. However, this approach does not make the imperial impregnation of biblical texts critically conscious. Another approach isolates a "canon within the canon" as the revealed center of scripture. The Pauline teaching of "justification by faith," or the baptismal formula of Gal 3:28, for instance, are offered as such a central canonical criterion of truth. However, others can argue on equally scriptural grounds that the virtues of empire, subordination, and obedience are central canonical norms.[79]

Thimmes, eds., *Escaping Eden: New Feminist Perspectives on the Bible* (Sheffield: Academic, 1999), 141–62.

77. Mary Ann Tolbert, "Protestant Feminists and the Bible," in Alice Bach, ed., *The Pleasure of Her Text: Feminist Readings of Biblical and Historical Texts* (Philadelphia, Pa.: Trinity, 1990), 11.

78. For a discussion of diverse hermeneutical discourses and a critique of the method of correlation see Francis Schüssler Fiorenza, "The Crisis of Hermeneutics and Christian Theology," in *Theology at the End of Modernity*, ed. Sheila Grave Davaney (Philadelphia, Pa.: Trinity, 1991), 117–40, esp., 128–30; see also his earlier article, "The Crisis of Scriptural Authority: Interpretation and Reception," *Interpretation* 44/4 (1990): 353–68.

79. See, e.g., John Howard Yoder, *The Politics of Jesus*, second and rev. edition (Grand Rapids, Mich.: Eerdmans, 1994), on "revolutionary subordination" and the discussion of it by Romand

A third approach is that of the "hermeneutics of correlation," which seeks in a continuous "to and from," to describe relations between a particular revealed principle within the canon and a particular ethical-the*logical principle today. For instance, this approach correlates the critical prophetical principle of scripture with the feminist critical principle of women's full humanity.[80] A similar hermeneutical approach personifies the biblical text or scripture as a pilgrim,[81] who has been the conversation partner of believing communities throughout the centuries and still is so today. Such a conversation between scripture and believer is ongoing, mutually corrective, and of reciprocal benefit, albeit by reducing the variegated power of biblical texts to abstract principle.

A fourth approach does not begin with a hermeneutics of acceptance but with one of suspicion placing on all texts the label: "Caution could be dangerous to your health and survival." This approach requires a rhetoric of inquiry and a critical hermeneutics of evaluation. For the articulation of this approach, I have found a classic the*logical teaching helpful which recognizes that the bible "*contains* revelation, namely in the form of a written record; but that not all of Scripture *is* revelation."[82] [emphasis added]

In line with Augustine and Thomas, this teaching articulates a criterion that limits revealed truth to matters pertaining to salvation or well-being: it says, the bible teaches "firmly, faithfully and without error that truth which God wanted put into sacred writings *for the sake of our salvation*."[83] [emphasis added] This the*logical criterion, "for the sake of our salvation," must be spelled out in the context of kyriarchal globalization as "for the sake of wo/men's salvation." Hence, this criterion may not be universalized as "for the sake of the Other"[84] or identified

Coles, *Beyond Gated Politics: Reflections for the Possibility of Democracy* (Minneapolis, Minn.: University of Minnesota Press, 2005), 109–38.

80. For such an approach see especially the work of Rosemary Radford Ruether, David Tracy, and Edward Schillebeeckx.

81. Such a hermeneutical approach has been consistently developed in the work of Phyllis Trible. See her biographical statement, "The Pilgrim Bible on a Feminist Journey," reprinted in *Daughters of Sarah* 15/3 (1989): 4–7.

82. *Dei Verbum, 11* see "Dei Verbum, Dogmatic Constitution on Divine Revelation," in W. Abbott and J. Gallagher, eds., *The Documents of Vatican II* (New York: America, 1966), 108–19.

83. Abbott and Gallagher, 119. The background of this text is discussed by Alois Grillmeier in Herbert Vorgrimler, eds., *Commentary on the Documents of Vatican II*, volume 3 (New York: Herder & Herder, 1969), 199–246.

84. "The Other," as moral summons, has been introduced by the work of Levinas. For the importance of Levinas to biblical studies, see Tamara Cohn Eskenzi, in Garry A. Phillips, and

with the biblical command to "love your neighbor as yourself."[85] One cannot do so because both the "generic" neighbor and the "face of the Other" have been conceptualized in terms of the masculine[86] and in terms of subordination.[87]

Focusing on the socio-political situation of wo/men on the bottom of the kyriarchal pyramid, the criterion "for the sake of wo/men's well-being" allows one to measure everything said in scripture as to whether it fosters wo/men's well-being[88] in particular social-political situations. This criterion allows one to reject the authority of those biblical texts that are inscriptions of empire and violence. It also allows one to free oneself from the internalized ethos of empire, in a process of critical reflection which traditionally is called the "discernment of the Spirit."

However, this criterion also asks for a critical and ongoing debate not only as to the meaning of a biblical text but also as to what constitutes particular wo/men's actual well-being. It requires that we claim the authority to challenge not only our interpretive traditions but also the biblical text itself, because texts and traditions are always embedded in forms of imperial power. To do so, we need to ask how the "power over" of empire is inscribed in a particular biblical text. We must ask which voices have been left out or marginalized in the text, and its interpretive tradition, and we must recognize that differential, decolonizing feminist interpretations are possible, and make sure that all voices are heard and given their due.[89] Biblical the*logy, as the "doing of the*logy," must be re-conceptualized in terms of the equality of the baptized by the reformation—not as an individualistic-privatized spiritual practice but instead as a radical democratic practice of the ekklēsia.

David Jobling, eds., *Levinas and Biblical Studies*, Semeia Studies 43 (Atlanta, Ga.: Society of Biblical Literature, 2003).

85. John J. Collins, *The Bible After Babel*, 156–58.

86. See Tamara Cohn Eskenazi, "Love Your Neighbor As An Other: Reflections on Levinas's Ethics and the Hebrew Bible," in *Levinas and Biblical Studies*, 145–57, and Susan E. Shapiro, "'And God Created Woman': Reading the Bible Otherwise," Ibid., 159–95.

87. Emmanuel Levinas, *Outside the Subject*, translated by Michael B. Smith (Stanford, Calif.: Stanford University Press, 1993), 44. "Gratuitous responsibility resembling that of a hostage. . . . Here, then, contrary to Buber's I—Thou, there is no initial equality. . . . Ethical inequality: subordination to the other, original diacony."

88. See my article "Understanding God's Revealed Word," *Catholic Charismatic* 1 (1977): 4-10, and my book *Bread Not Stone: The Challenge of Feminist Biblical Interpretation*, originally published 1985, Tenth Anniversary Edition (Boston, Mass.: Beacon, 1995), 23–42.

89. Georgia Warnke, "Feminism and Hermeneutics," *Hypatia* 8/1 (1993): 81–98 and Rosemary Hennessy, "Women's Lives/Feminist Knowledge," ibid.: 14 –34.

To sum up my argument: as the*logical subjects, Christian feminists have to insist on wo/men's spiritual authority to assess both the oppressive as well as the liberating imagination of particular biblical texts in the interest of wo/men's well-being. We must do so because of the imperial functions of authoritative scriptural claims that demand obedience and acceptance. By deconstructing the all-encompassing kyriarchal rhetorics and politics of obedience and subordination, we are able to generate new possibilities for engaging in emancipatory practices of biblical "meaning making" and political resistance to imperial globalization.

A critical biblical reading, in the ekklēsia of wo/men,[90] understands biblical authority not as something that requires subordination and obedience, but as a resource for creativity, courage, and solidarity. It understands truth not as something given once and for all, as hidden and buried, and ready to be unveiled and unearthed by a spiritual reading of biblical texts. It does not understand scripture as tablets of stone but rather as nourishing bread. It understands revelation as something ongoing, as fermenting yeast of the empowering presence of Divine Wisdom, which can be experienced and articulated only in and through the rejection of the violent power and ethos of empire. It does not understand the bible as an immutable archetype but as an historical prototype of Christian community and life,[91] as nourishing bread of Divine Wisdom that enables us to struggle against the violence and exploitation of empire in our daily lives.

As in *Rhetoric and Ethic*, I again quote Karen Baker-Fletcher here because she has glimpsed a dynamic vision of biblical interpretation that seeks justice and well-being for all wo/men without exception and she has likened this to the ceaseless motion of the sea:

> When I watch the wind tease and urge into dance the waves of the ocean, when I feel the moon's pull on the waters and on the cycles of my own body, I often think of the deep powerful waters of the ocean dancing with the spirit of God . . . Creation is born out of a loving, creative dance between Spirit and the elements of the cosmos. We humans are *adam*

90. For the elaboration of this notion, see Chapter 3.
91. See my book *In Memory of Her: A Feminist Theological Reconstruction of Christian Origins*, originally published 1983, Tenth Anniversary Edition (New York: Crossroad, 1994), 3–40, esp., 33ff; on the notion of prototype, see Rachel Blau Du Plessis, "The Critique of Consciousness and Myth in Levertov, Rich, and Rukeyser," *Feminist Studies* 3 (1975): 199–221, esp., 219.

(which means "earth creature" in Hebrew), dependent on all the elements of water, earth, air, sun. Our own nativity and the birth of our children's children is dependent on this power of life.[92]

If the scriptures were understood as the "deep powerful waters of the ocean dancing with the Spirit of G*d," biblical the*logy could then be seen as articulating and participating in "the creative dance between the Spirit and the elements" of the biblical traditions. In the critical deliberations of such an emancipatory-rhetorical paradigm of interpretation, biblical discourses could overcome their inscriptions of empire and violence and become Divine Wisdom-Sophia's power for life again.

92. Karen Baker-Fletcher, *Sisters of Dust, Sisters of Spirit: Womanist Wordings on God and Creation* (Minneapolis, Minn.: Fortress Press, 1998), 27.

Chapter 3

Empire and Ekklēsia

In the preceding chapter, I have explored empire as the context of our readings of scripture and the implications of this context for biblical studies, the*logy,[1] and biblical authority. In this exploration I asked how to read and evaluate the inscriptions of empire in early Christian writings, and I have called for practices of detoxifying or decolonizing interpretation. Biblical texts and their inscriptions of empire, I have argued, need not just to be understood but also adjudicated in a critical process of feminist interpretation. If such a critical process of interpretation is conceptualized as a radical democratic feminist practice of evaluation, it requires not only a different understanding of the power and authority of scripture but also a different understanding of language and interpretation.

To enable such a democratic process of adjudication and to protect the understanding of scripture from falling into the hands of fundamentalist literalism or academic positivism, it is necessary to articulate a radical democratic hermeneutical space that engenders such scriptural non-authoritarian adjudications. In my work, I have suggested the imaginary of the ekklēsia of wo/men as such a decolonizing space and feminist horizon from where to interpret and adjudicate biblical texts and interpretations in general and the biblical inscriptions of empire in particular. However, this theoretical proposal has not been widely discussed, perhaps because of the qualifier "wo/men"[2] or because it is assumed that ekklēsia means "church." Often those who are interested in church are not interested in wo/men and those engaged in feminist critique are not interested in church.

The expression is also misunderstood if it is reduced to "Western" notions of democracy. I have sought to defend against such a misunderstanding by adding

1. See footnote 6, Chapter 1: Introduction.
2. See footnote 21, Chapter 1: Introduction.

the qualifier "wo/men"[3] because neither Greece, the United States, nor any other democracy has established the full citizenship, equality, and well-being of all wo/men without any exceptions. Ekklēsia of wo/men is historically and theoretically conceptualized as the alternative—not the counter or anti–space—to empire. Ekklēsia is constituted not by super- and subordination but by egalitarian relationships. It is not a reversal of kyriarchal domination and subordination but a space that is "already" and "not yet." Elizabeth Castelli has rightly likened the notion of the ekklēsia of wo/men to an utopian space of "texts, institutions and worldviews that critique the historical or contemporary situation and promote an alternative vision of social and individual existence—generally a vision committed to more egalitarian and just stances."[4]

A Radical Democratic Imagination: The Ekklēsia of Wo/men

In the 1980s I coined the notion of the *ekklēsia gynaikōn* or "wo/men-church" as an in-between space that sought to overcome the dualistic feminist alternative: either "exodus" from church and religion or claiming church and religion wholeheartedly as "home," that is: "either religious or feminist." By introducing the radical democratic notion of the "ekklēsia of wo/men" as an alternative religious and symbolic space to the space evoked by the biblical images of "exodus" and "paradise/home," I sought to reframe, theoretically, the feminist "either/or" binary toward religion, which re-inscribes the dualistic division between religion and culture, religion and democratic rights, or religious and secular wo/men's movements. To overcome the dualistic evaluation of the bible as either liberative or oppressive, I suggested the ekklēsia of wo/men as such a political hermeneutical space.[5]

3. J'annine Jobling, *Feminist Biblical Interpretation in Theological Context: Restless Readings* (Burlington, Vt.: Ashgate, 2002), 32–59 and 142–62, discusses the concept of the *ekklēsia of wo/men* but chooses ekklēsia without the qualification of *wo/men* as her hermeneutical key concept in order to restrict the concept to the Christian feminist movement (143). In so doing she re-inscribes the division between the Christian and the so-called secular women's movements, which I sought to overcome by this radical democratic, alternative kyriarchal image.

4. Elizabeth A. Castelli, "The Ekklesia of Women and/as Utopian Space: Locating the Work of Elisabeth Schüssler Fiorenza in Feminist Utopian Thought," in *On The Cutting Edge: The Study of Wo/men in Biblical Worlds* (New York: Continuum, 2004), 36–52, esp., 38.

5. For the realizing practices of the ekklēsia of wo/men see also Mary E. Hunt, "Feminist

At the same time, my work sought to underscore the political-radical democratic aspects of the ekklēsia of wo/men. For conceptualizing the oxymoron ekklēsia of wo/men, I have built further on the discussions of radical democracy in feminist political theory[6] and on critical legal studies[7] that seek to reconceptualize legal discourses as a site of political struggles. By introducing the radical democratic notion of the ekklēsia of wo/men as an alternative religious symbolic concept to "exodus and paradise/home," I not only have sought to reframe theoretically the feminist either/or binary toward religion, I also have attempted to name an alternative emancipative the*logical and radical democratic theoretical space where different feminist movements and theoretical directions could articulate alternatives to global empire/kyriarchy. The following four aspects—the political, the semantic, the ekklesial and the the*logical—are important for understanding the ekklēsia of wo/men as such a critical hermeneutical "utopian" space.

The Political Dimension
The Greek word *ekklēsia* literally means the democratic assembly and is best translated as "democratic congress" of full decision making citizens. Democratic equality, citizenship, and decision making power are constitutive for the notion of ekklēsia. However, the Greek word *ekklēsia* is also determined by a Christian language context and is usually translated as "church" which robs the term of its political character. For that reason, I prefer not to translate ekklēsia as "church," a translation of the term that functions as a signifier that must be actively decoded in order to know what the Greek word actually means.

The root meaning of ekklēsia derives from the classical Greek institution of democracy, which, in theory, promised freedom and equality to all its citizens but, in practice, granted such rights only to imperial, elite, propertied, educated male heads

Catholic Theology and Practice: From Kyriarchy to Discipleship of Equals," in *Toward a New Heaven and a New Earth*, ed. Segovia, 459–472; and Marjorie Procter–Smith, "Feminist Ritual Strategies: the Ekklēsia Gynaikōn at Work," Ibid., 498–515.

6. See for instance, Seyla Benhabib, ed., *Democracy and Difference: Contesting the Boundaries of the Political* (Princeton, N.J.: Princeton University Press, 1996), and Chantal Mouffe, ed., *Dimensions of Radical Democracy* (London: Verso, 1992).

7. See for instance Mary Frug, *Postmodern Legal Feminism* (New York: Routledge, 1992); and Martha Minow, *Equality and the Bill of Rights* (Ithaca, N.Y.: Cornell University Press, 1992) and *Identities* (New Haven, Conn.: Yale University Press, 1991). See also H. Markus, R. Shweder, and M. Minow, eds., *The Free Exercise of Culture* (New York: Russell Sage Foundation, 2001).

of household by restricting full citizenship to them. The kyriarchal notion of equality grounded in sameness and uniformity—which is often labeled "Western"—has its roots in this restriction of democratic citizenship. Hence, the ekklēsia, understood as the radical democratic congress of citizen-subjects, has never been fully realized in history because neither the Greek *polis* nor the French and the American democratic revolutions fought for disenfranchised wo/men to become fully empowered decision making citizens. The struggles of the disenfranchised for full citizenship and civil rights, in the past three hundred years and more, have sought to correct this failure of modernity and to realize the vision of radical democratic equality. In short, the expression ekklēsia of wo/men calls for full citizens to come together not only critically to investigate cultural-religious traditions and texts but also to adjudicate them and make decisions in the interest of the well-being of the *cosmopolis*.[8]

According to the Greek philosopher Aristotle, democracy is best understood alternatively as a community of equals in the interest of the common good, or well-being, or as the independent, responsible rule of equal citizens who were not wo/men. Such a manner of government and rule was articulated and took place in the ekklēsia, the assembly of full citizens of the *polis* (the city-state), a term from which "politics" is derived. According to Hannah Arendt,

> . . . the political realm arises directly out of acting together, the sharing
> of "words and deeds." . . . The *polis* properly speaking is not the city-state
> in its physical location; it is the organization of people as it arises out of
> acting and speaking together, and its true space lies between people living
> together for this purpose, no matter where they happen to be. . . . action
> and speech create a space between the participants which can find its
> proper location almost any time and everywhere.[9]

With ekklēsia of wo/men I have thus in mind a heuristic and hermeneutical construct that is influenced by Hannah Arendt's notion of the polis as a space for "acting and speaking together,"[10] and has affinities to what Chandra Talpade

8. See the important book by Kwame Anthony Appiah, *Cosmopolitanism: Ethics in a World of Strangers* (New York: W.W. Norton & Co, 2006).

9. Hannah Arendt, *The Human Condition* (Chicago, Ill.: University of Chicago Press, 1958), 198.

10. Jennifer Ring, *The Political Consequences of Thinking: Gender and Judaism in the Work of Hannah Arendt* (New York: NYU Press, 1997), 259, argues that the text evokes "the destruction

Mohantia has called "the imagined community" of Third World oppositional struggles. Talpade Mohanti envisions it as the kind of space that provides

> political rather than biological or cultural bases for alliance. Thus it is not color or sex which constructs the ground for these struggles. Rather it is the way we think about race, class and gender,—the political links we choose to make among and between struggles. Thus potentially, women of all colors (including white women) can align themselves and participate in these imagined communities.[11]

Within the context of social movements for change,[12] one can theorize the ekklēsia of wo/men not only as a virtual utopian space[13] but also as an already partially realized space of radical equality, as a site of feminist struggles to transform social and religious institutions and discourses.

Theoretically, the oxymoron ekklēsia of wo/men seeks to develop "democratics" as the hermeneutic horizon for feminist struggles both in religion and society at large. I have borrowed the term "*democratics*" from Chela Sandoval, who has theorized it as one of the methods of the oppressed and delineated it in the following way:

> With the transnationalization of capitalism when elected officials are no longer leaders of singular nation-states but nexuses for multinational interests, it also becomes possible for citizen-subjects to become activists for a new decolonizing global terrain, a psychic terrain that can unite

---

of the Temple in Jerusalem and the Jewish diaspora. . . . The physical space that held the ancient Jews together was destroyed in fact, but the people lived on by means of 'organized remembrance'." She also points out that "The communal energy each time the congregation meets closely resembles Arendt's concept of action in the *Human Condition* and freedom in her discussion of the French resistance" (282).

11. Chandra Talpade Mohanti, "Introduction: Cartographies of Struggle," in *Third World Women and the Politics of Feminism*, eds. Chandra Talpade Mohanti, Ann Russo, and Lourdes Torres (Bloomington, Ind.: Indiana University Press, 1991), 1–47.

12. See Jill M. Bystydzienski and Joti Sekhon, eds., *Democratization and Women's Grassroots Movements* (Bloomington, Ind.: Indiana University Press, 1999).

13. See Elizabeth Castelli, "The Ekklesia of Women and/as Utopian Space," 39. Feminist fictional utopias literally map "the possible options for utopia in different conceptual and 'lived' spaces; elsewhere, in the borderlands between the 'real' and the 'possible,' and in the in-between space of the not-yet."

them with similarly positioned citizen-subjects within and across national borders into new, post-Western–empire alliances. . . . The new
countrypeople [of this imagined community] who fight for egalitarian
social relations under neocolonial postmodernism welcome citizenry to a
new polity, a new homeland. The means for entry is "the methodology of
the oppressed," a set of technologies for decolonizing the social [and reli-
gious] imagination. These technologies . . . are all guided by democratics,
the practitioners' commitment to the equal distribution of power. . . . [14]

The ekklēsia of wo/men could also be likened to the space delineated by
the justice seeking, "quilt-making" theory and method of black feminists as
developed by Patricia Hill Collins:

> Rather than being seen as yet another content area within Black feminist
> discourse, a concern with justice fused with a deep spirituality appears to
> be highly significant to how African-American women conceptualize crit-
> ical social theory. Justice constitutes an article of faith expressed through
> deep feelings that move people to action. For many Black feminist think-
> ers, justice transcends Western notions of equality grounded in same-
> ness and uniformity. Elsa Barkley Brown's discussion of African American
> women's quilting (1989) points us in the direction of conceptualizing an
> alternative notion of justice. In making their quilts Black women weave
> together scraps of fabric from all sorts of places. Nothing is wasted, and
> every piece of fabric has a function and a place in a given quilt. . . . [T]
> hose who conceptualize community via notions of uniformity and same-
> ness have difficulty imagining a social quilt that is simultaneously hetero-
> geneous, driven toward excellence, and just. [15]

Like Hill Collins' concept of "the social quilt," so the *democratics* of the oxy-
moronic construct "ekklēsia of wo/men" seeks to name a feminist space where
citizen-subjects can fight for justice and egalitarian relations that recognize the

14. Chela Sandoval, *Methodology of the Oppressed* (Minneapolis, Minn.: University of Minnesota Press, 2000), 183.
15. Patricia Hill Collins, *Fighting Words: Black Women & the Search for Justice* (Minneapolis,
Minn.: University of Minnesota Press, 1998), 248–49.

unique difference of each and every one. Ekklēsia of wo/men articulates a vision of radical equality for creating a world of justice and well-being. It wants to name the vision of justice and salvation which feminist movements seek and in which biblical religions share.

The Linguistic/Semantic Dimension

The expression *ekklēsia gynaikōn,* the ekklēsia of wo/men, is at the same time a linguistic tool and semantic means of critical reading and political conscientization. It seeks to bring into public consciousness the kyriocentric character of so-called generic language and the masculine overdetermination of ekklēsia in malestream[16] political discourses and religious representations. Since the signifier "woman" is still used to draw exclusive boundaries in societal democracies and biblical religions, it is important to mark linguistically the difference between democracy and church,—on the one hand a kyriarchal institution patterned after the Roman Empire, and on the other ekklēsia, the congress of decision making citizen subjects.

The qualification of ekklēsia with the split and differently articulated term *wo/men* serves as a linguistic tool for indicating how diversified and pluriform the social-sociological group wo/men in actuality is. Wo/men are not the same nor do they have an essence in common that makes them different from men. There are as many differences between wo/men and within wo/men as there are between men and wo/men. Wo/men are not just determined by gender, but also by race, class, ethnicity, culture, age, sexual preference, and religion. Identity is not stable, but changes over the course of time. Hence the oxymoron "ekklēsia of wo/men" should not be understood in the cultural terms of femininity as promoting the ideal of the White Lady. Rather, the oxymoron "ekklēsia of wo/men" thus seeks to signify the multiple forms in which radical democracy is lived today in order to presage the rich diversity of the radical democratic ekklēsia of the future.

Moreover, the expression "ekklēsia of wo/men" is an oxymoron, a contradiction in terms. Qualifying "ekklēsia" with "wo/men" seeks to lift into consciousness that democracy in antiquity and modernity has been a promise but not a lived reality. Church, society, and religion have been and still are governed by elite, mostly white, men who have been exclusive of wo/men and other servant-peoples for centuries, in order to protect their equality and prerogatives in democratic societies.

16. I have borrowed this term from feminist theorists and use it not in a pejorative way, but in order to signal that tradition, scripture, and language are elite male/masculine defined.

Because the elite male is the embodiment of ideals and agent of rights in ancient and modern democracies, one needs always to qualify ekklēsia with "wo/men" if one speaks of radical democracy in church and society. The expression seeks to communicate a vision that connects struggles for a more democratic and just church with global, societal, and political democratic movements for justice, freedom, and equality. I suggest that these movements have emerged again and again throughout the centuries because of the disparity between the professed vision of radical democratic equality in church and society and the actual reality of domination and subordination, which are experienced every day.

In sum, the oxymoron ekklēsia of wo/men seeks to articulate a radical democratic ethos. As Sheldon Wolin has succinctly remarked about Athenian democracy:

> Now while it is true that the *demos* refused to extend democratic citizenship to women, metics, and slaves, that refusal, unlike the refusal of the aristocrat to admit the *demos* to high office, would contradict the idea of democratic equality. Or, stated differently, democracy was and is the only political ideal that condemns its own denial of equality and inclusion.[17]

It is this fundamental contradiction that the oxymoron ekklēsia of wo/men seeks to lift into consciousness and to operationalize in the work of interpretation, as *democratics* which according to Chela Sandoval "is an ethical, ideological code that is committed to social justice according to egalitarian redistribution of power across such differences encoded as race, gender, sex, nation, culture or class distributions."[18] Throughout the centuries, democracy has been an elite male institution. It is necessary, thus, to qualify *ekklēsia* with *wo/men*, as long as wo/men remain second-class citizens in society and religion and as long as grammatically kyriocentric language prevails. Hence, the oxymoron ekklēsia of wo/men also seeks to provide a hermeneutical space from where to read. It opens up the possibility of interrupting a totalizing gender reading, which naturalizes the sex-gender system by identifying grammatical gender with

17. Sheldon S. Wolin, "Transgression, Equality and Voice," in *Demokratia: A Conversation on Democracies, Ancient and Modern*, eds. Josiah Ober and Charles Hedrick (Princeton, N.J.: Princeton University Press, 1996), 63–90, esp., 80.
18. Sandoval, *Methodology of the Oppressed*, 112.

natural gender and thereby erases the historical traces of actual wo/men from the kyriocentric record.

The Community Dimension

The expression ekklēsia of wo/men is not only a feminist theoretical symbolic construct, intending to overcome the dualistic split between religious and societal wo/men's movements, and a democratics for decolonizing the cultural and religious imagination. It is also a historical-communal term developed in terms of my own Christian Catholic context. Nevertheless, it could do the same critical work—albeit differently articulated—in terms of other religious visions and symbolic universes, such as for instance "synagogue of wo/men" or "umma of wo/men." Such a re-articulation of religion in the horizon of radical democratic equality is necessary if religion is to become an influence and power for radical democracy today.

Ekklēsia, as the decision making assembly of full citizens, insists on the ancient Roman and medieval democratic maxim: "that which affects all should be determined by every one" (or in Latin: *quod omnes tangit, ab omnibus judicetur*). In and through struggles for change and liberation, the vision of the ekklēsia, of G*d's life-giving and transforming power for community, becomes experiential reality in the midst of structural sin, which is constituted by death-dealing kyriarchal powers of exploitation and dehumanization.

In early Christian literature, the expression ekklēsia is the very name for the Christian community.[19] The very self-description of the early Christian communities was a radical democratic one.[20] The ekklēsia, understood as the force-field of Divine Wisdom-Spirit, is a "new creation," in which the Spirit-empowered people are all equal but not all the same. They all share in the multi-faceted gifts of Divine Wisdom-Spirit, all without exception: Jews, Greeks, Barbarians, wo/men and men, slave wo/men and free, those with high social status and those who are nothing in the eyes of the world.[21] The ekklēsia of wo/men, as this vision of G*d's renewed creation, is working toward a radical democratic society,

---

19. The word "synagogue" has a similar valence and means the "congregation of the people of G*d."

20. This is not unusual. Most organizational sociologists point out that most religions have an egalitarian self-understanding in the beginning.

21. See Schüssler Fiorenza, *In Memory of Her*, 160–99.

in which none are hungry, strangers, or outcasts but each cherishes the earth and struggles in solidarity with those who are oppressed by racism, nationalism, poverty, neo-colonialism, and hetero-sexism.

Although the word *ekklēsia* is usually translated in English as "church," the English word "church" derives from the Greek word *kyriakon*, i.e., belonging to the lord/master/father, but not from the Greek term *ekklēsia*.[22] The translation process, which has transformed "*ekklēsia*/congress" into "*kyriakē*/church," indicates a historical development that has privileged the kyriarchal/hierarchical form of church. Hence, the rendering of the Greek word *ekklēsia* with "church" promotes a Christian self-understanding that is derived from the kyriarchal models of household and state in antiquity, which were governed by the lord/master/father of the house, to whom freeborn wo/men, freeborn dependents, clients, and workers as well as slaves were subordinated as his property.[23]

It is misleading, thus, to translate this contradictory expression, *ekklēsia of wo/men*, as "wo/men-church," because in the process of translation ekklēsia tends to lose its radical democratic meaning. While the translation "wo/men-church" makes the connection between wo/men and church, it is not able to hold together the meaning of ekklēsia as both democratic assembly and as church, as political and as religious. As a result, the intended radical political valence of the term is lost. Yet, my goal in qualifying and circumscribing *ekklēsia* with the term *wo/men* has been precisely to raise into public consciousness the fact that neither church nor society are what they claim to be: ekklēsia, that is, the democratic congress of equal decision-making citizens who are wo/men.

The Global-Spiritual Dimension

The radical equality of the ekklēsia of wo/men is the*logically grounded in the conviction that all wo/men are created in the image of the Divine, each and

22. According to the Encarta Dictionary the word "church" is derived from the Old English *cir(i)ce*, from a prehistoric Germanic word that is also the ancestor of German *Kirche*, and ultimately from Greek *kuriakon doma* "house of the lord," from *kyrios* "lord." Microsoft® Encarta® Reference Library 2004. © 1993–2003 Microsoft Corporation. All rights reserved.

23. Schüssler Fiorenza, "A Discipleship of Equals: Ekklesial Democracy and Patriarchy in Biblical Perspective," in *A Democratic Catholic Church: The Reconstruction of Roman Catholicism*, eds. E.C. Bianchi and R. Radford Ruether (New York: Crossroad, 1992), 17–33.

every human being is precious in Her eyes, and that all have received multi-faceted gifts and "powers for" rather than "over." In all our differences, wo/men represent the Divine here and now because women are created in the Divine image and likeness. Every one is made in the image of Divine Wisdom, who has gifted and called every individual differently. The divine image is neither masculine nor feminine, white nor black, rich nor poor, but multicolored, multi-gendered, and more.

As a richly gifted people, the ekklēsia of wo/men envisions and works for a *cosmopolis*[24]—a world-community in which religious, racial, and class, but also heterosexual markers no longer signify and legitimate status differences and relations of kyriarchal domination and subordination. As a migrant/pilgrim people, the ekklēsia of wo/men may fail again and again, but it continues to struggle, to live in fullness and to realize its calling to be the radical democratic society in process.

This understanding of the ekklēsia of wo/men imagines society and religion as a reciprocal community of support, a dynamic alliance of equals. Its principle and horizon is a radical democratic vision and movement that creates community in diversity, commonality in solidarity, equality in freedom and love, a world-community that appreciates the "other" precisely as the other. This the*logical conceptualization of the ekklēsia of wo/men seeks not only fullness of being, all-encompassing inclusivity, but also dynamic multiplicity and the convergence of many different voices. In Christian terms, it is fore-shadowed in the image of Pentecost[25] where people from different regions and cultures could understand the Spirit in their own languages, an image that invites Christian wo/men in the power of the Spirit to struggle together with wo/men from other religions and persuasions for the realization of the ekklēsia of wo/men.

Such a the*logical vision was already articulated by the African American thinker Anna Julia Cooper in the nineteenth century,[26] albeit in different

---

24. For this philosophical political vision see especially Kwame Anthony Appiah, *Cosmopolitanism: Ethics in a World of Strangers* (New York: W.W. Norton & Co, 2006), xviii, who *explores* the final message of his father to him and his sisters: "Remember you are citizens of the world."

25. However it must not be overlooked that this text also has been used for legitimating colonial Christian missionary practices.

26. Her major work is *A Voice from the South* (Xenia, Ohio: Aldine, 1892; reprint New York: Oxford University Press, 1988).

terms. The work of Karen Baker-Fletcher points out that equality and freedom were not simply physical states for Anna Julia Cooper but political-spiritual realities.[27] Cooper believed that democratic progress was "a shadow mark of the creator's image" derived "from the essential worth of humanity." Cooper envisioned a future for humanity governed by the principles of equality, freedom, and democracy, which were ontological universal aspects of human nature. She asserts

> that progress in the democratic sense is an inborn human endowment—a shadow mark of the Creator's image, or if you will an urge-cell, the universal and unmistakable hall-mark traceable to the Father of all.[28]

Anna Julia Cooper insisted that democratic equality and freedom are G*d-given, inborn ontological capacities of every human being regardless of race, sex, class, and country. Against theories that claimed democracy, equality, and freedom as the property of the superior races of western European civilization,[29] Cooper insists that these democratic qualities are inherent in the fact of being human and hence can never be suppressed. The key-metaphor for G*d in Cooper's religious discourse, according to Baker-Fletcher, is a "Singing Something" that in every nation cries out for justice. As Baker-Fletcher puts it,

> What makes one human is one's inner voice, the voice of equality and freedom that is directly traceable to God. The voice of God, in this sense, sings through the human spirit and calls humankind to action,

27. Karen Baker Fletcher, *A Singing Something: Womanist Reflections on Anna Julia Cooper* (New York: Crossroad, 1994). See also idem, "A Womanist Ontology of Freedom and Equality," in *The Journal of Religious Thought* (2001): 60–71.

28. Anna Julia Cooper, "Equality of Races and the Democratic Movement," privately printed pamphlet, Washington, D.C., 1945, 5.

29. Like other Anglo-Saxon suffragists and social reformers, Elizabeth Cady Stanton was very much determined and limited by her social status and class position. She not only expressed anti-immigrant sentiments by arguing that the suffrage of women of her own class would increase the numbers of Anglo-Saxon voters, but she also appealed to ethnic and racial prejudices when she exhorted: "American women of wealth and refinement, if you do not wish the lower orders of Chinese, Africans, Germans, and Irish, with their low ideas of womanhood to make laws for you, demand that woman, too, shall be represented in the government" (as quoted by Barbara Hilkert Andolsen, *"Daughters of Jefferson, Daughters of Bootblacks": Racism and American Feminism* [Macon, Ga.: Mercer University Press, 1986], 31).

growth, development and reform. There is movement involved in the act of vocalization.[30]

While the notion of the ekklēsia of wo/men is theorized quite differently and speaks to a different rhetorical situation and historical context,[31] it nevertheless is a part of and continues this radical democratic vision. It also stands, as Elizabeth Castelli has pointed out,[32] in the utopian tradition of Christine de Pizan's *The Book of the City of the Ladies*[33] written 600 years ago in 1405 CE. In defense of wo/men, Christine constructs a strong and beautiful city, an allegorical dwelling-place where reason, righteousness, and justice prevail to show the world the truth of women's inherent value. The city is fashioned with the building blocks of reasoned argumentation as well as the exemplary stories of women of high honor, virtue, and achievement.[34]

This submerged feminist intellectual tradition of radical democratic religious agency, in which my own work stands, has claimed and continues to claim the authority and right of wo/men to interpret experience, scriptures, traditions, and religions from wo/men's perspectives and in our own many different voices. Although this feminist tradition of wo/men's religious authority and agency remains fragmented and has not always been able to overcome the limitations and prejudicial frameworks of its own time and social location, its critical knowledge and continuing vibrancy nevertheless remain crucial for contemporary radical democratic articulations of justice and well-being.

To sum up my argument: I have delineated the ekklēsia of wo/men as a radical democratic hermeneutical space that seeks to make connections between

30. Baker-Fletcher, *A Singing Something*, 192–93.

31. For discussion of this theoretical context, see for instance Anne Phillips, *Engendering Democracy* (Cambridge, Mass.: Polity, 1991); Judith Butler and Joan W. Scott, eds., *Feminists Theorize the Political* (New York: Routledge, 1992); Joan Cocks, *The Oppositional Imagination: Feminism, Critique and Political Theory* (New York: Routledge, 1989); Mary Lyndon Shanley and Carole Pateman, eds., *Feminist Interpretations and Political Theory* (University Park, Pa: The Pennsylvania State University Press, 1991).

32. Castelli, "The Ekklesia of Women," 36.

33. The title probably alludes to Augustine's *City of God*. See Bonnie A. Birk, *Christine de Pizan and Biblical Wisdom: A Feminist-Theological Point of View* (Marquette, Ind.: University Press, 2005), 155 n. 55.

34. Birk, *Christine de Pizan and Biblical Wisdom*, 121. See also Barbara Newman, *God and the Goddesses: Vision Poetry and Belief in the Middle Ages* (Philadelphia, Pa.: University of Pennsylvania Press, 2003).

ancient and modern democratic discourses. At the same time, I have argued that the radical democratic notion of ekklēsia needs to be qualified with "wo/men" in the differential, generic sociological sense because both ancient and modern forms of democracy, as well as of church, have excluded wo/men as second- or third-class citizens from political and religious decision making. This radical democratic political notion of the ekklēsia of wo/men also articulates a vision of the Christian community as one radical democratic assembly among many, in the *cosmopolis* of G*d's very different peoples.

The ekklēsia of wo/men is the hermeneutical space in which professional biblical interpretation, as well as that of the "common people," needs to take place. Its method is similar to that of Black wo/men who, according to Hill Collins, "weave together scraps of fabric from all sorts of places. Nothing is wasted, and every piece of fabric has a function and a place in a given quilt."[35]

Both forms of interpretation need to be guided by "democratics," which Chela Sandoval has defined as "bringing about new ethical and political standards in the name of egalitarian and democratic social change."[36] Sandoval's "democratics" is one of the emancipatory technologies of conscientization that needs to be put to work in biblical interpretation on both the historical and the contemporary levels of meaning making simultaneously. It needs to be seen, in rhetorical terms, as a debate taking place in the hermeneutical horizon of the ekklēsia of wo/men and using the method of democratics. Hence, in the next section I will stage the discussions on "Paul and Empire" as such a rhetorical debate in this hermeneutical space.

Debating Paul in the Ekklēsia of Wo/men

In the past decade "anti-imperial studies" have emerged under the leadership of Neil Elliott and Richard Horsley, among others, as a new direction in scholarship on the Pauline letters. This new scientific field of research is mostly oriented toward historical studies but does not eschew the reading of empire also on the contemporary level of meaning making.[37] Hence, it is surprising that

35. Hill Collins, *Fighting Words*, 248.
36. Sandoval, *Methodology of the Oppressed*, 114.
37. See for instance Neil Elliott, *Liberating Paul: The Justice of God and the Politics of the*

a debate has emerged between "anti-imperial studies" and feminist studies as to whether Paul has rejected the imperial order or whether he has re-enforced kyriarchal theories of subordination, which historically had been used by Greek and Roman elite men to support their own status prerogatives and to preserve the kyriarchal order of privilege and exploitation.

To approach this question, I will first discuss the ideological strategies determining the work of Pauline Studies, then with the help of an article by Robert C. Tannehill, I will sketch the debate between malestream and feminist work on "Paul and Empire." In a third step, I ask whether the notion of an anti-imperial Paul can be sustained in a reading of 1 Cor 11:2-16. Finally, I will indicate the theoretical shift that needs to take place, a shift from the rhetoric of Paul to the hermeneutical space of the ekklēsia of wo/men.

Rhetorical Strategies of Domination: Othering, Identity, and Identification
In my book *Rhetoric and Ethic: The Politics of Biblical Interpretation*, I have elaborated the ideological strategies that determine Pauline studies as a whole, and the anti-imperial studies of Paul in particular. Since these strategies countermine a reading of Paul in the hermeneutical horizon of the ekklēsia of wo/men, I need to summarize them here again. If one seeks to adjudicate whether Paul's gospel re-inscribes the gospel of Caesar they cannot be pushed off the table as "postmodernist critiques" to which a "modest form of the scientific method"[38] is an adequate antidote.

First: The Western "politics of identity and rhetorics of othering" establishes identity either by comparison to the other, as an inferior "same," or by emphasizing and stereotyping difference as the otherness of the other.[39] In its classical form, this politics of otherness is rooted in the practices of the andro-social Greek *polis*, its political-philosophical subtext is democracy, and its social

---

Apostle (Maryknoll, N.Y.: Orbis, 1994); Richard A. Horsley, *Religion and Empire: People, Power and the Life of the Spirit* (Minneapolis, Minn.: Fortress Press, 2003); Idem, *Jesus and Empire: The Kingdom of God and the New World Disorder* (Minneapolis, Minn.: Fortress Press, 2003).

38. Robert Jewett, "Exegetical Support From Romans and Other Letters," in Horsley, *Paul and Politics: Ekklesia, Israel, Imperium, Interpretation: Essays in Honor of Krister Stendahl* (Harrisburg, Pa.: Trinity International, 200), 58–71, esp., 60.

39. See Sandra Bartky, *Femininity and Domination: Studies in the Phenomenology of Oppression* (New York: Routledge, 1990).

formation is patriarchy or, better, kyriarchy, the governing dominance or supremacy of elite propertied men. The exclusion from democratic government of freeborn propertied wo/men, poor wo/men and men, slave wo/men and men, as well as barbarian wo/men and men required ideological justifications. It needed to be argued why only freeborn propertied Greek male heads of households could be full citizens if, as the Sophists maintained, all are equal by nature.[40] The articulation of dualisms, such as human-animal, male-female, slave-free, native-alien, and the assertion of the "natural" inferiority of freeborn wo/men as well as slave wo/men and men, are ideological constructs which articulate the politics of otherness. However, we must recognize that this politics does not elaborate generic man but rather the imperial Sovereign-Father or in black idiom, the Boss-Man, as the universal subject. Its totalizing discourse of male-female dualism masks the complex interstructuring of systems of exploitation and dehumanization in kyriarchal domination by Western societies and religions.

Such differences are established as "relationships of ruling,"[41] in which structures of domination and subordination are mystified as "naturalized" differences. This "politics of otherness" has found its way into the canon of Christian scriptures and permeates biblical writings and their contemporary interpretations. It is no accident, therefore, that the majority of scholars have constructed Paul's arguments as "normative" over and against Paul's so-called gnostic, libertine, or Jewish legalistic "opponents."[42] Exegetical discourses continue to understand the Pauline writings either the*logically, as documents of inner-Christian struggles between orthodoxy and heresy, or sociologically, as records of opposing sectarian groups that are defined in contrast to the ecclesiastically established church. In both instances, scholars understand canonical voices as right and true but vilify the submerged alternative arguments as false and heretical.

In this mode, the scholarly discourses on Paul's the*logy construct a series of dualistic religious, cultural, and political oppositions: such as orthodoxy vs. heresy,

40. Page duBois, *Centaurs and Amazons: Women and the Pre-History of the Great Chain of Being* (Ann Arbor, Mich: The University of Michigan Press, 1982).

41. For this expression see Dorothy E. Smith, *The Conceptual Practices of Power: A Feminist Sociology of Knowledge* (Boston, Mass.: Northeastern University Press, 1990).

42. For a renewed interest in the study of Paul's opponents, see the recent book by Stanley E. Porter, ed., *Paul and His Opponents* (Brill: Leiden, 2005); and the work of J. L. Sumney, *Identifying Paul's Opponents: The Question of Method in 2 Corinthians* (Sheffield: JSOT, 1990); Idem., *Servants of Satan, False Brothers and Other Opponents of Paul* (Sheffield: Sheffield University Press, 1999).

apostle vs. community, honor vs. shame, mission vs. propaganda, and the*logy of the cross vs. libertine enthusiasm. These dualisms seem to be naturalized facts or data and fail to underscore that they are, instead, the products of the*logical arguments over meaning and interpretation. This series of dualisms privileges the first terms of the opposition by reserving them either for Paul, Orthodoxy, or Christianity as a whole and constructs the second terms as the negative "other," by attributing them to diverse opponents such as Hellenistic propagandists, Jewish legalists, or other outsider groups. Such interpretive dualistic oppositions muddle and play down the linking and connecting terms, such as, "audience," "community," and "gospel," because these connecting terms are subsumed under one or the other pole of the opposition. A more adequate understanding would recognize in these connecting terms the opportunity for overcoming argumentative dualisms, which are constructed by Paul and by his interpreters.

The most telling dualistic construct is that of gender, which is already inscribed in the Pauline letters insofar as Paul understands himself as the "father" of the Corinthian community who is to present the community "as a pure bride to her one husband," namely, Christ (2 Cor 11:2-3). This gendering of the community has negative overtones, since it is connected with a reference to the seduction of Eve. Such a symbolic construct of gender dualism at once coheres in and undermines the other oppositions, insofar as it casts all speaking subjects (Paul, the opponents, contemporary interpreters, and so on) as masculine and construes their audiences (the Corinthian community, Judaism, or contemporary readers, etc.) in feminine terms as passive, immature, and gullible.

The politics of othering, with its series of dualisms that mystify and occlude relations of domination, bespeaks the logic and politics of identity. The logic of identity "consists in an unrelenting urge to think things together, in a unity," to formulate "an essence that brings concrete particulars into unity."[43] I would suggest that this drive to coherence, unity, and identity is the motivating methodological and ideological force in Pauline studies. This drive is expressed in the positivistic ethos of "scientific" exegesis as well as in the essentializing tendencies of Pauline the*logy.

This drive to coherence comes to the fore, for instance, in the attempts of Pauline scholarship to rearrange the extant text and to splinter it into discrete

43. Iris Marion Young, "Impartiality and the Civic Public," in Seyla Benhabib and Drucilla Cornell, eds., *Feminism as Critique* (New York: Routledge, 1993), 61.

rhetorical fragments in such a way that the symbolic coherence of Paul's
the*logical argument—as scholars have reconstructed it—is safeguarded. This
drive for coherence is at work in the attempts of scholars to declare texts such as
1 Thess 2:14-16, 1 Cor 11:2-16 and 14: 34-36, or Rom 13:1-7 as later inter-
polations because they do not cohere with their own reading of Paul's the*logy.
Still other scholars rearrange the extant text, and reconstruct the rhetorical situation of the diverse fragments of Paul's Corinthian or Philippian correspondence, in a way that safeguards the symbolic coherence of Paul's the*logical
argument for "radical obedience."[44]

The drive to coherence, unity, and identity is also the motivating ideological
force in the constructions of Pauline the*logy. Such a "logic of identity" with its
drive to univocality energizes, for instance, J. Christiaan Beker's reconstructive
model of coherence and contingency in Pauline the*logy. After discussing the
essentializing tendencies in the reconstruction of Paul's the*logy, he concludes,
that in the midst of a variety of theological expressions Paul was able to focus
on the central core of Christian faith.[45]

Although Beker is concerned with the *fluidity* of Paul's hermeneutic inter-
actions, he nevertheless asserts that Paul articulated the "abiding truth" of the
gospel and thereby gave to the church "the beginnings of a doctrinal 'orthodox'
structure."[46] Although Beker's coherence-contingency hermeneutical model
intends to be a "via media" between the "extremes of sociological analysis"—
which he calls the sociological captivity of Paul—and the dogmatist imposition
of a specific center on Paul's thought, he himself does not avoid speaking about
such an essentialized core.

Beker names the Holy Spirit as the site of the interaction between coherence and contingency, and speaks of a "pneumatic democracy." Nevertheless,
despite this dynamic and democratic vocabulary, his concern to safeguard the
the*logical master-voice of Paul forces him, again and again, to resort to the
logic of identity that must speak of a center, core, or essence. At stake in such an

44. Kittredge, *Community and Authority: The Rhetoric of Obedience in the Pauline Tradition*,
Harvard Theological Studies (Harrisburg, Pa.: Trinity International, 1998).

45. See J. Christiaan Beker, "The Method of Recasting Pauline Theology: The Coherence-
Contingency Theme as Interpretive Model," in *SBL 1986 Seminar Papers*, ed. Kent H. Richards
(Atlanta, Ga.: Scholars, 1986), 597.

46. Jouette M. Bassler, *Pauline Theology*, Vol I : Thessalonians, Philippians, Galatians, Philemon (Minneapolis, Minn.: Fortress Press, 1991), 19.

essentializing logics and rhetorics of identity is not just the the*logical authority of the master-voice of Paul but also the "orthodoxy" of the church.

Second: Such an essentializing politics of identity[47] results in a politics of identification, which re-inscribes malestream relations of privilege and orthodox relations of exclusion by inviting readerly identification with Paul and his arguments. Such an identification with Paul's the*logical rhetoric—for instance, that of his fatherly authority—allows ecclesial and academic "fathers" to claim Paul's authority for themselves. Moreover, by stressing an unbridgeable gulf between the past and the present, between Paul and himself, the exegete occludes the fact that Paul's meanings are present only in and through the words of his authoritative interpreter. Thereby he—and it is still mostly a he—surreptitiously can claim Paul's the*logical authority for his own interpretation.

The rhetoric that posits radical differences between past and present, moreover, complements the rhetoric of identification insofar as it serves to construct *sameness* between Paul and "his" communities.[48] It does so by identifying Paul's discourses with those of the communities to whom he writes, thereby suppressing and eradicating the historical voices and multiplex visions that differ from Paul's. Or, historical-critical studies view Pauline texts and their arguments— that is, the rhetorical situation construed by Paul—as identical with the actual historical-rhetorical situation. This equivalence serves to obscure the *difference* between Paul's the*logical rhetoric and that of his contemporary interpreters and also the differences among the early Christian communities, which Paul's text may misrepresent or silence.

The politics of identification, however, works not only on a the*logical but also on an historical level. Insofar as scholars tend to understand Paul as having the authority of the gospel to compel, control, and censure the persons or communities to whom he writes, they tend to read Paul's letters as authoritative rather than as argumentative interventions in the the*logical discourses of his

47. For the conceptualization of identity in "identity politics" see the important work of Linda Martín Alcoff, *Visible Identities: Race, Gender, and the Self* (New York: Oxford University Press, 2006).

48. For an exploration of sameness and difference in Pauline interpretation, see the intriguing work of Elizabeth Castelli, *Imitating Paul: A Discourse of Power* (Louisville, Ky.: Westminster/ John Knox, 1991) who uses Michel Foucault's theoretical framework for her analysis and now especially also Joseph A. Marchal, *Hierarchy, Unity, and Imitation: A Feminist Rhetorical Analysis of Power Dynamics in Paul's Letter to the Philippians* (Atlanta: SBL, 2005), 191–202.

audience. They thereby fail to understand that "Pauline Christianity" is a misnomer for the early Christian communities to whom Paul writes. These communities existed independently of Paul although we know about them only in and through the letters of Paul.

This analysis of the strategies of othering, identity, and identification sheds light on why, at least since Robin Scroggs's article on "Paul and the Eschatological Woman" which appeared in 1972,[49] Pauline scholars have been so persistent in their "defense of Paul against his feminist critics." For example, although he details the atrocities of the history of Pauline texts such as 1 Corinthians 14:34-35, even a liberationist scholar like Neil Elliott argues that this text is a later addition to the genuine Pauline letters. His desire to liberate Paul from his post-Pauline domestications, and to read his the*logy as liberating, compels him to jettison feminist objections to such a reading and to insist that "heard rightly, Paul's message could not be more appropriate for some of us, Christians in the first world, who [if we are honest] find ourselves in the place of the Corinthian elite. . . ."[50] Yet to place middle-class Americans in the position of the Corinthian elite does not justify Paul's politics of vilifying "othering."

The tacit context of such malestream defenses of Paul is their unconscious, taken-for-granted identification with Paul rather than, let's say, with the Corinthian wo/men prophets, as Antoinette Clark Wire suggests.[51] Such biases reflect a politics and rhetorics of interpretation which surmises that the actual rhetorical situation of the Pauline letters, and its historical power relations, are identical to and correspond with the rhetorical situation which Paul has inscribed in his correspondence.[52]

In other words, such a politics of interpretation presupposes both the "scientific" theoretical understanding of texts, either as windows or as mirrors, and the essentializing tendencies of orthodox the*logy. By mystifying and occluding the rhetoricity of Pauline language and text, the defense of Paul is able to privilege

49. Reprinted in Robin Scroggs, *The Text and the Times: New Testament Essays for Today* (Minneapolis, Minn.: Fortress Press, 1993), 69–95.

50. See Neil Elliott, *Liberating Paul*, 229; see also notes on pp. 282–87 for his critical discussion of Antoinette Clark Wire's work.

51. Antoinette Clark Wire, *The Corinthian Women Prophets: A Reconstruction through Paul's Rhetoric* (Minneapolis, Minn.: Fortress Press, 1990).

52. See Elizabeth Castelli, "Interpretations of Power in 1 Corinthians," *Semeia* 54 (1992): 159–96.

the "masculine" hegemonic voice inscribed in Pauline texts, rather than to particularize and relativize this voice by reconstructing a varied assembly of voices and arguments.[53] In short, read in the horizon of the ekklēsia of wo/men, *both* strategies reflect a hegemonic politics of meaning and re-inscribe the kyriarchal politics of subordination; they do so by valorizing the voice of Paul. The rhetoric of identity, identification, and othering is moreover at work not only in past Pauline Studies but also in the new research paradigm of "Paul and the Roman Imperial Order."

A Dual System's Construction: Feminist and "Political" Interpretation

In his introduction to "Paul and the Roman Imperial Order," Richard A. Horsley charts this new approach in Pauline Studies.[54] He points out that, in the aftermath of the Holocaust, two shifts have taken place in Pauline Studies, which had been dominated by the emphasis of Protestant the*logy on "justification by faith" and the modern emphasis on religion as a spiritual and private quest for salvation that is divorced from political and economic life. It was Paul, according to this interpretation, who was the founder of a new and universal religion that was the opposite of Jewish legalism.

A basic shift in the Protestant the*logical understanding of "Paul, the Apostle" was introduced when scholars recognized that Paul was a law-abiding Jew who remained within the confines of Judaism. Pauline Christianity is no longer defined over and against Judaism but recognized as an offspring of Judaism. Another basic shift in Pauline Studies was engendered by Krister Stendahl who argued that Paul did not intend to found a new religion nor did he convert to a new religion; rather, his "call" was the mission to both Jews and Gentiles.[55] Horsley argues that these two shifts did not suffice to introduce a basic change in the theoretical framework of Pauline Studies. This change is being brought about only with the recognition that Paul's context was the Roman Empire and that his the*logy was shaped by his experiences as a Jew living

53. See, for example, my article "Missionaries, Coworkers, and Apostles: Rm 16 and the Reconstruction of Women's Early Christian History," *Word and World* 6/4 (1986): 420-33.

54. Richard A. Horsley, "Introduction," in Richard A. Horsley, ed., *Paul and the Roman Imperial Order* (Harrisburg, Pa.: Trinity International, 2004), 1–23.

55. Krister Stendahl, "The Apostle Paul and the Introspective Conscience of the West," *HTR* 56 (1963): 199–215; reprinted in *Paul Among Jews and Gentiles* (Philadelphia, Pa.: Fortress Press, 1976), 78–96.

under Roman domination. Horsley sums up the tenets of this new approach in Pauline Studies:

> Focus on the Roman imperial order as the context of Paul's mission . . . is leading to another recognition. Instead of being opposed to Judaism, Paul's gospel of Christ was opposed to the Roman Empire. Paul, of course, was hardly a rabble-rousing revolutionary. . . . Rom. 13:1-7 is the virtual opposite of active revolution. He did not preach about how Rome oppressed subject peoples. . . . Instead, Paul set his gospel of Christ and the new communities he catalyzed in opposition to the Roman imperial order: the whole system of hierarchical values, power relations . . . at the apex of which stood the imperial savior.[56]

In a last paragraph, Horsley indicates awareness of the questions I have raised in terms of a "politics of interpretation"—albeit without citation—and concedes that insofar as Paul borrowed certain images and key terms of imperial discourse, he "perpetuates certain imperial images and patterns of social relations." Thereby he "bequeathed imperial images of Christ to the Church"[57] which were, after Constantine, used to support Western domination. Horsley views this as "irony" but does not allow this insight to challenge his interpretation of Paul as standing over and against the Roman imperial order.

Horsley does not problematize that the new paradigm in Pauline Studies, like the old one, is formulated in terms of dualistic othering and constructs an "over and against,"—although now the "other" is no longer Judaism but rather Paganism—in the form of the emperor cult.[58] According to this formulation, Christian identity still needs for its self-understanding the negatively constructed "other." Since he does not critically consider the imperial inscriptions in the Pauline literature, nor question the scholarly eagerness to read Paul as opposing the imperial order, Horsley (despite all rhetorical adaptations) can not take up the crucial question raised especially by feminist scholars.[59]

---

56. Horsley, "Introduction," in *Paul and the Roman Imperial Order*, 3.

57. Ibid., 23.

58. See also Ross Saunders, "Paul and the Imperial Cult," in Stanley E. Porter, ed., *Paul and His Opponents*, 227–38.

59. See the article of Jennifer Wright Knust, "Paul and the Politics of Virtue and Vice," 155–173 in *Paul and His Opponents*, who concludes that by using standard Greco-Roman moral discourse about sexuality Paul re-inscribes the sex-gender status presuppositions that underpinned the Roman imperial order.

In the horizon of the ekklēsia of wo/men one needs to insist on the question: Did Paul oppose the imperial order or did he co-opt its language, codes, and imagery for his own ends thereby understanding G*d, Christ, and the ekklēsia not in opposition but in analogy to the Roman imperial order? Is this a colonization of the Christian imaginary, which allowed for the Romanization and imperialization of the church under Constantine and his successors, to proceed without much resistance by the church?

Whereas in the previous "Protestant" the*logical research paradigm Christian identity is defined over and against Judaism, in this new anti-imperial paradigm it is defined over and against Paganism.[60] This opposition is clearly recognized and succinctly stated by N.T. Wright:

> To say that Paul opposed imperialism is about as politically dangerous as suggesting that he was in favor of sunlight. . . . What we are faced with throughout his writings is the fact that he was opposed to paganism in all its shapes and forms; . . . with the settled and unshakeable conviction that the God of Abraham, Isaac and Jacob, who was now revealed in and as Jesus of Nazareth, stood over against all other gods and goddesses, claiming unique allegiance. Paul, in other words was not opposed to Caesar's empire primarily because it was an empire, but because it was Caesar's, and because Caesar was claiming divine status and honors which belonged only to the one God.[61]

Has Pauline Studies distanced itself from an anti-Jewish reading of Paul in order to propagate an anti-Pagan one? Such a definition of Christian identity re-inscribes uncritically Paul's stance over and against Paganism; this would be understandable but not excusable in the present context of the American or the global capitalist empire. Hence, it must be critically investigated and rendered problematic rather than championed. The epithet "Jesus is Lord and G*d," taken over from the acclamation of the Roman emperor, must be approached with a hermeneutics of suspicion rather than of affirmation, since it has legitimated violence and domination not only against Jews but also against Pagans,

---

60. Although this construction of the "other" in terms of imperial Paganism is probably not intended by Horsley and others, it nevertheless is implicit in their focus on the imperial cult.

61. N.T. Wright, "Paul's Gospel and Caesar's Empire," in Horsley, ed., *Paul and Politics*, 160–83, esp., 164.

witches, infidels, and indigenous peoples throughout the centuries. Today, in a world where war and terrorism are again justified in the name of the one G*d, critical scholarship is called for that does not re-inscribe, in Christian terms, the violence and domination of empire.

In a perceptive article entitled "Paul as Liberator and Oppressor: How Should We Evaluate Diverse Views of First Corinthians?" Robert C. Tannehill seeks to stage a debate between malestream and feminist political interpretations of Paul. He attempts to elaborate a hermeneutic of indeterminacy and application by using this debate as an example. He does so by constructing an opposition between "two recent interpretations of Paul and 1 Corinthians that share a common concern—to demonstrate that New Testament Studies can support movements of liberation from social oppression—yet result in quite different pictures of Paul."[62] In other words, Tannehill constructs a dualistic model of feminist and what he calls "political" interpretations of Paul, albeit both directions share common liberationist goals.

Before addressing this issue, Tannehill explores introductory methodological issues, suggesting that rhetorical and historical situations result in a high degree of indeterminacy, and hermeneutical issues, suggesting an ethics of interpretation and the love commandment as a hermeneutical principle. Tannehill then proceeds to construct the differences between feminist and political interpretation, with reference, respectively, to Antoinette Clark Wire's and my own work as representing feminist studies, and to Neil Elliott[63] and Richard Horsley as representing "political" interpretation. He sums up the differences between the two directions in four points which can be tabulated as follows:[64]

---

62. Robert C. Tannehill, "Paul as Liberator and Oppressor: How Should We Evaluate Diverse Views of First Corinthians?" in Charles H. Cosgrove, *The Meaning We Choose: Hermeneutical Ethics, Indeterminacy and the Conflict of Interpretations*, JSOT 411 (London: T. & T. Clark International, 2004), 122–37, esp., 122. I am grateful to him for sending me this reference.

63. See Neil Elliott, "The Anti-Imperial Message of the Cross," in Horsley, ed., *Paul and Empire*, 167–183; idem., "The Apostle Paul's Self-Presentation as Anti-Imperial Performance," in Horsley, ed., *Paul and the Roman Imperial Order*, 67–88; and idem, "Paul and the Politics of Empire: Problems and Prospects," in Horsley, ed., *Paul and Politics*, 17–39.

64. Tannehill, "Paul as Liberator and Oppressor," 127. I added a fifth point which is not listed here but stated in the conclusion, 134.

Feminist	**Political**
1. attends to voice of the Corinthian wo/men	1. attends to voice of Paul
2. in reconstructing situation is suspicious of Paul	2. accepts Paul's view of situation
3. Corinthian wo/men experience new freedom in Christ as persons of low social status, whereas Paul had to relinquish his high social status	3. most Corinthians were of low status but some claimed high status
4. shares social commitments	4. new perspective, emphasis on imperial cult
5. 1 Cor 14:34–35 is authentically Pauline	5. 1 Cor 14:34 –35 is addition

In good liberal fashion, Tannehill concludes that the answer to his question "Was Paul a liberator or oppressor?" should be "He was both" because both reconstructions, the feminist and the "political," are possible in terms of sound biblical scholarship. However, he does not consider that his question might be the wrong one to ask. With Horsley,[65] he concludes that multiple interpretations are to be valued rather than avoided and with Clark Wire,[66] he asserts that the two different social experiences, those similar to the Corinthian wo/men prophets and those similar to Paul's, must be set in dialogue with each other in "the hope that deeper understanding and mutual acceptance may result."[67]

While I appreciate Tannehill's attempt at fair discussion and his hermeneutical-the*logical reflections, I have problems with his essentializing dualistic construction, which eliminates differences within the typified approaches, in the interest of creating unified oppositions. In so doing, he unwittingly seems to construct an ideological dualism according to which feminist studies are concerned with wo/men, gender, and patriarchy but not with politics,

---

65. Richard A. Horsley, "Introduction: Krister Stendahl's Challenge to Pauline Studies," in *Paul and Politics*, 1–16, esp., 15.

66. Wire, *The Corinthian Women Prophets*, 71: "Where conflicts with a religious tradition are understood in light of the different social experience of each party, it may be possible to move toward genuine mediation of the conflicts."

67. Tannehill, "Paul as Liberator and Oppressor," 135.

while political and postcolonial studies are concerned with empire but not with
wo/men. Rather than evaluating the arguments, Tannehill praises "political"
studies of empire as a new perspective, even though concern with the Roman
Empire as the context of early Christianity is not a new approach but much
older than "political" or feminist biblical studies.

It is curious that Tannehill does not refer to the response of Clark Wire to
Elliott and Horsley, which is also found in *Paul and Politics*, a collection of essays
which Horsley has edited, a response that stresses that "multiple interpretations
are to be valued and not avoided." Why not acknowledge the conversation that
has already taken place and reflect on the fact that one side of the two parties,
namely, feminist interpretation, has challenged the other side, namely, "political" interpretation? If Tannehill had paid attention to Antoinette Clark Wire's
response in the same volume, he could have recognized that her insistence on
different experiences is derived from a critical analysis of the rhetoric of Paul
and not just due to different background theories, which Tannehill characterizes as "in one case the Roman Empire as an ideological system, in the other
case, the church as a place of liberation for women."[68]

Clark Wire points out that Horsley, following Margaret Mitchell's analysis,[69]
had argued in his contribution to the volume that Paul draws on the same
rhetoric that was used in Greco-Roman cities, to belittle others for factionalism
and self-seeking and to champion the concord and order of the *Pax Romana*,[70]
although Horsley interprets this as applying only to the rhetoric of Paul's opponents in Corinth who are behaving in the same way as a city elite.[71] However,
what Horsley does not recognize, Clark Wire points out, is

> that it is aristocrats who practice this antifactionalist rhetoric against
> people who question their authority. In tarring the Corinthians with
> the brush of power-seeking, Paul is caught with the brush in his hand.
> And if Paul acts the aristocrat in his use of municipal rhetoric in this
> assembly, his protestations of modesty, simple speech, and service of

68. Ibid., 134.
69. Margaret Mitchell, *Paul and the Rhetoric of Reconciliation* (Louisville, Ky: Westminster
John Knox, 1992).
70. Greg Woolf, "Roman Peace," in John Rich and Graham Shipley, eds., *War and Society in
the Roman World* (London: Routledge, 1993), 171–94.
71. Horsley, "Rhetoric and Empire—and 1 Corinthians," 72–102, esp., 91.

unity are not counterindications but are recognizable elements in that rhetoric.[72]

She concludes with the observation that Horsley seems still to work with the model of opponents, which he had developed in the 1970s when he characterized "the Corinthians as connoisseurs of the Hellenistic Wisdom tradition in the mode of Philo and the Wisdom of Solomon."[73] Tannehill recognizes that Horsley and Elliott clearly favor Paul, when Paul is understood "as working against dangerous tendencies within the Corinthian community."[74] Yet, Tannehill does not refer to my response which pointed to the roots of this scholarly favoring of Paul. In this response to Elliott and Horsley, in the same volume, I diagnosed their "option for Paul" as part and parcel of the Western kyriocentric rhetorical strategy of "othering, identity and identification" that seem to hinder empire studies from critically interrogating Paul's re-inscription of empire.

The Anti-Imperial Paul and 1 Cor 11:2-16

In their mass-market book *In Search of Paul: How Jesus' Apostle Opposed Rome's Empire with God's Kingdom*, John Dominic Crossan and Jonathan L. Reed not only seek to trace Paul's anti-empire stance, but also ask what the difference in content was between Caesar's and Paul's vision and program.[75] To pursue this question is necessary, according to them, because all the "good words," such as peace, grace, salvation, justice, were available to both Caesar and Paul. Crossan and Reed define the Emperor Augustus's vision as "peace through victory" and Paul's vision as "peace through justice." To make this contrast, they focus on one crucial element in each program, which they define as "hierarchy within the global scenario of victory" for Caesar's program and "equality within that of global justice" for Paul's program which was following Jesus' radicality.

After discussing the imperial the*logy and turning to Pauline Christian the*logy, they respond to a possible objection, which proposes that Paul was as patriarchal and hierarchical as Augustus except on a much smaller scale.

72. Wire, "Response: The Politics of the Assembly in Corinth," 124–29, esp., 125.
73. Ibid., 126.
74. Tannehill, "Paul as Liberator and Oppressor," 134.
75. John Dominic Crossan and Jonathan L. Reed, *In Search of Paul: How Jesus' Apostle Opposed Rome's Empire with God's Kingdom: A New Vision of Paul's Words & World* (New York: HarperSanFrancisco, 2005), 70–123.

To address this objection, Crossan and Reed make a basic distinction between authentic and inauthentic Pauline letters and focus on the question of slavery and patriarchy, to match images, which are found on the altar (*Ara Pacis*) and forum, which is named after the emperor Augustus. Despite much feminist and other scholarship to the contrary, Crossan and Reed argue first, that Paul insisted that "a Christian mistress or master should not and could not have a Christian slave" and second, that "Christian women and men were as such equal in marriage, assembly, and apostolate. How could one be equal and unequal at the same time since *in Christ* all were equal before God?"[76]

In their view, it is the pseudo-Pauline literature that "deliberately muted" the radical equality in Paul's name which was championed by Paul. Given that they do not substantiate their claims with reference to other scholarship or by arguing explicitly against other interpretations, readers are not enabled to form their own judgment on the matter. The only direction they give is to stress, again and again, that such equality applies only to the Christian community and not to society.

Since I do not have the space to consider here all of their assertions, I will focus on their interpretation of one particular Pauline text: 1 Cor 11:2-16. In order to advance their argument that in 1 Cor 11:2-16 Paul advocates "equality in the assembly," Crossan and Reed have to move 1 Cor 14:33-36 out of the way, a text which also deals with wo/men speaking in the assembly. Like many exegetical defenders of Paul, they claim that this text is a later pseudo-Pauline interpolation, thereby abandoning the exegetical principle that the *lectio difficilior*—the more difficult reading—should be preferred.[77]

As many exegetes have done, Crossan and Reed begin by noting that the argumentation in 1 Cor 11: 2-16 is so "torturous" that there is no accepted scholarly consensus. If one notices, on the one hand, how the text oscillates and if one takes both sexes into account, on the other hand, then it becomes clear that 1 Cor 11:2-16 stresses *difference*. Paul takes for granted that both wo/men and men pray and prophecy, but insists on a different head-covering for each.

> The *difference* between women and men, however, that was customarily and socially signified, must be maintained, even while hierarchy and subordina-

76. John Dominic Crossan and Jonathan L. Reed, *In Search of Paul*, 75.
77. For an extensive discussion of this text see Wire, *The Corinthian Women Prophets*, 229–32.

tion was negated. . . . the text is emphatically not about hierarchical inequality but about differential equality. Paul presumes equality between women and men in the assembly, but absolutely demands that they follow the socially accepted dress codes of their time and place. Difference yes, hierarchy no.[78]

Crossan and Reed recognize that this is a very difficult passage—but not that their interpretation is very difficult to sustain. Rather they argue that it is "strongly confirmed" by the fact that wo/men were leading figures in the early Christian communities, as we still can see from Paul's accidental or polemical mentioning of them. Yet, instead of discussing wo/men's leadership as apostles, prophets, teachers, missionaries, founders and leaders of house-churches, they use the quaint Roman Catholic expression "women in the [male] apostolate." Moreover, the expression "equal but different" belongs to the same discourse of gender inequality which has been used in the past to keep wo/men out of academic, political, and societal leadership and is still used today—for instance, against wo/men's ordination. In defense of Crossan and Reed, some might object that such a choice of words does not mean they are wrong and that Paul could not have championed radical equality.

However, Paul begins in v. 3 with "But I want you to understand that the head of every man is Christ, the head of woman is man and the head of Christ is God," a verse which Crossan and Reed do not much discuss. The descending sequence—G*d, Christ, man, wo/man—denotes clearly a hierarchy, even if one translates kephalē = "head" with "source."[79] While head conveys directly the notion of "power over," source does so too, in its present meaning context of a descending chain of dependency. To say that G*d is the source of Christ, Christ is the source of man, and man is the source of wo/man articulates a chain of dependency and subordination.[80] This is clearly spelled out in v. 7, which argues alluding to Genesis 2 that "man is the image and glory of God, but woman is the glory of man." As Mary Rose D'Angelo succinctly observes,

78. Crossan and Reed, In Search of Paul, 114.

79. See e. g. Linda L. Belleville, "ΚΕΦΑΛΗ & the Thorny Issue of Head Covering in 1 Cor 11:2-16," in Trevor J. Burke and J. Keith Elliott, eds., Paul and The Corinthians: Studies on a Community in Conflict (Leiden: Brill, 2003), 215–32.

80. See Kittredge, "Corinthian Women Prophets and Paul's Argumentation in 1 Corinthians," in Paul and Politics, 103–109, with reference to Christ's subordination in 1 Cor. 15:28.

"In such a context 'head' as 'source' does not exclude 'head' as 'ruler' but justifies it."[81]

Like Crossan and Reed, Francis Watson also stresses that one should not construct an "hierarchical" and "egalitarian" polarity, because such an approach does not allow one to see that this text speaks about the interdependence of men and wo/men. With reference to 11:11-12, and with a note invoking Irigaray, Watson asserts that "interdependence rather than equality is the concept that is at the heart of Paul's concern." This principle, of the irreducible difference between men and wo/men,

> finds its concrete application in the communal practices of prayer and
> prophecy in which women and men both participate. Fearing that women
> who fulfill these prominent roles expose themselves to male erotic fantasy.[82]

In order to protect these wo/men from the erotic gaze of men, Paul requires not just a head-covering such as a scarf but the veil covering the face. However, in spite of Paul's language to the contrary, Watson asserts, "the concept of hierarchy is marginal to this passage."[83]

Adopting a much more sophisticated Irigarayan reading, Jorunn Økland comes at first glance to an opposite conclusion but one that has a similar result, which advocates the veiling of wo/men so that their face can no longer be seen in history. She argues that we do not know what Paul means by the term "*gynē*," since gender understandings change. Paul is not concerned about "real" wo/men but about transforming the ekklēsia from *oikia* space into ritual space. "Gender is present in the structure of our language" and "there is no female essence that makes it possible to speak transhistorically about women."[84] She sums up her reading of 1 Cor 11–14:

81. Mary Rose D'Angelo, "Veils, Virgins, and the Tongues of Men and Angels: Women's Heads in early Christianity," in Howard Eilberg-Schwartz and Wendy Donninger, eds., *Off With Her Head! The Denial of Women's Identity in Myth, Religion and Culture* (Berkeley, Calif.: University of California Press, 1994), 131–64, esp., 133.

82. Francis Watson, "The Authority of Voice: A Theological Reading of 1 Cor 11:2-16," *New Testament Studies* 46 (2000): 520–36, esp., 522.

83. Ibid., 528.

84. Jorunn Økland, *Women in Their Place: Paul and the Corinthian Discourse of Gender and Sanctuary Space* (London: T. & T. Clark International, 2004), 14, 15.

The text is concerned with the construction of ritual space, where women's places and men's places, patterns of action, . . . clothing and so forth should be kept distinct and hierarchically ordered. This reflects a cosmos. . . .which is also gendered and the ritually constructed sanctuary space should be gendered in the same way. . . . Therefore Paul is not necessarily intent on gendering the ekklesia, not on putting a particular view of women into practice. . . .The women's utterances of this section form part of the much broader project of ritual, order, and place construction.[85]

Økland notes that some might object that, in this reading, individual "'real' women and men disappear" and she affirms that this understanding is correct. "If gender discourse constantly produces 'men' and 'women', I think it is more important to focus on this discourse than on its effects or products, people situated as men and women."[86]

Like Økland, Caroline Vander Stichele and Todd Penner also engage in a gender-critical cultural analysis, in an article that provides an excellent survey of the vast literature on 1 Cor 11:2-16. However, they do not use a totalizing deconstructive gender analysis but explore the rhetorical function of Paul's argument for maintaining the different practices of head-covering of men and wo/men, by grounding sexual differentiation in nature (1 Cor 11:7-12) as he does in Rom 1:26-27 and 2:27.[87] A comparison with similar ontological arguments in philosophical–cultural discourses of the time shows, they conclude, that "grounding gender distinctions in nature represents a powerful means to establish superiority and/or relegate others to inferiority in the competitive world of ancient (and modern) identity formations."[88]

Their argument could be made even stronger if they had recognized that this ontological gender discourse is part and parcel of the ontological philosophical discourse about the "chain of being."[89] Page duBois has argued that a "series

85. Økland, *Women in Their Place*, 217.
86. Økland, *Women in Their Place*, 218.
87. Caroline Vander Stichele and Todd Penner, "Paul and the Rhetoric of Gender," in Caroline Vander Stichele and Todd Penner, *Her Master's Tools? Feminist and Postcolonial Engagements of Historical-Critical Discourse* (Atlanta, Ga.: Society of Biblical Literature, 2005), 287–310.
88. Stichele and Penner, "Paul and the Rhetoric of Gender," 308.
89. Following Page duBois, I had pointed out in *But She Said* that this ontological democratic discourse is not only a gender discourse but a kyriarchal discourse that also negotiates slavery and ethnicity in a pyramid of multiplicative oppressions. See Schüssler Fiorenza, *But She Said*, 114–20.

of oppositions articulated by Thales[90]—Greek/Barbarian, human/animal, man/ woman—is a catalogue through which the Greek, human, male citizen defined himself over and against the 'others.'" This democratic difference-discourse of the fifth century BCE "relied on definition through separation, and the polarization of kinds of Beings."[91] However, according to her this discourse changed in the fourth century BCE when anti-democratic philosophers such as Plato and Aristotle formulated hierarchical—or as I would say kyriarchal—ideas of difference. This kyriarchal discourse "rationalizes and justifies an order in the world in which some beings in the hierarchy dominate others." Those who dominate claim an innate superiority that was given to them by "nature" or by G*d.

> It must be remembered that not only *barbaroi*, foreigners, were seen by Plato as deprived of reasoning ability. Women and slaves as well as animals formed part of a "chain" which descended from the Ideas, from the Idea of the good, from god. The hierarchy which Plato fixed among kinds endured for many centuries and still operates in Western discourse about difference.[92]

A similar logic seems to be at work in the discourse of Paul since he clearly establishes, in the*logical terms, such an ontological chain in 1 Cor 11 in which wo/man is placed on the lowest rank. Rather than championing "equal but different" or "interdependence," Paul seems to have operated within the onto-logical philosophical "chain of being." In 1 Cor 11:2-16 he does not advocate difference but asserts kyriarchal differences using the biblical language of creation to construct his argument. In short, Crossan and Reed's argument that the Pauline gospel is different from that of Caesar cannot be sustained. Yet, this does not mean that Paul and the Corinthian community did not know of such a gospel of "equality within the global scenario of justice" which was different from that of Caesar's "hierarchy within the global scenario of victory." To the contrary, the convoluted response of Paul would not have been necessary if such a gospel had not been practiced in the Corinthian community.

90. Similar statements are found in variations in other classical texts which state that men should give thanks to the Gods that they were not created uneducated, as barbarians or as wo/men. This saying was known in Jewish tradition and is probably rejected in the baptismal tradition of Gal. 3:28.

91. DuBois, *Centaurs & Amazons*, 90 ff.

92. Ibid., 13.

We are not able to get hold of this anti-imperial gospel, however, if we continue to defend the kyriarchal rhetoric of Paul or concentrate on gender constructions that eliminate "real" wo/men. Instead we need to read against the grain of kyriocentric language and ideology, which keeps "the gospel of domination" in place. As the studies discussed above have shown, what is necessary is not to follow Paul's lead of ritualizing and hierarchalizing—or better kyriarchalizing—the space of the ekklēsia but to re-imagine this space as the ekklēsia of wo/men that is "already" and "not yet."

What Difference Does Difference Make? Empire and Ekklēsia

For these reasons, I would argue that, in addition to the shift from Paul the the*logian who stands over and against Judaism on the one hand, and the shift that seeks to contextualize Paul within the power politics of the Roman Empire on the other, an even more drastic paradigm shift is necessary in Pauline studies. This shift would be a shift from focusing on Paul to reading or "hearing the ekklēsia of wo/men into speech"—to paraphrase a saying of Nelle Morton—the ekklēsia of which Paul has been a member. This would entail a shift from the hermeneutics of othering and identification to a hermeneutics of ekklēsia, tracing its footprints which are also inscribed in Paul's texts.[93] Ekklēsia is to be understood in radical democratic terms and it must be qualified with "wo/men." To interrupt the writing of "wo/men" intends to signify wo/men as a social-political group. It seeks to overcome the dualistic constructions of gender that "veil" or obscure those of race, class, heterosexuality, and nation that determine "real" wo/men's lives. It also means to stand linguistic gender construction on its head by using wo/men and not men as the generic term for human. Understood within the logic of democracy, ekklēsia means then a pluriform assembly of fully responsible "adult" wo/men-citizens who have equal standing, rights, and responsibilities, whether they are free or slave men or wo/men, Jewish, Roman, Greek, or Pagan men or wo/men.

Yet such a shift in Pauline studies can come about only if one deconstructs the gendered identification between Paul and his interpreters, which underwrites the authority claims of biblical scholars. This deconstruction would require that one replace the politics of othering, marginalization, and elision with

---

93. I have argued in *In Memory of Her* that as a basic methodological rule we must cease to read prescriptive texts as descriptive of the reality they seek to prescribe. Rather they must be seen as rhetorical arguments which presuppose a different reality into which they seek to intervene.

a critical rhetorics and logics of ekklēsia which can comprehend the disputes in the early Christian ekklēsia of wo/men in terms of debate and *parrēsia*—the free speech of citizens—rather than cast them in terms of confessional internecine altercations or imperial market competition.[94] These debates must be staged as exchanges attempting to spell out the gospel of "equality within justice," rather than the imperial gospel of hierarchy or kyriarchy.

In the first part of the chapter, I have elaborated that my own work has sought to develop and refine such a reconstructive historical politics of ekklēsia[95] that valorizes difference, many voices, argument, persuasion, and the democratic participation of all those excluded from or subordinated by the*logical discourses. Antoinette Clark Wire has done so by carefully analyzing 1 Corinthians in order to discover the voices of the wo/men prophets "in the voice of Paul." Joseph A. Marchal has done so by focusing on the power dynamics in the letter of Paul to the Philippians.[96] Cynthia Briggs Kittredge has examined the rhetoric of obedience in the letters attributed to Paul, and in particular has focused on the rhetoric of Philippians and Ephesians. By distinguishing between the inscribed rhetorical and the possible historical situation, her work is able to trace in these letters the struggle between a rhetoric of ekklēsia and one of kyriarchal submission.

94. See Dieter Georgi, *Theocracy in Paul's Praxis and Theology* (Minneapolis, Minn.: Fortress Press, 1991) for this expression.

95. It is troubling that feminist interpreters of the Pauline writings are often bent to reduce my work to my book *In Memory of Her* which they then misread in positivist historicist or Protestant terms of golden origins, while at the same time co-opting rather than engaging its different theoretical framework. While this is understandable in terms of anti-feminist or market politics, it is destructive (not deconstructive) in terms of feminist politics because it colludes with the kyriocentric text to "write wo/men out of history." See for instance, Økland, *Women in Their Place*, 7, n. 3, who has only short references to *In Memory of Her*, relegating the book to feminist naïve beginnings. She can do so because she sees my other writings just as a restatement rather than as a theoretical clarification, correction, and development of this work. Without question, her deconstructive Irigarayan theoretical frame is clearly different from my own socio-critical one. However, rather than discussing this difference, she chooses to displace it.

96. Joseph A. Marchal, *Hierarchy, Unity, and Imitation: A Feminist Rhetorical Analysis of Power Dynamics in Paul's Letter to the Philippians* (Atlanta, Ga.: Society of Biblical Literature, 2006). See also his "Military Images in Philippians 1–2: A Feminist Rhetorical Analysis of Scholarship, Philippians, and Current Contexts," in *Her Master's Tools?* 265–86; and "Mutuality Rhetorics and Feminist Interpretation: Examining Philippians and Arguing for Our Lives," *Bible and Critical Theory* 1:3 (August 2005)—an online, peer-reviewed journal: http://publications.epress. monash.edu/loi/bc.

In both Philippians and Ephesians, the authors use the language of obedience to respond to alternative languages and symbolic universes within
early Christian communities. Evidence of these visions survives in the
early Christian traditions that Paul and the Pauline author employ in
their arguments.[97]

In order to recover the authorship and authority of the ekklēsia, it is necessary to decenter the single authorship and unquestioned authority of Paul. This
does not mean that we do not need to study Paul. It only means that we recognize him as one among many others who struggled to articulate the meaning of
the gospel of Jesus. Hence, Pauline Studies need to rediscover the democratic
arguments of the ekklēsia and revalorize the early Christian egalitarian traditions, if they are to show that the gospel of Jesus Christ is different from that
of Caesar which preached domination and subordination. Crossan's and Reed's
references to wo/men's leadership, for confirming their interpretation of 1 Cor
11:2-16, are a pointer to the ekklēsia which was struggling to live such a different gospel and was debating how to do so. To read Paul's letter as taking part in
such a debate opens up the possibility to reconstruct it in such a way that ac-
knowledges that communities today are still participating in it. To quote Briggs
Kittredge again:

> A model which envisions Christian communities as true conversations
> within the ekklēsia can function more helpfully in creating dialogical inter-
> pretive communities in the complex contemporary hermeneutical context.
> A model in which Paul is a participant but not the center can function to
> envision a democratization of contemporary interpretive communities.[98]

In short, in order to displace the politics and rhetorics of subordination
and otherness, which is constitutive of the gospel of Caesar but also inscribed
in the "Pauline" correspondence, Pauline Studies need to articulate the politics
and rhetorics of equality, justice, and responsibility of ekklēsia, which are also

---

97. Kittredge, *Community and Authority,* 178.
98. Kittredge, "Rethinking Authorship in the Letters of Paul: Elisabeth Schüssler Fiorenza's
Model of Pauline The*logy," in Shelly Matthews, Cynthia Briggs Kittredge, and Melanie Johnson
DeBaufre, *Walk in the Ways of Wisdom,* 318–33, esp., 331.

inscribed in this correspondence. Such an approach conceives of early Christian communities as taking part in the emancipatory struggles and discourses of antiquity and conceptualizes early Christian communities as radical democratic assemblies (ekklēsia) of differing the*logical voices and sociorhetorical practices.

Luzia Sutter Rehman, however, has objected to a feminist reading that valorizes the ekklēsia over and against Paul because such a reading allegedly simply puts the malestream reading of Paul on its head.[99] This objection arises because she believes that this North American feminist approach reads Paul negatively, and his "opponents" the Corinthian wo/men prophets, positively, while malestream interpreters have negatively constructed the "opponents" of Paul. Yet, this objection overlooks several things.

For one, the construction of "opponents" sees them in negative terms as working over and against the authority of Paul and the integrity of the gospel, whereas the ekklēsia approach sees Paul as one among many and tries to show that his rhetoric seeks to obfuscate his relative status. It does not seek for wo/men behind or beneath Paul's text but *within* Paul's text. It argues that one cannot take Paul's rhetoric at face value but must read it against its kyriocentric grain to find the ekklēsia and its debates within the text of Paul.

To see Paul not as the authoritative leader but as one of many within the ekklēsia of wo/men recognizes that Paul and his gospel stands within an ekklesial tradition. Alan Segal has pointed out that Paul underwent a "conversion" not to another religion but to another sect.

> Of course Paul continues to be a Jew and he continues to believe that this new faith is part of Judaism. . . . It may be that Paul was not entering a fully defined Christian community. . . . But there were identifiable Christian communities . . . to be concerned about when he was a Pharisee. And, of course, after his conversion he spent many years in that community before writing his major letters, pointing up Paul's long association with the issues in Christianity before he wrote.[100]

---

99. Lucia Sutter Rehmann, "Die Paulinischen Briefe in der Feministischen Exegese," *lectio difficilior* 1/2001: 1–13, http://www.lectio.unibe.ch/01_1/w.htm.

100. Alan F. Segal, "Some Aspects of Conversion and Identity Formation in the Christian Community of His Time," in *Paul and Politics*, 184–90, esp., 185.

Sutter Rehmann herself, moreover, displaces one opposition with another when she rhetorically asks: "Can we imagine a Paul who does not think in terms of the opposition of Jews and Christians but in that of Jews and Pagans; a Paul who fights on the side of the Jewish losers against the repressive structures of the Roman Empire?"[101] She then goes on to outline the same communal approach for which she criticizes North American feminists, while claiming that this approach is now being developed by German-speaking feminists.[102] If that is the case, then there is less conflict here than she assumes, except that what she calls a German-speaking feminist approach continues to valorize Paul's voice.[103]

In contrast to her, I argue that hand-in-hand with a critical deconstruction of the kyriarchal arguments of Paul must go a critical recovery of the ekklēsia-traditions which are also inscribed in the Pauline correspondence and in other early Christian texts.[104] Although these traditions are submerged, they are still "readable" and indicate that the democratic ethos of the ekklēsia—the public assembly or congress—was at work in a community living under Roman rule in an urban colonial center such as Corinth. Key symbols of their self-understanding emerge from Paul's letter—not only ekklēsia but also *sōma* or body/corporation of Christ/Messiah. However both community designations do not completely overlap because they draw on quite different meaning contexts.[105] Both terms evoke an emancipatory political symbolic universe and vision if conceptualized not in anthropological gender but in socio-political terms.[106]

101. Lucia Sutter Rehmann, "Die Paulinischen Briefe," 7 (my translation).

102. See also her contribution, "Die aktuelle feministische Exegese der Paulinischen Briefe: Ein Überblick," in Claudia Janssen, Luise Schottroff, und Beate When, eds., *Paulus. Umstrittene Traditionen—lebendige Theologie. Eine feministische Lektüre* (Gütersloh: Chr. Kaiser Gütersloher Verlagshaus, 2001), 10–22, which is practically the same essay as the one mentioned in note 99.

103. See the contributions in *Paulus. Umstrittene Traditionen—lebendige Theologie. Eine feministische Lektüre,* and especially also Kathy Ehrensperger, *That We May be Mutually Encouraged: Feminism and the New Perspective in Pauline Studies* (New York: T. & T. Clark, 2004); However, this is also the case for apologetic feminist North American interpretation. See, e.g., Sandra Hack Polaski, *A Feminist Introduction to Paul* (St. Louis, Mo.: Chalice, 2005). My project seeks to navigate between a rejectionist and an apologetic reading of Paul.

104. Schüssler Fiorenza, "A Discipleship of Equals," 17–33.

105. See Robert Banks, *Paul's Idea of Community: The Early House Churches in their Historical Setting,* Revised Edition (Peabody, Mass: Hendrickson, 1994), 37–46, 58–66.

106. In this insistence I follow the Jewish philosopher Jacob Taubes, *Die politische Theologie des Paulus,* ed. Aleida Assmann and Jan Assmann (Munich: Wilhelm Fink Verlag, 1993), 178–80.

A totalizing gender reading identifies the metaphor of the "body" in anthropological terms as male body which is hierarchically arranged.[107] Jorunn Økland reasons: "Since the body that is the Corinthian ekklesia carries a male name, Christ, I treat it as a male body."[108] However, the *sōma* = body is not the body of Jesus, nor does the masculine grammatical pronoun for *Christ/in Christ* signify natural gender. Anthropological understandings of the body of Christ as male do not constitute the only possible or probable meaning. *Sōma* = body can also be understood, in corporate terms, as a body of people. Since the ekklēsia is such a corporate body of people, this corporate meaning is more likely. Hence, *sōma* = body is best contextualized within the popular political discourses of antiquity that understood the *polis* or city state as a "body politic"[109] which has a multiplicity of members who are different but interdependent.[110] Read against the androcentric grain, the metaphor of the "body" describes "being in Christ" with the political language of the day.

> For just as the corporation[111] [*sōma*] is one and has many members, and all the members of the corporation, though many, constitute one corporation, so is it with Christ. For by one Spirit we were all baptized into one corporation—Jewish wo/men or Greek wo/men, slave wo/men or free wo/men—and all were made to drink of one Spirit.
> (1 Cor 12:12-13)

Taubes argued that the "people of G*d" are to be envisioned as a historical community free of domination. The explosive Power of the political theology of Israel consists in the fact that according to it the people replace the king as the representative of G*d. However one must not forget that in the horizon of Jewish thought the institutions of domination of people by people cannot and may not represent the Messiah. The messianic may not legitimate the political order; instead it relativizes and replaces it.

107. See Dale B. Martin, *The Corinthian Body* (New Haven, Conn.: Yale University Press, 1995), 34: "Each body held its hierarchy within itself, and every body occupied its proper place in the hierarchy of society and nature."

108. Økland, *Women in Their Place,* 212.

109. For the phallic overdetermination of the "body politic" in classical Athens, see David Halperin, "The Democratic Body: Prostitution and Citizenship in Classical Athens," *differences* 2/1 (1990): 1–28; John Winkler, "Phallos Politikos: Representing the Body Politic in Athens," Ibid., 29–45.

110. For extensive discussion of the literature. See Mitchell, *Paul and the Rhetoric of Reconciliation,* 157–64.

111. Such a translation refers to the global power of multinational corporations and asks whether and what Christian the*logy can contribute to a "corporate" global ethos that could contribute to the well-being of all wo/men in the global village.

Moreover, if read not in later Christian but more appropriately in Jewish terms, Christ here is to be understood as the Messiah and the body of Christ as the Messiah-people[112] who are a messianic corporation. In the messianic body-politic all have equal access to the gifts of the Spirit albeit these gifts are different. This equality in the Spirit does not mean that all are the same. Rather, the gifts of the members vary and their individual functions are irreplaceable.[113] No one can claim to have a superior function because all functions are necessary and must be equally honored for the building up of the "corporation."[114] Solidarity and collaboration are the "civic" virtues in the political order (*politeuma*) of the Messiah, which is best characterized with J. Christiaan Beker as a "pneumatic or charismatic democracy."

"In Christ," i.e., in the body politic, the messianic sphere of power, ethnic-religious privileges and social status inequalities between Jews and Gentiles, Greeks and Barbarians, slave and free—both wo/men and men—no longer define the identity of those who are "in Christ," i.e., in the messianic corporation (Gal 3:28).[115] They are all called, elect, and holy, adopted children of G*d.[116] All without exception—Jews, pagans, slaves, free, poor, rich, both wo/men and men, those with high status and those who are "nothing" in the eyes of the world. Like religious cults, voluntary associations, professional clubs, funeral

112. See also, N. T. Wright, "Paul's Gospel and Caesar's Empire," 167, who however understands Messiah as the corporate king.

113. Andreas Lindemann, "Die Kirche als Leib," *Zeitschrift für Theologie und Kirche* 92 (1995): 140–65, reviews the uses of this metaphor of the body and concludes that Paul takes over the political democratic interpretation rather than the hierarchical one, because the explication of the image of the body conceives of the members of the body as completely equal and interdependent. However, it is also possible that the Corinthian community had this democratic egalitarian understanding and Paul is introducing a ranking.

114. It seems that it was Paul who introduced in 1 Cor 12:28-30 a ranking of spiritual gifts. The introduction of "hierarchical governance structure [is] another response to the divisions within the church. . . ." (M. Mitchell, p. 164). See also J. H. Neyrey, "Body Language in 1 Corinthians: The Use of Anthropological Models for Understanding Paul and His Opponents," *Semeia* 35 (1986): 129–64. For Paul's use of the rhetorics of power see Castelli, *Imitating Paul: A Discourse of Power*.

115. Elisabeth Schüssler Fiorenza, "Justified by All Her Children: Struggle, Memory, and Vision," in The Foundation of Concilium, eds., *On the Threshold of the Third Millennium* (London: SCM, 1990), 19–38, esp., 32–35, and Elisabeth Schüssler Fiorenza, *Rhetoric and Ethic*, 149–73.

116. See also Reinhold Reck, *Kommunikation und Gemeindeaufbau. Eine Studie zur Entstehung, Leben und Wachstum paulinischer Gemeinden in den Konmmunikationsstrukturen der Antike* (Stuttgart: Katholisches. Bibelwerk, 1991), 232–85.

societies and the Jewish synagogue,[117] the ekklēsia gathered *en oikō* = in house. These "private" organizations did not adopt the structures of the patriarchal household, however, but utilized rules and offices of the democratic assembly, i.e., the ekklēsia of the polis. Such assemblies were often socially stratified but conceded an equal share in the life of the association to all their members. The equality of the messianic people is given by the Spirit and expressed in alternating leadership and partnership,[118] in equal access for everyone, Greeks, Jews, Barbarians, slaves, free, rich, poor—both wo/men and men. The "messianic people," therefore, call their assembly by the democratic name *ekklēsia* and claim their location in the messianic *sōma*.

In sum, the Pauline letters and the whole of scripture still allow one to glimpse the practical-the*logical struggles which sought to realize the radical democratic religious vision of ekklēsia in a socio-political and religious situation of Roman colonial imperialism. However, one would be ill-advised if one were to tackle the question as to whether scripture supports a radical democratic church, society, and the full citizenship of wo/men in an apologetic fashion. For, it is not possible methodologically to "prove" that the bible advocates egalitarian democracy rather than kyriarchal empire, since both forms of social organization are inscribed in the socio-symbolic universe of Pauline and other early Christian writings.

Such a radical democratic vision of ekklēsia is not simply a given fact nor is it just an ideal. Rather it is an active process of struggle[119] moving toward greater equality, freedom, and responsibility, as well as toward communal relations free of domination. All wo/men silenced and marginalized by kyriarchal-hierarchic

117. See Bradley McLean, "The Agripinilla Inscription: Religious Associations and Early Church Formation," in Bradley McLean, ed., *Origins and Method: Toward a New Understanding of Judaism and Christianity* (Sheffield: Academic, 1993), 239–70; Wayne O. McCready, "Ekklēsia and Voluntary Associations," in John S. Kloppenborg and Stephen G. Wilson, eds., *Voluntary Associations in the Greco-Roman World* (New York, NY: Routledge, 1996), 59–73; Carsten Claussen, "Meeting, Community, Synagogue—Different Frameworks of Ancient Jewish Congregations in the Diaspora," in Birger Olsson and Magnus Zetterholm, eds., *The Ancient Synagogue from Its Origins Until 200 C.E.* (Stockholm: Almqvist & Wicksell International, 2003), 144–67 and Thomas Schmeller, *Hierarchie und Egalität: Eine sozialgeschichtliche Untersuchung Paulinischer Gemeinden und griechisch-römischer Vereine* (Stuttgart: verlag Katholisches Bibelwerk, 1995).

118. For the understanding of *koinonia* as consensual *societas* and reciprocal partnership, see J. P. Sampley, *Pauline Partnership in Christ: Christian Community and Commitment in Light of Roman Law* (Philadelphia, Pa: Fortress Press, 1980).

119. For this distinction see Phillips, *Engendering Democracy*, 162.

structures of domination are crucial in this ekklesial process of struggle for a radical democratization that is inspired by an eschatological vision of a society and world free of exploitation, domination, and evil.

Contrary to popular opinion, the bible does not speak for itself. Rather, interpretations of biblical texts and reconstructions of early Christian history are shaped by the contemporary interests of the biblical historian, the*logian, or general reader just as much as they were in the case of people in the first century. In order to read Paul in the horizon of the ekklēsia of wo/men, as I have proposed in the beginning of this chapter, we need to think about interpretation and history writing as "quilting,"[120] as piecing scriptural remnants of the gospel of equality, in the debates of the ekklēsia, together into a new design.

Without such "alternative" models or "imaginative designs" we would have no basis for comprehending the past which requires interpretation. The past is not simply there in the text, waiting for us to discover how things really were or what Paul really meant. In other words, those biblical interpreters who favor an ekklēsia model of church will emphasize the radical democratic elements inscribed in Pauline texts and those who favor a "hierarchical" one will stress the authoritative voice of Paul. Those who emphasize an ekklēsia model of church will either identify with Paul or with the members of the communities depending on their social location in the kyriarchal pyramid. For our experience functions as what the anthropologist Clifford Geertz calls "a model" of reality.[121] The notions and beliefs we hold today inform how we read the texts of the past. Variations upon both models—*ekklēsia* and empire/*kyriarchē*—are inscribed in the Pauline traditions and, at the same time, shape our readings today because egalitarian and imperial structures of reality are still at work in our times. We must still choose today between the "gospel of Caesar, the gospel of subordination" and the "messianic gospel of radical equality" which was and is also preached in the name of Jesus and we must do so conscious of our sociopolitical location within the kyriarchal pyramid of power.

---

120. See my article "The Quilting of Women's Early Christian History," in *Lessons from Women's Lives*, Maxwell Summer Lecture Series (Syracuse: Syracuse University Press, 1984), 22–29.

121. Clifford Geertz, "Religion as a Cultural System," in M. Banton, ed., *Anthropological Approaches to the Study of Religion* (London: Tavistock, 1966), 1–46.

Chapter 4

Toward a Critical Feminist
Decolonizing Interpretation

In the previous chapter, I have elaborated the imaginary of the ekklēsia of wo/men,[1] as a decolonizing[2] intellectual and practical space or feminist horizon from where to interpret and adjudicate biblical texts and interpretations, in general, and the biblical inscriptions of empire, in particular. Ekklēsia is historically and theoretically the alternative—not the counter or anti–space—to empire, because it is not constituted by super- and subordination but by radical egalitarian relationships. "Decolonizing" indicates the process by which this is accomplished.

This chapter focuses on how to read the inscriptions of empire in a particular biblical text, the book of Revelation, and its contemporary interpretations, as well as on the method and approach for doing so. A rhetoric of inquiry does not just have the task of adjudicating, on exegetical-textual grounds, which interpretations advocate imperial power and which are resisting it. Rather, its task is to assess ethically and politically the kinds of reality and visions that are generated by texts and interpretations. Moreover, this inquiry must clarify the underlying methodological assumptions and interpretative lenses that are used in readings and assess their implications for shaping the symbolic/moral

---

1. In order to lift into consciousness the linguistic violence of so-called generic male-centered language, I write the term "wo/men" with a slash—see footnote 21, Chapter 1: Introduction. *Ekklēsia* (Gr. "assembly") is usually translated as a religious term, "church," but is primarily a political term of ancient democracy—see also the discussion in Chapter 2.

2. I use the verb form "decolonizing" rather than the adjective "postcolonial" in order to indicate an active continuing dynamic process rather than one already concluded. See also Fernando Segovia, *Decolonizing Biblical Studies: A View from the Margins* (Maryknoll, N.Y.: Orbis, 2000), XI, who argues "that the discipline of biblical criticism has witnessed, over the last quarter of a century, a process of decolonization and liberation. . . ." which, I would add, is still ongoing.

universe of texts and interpreters. Since the emerging postcolonial biblical criticism[3] interrogates the power of empire, it seems that a postcolonial approach would be the best method to use for such a critical adjudication of power that is inscribed in scripture. However, as R. S. Sugirtharajah, one of the leading postcolonial biblical critics, among many others, has pointed out, "postcolonialism has a multiplicity of meanings" and is more "a mental attitude rather than a method, a subversive stance toward the dominant knowledge."[4] In a similar vein, Ato Quayson states, "Like postmodernism and poststructuralism, postcolonialism designates a critical practice that is highly eclectic and difficult to define."[5] Moreover, both postcolonialism and poststructuralism have been developed without taking feminist questions into account. Hence, postcolonialism cannot be adopted without feminist re-articulation.

Although an enormous quantity of academic discourse on the postcolonial and postcolonialism has been produced, and a whole field of study has been developed in the last four decades or so, the meaning of the nomenclature *postcolonial* itself is still hotly debated. For that reason, it is important to interrogate, from a critical feminist perspective, the divergent analytical practices of postcolonial criticism. In order to develop a praxis of critical political reading in the center of the American global empire, I will focus here on the theoretical intersections of a critical feminist interpretation and method of rhetorical analysis—my own hermeneutical approach—with a postcolonial theory and method of oppositional consciousness that is able critically to read the inscriptions of empire in the bible for constructing "dissident globalization," in place of the neo-colonializing forces of postmodernism.

3. For ground-breaking work in postcolonial biblical studies, see the work of Kwok Pui-lan, Laura Donaldson, Musa W. Dube, Fernando Segovia, and R. S. Sugirtharajah. See also the contributions of Musa W. Dube, "Ahab Says Hello to Judith: A Decolonizing Feminist Reading," Kwok Pui-lan, "Engendering Christ," Fernando Segovia, "Liberation Hermeneutics: Revisiting the Foundations in Latin America," R. S. Sugirtharajah, "The End of Biblical Studies?" and Richard A. Horsley, "Subverting Disciplines: The Possibilities and Limitations of Postcolonial Theory for New Testament Studies,"—all in *Toward a New Heaven and a New Earth: Essays in Honor of Elisabeth Schüssler Fiorenza*, ed. Fernando F. Segovia (Maryknoll, N.Y.: Orbis, 2003). See also his article "Feminist Scholarship and Postcolonial Criticism: Subverting Imperial Discourse and Reclaiming Submerged Histories," in *Walk in the Ways of Wisdom*, eds. Shelly Matthews, Cynthia Briggs Kittredge, Melanie Johnson-DeBaufre, 286–96.

4. R. S. Sugirtharajah, "A Postcolonial Exploration of Collusion and Construction in Biblical Interpretation," in *The Postcolonial Bible* (Sheffield: Sheffield Academic, 1998), 93.

5. Ato Quayson, *Postcolonialism: Theory, Practice or Process?* (Oxford: Polity in Association with Blackwell, 2000), 1.

Since Fernando Segovia, a major postcolonial biblical critic, has invited a rigorous theoretical discussion on the emerging field of postcolonial biblical studies,[6] I will take up this invitation. If I raise critical questions, I do so not in order to distance myself from postcolonial interpretation, but in order critically to engage it. In the first part of this chapter, I will look very briefly at the optic of postcolonial criticism and of postcolonial feminist biblical studies, which stress a dual systems analysis—patriarchy and imperialism—rather than a kyriarchal analysis of intersecting dominations. The differences between a dual systems analysis of patriarchy and imperialism, on the one hand, and a complex intersecting systems analysis of kyriarchy, on the other, will turn out not to be differences of identity—postcolonial and white feminist—but differences of analytic frameworks. In order to illustrate what is at stake in this debate, I will discuss the visions of Babylon and the New Jerusalem in the book of Revelation, which represent the Roman Empire and G*d's alternative world.

Postcolonial Criticism and Feminist Criticism

Just as critical feminist studies, so also the field of postcolonial studies has been introduced into the American Academy in the 1970s and many would date its beginnings to the appearance of Franz Fanon's work *The Wretched of the Earth* in 1963[7] and Edward Said's very influential book *Orientalism* in 1978.[8] As the term indicates, postcolonial criticism began as the study of the literature of Europe's former colonies and examines the interaction between the European Empires and their former colonies in the modern period.

Central to such studies has been an analysis of ideologies that allege the inherent superiority of Europeans, which has legitimated colonial domination and exploitation. Hence, one would expect that postcolonial studies would be at home in social and political studies. Yet, this seems not to be the case. Rather,

---

6. Segovia, *Decolonizing Biblical Studies*, 133f.

7. Franz Fanon, *The Wretched of the Earth* (New York: Grove, 1963); idem, *Black Skin, White Masks* (New York: Grove, 1967); *A Dying Colonialism* (New York: Grove, 1970); *Toward the African Revolution* (New York: Grove, 1970). See also Lewis R. T. Gordon, Deneon Sharpley-Whiting and Renee T. White, eds., *Fanon Critical Reader* (Oxford: Blackwell, 1996).

8. Edward Said, *Orientalism* (Hammondsworth: Penguin, 1978); *Culture and Imperialism* (London: Vintage, 1993); *The World, The Text, The Critic* (London: Vintage, 1993).

because of its focus on representation, identity, hybridity, and cultural location, postcolonial criticism has found its home primarily in literature or cultural studies departments.[9] Moreover, because of its indebtedness to postmodernism and poststructuralism, postcolonial criticism tends to focus on representation. These theoretical and academic locations raise several issues.

Postcolonial Criticism and Neo-liberal Globalization
Many have critiqued the dualistic rhetoric of postcolonial discourse, which tends to set up the "West and the Orient," or the "Colonizer and the Colonized," as two monolithic totalities. This Manichean construction has also been problematized within postcolonial studies. Since this dualistic rhetoric constructs the "either/or" choice between the West and the "rest of the world," it does not leave room for the complexity of world politics.[10] In addition, because of their academic location, the discourses of postcolonial studies respond to the questions of the academy and are greatly determined by the academic frameworks of postmodernism and poststructuralism.[11] As Leela Gandhi has observed in her Preface to *Postcolonial Theory*:

9. For introductions to this area of study, see Bill Ashcroft, Gareth Griffin, and Helen Tiffin, eds., *The Empire Writes Back: Theory and Practice in Post-colonial Literatures* (New York: Routledge, 1989); Bill Ashcroft, Gareth Griffin, and Helen Tiffin, eds., *The Post-colonial Studies Reader* (New York: Routledge, 1995); Bill Ashcroft, Gareth Griffin, and Helen Tiffin, eds., *Key Concepts in Post-colonial Studies* (New York: Routledge, 1998); Peter William Patrick Childs, *An Introduction to Post-colonial Theory* (London: Harvester Weatsheaf, 1997; Loomba Ania, *Colonialism/Postcolonialism* (London: Routledge, 1997); John McLeod, *Beginning Post-colonialism* (Manchester: Manchester University Press, 2000); Robert Young, *Postcolonialism: An Historical Introduction* (Oxford: Blackwell, 2001).

10. Kwame Anthony Appiah, "Is the 'Post' in 'Postcolonial' the 'Post' in 'Postmodern'?" in *Dangerous Liaisons: Gender, Nation, & Postcolonial Perspectives*, eds. Anne McClintock, Aamir Mufti, & Ella Shohat (Minneapolis, Minn.: University of Minnesota Press, 1997), 420–44, esp., 439.

11. My main disagreement is not with postcolonial theory but with its sometimes wholesale adoption of some of the so-called French school of theory and its construction of "difference." It seems to me that "imperial identity" has not so much been established by the denial of difference, in the interest of the "same," but rather that kyriarchal domination has been forged in and through the ideological articulation of the differences between colonizers and colonized, white and black men and women, West and Orient, rich and poor in subordinationist dehumanizing terms. See also R. S. Sugirtharajah, *Asian Biblical Hermeneutics and Postcolonialism, Bible and Liberation* (Maryknoll, N.Y.: Orbis, 1998), 15, who criticizes the French school of theory for its Eurocentrism, lack of a theory of resistance and a transformative agenda, its celebration of the local and of differences which lead to horizontal violence, the assignment of subalterns to their space of Otherness, and its skepticism toward grand narratives that "fails to take into account liberation as an emancipatory metastory."

... "postcolonialism" remains a diffuse and nebulous term. Unlike Marxism or deconstruction, for instance, it seems to lack an "originary moment" or a coherent methodology. . . . In my reading of this field, there is little doubt that in the current mood postcolonial theory principally addresses the needs of the Western academy. It attempts to reform the intellectual and epistemological exclusions of this academy, and enables non-Western critics located in the West to present their cultural inheritance as knowledge. This is, of course, a worthwhile project. . . . But, of course, what postcolonialism fails to recognise is that what counts as "marginal" in relation to the West has often been central and foundational in the non-West.[12]

If the optic and self-understanding of postcolonial criticism is shaped by its oppositional rhetoric to that of the West, on the one hand, and by the Western academy, on the other, then one must ask how it is able theoretically to reflect on the liberation struggles of wo/men, who are at the bottom of the kyriarchal pyramid of domination in a world of global capitalism? Economic globalization[13] has been created with the specific goal of giving primacy to corporate profits and values and installing and codifying such market values globally. Globalization has been designed to amalgamate and merge all economic activities, around the world, within a global monoculture. In many respects wo/men are suffering not only from the globalization of market capitalism but also from the sexual exploitation instigated by it.

In the time of capitalist neo-liberal globalization, the line between the "haves" and the "have-nots" increasingly spans the entire globe, with the West (i.e., Europe and the United States) becoming more and more part of this global "equalization of the oppressed." According to this process of capitalist globalization, eighty countries have per capita income that is lower than a decade ago. In 1960 the income gap between the fifth of the world's people who are living in the richest countries and the fifth in the poorest countries was 30 to 1; in 1998

12. Leela Gandhi, *Postcolonial Theory: A Critical Introduction* (New York: Columbia University Press, 1998), viii–ix.

13. See Jan Nederveen Pieterse, ed., *Christianity and Hegemony* (Oxford: Berg, 1992), 11–31; see also Paul E. Sigmund, "Christian Democracy, Liberation Theology: the Catholic Right and Democracy in Latin America," in *Christianity and Democracy in Global Context*, ed. John Witte, Jr., (Boulder, CO: Westview, 1993), 187–207.

it was 74 to 1. From 1995 to 1999 the world's 200 wealthiest people doubled their net worth to one billion dollars, whereas three billion people presently live on two dollars or less a day. Two billion people suffer from malnutrition, including 55 million in industrialized countries.

Neo-liberal globalization is evoking a future where a handful of the world's most well-to-do families may pocket more than 50 percent of the world's $90 trillion in assets and securities (stocks, bonds, etc). As of 1996, the biologically productive area, which is needed both to produce the natural resources that we consume and to absorb the carbon dioxide that we emit, was 30 percent larger than the area available. Relentlessly rising global temperatures are bound to create catastrophic conditions worldwide and the poor of the world will be the hardest hit.[14] The predictable results of the neo-liberal economic model, which has been made in the United States, are socially unjust, politically destabilizing, culturally destructive, and ecologically unsustainable.

Because of its alliance with postmodernism and its academic location in literature departments, however, the tendency of postcolonial criticism has been to privilege the act of reading over socio-political analysis. As a consequence postcolonial criticism has not sufficiently focused on global structures of exploitation and domination. In response to Ella Shoat's question "When exactly does the postcolonial begin?"[15] Arif Dirlik at first answers facetiously: "When Third World intellectuals have arrived in First World academy," but then concludes more seriously:

It begins with the emergence of global capitalism, not in the sense of an exact incidence in time but in the sense that the one is a condition of the other. . . . What is remarkable, therefore is not my conclusion here but that a consideration of the relationship between postcolonialism and global capitalism should be absent from the writings of postcolonial intellectuals: this is all the more remarkable because this relationship is arguably less abstract and more direct than any relationship between global capitalism and postmodernism, since it pertains not just to cultural/epistemological but to social and political formations.[16]

---

14. According to the *United Nations Human Development Program Report of 1999.* These statistics are taken from Jeff Gates, "Modern Fashion or Global Fascism," *Tikkun* 17/1 (January/February 2002): 30–32.
15. Ella Shohat, "Notes on the Postcolonial," *Social Text* 31/32 (1992): 103.
16. Arif Dirlik, "The Postcolonial Aura: Third World Criticism in the Age of Global Capitalism," *Dangerous Liaisons,* 501–58, esp., 519 ff.

Only when it takes this political contemporary context into account, I suggest, does postcolonial biblical criticism provide analytic approaches that can identify the kind of power inscribed in scripture, as well as the Bible's power of persuasion in the context of the global capitalist empire which conditions all biblical readings today.

Postcolonial and Feminist Theory

According to Leela Gandhi, the theoretical resistance movements of postcolonialism and feminism have pursued "a path of convergent evolution"[17] and have developed "a remarkably similar theoretical trajectory" insofar as both have tended to invert "prevailing hierarchies of gender/culture/race" and have increasingly resorted to poststructuralist and postmodernist theory.

> It is only in the last decade or so, however, that these two parallel projects have finally come together in what is, at best, a very volatile and tenuous partnership. In a sense, the alliance between these two disciplinary siblings is informed by a mutual suspicion, wherein each discourse constantly confronts its limits and exclusions in the other.[18]

Gandhi points to the following three "collisions and collusions" between feminist and postcolonial theory. In the first collusion, feminist theory is alleged to represent the Third World Wo/man solely as a victim of oppression. Yet, in Gandhi's view, leading postcolonialist critics are also in danger

> [of] idealis[ing] and . . . essentialis[ing] the epistemological opacity of the "real" third-world woman. By making her the bearer of meanings/experiences which are always in excess of Western analytic categories, these critics paradoxically re-invest the "third-world woman" with the very iconicity they set out to contest.[19]

The second area of contention, according to Gandhi, is the tendency of Western liberal feminism to "orientalize" the "third-world wo/man" and to exoticize her for imperial consumption. The third quarrel pertains to the question

17. Ashcroft, et al., eds., *The Empire Writes Back*, 249.
18. Gandhi, *Postcolonial Theory*, 83.
19. Ibid., 88.

as to which comes first: female emancipation and equality or cultural-national emancipation, feminist, or postcolonial struggle? Yet, Gandhi believes that a productive collaboration between feminist and postcolonial theory has emerged in a fourth area, which investigates the "aggressive myth of both imperial and nationalist masculinity."[20]

In *A Critique of Postcolonial Reason*, Gayatri Chakravorty Spivak in turn charts her progress from colonial discourse studies to trans-national cultural studies.[21] She understands her book as a feminist book that seeks to foster "the literary habit of reading the world" and an "acknowledgment of complicity." How such a "reading of the world" and "acknowledgment of complicity" works becomes obvious in her telling of an incident in a migrant community in London. She refers to this incident in order to illustrate the hypothesis of Gramsci, that "American expansionism would use African-Americans to conquer the African market and the extension of American civilization."[22] She applies it to the New Immigrant intellectuals and their countries of national origin taking herself as an example. When she insisted that "we show evidence of the fact that ethnic entrepreneurs were pimping for the trans-nationals and selling their women into sweat labor," the response was not to show "sexist exploitation within the community" but only to point to white racism. Because of this cultural politics of reverse racism—expressed by the idea that whites are all bad and black migrants are all good—it was not possible, in Chakravorti Spivak's view, to lift the interconnectedness of global exploitation into public consciousness. She concludes:

> Rather than continue to celebrate the essentializing moralism of Colonizer/Colonized, White/Black, it had seemed necessary to me to make visible to the viewing public what the activists in the field knew. That the keeping apart of migrancy and development allowed the setting of thousands of unskilled female Bangladeshi homeworkers in London's East End in unwitting competition with thousands of unskilled female workers in the export-based garment industry in Bangladesh proper. The

---

20. Ibid., 98 ff.
21. Gayatri Chakravorty Spivak, *A Critique of Postcolonial Reason: Toward a History of the Vanishing Present* (Cambridge, Mass: Harvard University Press, 1999), x.
22. Ibid., 376.

latter were winning because they cost £500 less per head a year. . . . Ethnicization of female super-exploitation is a global story, an episode in the same large-scale story that creates our demand for cross-culturalism: successful pimping requires it.[23]

It is this global interconnectedness of exploitations that challenges us to "learn to be responsible as we must study to be political."[24] Hence, Chakravorty Spivak is highly critical of "much of U.S. academic postcolonialism" that seems to be "as much a strategy of differentiating oneself from the racial underclass as it is to speak in its name."[25]

Postcolonial Biblical Studies

In his book *Empire and Apocalypse* Stephen Moore[26] seeks to map the emergent field of postcolonial biblical criticism. He argues that postcolonial biblical criticism has emerged from three clusters of study: historical criticism and contextual liberation hermeneutics, empire-studies, and the engagement of biblical scholars with the field of extra-biblical postcolonial studies.[27] Surprisingly (or not?) he does not mention the variegated field of feminist biblical studies and its engagement with feminist theory which preceded the emergence of extra-biblical and biblical postcolonial studies in the American academy.

Although postcolonial theory has arrived in biblical studies at a very late point in the discussion, it nevertheless has already made invaluable contributions to a political emancipative biblical criticism. This late arrival of both postcolonial cultural and postcolonial feminist biblical studies, which has been pioneered by Laura Donaldson, Kwok Pui-lan, and Musa W. Dube,[28] might be

23. Ibid., 377 ff.
24. Ibid., 378.
25. Ibid., 358.
26. Stephen D. Moore, *Empire and Apocalypse: Postcolonialism and the New Testament* (Sheffield: Phoenix, 2006), 14–23. He credits Michael Prior, *The Bible and Colonialism: A Moral Critique* (Sheffield: Sheffield Academic, 1997) as the first monograph with the title topic.
27. See, Laura E. Donaldson, ed., *Postcolonialism and Scriptural Reading*, Semeia 75 (Atlanta, Ga.: Scholars, 1996); R.S. Sugirtharajah, *Asian Biblical hermeneutics and Postcolonialism* (Maryknoll, N.Y.: Orbis, 1998); R.S. Sugirtharajah, ed., *The Postcolonial Bible* (Sheffield: Sheffield Academic, 1998); Stephen D. Moore and Fernando F. Segovia, eds., *Postcolonial Biblical Criticism: Interdisciplinary Intersections* (New York: T. & T. Clark International, 2005).
28. See, e.g., Laura E. Donaldson, *Decolonizing Feminisms: Race, Gender & Empire Building* (Chapel Hill, N.C.: University of North Carolina Press, 1992); Laura E. Donaldson and Kwok

an advantage insofar as postcolonial biblical studies are able to learn from the trials and errors of postcolonial cultural studies. It also can be a liability, since the conceptualization of the field seems to perpetuate the split between cultural and Marxist studies, a split provoked by malestream postcolonial criticism. Whereas Sugirtharajah and Segovia are advocating cultural postcolonialism, Horsley seems to have adopted an implicit Marxist approach. In postcolonial *feminist* biblical criticism a similar split is provoked when a dual systems analysis—patriarchy and imperialism—is advocated.

In biblical studies, a postcolonial and a critical feminist hermeneutics, I argue, have not followed "a path of convergent evolution."[29] Rather, historically speaking, feminist biblical criticism and liberation the*logy have paved the way for postcolonial biblical criticism within the academy and in the churches.[30] That the feminist roots of postcolonial biblical studies must remain an integral part of decolonizing interpretation seems to be forgotten by some. Instead,

---

Pui-lan, eds., *Postcolonialism, Feminism, & Religious Discourse* (New York: Routledge, 2002); Kwok Pui-lan, "Claiming a Boundary Existence: A Parable from Hong Kong," in "Special Section: Asian Women Theologians Respond to American Feminism," *Journal of Feminist Studies in Religion* 3:2 (Fall 1987): 121–24. Kwok Pui-lan, "Speaking from the Margins," in "Special Section: Appropriation and Reciprocity in Womanist/Mujerista/Feminist Work," *Journal of Feminist Studies in Religion* 8:2 (Fall 1992): 102–5; Kwok Pui-lan, *Discovering the Bible in the Non-Biblical World* (Maryknoll, N.Y. Orbis, 1995); Kwok Pui-lan, "Mercy Amba Oduyoye and African Women's Theology," *Journal of Feminist Studies in Religion* 20:1 (Spring 2004): 7–22; Kwok Pui-lan, *Introducing Asian Feminist Theology* (Sheffield: Academic, 2000); Musa W. Dube Shomanah, "Postcolonial Biblical Interpretation," in *Dictionary of Biblical Interpretation*, ed. John H. Hayes (Nashville, Tenn.: Abingdon, 1999), 299–303; Musa W. Dube, *Postcolonial Feminist Interpretation of the Bible* (St. Louis, Mo.: Chalice, 2000); Musa W. Dube, "Villagizing, Globalizing and Biblical Studies," in *Reading the Bible in the Global Village: Cape Town*, eds. Justin S. Upkong, et al. (Atlanta, Ga: Scholars, 2002), 41–64; Musa W. Dube, ed., *Other Ways of Reading: African Women and the Bible* (Atlanta, Ga.: SBL, 2001); Musa W. Dube and Musimbi Kanyoro, *Grant me Justice: HIV/AIDS & Gender Readings of the Bible* (Maryknoll, N.Y.: Orbis, 2004); and the contributions of Elsa Tamez, Renita Weems, Ivoni Richter Reimer, Mukti Barton, Sarojini Nadar, and Gloria Kehilwe Plaatjie, among others, in *Voices from the Margins: Interpreting the Bible in the Third World*, ed. R. S. Sugirtharajah, second edition (Maryknoll, N.Y.: Orbis, 1995).

29. See Fernando F. Segovia, *Decolonizing Biblical Studies* (Maryknoll, N.Y.: Orbis, 2000), 119–56.

30. Catherine Keller, Michael Nausner, and Myra Rivera, eds., *Postcolonial Theologies: Divinity and Empire* (St. Louis, Mo.: Chalice, 2004), 5 ff., argue that "the engagement of theory by theology is incoherent outside the effects of liberation theology," but surprisingly subsume feminist the*logies of liberation under the heading of liberation the*logy rather than understanding them as rooted in the women's liberation movement and having developed a different hermeneutics of liberation.

postcolonial biblical criticism tends to engage in a progressivist dichotomizing rhetoric, showing what is wrong with feminist or liberation the*logy rather than arguing for a collaborative hermeneutics, which would require the recognition of existing liberationist feminist approaches.

If in the following I give an example of this tendency, I seek to make visible its implications in order to strengthen the field. For instance, Fernando Segovia, who has made invaluable contributions to this emerging field of study, recognizes the affinity between the postcolonial discourse of resistance and emancipation with "other discourses of resistance and emancipation in Biblical Studies—such as socioeconomic (Marxist) or feminist criticism." However, he does not then go on to identify the common theoretical assumptions and practical goals of such postcolonial, materialist, and feminist discourses in terms of an ethics of solidarity, but states categorically that "neither the project of Marxism nor the project of feminism suffices in and of itself, since they both reflect their own origins in the West."[31]

Moreover, he charges that despite the "exalted ideal of feminism" the "women's movement has been not only feminist but also racist in orientation."[32] While this critique certainly applies to some quarters and practices of the women's movement and to essentialist forms of gender theory, it conveniently overlooks that postcolonial discourse could be critiqued in the same way. Third-World feminists have equally indicted postcolonial theory and liberation the*logy as male supremacist and sexist.

The disqualification of feminism/Marxism because of their origins in the West, moreover, not only essentializes the West as a unitary entity but also overlooks the fact that, according to Leela Gandhi, "the intellectual history of postcolonial theory is marked by a dialectic between Marxism, on the one hand, and post-structuralism/postmodernism on the other,"[33] both of which have their origins in the West. Finally such dichotomizing and essentializing rhetoric allows postcolonial scholars to disregard rather than to engage feminist theoretical work.[34]

31. Segovia, *Decolonizing Biblical Studies*, 140.
32. Ibid., 141.
33. Gandhi, *Postcolonial Theory*, viii.
34. See e.g the discussion of this problem by Joseph A. Marchal, "Imperial Intersections and Initial Inquiries: Toward a Feminist, Postcolonial Analysis of Philippians," *Journal of Feminist Studies in Religion* 22/2 (2006): 5–32.

Postcolonial rhetoric of "the West and the Rest," and re-inscription of this dualism in terms of Western white wo/men as colonizers and wo/men of the Third World as the colonized, perpetuate a reverse "othering." This dynamic of "othering" does not take into account that "postcolonial intellectuals, in their First World institutional locations, are ensconced in positions of power not only vis-à-vis the 'native' intellectuals but also vis-à-vis their First World neighbors."[35] To reverse the polarizing dualism "the West and the Third World" is to become complicit in its totalizing power.

Colonized as well as Western peoples are highly diverse in their self-understanding, social status, economic resources, and national history. They differ not just from colonizing peoples but also from each other. To essentialize the colonized and the colonizers, the West and the Third World, means to construct a dichotomy. Such a dichotomy makes a "mystical One" out of many different peoples, while opposing this "mystical One" to the "Other," which is conceived also as a unitary entity or One rather than as many.

Feminist Postcolonial Biblical Studies

The "coming together" of postcolonial and feminist theories in biblical studies and the*logy is of even more recent vintage.[36] Laura Donaldson, Kwok Pui-lan, and Musa W. Dube have been path-breaking[37] and their work has immensely enriched and sharpened feminist studies in religion. My critical questions are not a criticism of their whole work which has quite different theoretical moorings. Rather, I focus here only on one aspect of its theoretical frame. I do so by referring to a summary account of postcolonial feminist studies by Kwok Pui-lan.[38] In her collection of essays, *Postcolonial Imagination & Feminist Theology*, Kwok Pui-lan outlines the following five characteristics that define postcolonial feminist the*logy and biblical interpretation:

35. Dirlik, "The Postcolonial Aura," 513.

36. See especially the path-breaking collection of essays by Laura E. Donaldson & Kwok Pui-lan, eds., *Postcolonialism, Feminism, & Religious Discourse* (New York: Routledge, 2002).

37. See also Gale Yee, *Poor Banished Children of Eve: Woman as Evil in the Hebrew Bible* (Minneapolis, Minn.: Fortress Press, 2003).

38. See, however, the excellent article by Marchal, "Imperial Intersections and Initial Inquiries," esp., 17 ff., who fruitfully engages these points for the interpretation of Paul's letter to the Philippians.

1. Feminist postcolonial criticism indicts Western scholarship and inter-pretation as totalizing, pointing out its co-optation by imperial interests.

2. It is a counter-hegemonic discourse which pays special attention to the hidden and neglected voices in the bible.

3. It pays special attention to the multi-faith contexts of Third World situations.

4. It welcomes and fosters contributions from marginalized groups such as the Dalits, indigenous peoples, migrants, those living in the border-lands, diaspora, and at many different margins and "especially women in these communities."

5. It interacts with and draws on other hermeneutical frameworks such as postmodernism and post-structuralism.[39]

While these five methodological points are important, in their delineation of the relationship between postcolonial imagination and feminist the*logy, the overall conceptualization is troublesome. When critically discussing its tendencies, I do not identify Kwok Pui-lan or any other individual author with these tenden-cies. To personalize these tendencies would mean to shut off a critical discussion of their ideological mechanisms. First of all, postmodernism and poststructuralism but not feminist theory are recognized here as hermeneutical frameworks. The omission of feminism as a hermeneutical framework is worrisome if one does not assume that it is implied in the name *postcolonial feminist the*logy*. But how so, if *feminist the*logy* that is not qualified with *postcolonial* is attributed to the West?

It is unfortunate, moreover, that this new emerging feminist postcolonial biblical scholarship also has the tendency to construct a Manichean dualism between wo/men in the Third World and wo/men in the First World, which homogenizes and essentializes wo/men in either world.[40] How is one to locate within this dualistic scheme the work of feminists who live in both worlds? For instance, Gabrielle Dietrich,[41] who was born and educated as a German, has

---

39. Kwok Pui-lan, *Postcolonial Imagination & Feminist Theology*, 64.

40. Kwok Pui-lan, *Postcolonial Imagination & Feminist Theology*, 24: "Feminist theology from the Third World, whether using an explicitly postcolonial framework or not, deals with the intersection of national independence, cultural politics, and social transformation. Chapter 6 highlights the contributions of women from the Third World to political theology and points to the difference of their approaches from those of women of the First World."

41. See Lalrinawmi Ralte, "Interview with Gabrielle Dietrich," in *Waging Peace, Building*

lived her adult life as a naturalized citizen of India and has been engaged as a feminist activist in Indian and trans-national peoples' movements.[42] It seems that a rethinking of the First-Third World/Colonizer-Colonized dichotomy could be fruitfully undertaken if other postcolonial concepts, such as hybridity, diaspora, resident alien,[43] or migrancy were taken into account, which could delineate more effectively different feminist locations.

Such a homogenizing tendency and dualistic rhetoric seems to have a difficult time, moreover, acknowledging either its social location in the "First World" academy or its variegated Western feminist contexts. It does not enable readers to acknowledge how much postcolonial feminism has learned from critical feminist work in biblical studies, albeit this work has been developed in the West. Rather, in good "Western" academic fashion, it seems bent on proving its "novelty" and "uniqueness" by silencing its critical feminist roots.[44] Since the oppressed/colonized also have internalized the ethos of domination, as Paolo Freire has argued some time ago, it is important that we explore such rhetorical tendencies and internalizations in a critical feminist discourse of liberation.

---

a World in which Life Matters: Festschrift to Honor Gabrielle Dietrich, eds. Lalrinawmi Ralte and Stella Faria (Delhi: Indian Women in Theology/ISPCK, 2004), 10–33.

42. See, for instance, her article "People's Movements, the Strength of Wisdom and the Twisted Path of Civilization," in *Toward a New Heaven and a New Earth*, ed. Segovia, 407–21, and her book *A New Thing on Earth: Hopes and Fears Facing Feminist Theology: Theological Ruminations of a Feminist Activist* (Delhi: ISPCK, 2001).

43. For the development of this notion, see my book *Grenzen überschreiten. Der theoretische Anspruch feministischer Theologie* (Münster: Lit Verlag, 2004), 25–40.

44. I have been puzzled why some postcolonial feminist scholars have singled out my work for harsh criticism (see the widely quoted book of Dube, *Postcolonial Feminist Interpretation of the Bible*) or why this criticism has been repeated almost verbatim without critically engaging my arguments (e.g., Kwok Pui-lan; Gay Byron) while neglecting to scrutinize feminist academic works that focus exclusively on gender, or on wo/man, without paying any attention to Two-Third World wo/men. While I appreciate critical engagement with my work, I am disappointed that postcolonial feminists feel entitled to such mis-readings in the name of Two-Thirds World Christian wo/men, many of whom have found my work helpful. Moreover, this criticism focuses on *In Memory of Her* without taking into account my other works. The following observation of K. A. Appiah on art has shed some light on this depressing experience: "It is an important question why this distancing of the ancestors should have become so central a feature of our cultural lives. . . . To sell oneself and one's products as art in the marketplace, it is important, above all, to clear a space in which one is distinguished from other producers and products—and one does this by the construction and the marking of differences" (Kwame Anthony Appiah, "Is the 'Post' in 'Postcolonial' the 'Post' in 'Postmodern'?" 426). It seems that feminist postcolonial criticism needs not only to discuss the economics of academia but also the ideological patterns that prohibit the formation of a feminist intellectual tradition in biblical and other studies.

Whereas the emerging feminist post-colonialist voices have the tendency to forgive the absence of critical feminist theoretical arguments in the emerging field of postcolonial biblical studies, they seem inexplicably harsh in their judgment of critical feminist studies.[45] This rhetoric unwittingly supports the malestream academic disqualification of critical and liberationist feminist biblical studies, which have struggled, since the 1970s, for recognition of the marginalized and silenced voices of wo/men in the academy and in organized religious communities. Because it does not engage in a critical theoretical discussion of an intersectional feminist theoretical analytic in biblical studies that is different from a postcolonial analytic, this rhetoric inadvertently re-instates a "dual systems"[46] approach to feminist discourse. Such a dual systems approach conceptualizes colonialism and patriarchy as two independent systems of oppression. Therefore it deploys a "patriarchy/gender" and a "postcolonialism/imperialism" analytic rather than an intersectional analysis of the interstructuring of heterosexism, race, gender, class, and imperialism, which can pay attention to the multiplicative intersecting structures of domination.

In short, feminist postcolonial biblical criticism is an exciting new field of study which nevertheless needs to be engaged in a critical constructive conversation and debate. For just as postcolonial studies, in general, so also postcolonial feminist biblical criticism seems to construct an essentializing Manichean opposition between Western white feminists and feminists from the Third and Fourth Worlds, even though such a split is against its very own explicit intention.

In their path-breaking collection of essays *Postcolonialism, Feminism & Religious Discourse*, the editors Laura Donaldson and Kwok Pui-lan expressly state that they seek to "shift the dialogue among women of the Third and Fourth Worlds and those of the First [and I would add also of the previous Second World] from a moral to an epistemological paradigm."[47] Such an epistemological

45. Both Kwok Pui-lan (in *Postcolonial Imagination & Feminist Theology*, 7–8) and Musa W. Dube (in *Postcolonial Feminist Interpretation*, 118) have recognized that postcolonial critics have "left out the gender dimension," in Kwok Pui-lan's words, and they are well aware that it does not suffice just "to add gender and stir" to the postcolonial theoretical mix.

46. Such a dual systems approach was first articulated in terms of feminism and Marxism. See the review of Valery B. Ryson, *Feminist Debates: Issues of Theory and Political Practice* (New York: New York University Press, 1999), 16–25.

47. Laura E. Donaldson, "The Breasts of Columbus," in *Postcolonialism, Feminism & Religious Discourse*, 45.

paradigm will be able to explore the numerous historical and political linkages between wo/men in the metropolitan centers and the colonies.[48]

To engage in such an epistemological discussion, I will reflect here on my own theoretical approach. As is well known, since the early 1970s I have sought to develop, in the context of global feminist movements, a critical feminist epistemological paradigm. I have not named this paradigm *postcolonial*, although I have learned from postcolonial discourses and have emphasized the decolonizing task of biblical interpretation in the process of conscientization. I have not done so because of the positive valuation of nationalism[49] in some postcolonial discourses, their often heavy reliance on the French school of theory,[50] and the lack of feminist analysis in key postcolonial articulations. Instead, I have used an eclectic syncretism of methods and theories—including postcolonial ones—and have named this epistemological paradigm a *critical feminist interpretation for liberation*. Such a critical emancipative rhetorical approach could appropriately be called *decolonizing* but not *postcolonial* in the strict sense of the word.

My own formulations have been conditioned and limited, of course, by my social-religious-geographical locations as well as by my theoretical, academic discursive contexts.[51] Nevertheless, even while admitting this conditioning, I want to stress that a critical feminist epistemological paradigm cannot be formulated simply in terms of identity politics if it should be able to make possible critical alliances between feminists of all worlds—alliances which are so necessary in a globalizing world that is characterized by increasing violence and exploitation of wo/men.

Such a critical feminist theory and praxis for transformation has sought to work out both a systemic analysis of domination and a radical democratic vision

48. Kwok Pui-lan, "Unbinding Our Feet," ibid., 78.

49. For an exploration of this question, see "Feminist Studies in Religion and Theology In-Between Nationalism and Globalization," *JFSR* 21 (2005): 113–22.

50. See Stephen D. Moore, *Empire and Apocalypse*, 1-8, 77–96.

51. Because of this location of my work in the Euro-American wo/men's movements and academy, for instance, I have sought to articulate analytically the interstructuring of gender, sex, race, class, nationalism/imperialism. However, I have spoken, for instance, in *In Memory of Her* of the Greco–Roman world following the language practice of social-world discourses and less of Roman imperialism—as Musa Dube rightly points out. Yet, she seems not to be aware that I have consistently done so in terms of structures of domination, particularly in my work on the book of Revelation, since the imperial power of Rome takes center stage in this writing. If my early work is read through this lens, it cannot be misread as being uncritical of Roman imperial power. Moreover, such a misreading is only possible if *But She Said* is not taken into account.

and decolonizing space for change and transformation. From the beginnings, I have articulated epistemologically that a feminist biblical rhetoric and hermeneutic must be conceptualized theoretically not simply in terms of gender but with regard to the intersecting pyramidal structures of domination. It must be articulated from the perspective and standpoint of wo/men who struggle for survival and justice at the bottom of the kyriarchal pyramid of dominations and subordinations, oppressions and exploitations,[52] whether these wo/men be geographically located in the Third or First worlds. Since the kyriarchal pyramid of global capitalism is not static but consists of ever-shifting and intersecting structures of domination and exploitation, it cannot be reduced to fixed geographical localizations.

I have tried to use this critical feminist theoretical optic for reading and interpreting biblical texts as well as for elaborating such an approach to interpretation, not only as a critical hermeneutics of liberation[53] but also as a critical emancipative rhetoric and ethic of inquiry,[54] which lends itself to investigating biblical texts and history as well as contemporary ways of interpretation. A critical rhetoric of inquiry treats biblical texts and their interpretations as arguments rather than as scientific or revelatory facts. It investigates not only how biblical texts "mean" but also what they "do" to those who submit to their world of vision. Such an understanding of biblical texts and interpretation as rhetorical agrees with the following epistemological principle stated by Edward Said, "Texts are worldly, to some degree they are events, and even when they appear to deny it, they are nevertheless a part of the social world, human life, and of course the historical moments in which they are located and interpreted."[55] Yet, a feminist rhetoric of inquiry accentuates this insight in a critical feminist mode.

Moreover, the method that I have employed in *In Memory of Her*[56] for a critical feminist interpretation of Christian origins, and with which I sought to reconstruct early Christian history in terms of struggle, has affinities with Said's notion of contrapuntal reading. In his book *Culture and Imperialism*, Said

52. See Elisabeth Schüssler Fiorenza, *Discipleship of Equals: A Critical Feminist Ekklesia-logy of Liberation* (New York: Crossroad, 1992).

53. See my books *Bread Not Stone; But She Said; Sharing Her Word;* and *Wisdom Ways.*

54. See Elisabeth Schüssler Fiorenza, *Rhetoric and Ethic: The Politics of Biblical Studies* (Minneapolis, Minn.: Fortress Press, 1999).

55. Edward Said, *The World, the Text and the Critic* (Cambridge, Mass: Harvard University Press, 1983), 4.

56. See Schüssler Fiorenza, *In Memory of Her.*

distinguished such a contrapuntal from a unitary reading and defined it as follows: to read contrapuntally is to read "with a simultaneous awareness both of the metropolitan history that is narrated and of those other histories against which (and beyond which) the dominating discourse acts."[57]

While not explicitly developed in postcolonial terms, my analytical and reconstructive concepts of kyriarchy, which articulates the pyramid of intersecting structures of domination and exploitation, and that of the ekklēsia of wo/men, which is understood as a radical, democratic, decolonizing, egalitarian space of equal rights and respect for all in the diversity of their identities, are not just religious but also anti-imperial political concepts. To claim that they are "Western" concepts is to overlook that they seek to correct Western imperialism.[58] The definition of kyriarchy as "rule of the emperor, lord, slave master, father, husband"—as the domination by elite propertied colonizing men— interstructures imperialism with hetero-sexism, gender injustice, and class exploitation, racism, nationalism, and ageism in multiple ways. With ekklēsia of wo/men, in turn, I have a heuristic construct in mind that is similar to what Chandra Talpade Mohanti has called the "imagined community of Third World oppositional struggles."[59] She envisions it as the kind of space that provides a political, rather than a biological or cultural, basis for alliances between wo/men

57. Edward Said, *Culture and Imperialism* (London: Chatto & Windus, 1993), 59.

58. Musa Dube states in her book that my "theoretical articulations of *kyriarchy* and *ekklesia* of women go a long way toward countering imperialism if followed. The question is, therefore, does Schüssler Fiorenza honor her theoretical goals in her rhetorical hermeneutical practice?" (*Postcolonial Feminist Interpretation of the Bible*, 37). However, rather than engaging my epistemological proposals on theoretical grounds, she goes on to caricature them and to fault me for not practicing my "goals." Instead of arguing why her dual-systems analysis—patriarchy and imperialism—does better critical feminist work than my intersectional analysis of kyriarchy, she misconstrues my arguments. For instance, she summarizes her claims: "In short, the logic of radical democracy invites international wo/men to the ekklesia as long as they speak the language of the 'civilized' and the 'cultured' and not necessarily to bring traditions that were devalued by Western kyriarchal traditions. . . ." (39) without giving any examples as to how I do so. Moreover, she seems to think that I identify the ekklēsia of wo/men or wo/men-church, understood as a feminist hermeneutical center, with the institutional church when she claims that "for survivors of imperialism the invitation to inhabit the 'ekklesia,' the white male, most hierarchical and exclusive of centers, dangerously befriends the ideology of imperialism. . . ." However, such a misreading of my concept is only possible because she leaves out my qualification of "ekklēsia" with "wo/men" and does not recognize the theoretical import of this qualification. See Musa W. Dube, "Toward a Feminist Postcolonial Interpretation of the Bible," *Semeia* 78 (1997): 11–26, esp., 21 n.15.

59. See Chapter 3 for a fuller theoretical development of this.

of all colors and seeks to move away from essentialist notions of Third World feminisms.

In this way, I have sought to follow the lead of critical feminist postcolonial theorists who have drawn attention to two crucial theoretical issues in emancipative struggles. On the one hand, they have pointed out that cultural and religious essentialisms fashion identity discourses of sameness rather than discourses of rich diversity.[60] On the other hand, they have argued that emancipative struggles need to imagine alternatives[61] to the structures of domination and envision discursive communities that are not simply idealized political or religious fantasies but already have been partially realized in history.[62]

Such a mapping of the decolonizing space, which I have named the ekklēsia of wo/men, requires that we move beyond the "confessional stance" of identity politics or the dichotomy of the West and the rest, the Colonizers/Colonized. Instead we need to adopt a critical analytic for interpreting the inscriptions of kyriarchal power in biblical texts and their possible internalizations by biblical readers. To that end, it is important also to trace emancipatory discourses inscribed in biblical texts in terms of Sandoval's "democratics," which seeks to equalize unequal power relations. Such a decolonizing approach always has to operate on two levels: the historical level of the text and the contemporary level of its interpreters since the colonizing power of empire determines both levels. In the second part of the chapter, I will engage such an interpretation for "dissident consciousness" and both its inscriptions of empire as well as its alternative visions of well-being, with respect to the book of Revelation, the last book of the Christian canon.

60. See Uma Narayan, "Essence of Culture and a Sense of History: A Feminist Critique of Cultural Essentialism," in *Decentering the Center: Philosophy for a Multicultural, Postcolonial, and Feminist World*, eds. Uma Narayan and Sandra Harding (Bloomington, Ind.: Indiana University Press, 2000).

61. For the importance of imagination in decolonization, see the contributions in *The Decolonization of Imagination: Culture, Knowledge and Power*, in eds. Jan Nederveen Oieterse and Bhikhu Parekh (London: Zed, 1995).

62. See for instance Alison M. Jagger, "Globalizing Feminist Ethics," in *Decentering the Center*, 1–25.

A Decolonizing Interpretation of the Book of Revelation

Whereas postcolonial studies have only recently focused on the power of empire inscribed in early Christian texts, scholarship on the book of Revelation has always wrestled with this question.[63] It has either praised the book because of its critique of the Roman Empire or condemned it as a sub-Christian writing of hatred because it denigrates Roman culture and civilization.[64] In the following I do not want to repeat my work on the whole book of Revelation but only focus on the discussion of the feminine figuration of the Roman Empire in chapters 17–18.

Exegetes have understood the feminine gendered figure of Babylon in essentializing and generalizing terms as a sign for the general decadence of civilization, the fleeting character of power and wealth, the symbol of the archetypal enmity against G*d, or as embodiment of all evil. Such an essentializing approach depoliticizes and dehistoricizes Babylon as a steno-symbol for the imperial power of Rome.

In the past fifteen years or so, feminist interpretation seems to have also adopted such an archetypal essentializing gesture[65] by identifying the gendered

63. I have already analyzed Revelation in political terms in my dissertation, *Priester für Gott: Studien zum Herrschafts- und Priestermotiv in der Apokalypse*. Neuetestamentliche Abhandlungen n.s. 7. (Münster: Aschendorff, 1972), and in my articles, "Religion und Politik in der Offenbarung des Johannes," *Biblische Randbemerkungen: Schülerfestschrift für Rudolf Schnackenburg zum 60. Geburtstag*," in eds. Helmut Merklein und Joachim Lange (Würzburg: Echter Verlag,1974), 261–72, and "Redemption as Liberation: Apoc 1:5 ff. and 5:9 ff," *Catholic Biblical Quarterly* 36, no. 2 (1974): 220–32.

64. See my commentary *Revelation: Vision of a Just World*, Proclamation Commentaries (Minneapolis, Minn: Fortress Press, 1991), and my collection of essays, *The Book of Revelation: Justice and Judgment*, original edition, 1985; 2nd edition with a new epilogue (Minneapolis, Minn.: Fortress Press, 1998) which stress the problematic reinscription of imperial language for G*d and Christ and its internalizations in the process of reading and proclaiming Revelation as sacred scripture. Stephen D. Moore's book *Empire and Apocalypse* does not indicate that he is aware of this argument and my work.

65. See for instance, Tina Pippin, *Death and Desire*, 47, who states: "I want to focus on the clearly identified women in the text who are destroyed and on the general 'apocalypse of women' brought about in the utopian vision of the New Jerusalem. By the 'apocalypse of women' I mean the misogyny and disenfranchisement that are at the root of gender relations, accompanied by (hetero)sexism and racism along with violence, poverty, disempowerment and fear. . . . The text of the Apocalypse, with its female archetypes of good and evil, virgin and whore is an account of a political and religious and also gender crisis of the end of the first century CE." See also her article "The Heroine and the Whore: The Apocalypse of John in Feminist Perspective," in *From Every People and Nation: The Book of Revelation in Intercultural Perspective*, ed. David Rhoads (Minneapolis, Minn.: Fortress Press, 2005), 127–45.

symbolization of Babylon not just as a feminine figuration but as a "whoring woman"[66] and that of the New Jerusalem as a "chaste bride."[67] A lively discussion, on the function of the feminine figurations of Babylon and the New Jerusalem, has ensued that does not indict Revelation in defense of civilization but rather for misogyny. In the course of this feminist debate, I have argued that the Book of Revelation cannot be adequately understood using an essentializing gender analysis, because gender is always constructed and inflected by relations of domination such as race, class, age, nation, and colonization.[68]

A reading of Revelation in terms of the multiplicative structures of domination—which does not identify with actual wo/men the feminine gender figuration of things such as cities, countries, or institutions—can correct a dualistic-androcentric gender lens, I have maintained, and can enable contemporary interpreters to read "against the grain" of their own cultural religious assumptions or prejudices as well as against those of the grammatically and symbolically kyriocentric text.[69] A feminist rhetorical-political reading of Revelation uses gender as one but not as the sole lens of interpretation. It does

66. For instance, in her contribution to the *Women's Bible Commentary* (Susan R. Garrett, "Revelation," in *The Women's Bible Commentary*, eds. Newsome and Ringe (Louisville, Ky.: Westminster John Knox, 1998), 377, Susan Garrett has elaborated the significance of reading Revelation in terms of gender: "Each of these symbols reflects the male-centered view of the first century: women are caricatured as virgins, whores or mothers. . . . The stereotyped feminine images in the book do not represent the full spectrum of authentic womanhood, either in John's day or in our own. . . . Exploring the cultural roots of John's metaphoric language about women will enable us to understand what he was trying to say at those points, but the dehumanizing way in which he phrased his message will remain deeply troubling."

67. Most recently Jorunn Økland, "Why Can't The Heavenly Miss Jerusalem Just Shut Up?" in *Her Master's Tools*, eds. Caroline Vander Stichele and Todd Penner, 311–32.

68. See the works on which I draw here: the epilogue to my book, *The Book of Revelation: Justice and Judgment*, 205–36, and my article, "Babylon the Great: A Rhetorical-Political Reading of Revelation 17–18," in *The Reality of Apocalypse: Rhetoric and Politics in the Book of Revelation*, ed. David L. Barr (Atlanta, Ga.: Society of Biblical Literature, 2006), 243–69.

69. Caroline Vander Stichele, "Just A Whore: The Annihilation of Babylon According to Revelation 17:16," in the internet journal *lectio difficilior* 1(2000): 1–13, esp., 6, misreads my argument that the feminine gendered figurations of Revelation are "conventional" language, as denying the androcentrism of Revelation. She insists that, "In the case of Babylon, the woman/city represents the other, viewed as alien territory to be conquered and eventually destroyed, thus presuming and affirming an analogy between military and sexual invasion, the colonizer presented as male, the colonized as female. Gender then is more than just a matter of convention but plays a role in the message to be delivered." I could not agree more, but the question is: does Revelation want to deliver the message that Rome represents the colonized female to be conquered and raped?

not naturalize and reify the text in terms of the dualistic kyriocentric Western sex-gender system. Instead it points out that gender is an ideological construct that is produced by and in turn legitimates and "naturalizes" relations of domination. Hence the political constructedness of gender[70] in texts and interpretations can come to the fore only when inherent structures of domination become the focus of feminist readings.

While a feminist reading of Revelation primarily in terms of gender underscores the ways the discursive sex/gender system determines the rhetoric of Revelation and our own readings of it, an interpretation of Revelation in terms of the political "imperial" code insists that gender is not a discrete category but that it is inflected by other relations of domination, such as race, status, religion, and colonial imperialism. It points out that a gender analytic tends to focus on the sex/gender system but not on the systemic structures of heterosexuality, class, race, ethnicity, or colonialism. It also tends to subsume an imperial reading under that of gender. It privileges feminine markers when reading Revelation whereas an intersecting dominations analysis stresses the political language and gendered imperial rhetoric of the book.[71] Both types of analysis must remain interactive with each other if they are to reciprocally and fruitfully correct each other. Such a correction and fine-tuning of the feminist lens and interpretive focus are especially necessary for those who read from the social location of Western elite male status and imperial privilege.[72] A rhetoric of inquiry must therefore be accompanied by an ethics of inquiry that is able to assess critically the scholarly frameworks and interpretive patterns that determine all interpretation of Revelation in light of its utopian vision of justice and well-being for all, which is signified by the city of G*d, the New Jerusalem.

70. I could not agree more with H. Stenström (quoted by Vander Stichele, "Just A Whore," 7) that "to speak about gender is to speak about a structure of power. To speak about power structures is to speak about something political." However, I would add, to speak about gender is not necessarily to speak about actual wo/men.

71. See, e.g., Allen Dwight Callahan, "Revelation 18: Notes on Effective History and the State of Colombia," in *Walk in the Ways of Wisdom*, 269–85.

72. Such elite male status, of course, is not only found in the West; it is to be understood not in essentialist gender terms but as a socio-political historical location.

Reading the Feminine Figuration of Babylon/Rome

To read the feminine gendered figuration of Babylon, it is important to look care-fully at both the book of Revelation's arguments as well as at one's own frames of meaning[73] and understanding of language "as a reality-generating system."[74] Although Babylon is figured as a queen and a whore, an elite wo/man of great power, the rhetorical-symbolic discourse of Revelation clearly wants us to under-stand it as an imperial city and not as representing an historical wo/man. Revela-tion 17:18 unambiguously states: "And the woman that you saw is the great city which has dominion over the kings of the earth." Just as the figure of "beast" or the "lamb" does not connote "animal," nor does that of the "ten horns" connote an animal's "bony outgrowth," so "harlot" does not connote "woman" nor does it mean actual "prostitutes" in the rhetoric of Revelation. The rhetorical markers in the text, again and again, refer the reader to a certain "city" and not to an actual wo/man. Just as "Lady Liberty" refers not to the freedom of American wo/men but symbolizes America as a powerful nation, so also the "Whore Babylon" refers not to actual wo/men living in the Roman Empire but rather signifies seductive imperial power.

The narrative sequence concerning Babylon in 17:1—19:10 may be com-pared to a triptych with three panels. After a general introductory headline in 17:1-2, the first panel (17:3-18) describes and interprets the world capital, Babylon. The second panel (18:1-24)[75] differs stylistically insofar as the destruc-tion of the great city is not described but only reflected in the dirges of the kings, merchants, and ship owners. The legal claim of the persecuted victims against Babylon is now granted. The powerful capital of the world is destroyed not just because it has persecuted Christians but also because it has unlawfully killed many other people. Revelation 18:24 is therefore best understood as the hermeneutical key to the whole Babylon series of judgments. That the question of justice is at the heart of Revelation's politics of meaning is also underscored by the third panel (19:1-10) which presents a heavenly liturgy praising the jus-tice of G*d's judgments and announcing the marriage feast of the Lamb.[76]

73. For the theoretical elaboration of this expression see Rosemary Hennessy, *Materialist Feminism and the Politics of Discourse* (New York: Routledge, 1993) and my book *Jesus: Miriam's Child, Sophia's Prophet: Critical Issues in Feminist Christology* (New York: Continuum, 1994).
74. M.A.K. Halliday, "Anti-languages," *American Anthropologist* 78 (1976): 570–84.
75. Susan M. Elliott, "Who Is Addressed in Revelation 18:6-7?" *BR* 40 (1995): 98–113.
76. When read literally we have here a marriage between an animal and a wo/man. However,

Whereas in chapter 17, Babylon is seen primarily as a feminine figure (17:1-7, 9, 15-16) and secondarily as a city (17:5, 18), in chapter 18 Babylon is primarily characterized as an imperial city (18:2, 4, 10, 16, 18-19, 21) and only three times as a "woman" (18:3, 7, 16). This reversal in emphasis indicates that the rhetorical argument shifts from feminine figuration to that of imperial city. The author's explanatory identification of "the woman" vision, as that of the "the great city which has dominion over the kings of the earth" in 17:18, serves as a rhetorical directive telling readers that they should understand this sequence of visions in terms of imperial Rome.[77] The feminine figuration of Babylon is not a metaphor but a steno-symbol which is to be read as having a one-to-one meaning.[78] Babylon equals imperial city. At no time does Revelation 17–18 refer to any individual flesh-and-blood wo/man but only to a feminine figuration.[79]

This whole narrative rhetoric ratifies Rev 14:8, the announcement of imperial Babylon/Rome's judgment, which the second angel proclaims in traditional prophetic language (cf. Isa 24:19; Jer 51:7 ff; Dan 4:27). The expression "Babylon the Great" recurs in Rev 16:19; 17:5 and 18:2, 10, 21. Most exegetes hold that, in the context of Revelation, Babylon is a prophetic name for Rome, since Rome was understood in Jewish (4 Esth 3:1-2, 28, 31; Apoc Barn 10:1-3; 11:1; 67:7; *Sibylline Oracles* 5:143, 159) and early Christian literature of the time as "Babylon." Both Babylon and Rome shared in the dubious distinction of having destroyed Jerusalem and the temple. Revelation uses the name "Babylon" in order to evoke a whole range of scriptural-theological-political meanings to characterize imperial Rome.[80]

---

scholars do not read "lamb" as "animal" but see it as a figuration of Christ.

77. For the imperial context of Revelation, see also D. Aune, "The Form and Function of the Proclamations to the Seven Churches (Rev 2–3)," *NTS* 36 (1990): 182–204; also, his "The Influence of Roman Imperial Court Ceremonial on the Apocalypse of John," *BR* 28 (1983): 5–26; and the most recent discussion by Heinz Giesen, "Das Römische Reich im Spiegel der Johannes-Apokalypse," *ANRW* II/26 (1996): 2501–2614; H.J. Klauck, "Das Sendschreiben nach Pergamon und der Kaiserkult in der Johannesoffenbarung," *Biblica* 73 (1992): 153–82.

78. See P. Wheelwright, *Metaphor and Reality*, 6th edition (Bloomington, Ind.: University of Indiana Press, 1975), makes the distinction between steno- and tensive symbol. Whereas a steno-symbol always bears only a one-to-one relationship and is mostly used in definitions, the tensive symbol can evoke a whole range of meanings and can never be exhausted or adequately expressed by a single referent.

79. The study of gender has amply documented that gender does not refer to actual wo/men but is a discourse of domination.

80. Jean Pierre Ruiz, *Ezekiel in the Apocalypse: The Transformation of Prophetic Language in Revelation 16:17—19:10* (New York: Peter Lang, 1989).

For its feminine figuration of the imperial city as "whore," Revelation not only uses the conventional feminine metaphor for a city or country—a verbal practice that is still in vogue today—but also relies on the prophetic language of the Hebrew Bible that indicts Jerusalem and the people of Israel for idolatry, which is metaphorically likened to prostitution,"[81] a figure of speech which was by then conventional language and would have been understood by the hearers/readers of Revelation as such. Just as, for example, the image of the Lamb refers to an actual historical person Jesus (who was not a lamb) rather than to an actual sheep-animal, so the label of prostitute refers to an actual imperial city rather than to an actual wo/man. In short, the vision of Babylon "the Great" does not tell us anything about Revelation's understanding of actual wo/men. This is not to say that readers have not and will not interpret Revelation 17–18 in misogynist terms, since they are used to identifying grammatical gender and feminine figuration with natural gender and wo/men.

The controverted question remains whether Revelation activates this feminine figuration of Babylon for misogynist ends or whether it intends it as an argument against the imperial domination of Rome. For in the classical prophets the language of prostitution and immorality signifies unfaithfulness to Israel's G*d, which was enacted in foreign alliances and the worship of other Gods. It is therefore not femininity and sexual morality but the politics of power that is central to the argument of Revelation. As Adela Yarbro Collins has pointed out:

> Like Nineveh, Rome has seduced many nations into alliance because of its overwhelming and attractive power. Like those of Tyre, its commercial enterprises are widespread, enriching some and making the poverty of others harder to bear. Idolatry is a factor here as well, although the image has shifted. Rather than depicting the people of God as a prostitute who has lusted after male gods. . . . instead of remaining faithful to Yahweh, Revelation presents the foreign god as female, as a prostitute who seduces the inhabitants of the earth.[82]

81. For a feminist discussion of this language tradition of idolatry as prostitution and the rhetoric of Israel as harlot, see Renita Weems, *Battered Love: Marriage, Sex and Violence in the Hebrew Prophets* (Minneapolis, Minn.: Fortress Press, 1995).

82. Adela Yarbro Collins, "Feminine Symbolism in the Book of Revelation," *Biblical Interpretation* 1/1 (1993): 27. Such an archetypal gender reading depoliticizes Revelation's imperial language and imagery in order to make sense out of the feminine figuration of Rome as

In short, if one reads the sexually charged language of Revelation not just in gender but in political terms, one can discover a critique of empire in the conventionally coded feminine language for a city, which uses gender for constructing power. Clarice Martin's womanist reading of Rev 18:13, for instance, underscores John's critique of Rome's exploitation through the system of slavery which "rendered a sharply polemical indictment of the pervasive and baleful commodification and trafficking of human beings throughout the Roman Empire."[83] Martin's approach does not eclipse a feminist reading but draws on African American slave wo/men's experience of the slave mistress to enhance our understanding of Rome's economic power gained in and through the institution of slavery.

Whereas an analysis solely in terms of essentializing gendered representation focuses on Revelation's references to *porneia/porneuein* as expressions of sexual abuse, a complex-rhetorical-political analysis argues that the sexual metaphor of "whoring" or "practicing immorality" is a *conventional metaphor* connoting idolatry and exploitation. Since the "harlot" trope is taken over from the classical prophets, who also spoke of nations and cities as prostitutes and harlots (Nah 3:4-7 Nineveh; Isa 23: Tyre and Sidon; Isa 1:21; Hos 1–4; Jer 3:6-10; Ezra 16: Jerusalem and Israel), this trope must be problematized as engendering an ideological tradition that has been and is activated against wo/men in the interest of a misogynist politics. Revelation's gendered language of "whoring" must be scrutinized not only for its ideological-misogynist evocation but also for its religious exclusivist bias and its economic strength based upon a slave-holding system.

Yet, Revelation does not use the metaphor of "whoring" as the prophets of the Hebrew Bible did, in such a way as to indict the Christian community as unfaithful to G*d. Rather, the text foregrounds the economic-political realities of kyriarchal exploitations by the Empire. "The wine of its fornication," from which the "dwellers of the earth have become drunk," stems from the "intercourse" of Babylon with the "kings of the earth" by which "the wealth of its wantonness" has enriched the merchants of the earth.[84] Not sex but power, wealth, and

prostitute. This Jungian perspective finds in the depiction of Rome as the Great Mother "a struggle of Christian faith as a religion of individuation to free itself" from Greco-Roman "participation mystique."

83. Clarice J. Martin, "Polishing the Unclouded Mirror: A Womanist Reading of Revelation 18:13," in *From Every People and Nation*, 82–109, esp., 86.

84. See J. Nelson Kraybill, *Imperial Cult and Commerce in John's Apocalypse* (Sheffield:

murder are the ingredients of Babylon/Rome's "fornication." The conventional use of "practicing immorality" as signifying idolatry is here redefined as political "intercourse" that negotiates wealth, power, and violent death. The trope of "whoring" is not used in the interest of imperial power but against it.

Revelation's political critique of imperialism points to the death-dealing powers of Empire. Whereas the merchant ship owners, kings, and all the nations of the earth were "drunk" with Babylon's wantonness, i.e., their sharing in its power and wealth, Babylon is drunk with "the blood of the witnesses of Jesus" (17:6), and that of "prophets, and of saints, and of all who have been slain on earth" (18:24). If one reads the problematic statement "these who have not defiled themselves with women" (Rev 14:4)[85] in light of the rhetorics of Revelation 17–18, then it becomes clear that Revelation's use of conventional Hebrew Bible language[86] does not refer to actual prostitutes or illicit sexual intercourse with flesh and blood wo/men.

Reading Revelation in Terms of Gender Dualism

A dualistic reading of Revelation just in terms of gender is also in danger of re-inscribing the wide-spread cultural-religious dichotomy between the "good" and the "bad woman." Barbara Rossing's work has convincingly shown that the author of Revelation was familiar with the feminine coding of the dualistic cultural pattern of ethical choice as found in Greco-Roman and in Jewish Wisdom literature.[87] Yet, it must not be overlooked that this ethical dualism, which is symbolized by two feminine figures, is embedded in an overarching tripartite

---

Sheffield Academic, 1996), 102–43.

85. Pablo Richard, *Apocalypse: A People's Commentary on the Book of Revelation* (Maryknoll, N.Y.: Orbis, 1995), 120, suggests the following translation of 14:4a: "these are those who did not contaminate themselves with idolatry, for they are clean of heart." However, as I have pointed out above, "idolatry" must not be misread in a purely religious modern sense but must be understood as economic, political, and religious perfidy.

86. See Judith Plaskow, *Standing Again at Sinai* (San Francisco, Calif: Harper & Row, 1990), who has problematized Exod 19:15, "Be ready on the third day; do not go near a woman." According to her, for a feminist, this is one of the most disturbing verses in the bible because wo/men are rendered invisible at the central moment in Jewish history.

87. Barbara Rossing, *The Choice Between Two Cities: Whore, Bride, and Empire in the Apocalypse* (Harrisburg, Pa.: Trinity International, 1999). For a more deconstructive reading of the Wisdom language in Revelation, see Tina Pippin, "Wisdom and Apocalyptic in the Apocalypse of John: Desiring Sophia," in *In Search of Wisdom*, ed. Leo Purdue (Louisville, Ky.: Westminster John Knox, 1993), 285–95.

symbolism. A binary reading of Revelation's feminine representations, as "good woman" and "bad woman," does not appreciate that the author introduces and relates, one to another, three, and not just two, powerful feminine figures—Babylon, the Whore, and New Jerusalem, the Bride. Revelation does not work with a simple "either/or" dualism but rather dialectically[88] mediates this ethical dualism by inserting, as a third figure, the birthing Wo/man (not the Mother) of chapter 12.[89] They symbolize in a dialectical fashion the Powerful Queen of Heaven, the Powerful Queen of Earth, and the Powerful Queen of the New Heaven and New Earth. Such a three-part structure also can be observed in Revelation 17–18 and in chapter 12, as well as in the New Jerusalem segment.[90]

Chapter 12 takes the form of an inclusion. Between the great portent of the glorious wo/man and the powerful dragon (12:1-6), on the one hand, and the vision of the dragon's persecution of the wo/man (12:13-17), on the other, John inserts the vision about war in heaven waged by the dragon (12:7-12). He first draws the audience's attention to the glorious sign in heaven, but at the end of each section he shifts the focus again toward the earth. The whole vision appears to be a mythological elaboration of the *eschatological war* motif already sounded in 11:7.

The myth of the Queen of Heaven with the divine child was—as Adela Yarbro Collins has shown[91]—internationally known at the time of John. Variations appear in Babylonia, Egypt, Greece, Asia Minor, and especially in texts about astral religion. Elements of this myth include: the Goddess and the divine child, the great red dragon and his enmity to mother and child, and the motif of the protection of mother and child. Revelation 12 also incorporates these elements. As in other versions of the myth, the dragon seeks the child who is not yet born

---

88. Roger Fowler, *Linguistic Criticism* (Oxford: Oxford University Press, 1986), 146, points to "the dialectical semantics" of anti-language at work.

89. See Edith McEwan Humphrey, *The Ladies and the Cities: Transformation and Apocalyptic Identity in Joseph and Aseneth, 4 Ezra, the Apocalypse and The Shepherd of Hermas*, 103–11, who argues against Yarbro Collins' disassociation of the wo/men in chapters 12 and 21 (*Combat Myth in the Book of Revelation*; Missoula, Mont.: Scholars, 1976, 233–35). Humphrey argues that the two figures "have a close relationship, but not an exact identity," (110). However, she does not explore the links between the three "queen" figures in Revelation.

90. It must not be overlooked that the feminine metaphor of the bride, which serves to allude to Synoptic messianic banquet traditions, is quickly replaced by that of the city, the New Jerusalem. Contra Jan Fekkes III, "Revelation 19–21 and Isaian Nuptial Imagery," *JBL* 10/2 (1990): 283 who argues that Rev 21:18-21 is a continuation of the bride scheme.

91. See Yarbro Collins, *Combat Myth*.

in order to devour and kill it. The dragon therefore pursues the pregnant wo/man because of the child she carries. In other forms of the myth, the wo/man is either carried away in order to give birth in a protected place, or she gives birth in a miraculous way and, together with the newborn, escapes the onslaught of the dragon. In Revelation 12 the child is exalted to heaven while the wo/man is carried to the desert for the sake of her own protection.[92]

Some features of this international myth appear also in the Roman imperial cult. A coin of Pergamum, for example, shows the goddess Roma with the divine emperor. In the cities of Asia Minor, Roma, the Queen of Heaven, was worshiped as the Mother of the Gods.[93] Her oldest temple stood in Smyrna. Her imperial child was celebrated as the "world's savior," incarnation of the Sun-God Apollo. Revelation probably intends such an allusion to the imperial cult[94] and the Goddess Roma but it pictures the wo/man clothed with the sun as the anti-image of Babylon, the symbol of the world-power of his day and its allies (Revelation 17–18), because it reinterprets this international ancient myth in terms of Jewish expectations. Its emphasis on the travail of the wo/man does not derive from the ancient pagan myth but takes inspiration from the Hebrew Bible's image of Israel-Zion in messianic times.

The vision of the wo/man in labor pains alludes to Israel-Zion seen as a pregnant wo/man awaiting the delivery of the messianic age in Isa 26:16-21; 54:1; 66:7-9 (cf. also Mic 4:9-10).[95] With the symbolic language of Isaiah and

92. In her "Response to Tina Pippin, 'Eros and the End'" in *Ideological Criticism of Biblical Texts*, Semeia (Atlanta, Ga.: Scholars, 1992), 220, Jane Schaberg comments: "helped by the wings of the great eagle (12:14) and by the earth (v. 16), she almost seems like a character from the Native American traditions. She represents a third option: she does not follow the beast, nor is she a martyr/companion/bride of the Lamb. Refusing this either/or she flees. She has become interesting in a new way." However, Schaberg overlooks the positive understanding of the "earth" in Revelation (see also the hymn 11:18 where judgment is announced as "destroying the destroyers of the earth") when she claims that reverence for the earth is missing from Revelation (223). See also Barbara Rossing, "For the Healing of the World: Reading Revelation Ecologically," in *From Every People and Nation*, 165–82.

93. See Ronald Mellor, *Thea Roma: The Worship of the Goddess Roma in the Greek World* (Göttingen: Vandenhoeck & Ruprecht, 1975). See also his "The Goddess Roma," in *Aufstieg und Niedergang der Römischen Welt II, 17.2*, ed. Wolfgang Haase (New York: de Gruyter, 1981), 950–1030.

94. S. R. F. Price, *Rituals and Power: the Roman Imperial Cult in Asia Minor* (Cambridge: Cambridge University Press, 1984); see also Steven J. Friesen, *Neokoros: Ephesus, Asia and the Cult of the Flavian Emperors* (Leiden: E.J.Brill, 1993).

95. See Claudia Suter Rehmann, *Geh frage die Gebärerin; feministisch-befreiungstheologische Untersuchungen zum Gebärmotiv in der Apokalyptik* (Gütersloh: Gütersloher Verlagshaus, 1995).

this ancient pagan myth, Revelation invokes the image of the messianic child being born accompanied by the birth-pangs of the messianic woes. The messianic community, Judaism, is protected and nourished in the wilderness, during the time of the dragon, representing imperial death-dealing power of Rome. Probably written after the Roman imperial army's destruction of Jerusalem in 70 CE, Revelation nevertheless asserts that the messianic community Israel is nonetheless protected during the end time. Again, the text does not speak about an actual woman but it speaks in gendered terms about the messianic community.

Reading Gender in Political Terms

While the "wo/man clothed with the sun" is clearly a female metaphor, as Rossing has elaborated, the vision of G*d's alternative world, the New Jerusalem, like Babylon is a steno-symbol referring to a cosmic city. If a dualistic contrast is intended, it is the *political contrast* between the capital of the world of oppression and the capital of the world of G*d in which tears, hunger, and death—the characteristics of the world of injustice—have passed away. The contrast is not between two types of wo/men but between two types of world. The "first" heaven and earth now belong to the past. The antagonistic dualism no longer exists: between the reign of G*d and Christ in heaven, the world of G*d, on the one hand, and that of Babylon, the Dragon, and his allies on earth and in the underworld, on the other hand. The "new heaven and earth" stands in continuity with the former heaven and earth[96] but they form a qualitatively new and unified world. This new reality is characterized by G*d's presence among the peoples of G*d. The vision of the New Jerusalem, arrayed like a bride in the splendor of the "righteous deeds of the saints,"[97] makes symbolically present G*d's eschatological salvation and reign which entails that heaven will move down to earth.[98] Read in rhetorical-political terms, Revelation

96. See the ecological analysis of Barbara R. Rossing, "For the Healing of the World: Reading Revelation Ecologically," in *From Every People and Nation*, 165–82.

97. Pippin stresses that the New Jerusalem is a controlled and subdued female figure (see her "Reading for Gender in the Apocalypse of John," 195). However, there is no evidence for this in the text which does not stress wifely subordination but splendor, bliss, and well-being.

98. Richard, *Apocalypse*, 172: This "is not the end of history, but rather a new creation within history. It is a transcendent world, not because it is beyond history, but rather a new creation within history. This new creation is the final achievement of our history."

speaks not of gender and sex but of power used either for destruction or for well-being.

The last series of visions in 21:9—22:9 magnificently elaborate, in visionary symbolization, the eschatological salvation announced in 21:1-8. This series is structurally designed to form the third panel in the triptych 17:1—22:9, insofar as like the Babylon visions, it is introduced by one of the seven bowl angels (21:9 cf. 17:1) and concludes with a dialogue between the angel and the seer (22:6-9 cf. 19:9-10). In contrast to 17:1 where John is carried into the wilderness, in 21:10 he is carried to a great mountain, where one of the bowl angels shows him the "bride, the wife of the lamb"[99] (21:9) as a contrasting image to the "great harlot," Babylon/Rome (17:1). Just as Babylon is arrayed in scarlet and purple, adorned with gold, jewels and pearls (17:4, 16-17), so the New Jerusalem sparkles with precious jewels and pearls (21:18-21). It radiates from the glory of G*d like a most rare precious gem, like jasper, clear as crystal (21:11). Nothing "unclean" and no abomination scars the beauty of the New Jerusalem (21:27; 22:3a) in contrast to the gaudy appearance of Babylon who is called "the mother of abominations" (17:5). Just as Babylon has a "name on its forehead" (17:5) so the citizens of the New Jerusalem have "God's name on their foreheads" (22:4). Their names are written in the "Lamb's book of life" (21:27) in contrast to Babylon's followers whose names are "not written in the book of life" (17:8). The "kings of the earth," who are not only vassals of Babylon/Rome but also destroy it (17:15-18), bring their glory to the New Jerusalem (21:24). Thus Revelation depicts the eternal glory of the New Jerusalem as the dwelling place of G*d (21:10—22:5) by contrasting it with Babylon's doom as the dwelling place of demons (18:1-3, 9-19).

However, Revelation does not construct an absolute dualism in which the world of G*d mirrors and mimics the empire of Rome. Rather, it constructs an ethical dualism that seeks to attract people to decide against the violent destructive power of empire. Through its rhetorical contrasts, Revelation draws the picture of the New Jerusalem as the alternative and not the counter image of the Great City Babylon/Rome. Revelation contrasts the splendor and power of the Roman Empire with that of the empire of G*d and Christ in order to encourage readers to resist the murderous power of Rome.

---

99. Note that here the masculine-feminine dualism is interrupted through the figuration of Christ as well as of the imperial power of Rome as animals, which does not mean that the text is talking about animals.

Revelation's narrative symbolization of the city of G*d, the New Jerusalem, evokes a range of rich meanings that appealed both to Jewish imagination and Greco-Roman desires. The symbolization of the eschatological city reflects much of the Hellenistic hope for the ideal city. It also alludes to Rome's proud claim to be the "Eternal City," a claim found on coins and descriptions of the time.

Like Hellenistic cities, the New Jerusalem does not have a temple area as its center but a broad main street for procession, commerce, and public discourse. Its citizens have the power of ruling but this rule is not domination over others but rather the life-giving "power for." Like priests they have direct access to the Divine. G*d's ideal city is not only a universal and inclusive city with a population drawn from all nations but it is also magnificent and beautiful radiating with gold and pearls, the treasures of kings and nations. Life in G*d's city is free of injustice and abomination, curse and the evil powers of the "sea." Tears, crying, pain, sorrow, hunger, thirst, death are no longer found in it. Although there are still "insiders and outsiders," the gates of G*d's city, on which are inscribed the twelve tribes of Israel, are permanently open. Moreover, the city wall, which is clearly marked as being built on the foundation of the apostles and thereby as signifying the Christian community, are minuscule in relation to the overall size of the city which is approximately 1,200 miles; the wall is about 144 feet.

In short, Revelation images G*d's final salvation not as a cosmic counter-image to the Roman Empire but as a world in which nature and culture are integrated. The New Jerusalem also fulfills Roman idyllic as well as Jewish apocalyptic hopes for the "golden age" and "paradise." Through the center of the city flows the "river of life;" the leaves of the "tree of life" have the power to heal the nations. Thus the narrative symbolization of G*d's cosmopolitan city integrates "heaven and earth." A series of dichotomies are integrated: the world of G*d vis à vis the world determined now by imperial Roman power, metropolis and colonized nations, culture and nature, sacred and profane, Israel and the messianic community of the followers of the Lamb, bride and harlot, Rome and Jerusalem, center and margins. Revelation's final visions imagine heaven as world, world as cosmopolitan city in feminine gendered terms, G*d's cosmopolis as an open, inclusive place of citizenship and well-being for all.

The Reinscription of the Language of Empire

My cursory discussion of Revelation 17–18, has underscored the anti-imperial rhetoric of the book and argued that the feminine gendered figurations of the metropolitan cities of the Roman Empire, and of the Divine empire, do not speak about actual wo/men but are gendered symbolizations of imperial power. However, because of my focused attention to the feminist gender debate, I have not paid sufficient attention to the process of the re-inscription of the language of empire that transfers the attributes of Roman power to G*d, the Lamb and its followers. The power of G*d is thereby conceived by analogy to Roman imperial power. This analogy is proclaimed by the seventh trumpet angel in 11:15: "The empire of the World has become the empire of our Lord and of his Messiah and he will reign forever and ever." The anti-language of Revelation asserts: empire does not belong to Rome but to the followers of the Lamb. They have been constituted as a *basileia*, as an empire in the redemption from the slavery of empire through Christ. Hence, they now have imperial rule over the earth (1:6; 5:10) and as citizens of the New Jerusalem, they will reign forever (22:5). If such anti-language is internalized through the reading of Revelation, it determines the self-understanding of Christians today. Such imperial self-understanding projects evil onto the "others" who do not follow Christ, the poor, prostitutes, homosexuals, the feminists, and other powerful or objectified wo/men.

In the feminist debate about the gendered figuration of Babylon and the disagreement about the misogyny of Revelation, I have argued against an essentializing and naturalizing tendency, which claims that the metaphor of the whore Babylon connotes a wo/man rather than a city. Instead I have argued for an intersectional systems (kyriarchal) analysis that foregrounds Roman imperialism[100] while analyzing the multiple intersecting structures of domination. However, it is still important to study the gendered violent language of the book and to reject its kyriocentrism. My argument is not that the feminine images of Revelation have not and do not produce misogynist readings because they have done so and continue to do so. Rather, I stress that one must avoid absolutizing gender as an essentializing category of analysis and cease to identify gendered figurations with actual wo/men.[101]

---

100. For a political reading of Rev 17–18, see Klaus Wengst, "Babylon the Great and the New Jerusalem: The Visionary View of Political Reality in the Revelation of John," in *Politics and Theopolitics in the Bible and Postbiblical Literature*, eds. Henning Graf Reventlow, Yair Hoffman, and Benjamin Uffenheimer (Sheffield: Sheffield University Press, 1994), 189–202.

101. The only text that vilifies an actual wo/man is Rev 2:20–23 where John argues violently against a leading wo/man prophet whom he calls "Jezebel," but he does so not because she is a wo/man but because she and her followers are advocating adaptation to Roman society. For the

I have tried to show, therefore, that a reading of Revelation, in terms of a dualistic gender framework, inscribes or re-inscribes the Western sex/gender system,[102] whereas a rhetorical-political reading, in terms of kyriarchy, is able to underscore the socio-political-religious power of Roman imperialism that affects wo/men differently. I have argued further that a rhetorical-political analysis, which reads Revelation in terms of the structures of domination inscribed in the text, is more appropriate for a historical-postcolonial reading, whereas a gender reading is more apt to underscore the Western sex-gender frame and misogynist assumptions of biblical texts and their readings.

A feminist decolonizing reading of Revelation, in terms of an additive reading of gender and colonialism, however, is also problematic. In a new and interesting postcolonial interpretation of Revelation 17, Jean Kim has argued that

> [t]he metaphor "whore" is a double entendre, standing not only for the city of Rome (colonizing power) but also for a decolonized woman who is sexually exploited by two sets of men (foreign and natives); secondly I will show that the feminization of the city as a whore is due to national-ist (Jewish) ideology; and lastly, I will emphasize the importance of a inter(con)textual reading of the text from a deconstructionist perspective which uses woman's marginality as a starting point for the sake of produc-ing a new meaning out of Revelation 17.[103]

She rightly goes on to detail the interface between slavery and prostitution and between war and the fate of whores in the Roman Empire as well as the sexual control enacted by the policies of Augustus. In addition, she argues that the prophetic inter(con)texts that have shaped the rhetoric of Revelation 17–18 are, like the text of Revelation, addressed to subaltern men and express their nationalist (Jewish) ideology.

---

exploration of the figure of queen Jezebel, see the interesting postcolonial but essentializing read-ing of Judith McKinley, *Reframing Her: Biblical Women in Postcolonial Focus* (Sheffield: Sheffield Phoenix, 2004), 57–95, 140.

102. For this expression see my book, *Jesus: Miriam's Child, Sophia's Prophet*, 33–43.

103. Jean K. Kim, "Uncovering Her Wickedness: An Inter(con)textual Reading of Revela-tion 17 from a Postcolonial Feminist Perspective," *JSNT* 73 (1999): 61–81, esp., 64.

In biblical narrative, sexuality/gender and race/ethnicity are thus crucial characteristics in terms of judging whether female characters are good women or whores: faithful Israel is sexually controlled while her faithless anti-type is sexually loose. . . . when nationalism and religion coalesce there is always the danger of deifying the nation.[104]

Kim concludes that "this Jewish national feeling is still found in the book of Revelation."[105] She agrees with Tina Pippin's judgment that the book is dangerous for wo/men, but points out that Pippin fails to recognize the force of "male discourses such as colonialism and gendered nationalism on women's bodies."[106]

Kim's postcolonial reading of Revelation in terms of masculine Jewish nationalism comes close to Christian anti-Jewish interpretations of Revelation, which judge the book as Jewish and not fully Christian. Yet, Kim is to be commended for attempting a postcolonial gender reading that does not just focus on feminine characterization but analyzes gender as pertaining to both women and men. Moreover, she does not just read in terms of gender but also in terms of class and nation. However, Kim seems to read in an essentializing fashion at times. When looking at the violence against wo/men which is graphically told in the judgment of Babylon, for instance, she claims that we have to identify ourselves with the feminine character or "to betray our sexual identity in order to share the perspective of the author/God."[107]

But why should a conquered, exploited, enslaved, and prostituted Jewish wo/man not rejoice in the downfall of the imperial power Rome that has destroyed her home and crucified her son, even though Rome is figured in feminine terms? Why should we assume that such a wo/man has to deny her own sexual identity if she looks hopefully at the visionary destruction of the imperial power of Rome? Since the imperial power of Rome is figured as an "elite woman" (*kyria*), why shouldn't a wo/man at the bottom of the kyriarchal pyramid experience and resent this power as a violent force which enslaves and exploits her? Paying attention to the national and class distinctions between

104. Ibid., 76.
105. Ibid., 77.
106. Ibid., 77.
107. Ibid., 61.

wo/men would enable us to read Revelation not as preaching "sexual violence against wo/men" but as highlighting the exploitation and violence of Empire against wo/men.

Hence, I want to take up Kim's insight of "double entendre" but read it not in terms of gender but in terms of Empire. Babylon then is the feminine figuration of the imperial power Rome and signifies "the essence" of empire as engendering prostitution and violence against wo/men.[108] Imperialism and colonization then cannot be adequately understood without paying attention to the sexual and economic exploitation of wo/men. Such was the case in antiquity and is still the case today: The "essence" of globalizing capitalism's exploitations can be seen in the international sex-trade and in violence against wo/men and children in war, poverty, migration, and global exploitation.

In this chapter I have juxtaposed two different feminist strategies of reading Revelation in general, and the female images of the book in particular, in order to clarify the interaction between a critical feminist and a postcolonial interpretation. One reading strategy subscribes to an essentializing gender or empire politics, the other reads gender or empire in contextual-rhetorical-political terms. A rhetoric and ethics of inquiry can alert us to the fact that the disagreement between these two reading strategies is not exegetical-textual but rather rhetorical-hermeneutical.

Whereas a scientific-positivist paradigm of interpretation would argue for one interpretation over the other as the only correct one, a rhetorical paradigm seeks to understand why and on what grounds different interpretations privilege different rhetorical markers in the text. The determination of which interpretation is most appropriate, however, cannot be settled on purely exegetical grounds but only in terms of a rhetoric and ethics of inquiry. Both the essentializing and the rhetorical reading strategies highlight important aspects of the discourse of Revelation.

108. This is recognized but elided by Carolyn Vander Stichele, "Just a Whore," 8. She sees herself caught in a double bind because she "shares the critique of a violent regime, while I resist the violence done to the whore. . . . as a citizen of Fortress Europe, I rather find myself identified with Babylon as locus of colonial power and oppression." But rather than accepting the judgment of Revelation as someone who benefits from colonial power and oppression, she displaces it onto wo/men who refuse to participate in the sex-trade. "The fate of Babylon described in Rev 17:16 reminds me of the violence done to wo/men who refuse to prostitute themselves."

As I have pointed out almost fifteen years ago,[109] when reading Revelation, contemporary "audiences" always interpret the text in terms of the sex-gender system, since they are bound to activate unconsciously the most prominent reading paradigm in Western culture and religion. Hence, the work of feminists who uncover and demystify the gender code of Revelation is crucially important as long as it does not "naturalize" gender. As I have argued throughout this chapter, a reading approach that single-mindedly focuses on gender, and identifies gender constructs with actual wo/men, is in danger of re-valorizing the symbolic sex-gender system of the text in modern Western terms even while seeking to deconstruct it. Equally, an interpretation that essentializes the inscriptions of empire cannot but reinscribe empire in the process of reading.

Conversely, a reading focused on imperial inscriptions of power needs critically to lift into consciousness the rhetorical functions of language either as anti-language or as alternative language. By constructing the cosmic city of G*d/New Jerusalem as anti-image of Babylon/Rome in terms of essentalizing dualism, and then claiming the ruling power of empire for G*d and the inhabitants of the New Jerusalem, such an essentializing dualistic reading is liable to inculcate imperial values and visions of Revelation anew in the process of reading/interpretation. Hence, all readings need to remain embedded in a decolonizing socio-political-religious rhetoric and ethics of inquiry that does not reproduce dichotomous dualism.[110] Such an inquiry can debate and adjudicate which texts and interpretations of Revelation re-inscribe colonialist misogyny, and other languages of domination, and in which situations of contemporary contexts of imperial globalization they do so. While the language and ethos of empire has deep roots not just in Revelation and apocalyptic literature but in sacred scriptures on the whole, a feminist decolonizing reading in the interest of wo/men struggling at the bottom of the kyriarchal pyramid of domination must not only name the violent powers of empire inscribed in the bible but also valorize those alternative utopian rhetorical elements and imaginations of a "different" world and power for justice and well-being which are also inscribed in sacred scriptures.

109. Elisabeth Schüssler Fiorenza, "The Followers of the Lamb: Visionary Rhetoric and Social-Political Situation," in *Discipleship in the New Testament*, ed. F. Segovia (Philadelphia, Pa.: Fortress Press, 1985).

110. For such a dichotomous essentializing reading of Revelation see Stephen D. Moore, *Empire and Apocalypse*, 97–121, who relies heavily on the work of Homi K. Bhabha.

Chapter 5

Empire and the Rhetoric
of Subordination[1]

In the preceding chapter, I have analyzed the inscription of empire in the book of Revelation and argued that a dual systems analysis, in terms of gender/patriarchy and imperialism, tends to naturalize and essentialize gender and to degenderize imperialist domination. Rather than using such a dualistic epistemology, I have proposed an intersectional kyriarchal analysis that can decode the complex power of domination inscribed in biblical texts. Biblical texts shaped by the rhetoric of empire, I have argued, must be detoxified in a critical process of decolonizing interpretation.

In this chapter, I explore the inscriptions of the ethos of empire—kyriarchy—in the First Epistle of Peter and I do so on the historical level as well as on the contemporary level of interpretation since every "faithful" reading internalizes this kyriarchal ethos. In the process of "making sense" out of sacred kyriocentric texts, we imbibe their ethos because it resonates with the contemporary structures of domination and subordination that have become for us "common sense." Hence, I will introduce seven hermeneutical practices that facilitate a critical decolonizing interpretation of biblical texts (as well as other kinds of texts) by both expert and engaged bible readers.

The work of Nathan Hatch has shown that a democratic understanding of bible reading has led to multiple forms of fundamentalism. According to

---

1. This chapter draws on the materials in my articles "The First Letter of Peter," in *A Postcolonial Commentary of the New Testament Writings*, eds., Fernando F. Segovia and R. S. Sugirtharajah (*The Bible and Postcolonialism*; London-New York: T. & T. Clark International, forthcoming, 2007), and "Invitation to Dance in the Open House of Wisdom: Feminist Study of the Bible," in *Engaging the Bible: Critical Readings from Contemporary Women*, eds. Choi Hee An and Katheryn Pfisterer Darr (Minneapolis, Minn.: Fortress Press, 2006), 81–104.

him "deep and powerful undercurrents of democratic Christianity distinguish the United States from other modern industrialized democracies,"[2] on the one hand, but on the other, these populist movements also have led to authoritarianism and biblicist literalism because they stand in opposition to liberal secular and religious elites.[3]

Since the American democratic symbolic universe has not been matched by the construction of a radical egalitarian biblical symbolic universe, challenges to authority in the name of the bible have not been directed to the authoritarianism of fundamentalist leadership. The ironic consequence is that biblicist authoritarianism is bolstered, valorizing anti-democratic biblical texts and anti-egalitarian exclusivist biblical arguments.

All shades of fundamentalism skillfully, moreover, use the modern media and vast communications industry to spread their "common sense" biblical messages of hatred and exclusion. They promise security to common people who struggle for survival if they follow their fundamentalist message of exclusion and condemnation. Biblical fundamentalisms have this effect because they assert that people have the democratic ability to read the bible for themselves. However, in reality American Evangelicalism does not grant to people the democratic ability to adjudicate and evaluate the authority of biblical texts, because this movement insists that only a literalist reading does justice to the bible's authority. At the same time, its leaders polemicize against those who read critically and evaluate the bible in terms of ethical norms—labeling them as "educated elites" who despise the common people. Thus, for authoritarian political ends, they can abuse the democratic aspirations of the people. Conversely, biblical scholarship also does not enable a democratic reading of the bible but restricts it to expert readers. Hence, it is important to develop a democratic method of critical bible reading that is not restricted to the*logical experts and biblical scholars but can be engaged by everyone.

2. Nathan O. Hatch, *The Democratization of American Christianity* (New Haven, Conn.: Yale University Press, 1989), 5.

3. Hatch, *The Democratization of American Christianity*, 219.

The Ethos of Kyriarchy: Intersecting Discourses of Domination

It is no accident that the antifeminist Christian Right has made the family, sexuality, and the reproductive rights of wo/men[4] the central cornerstone of its political rhetoric.[5] The bible is invoked because it teaches the divinely ordained subordination of wo/men and the creational differences between the sexes as well as the abomination of homosexuality. As the 2004 presidential election showed, this right-wing political rhetoric is so effective because it defends the American family in the name of biblical Christianity.[6]

We find a series of texts in the Christian Testament (CT) which demand submission to the *kyrios*, the emperor, as well as to the head of the household, the lord, slave master, father—that is, to the elite propertied male colonizer. These texts which are classified as household code—a label derived from Lutheran teaching on social status and roles (*Ständelehre*)—are concerned with seemingly three sets of relationships: wife and husband, slave wo/men and

4. In order to lift into consciousness the linguistic violence of so-called generic male-centered language, I write the term "wo/men" with a slash—see footnote 21, Chapter 1: Introduction. This writing of wo/men signifies that the expression wo/men is inclusive of men as well as that the power differences within wo/men and between wo/men can be greater than those between wo/men and men of the same race, class, nation, culture, or religion.

5. Shirley Rogers Radl, *The Invisible Woman: Target of the Religious New Right* (New York: Dell, 1981); Judith Stacey, "Sexism by a Subtler Name? Postindustrial Condition and Postfeminist Consciousness in the Sillicon Valey," *Socialist Review* 96 (1987): 7–28; Sara Diamond, *Spiritual Warfare: The Politics of the Christian Right* (Boston, Mass.: South End, 1989); Hans Küng and Jürgen Moltmann, *Fundamentalism as an Ecumenical Challenge* (Concilium; London: SCM, 1992); "Fundamentalismen," *Beiträge zur feministischen Theorie und Praxis* 32 (1992); R. Marie Griffith, *God's Daughters: Evangelical Women and the Power of Submission* (Berkeley, Calif.: University of California Press, 1997); W. Howland, ed., *Religious Fundamentalisms and the Human Rights of Women* (New York: Palgrave, 1999); Carol Mason, *Killing for Life: The Apocalyptic Narrative of Pro-Life Politics* (Ithica, N.Y.: Cornell University Press, 2002); Sally Gallagher, *Evangelical Identity and Gendered Family Life* (New Brunswick, N.J.: Rutgers University Press, 2003); Julie Ingersoll, *Evangelical Christian Women: War Stories in the Gender Battles* (New York: NYU Press, 2003).

6. See especially the work of Erin Runions, "Biblical Promise and Threat in U.S. Imperialistic Rhetoric, Before and After 9/11," in Elizabeth A. Castelli and Janet R. Jacobsen, eds., *Interventions: Activists and Academics Respond to Violence* (New York: Palgrave Macmillan, 2004), 71–88 and "Desiring War: Apocalypse, Commodity Fetish, and the End of History," in R.S. Sugirtharajah, ed., *The Postcolonial Biblical Reader* (Oxford: Blackwell, 2006), 112–128; "Refusal To Mourn: U.S. National Melancholia and Its Prophetic Precursors," *Postscripts* 1/1 (2005): 9–45; and "Queering the Beast" in *Queering the NonHuman*, ed. Myra Hird and Noreen Giffney (New York: Ashgate, forthcoming, 2007).

master, and son/children and father. However, it must not be overlooked that in each case it is the *kyrios*/father—the head of the household—to whom the members of the household owe submission. The central interest of these texts consists in bolstering the authority of the *kyrios*, the *pater familias*, by demanding submission and obedience from the socially weaker group—wives, slaves, and children and the whole community.

Familia did not mean "nuclear family" in the Roman Empire but encompassed all those who were under the authority of the *pater familias*—the *mater familias*,[7] children, relatives and slaves—whereas the *domus*, the household (Gk *oikos*) included all those affiliated with it, not only the members of the *familia* but also clients, day-workers and even visitors. The household[8] in the Roman Empire was an economic production center, a central site of education and training in trade and craft skills, and the guarantor of social services and locus of religious life.[9]

Politically, the household was the microcosm of the Empire and the "nursery" of the state. As Cicero succinctly states:

> The first bond of union is that between husband and wife; the next that between parents and children; then we find one *domus* with everything in common. And this is the foundation of civil government, the nursery (seminarium), as it were of the state. (*De officiis* 17.54)

The emperor was called *pater patrum*, the father of all fathers, and the *pater patriae*, the father of the fatherland. The emperor was the ultimate father and lord (*kyrios*) par excellence. He was king of kings, lord of lords, and supreme

7. Richard Saller, "Pater Familias, Mater Familias, and the Gendered Semantics of a Roman Household," *Classical Philology* 94 (1999): 182–97.

8. See Keith R. Bradley, *Discovering the Roman Family: Studies in Roman Social History* (New York: Oxford University Press, 1991); Suzanne Dixon, *The Roman Family* (Baltimore: Johns Hopkins University Press, 1992); Cheryl A. Cox, *Household Interests: Property, Marriage Strategies, and Family Dynamics in Ancient Athens* (Princeton, N.J.: Princeton University Press, 1998); Jane Gardner, *Family and familia in Roman Law and Life* (Oxford: Oxford University Press, 1998); Shaye Cohen, *The Jewish Family in Antiquity* (Atlanta, Ga.: Scholars, 1993); David Balch and Carolyn Osiek, eds., *Early Christian Families in Context: An Interdisciplinary Dialogue* (Grand Rapids, Mich: Eerdmans, 2003).

9. See John M. G. Barclay, "The Family as the Bearer of Religion in Judaism and Early Christianity," in *Constructing Early Christian Families: Family as Social Reality and Metaphor*, ed. Halvor Moxnes (London: Routledge, 1997), 66–80.

father. According to Greco-Roman political ideology, a male citizen's authority rested in his dominance over his extended household.[10] Those male citizens who could not control their households risked losing control of the state. Hence the emperor, like any other elite male, had to project and maintain a firm patriarchal image and to appear in full control of his household in order to show that he was to be trusted as the ruler of the empire. As Price observes:

> The stability of the imperial rule was perceived to lie in the transmission of power within the imperial family and, in consequence, considerable importance was attached to the whole imperial house. . . . [11]

According to this kyriarchal ideology, the order of subjection/subordination of the empire was mirrored in the order of submission of the kyriarchal household. Since the word *kyriarchal* is derived from the Greek word *kyrios*, and the word *archein*, which means "to rule," to question this kyriarchal order and to destabilize the kyriarchal household was a threat to the order of the state.

The Christian Testament (CT) teaching on "male headship and female subordination" reflects this *oikos*-ethos of empire[12] that calls for submission and subjection from members of the household, officers of the empire, citizens, vassals, and provinces. It does not just affect elite married men and wo/men and their relationships, but it calls for submission and subordination of all the subjects of the Roman Empire, freeborn men and wo/men, slave wo/men and

10. Richard Saller, *Patriarchy, Property, and Death in the Roman Family* (Cambridge: Cambridge University Press, 1994); also his chapter, "Women, Slaves, and the Economy of the Roman Household," in *Early Christian Families in Context: an Interdisciplinary Dialogue*; and his chapter, "Corporal Punishment, Authority, and Obedience in the Roman Household," in *Marriage, Divorce, and Children in Ancient Rome*, ed. Beryl Rawson (Canberra: Humanities Research Center, 1991), 144–65.

11. S.R.F. Price, *Rituals and Power: The Roman Imperial Cult in Asia Minor* (Cambridge: Cambridge University Press, 1984), 162; see also Susan Fischler, "Imperial Cult: Engendering the Cosmos," in *When Men were Men: Masculinity, Power and Identity in Classical Antiquity*, eds. Lin Foxhall and John Salmon (New York: Routledge, 1998), 165–83.

12. See Eva-Marie Lassen, "The Roman Family: Ideal and Metaphor" in *Constructing Early Christian Families*, 103–20; Dale B. Martin, "The Construction of the Ancient Family: Methodological Considerations," *Journal of Roman Studies* 86 (1996): 40–60; Rawson, *Marriage, Family and Divorce in Ancient Rome*; and also his "Children as Cultural Symbols: Imperial Ideology in the 2nd Century," in *Childhood, Class, and Kin in the Roman World*, ed. Suzanne Dixon (London: Routledge, 2001).

men, clients and resident aliens. However, it must be kept in mind that these texts are not descriptive but prescriptive. They are responses to the egalitarian ethos of ekklēsia = the democratic assembly which met "in house" (en *oikō*).[13]

The Christian Testament texts of subordination have been erroneously classified simply as "household code"—a label derived from Lutheran teaching on social status and roles (*Ständelehre*).[14] These texts are not only concerned with three sets of household relationships: wife and husband, slave wo/men and master, and father and son, but also with submission to the emperor. The central interest of these texts lies in enforcing the submission[15] and obedience

13. See my book, *In Memory of Her: A Feminist Theological Reconstruction of Christian Origins*, original edition, 1983; Tenth Anniversary Edition (New York: Crossroad, 1994), for this argument. Most recently, Carolyn Osiek and Margaret Y. MacDonald have revisited this argument in light of the research of the last twenty-five years but without crediting my work. Rather they caricature the polarity "patriarchy-discipleship of equals" (note my alternative has been patriarchy/kyriarchy–ekklēsia of wo/men) and instead opt for the polarity honor-shame. While their other two assumptions—masculine titles do not just refer to men; and wo/men participated in all the activities of the house-church—also have been discussed at length in *In Memory of Her*, they do not refer to them nor do they engage my theoretical reconstructive model. See *A Woman's Place: House Churches in Early Christianity* (Minneapolis, Minn.: Fortress Press, 2006).

14. Dieter Lührmann, "Wo man nicht mehr Sklave und Freier ist: Überlegungen zur Struktur frühchristlicher Gemeinden," *Wort und Dienst* 13 (1975): 53–83; Klaus Thraede, "Aerger mit der Freiheit: Die Bedeutung von Frauen in Theorie und Praxis der alten Kirche," in *Freunde in Christus werden*, ed. Gerda Scharffenroth (Gelnhausen and Berlin: Burckhardthaus, 1977), 35–182; Clarice Martin, "The Haustafeln (Household Codes) in African American Biblical Interpretation: 'Free Slaves' and 'Subordinate Women,'" in *Stony the Road We Trod: African American Biblical Interpretation*, ed. Cain Hope Felder (Minneapolis, Minn.: Fortress Press, 1991), 206–31; James D.G. Dunn, "The Household Rules of the New Testament" in *The Family in Theological Perspective*, ed. S.C. Barton (Edinburgh: T. & T. Clark, 1996), 43–63. For a christological justification of this pattern of subordination, see Else Kähler, *Die Frau in den Paulinischen Briefen* (Zürich: Gotthelf Verlag, 1960). For a feminist evangelical interpretation of the pattern as a pattern of "mutual submission," see, for instance, Virginia Ramey Mollenkott, *Women, Men, and the Bible* (Nashville, Tenn.: Abingdon, 1977), and Letha Scanzoni and Nancy Hardesty, *All We're Meant to Be: A Biblical Approach to Women's Liberation* (Waco, Tex: Word, 1975); Esther Yue L. Ng, *Reconstructing Christian Origins?* (Carlisle, U.K.: Paternoster, 2002); Virginia Ramey Mollenkott, "Emancipative Elements in Ephesians 5: 21–33: Why Feminist Scholarship Has (Often) Left Them Unmentioned, and Why They Should Be Emphasized," in *A Feminist Companion to the Deutero-Pauline Epistles*, ed. Amy-Jill Levine (New York: Continuum International, 2003), 37–58; David M Scholer, "1 Tim 2:9-15 and the Place of Women in the Church's Ministry," in *A Feminist Companion to the Deutero-Pauline Epistles*, 98–121.

15. The code is said to be completely incorporated in Colossians 3:18—4:1 and Ephesians 5:22—6:9. However, as in 1 Peter 2:18—3:7 it is not found completely in the remaining passages: 1 Timothy 2:11,15; 5:3-8; 6:1-2; Titus 2:2-10; 3:1-2; 1 Clement 21:6-8; Ignatius to Polycarp 4:1—6:2; Polycarp 4:2—6:1; Didache 4:9-11; Barnabas 19:5-7. Hence, it would be better to call it the "pattern of submission" which can be used in various circumstances.

of the socially weaker groups—the whole community, wives, slave wo/men, and children—on the one hand, and in bolstering the authority of the head of the household, the *pater familias*, on the other, which in the case of the emperor encompassed the whole empire.[16]

This pattern of domination and subjection need not always include all the four social status groups (freeborn *patres familias* as well as slave wo/men, wives and children) which are addressed in Colossians[17] and Ephesians. In other texts, only some of the subordinate groups are mentioned. Most important, the imperial code demands obedience to the political powers of the Roman Empire and is used to ensure the ethos of submission for the household and the Christian community, which is understood as household of G*d.[18] The injunction to submissiveness already occurs in the authentic Pauline letters, for example, in Romans 13 and 1 Corinthians 14.[19] It therefore cannot be attributed solely to what exegetes call early Catholicism. While this pattern of submissiveness functions differently in different early Christian documents and their social-ecclesial-historical contexts, the imperial pattern of submission seems to be characteristic throughout. This ethos of submission conceives not only of family but also of state and church in terms of the kyriarchal household.

Susan Moller Okin, a feminist political philosopher, has shown that the Aristotelian political ethics of the household code still operates in contemporary American democratic society. Although kyriarchal household and family have been modified in the course of history, political philosophy still accepts the Aristotelian premise that the free, propertied man is the full citizen, whereas

> all the other members of the population—slaves and artisans as well as women—exist in order to perform their respective function for the few

16. Ronald Syme, *The Roman Revolution* (Oxford: Oxford University Press, 1939), 509–24.

17. See Robert Scott Nash, "Heuristic Haustafeln: Domestic Codes as Entrance to the Social World of Early Christianity: The Case of Colossians," *Religious Writings and Religious Systems: Systemic Analysis of Holy Books in Christianity, Islam, Buddhism, Greco-Roman Religions, Ancient Israel, and Judaism,* in Jacob Neusner, Ernest S. Frerichs, and A.J. Levine, eds. (Atlanta, Ga.: Scholars, 1989), 25–50. See also Angela Standhartinger, "The Origin and Intention of the Household Code in the Letter to the Colossians," *JSNT* 79 (2000): 117–30.

18. See footnote 6, Chapter 1: Introduction.

19. See Kittredge, *Community and Authority in Paul: The Rhetoric of Obedience in the Pauline Tradition* (Harrisburg, Pa.: Trinity International, 1998).

free males who participate fully in citizenship. The "natures" of all these groups of people are defined in terms of their satisfactory performance of their conventional functions.[20]

In antiquity, the sphere of the household was important primarily as an economic base, whereas in modern times the bourgeois family is crucial for affective life. Since the bourgeois wife is responsible for the private sphere of the household, even a liberal philosopher such as John Stuart Mill asserts that she can only take on outside responsibilities after she has successfully taken care of *her* domestic ones.

Even though liberalism is supposed to be based on individualism and to understand society as constituted of "independent, autonomous units," it is clear, according to Moller Okin, that in spite of this individualistic rhetoric, the "nuclear patriarchal family," and not the adult human individual is the basic political unit of liberal and non-liberal political philosophy. The adult members of the family are assumed to share all the same interests. Yet, whenever a conflict of interest occurs between husband and wife, the presumption in political and legal philosophy has been that a conflict of interest must be decided by the male head of the household. Moreover, the public political sphere is defined by competition and self-interest, not by values of compassion, love, and altruism, since such values are relegated to the private sphere of the home as the domain of wo/men, children, and servants. Legally and politically to recognize wo/men as individual citizens in their own right would entail, therefore, a change in both the family structure and in political philosophy. Moller Okin concludes:

> If our aim is a truly democratic society, or a thoroughly democratic theory, we must acknowledge that anything but a democratic family with complete equality and mutual interdependence between the [adult members of the household] will be a severe impediment to this aim.[21]

In short, Moller Okin has convincingly argued that the Aristotelian political ethics of natural inequality has shaped Western political philosophy and society. A truly democratic society would necessarily presuppose not only a radical

---

20. Susan Moller Okin, *Women in Western Political Thought* (Princeton, N.J.: Princeton University Press, 1979), 276.

21. Ibid., 289. See also her book, *Justice, Gender, and the Family* (New York: Basic, 1989).

change of the patriarchal family but also a radical transformation of civic society and political philosophy. Moller Okin has recognized the historical, political, and philosophical interconnections among spheres of state, civil society, and the family, both in antiquity and modernity. Nevertheless, her analysis remains within the analytic framework of gender analysis rather than being formulated in terms of intersecting structures of domination.

White feminist theory has used as key analytic categories wo/man (female), gender (feminine-masculine construction) and patriarchy (the domination of the father/male over wo/men) and has distinguished between sex and gender.[22] However, such a dualistic approach has been seriously questioned by Two-Thirds World feminists who point to the multiplicative structures of domination that determine wo/men's lives.[23] In order to theorize structures of domination in antiquity and the multiple intersections of gender, race, class, and ethnicity in modernity,[24] I have sought to articulate kyriarchy with reference to classical political philosophy and the Christian Testament texts of subordination. I have developed a feminist heuristic model since the 1980s that is able to articulate intersecting structures of race, gender, class, ethnicity, and imperialism.[25] Hence, I have replaced the notion of patriarchy/patriarchalism with the neologism *kyriarchy* as a key analytic concept.[26]

22. See Herta Nagl-Docekal, *Feminist Philosophy* (Boulder: Westview, 2004); Giovanna Miceli Jeffries, *Feminine Feminists: Cultural Practices in Italy* (Minneapolis, Minn.: University of Minnesota, 1994); Marianne Dekoven, ed., *Feminist Locations: Global and Local Theory and Practice* (New Brunswick, N.J.: Rutgers, 2001); Sylvia Walby, *Patriarchy at Work* (Minneapolis, Minn.: The University of Minnesota Press, 1986). Mary Lyndon Shanley & Caroline Pateman, eds., *Feminist Interpretations and Political Theory* (University Park, Pa.: Penn State University Press, 1991); Hadumond Bussman and Renate Hof, *Genus. Geschlecherforschung/ Gender Studies in den Kultur und Sozialwissenschaften* (Stuttgart: Kröner, 2005).

23. See Valerie Bryson, *Feminist Debates: Issues of Theory and Political Practice* (New York: NYU Press, 1999) and especially Chela Sandoval, *Methodology of the Oppressed* (Minneapolis, Minn.: University of Minnesota Press, 2000). For this discussion in feminist the*logy, see, e.g., María Pilar Aquino, Daisy L. Machado, and Jeanette Rodrigues, eds., *A Reader in Latina Feminist Theology* (Religion and Justice, Austin: University of Texas Press, 2002). Ellen T. Armour, *Deconstruction, Feminist Theology and the Problem of Difference: Subverting the Race/Gender Divide* (Chicago, Ill: University of Chicago Press, 1999).

24. See, e.g., France Winddance Twine & Kathleen M. Blee, eds., *Feminism & Antiracism: International Struggles for Justice* (New York: University Press, 2001); Joan Acker, *Class Questions: Feminist Answers* (Lanham: Rowman & Littlefield, 2006).

25. For a discussion of Roman imperialism, see Craige B. Champion, ed., *Roman Imperialism: Readings and Sources* (Malden, Mass.: Blackwell, 2004).

26. For the development of this concept and bibliographic documentation, see my books

Kyriarchy means the domination of the emperor, lord, slave master, husband, the elite freeborn educated and propertied male colonizer who has power over all wo/men and subaltern men. It is to be distinguished from kyriocentrism, which has the ideological function of naturalizing and legitimating not just gender but all forms of domination. Kyriarchal relations of domination are built on elite male property rights over wo/men who are marked by the intersection of gender, race, class, imperial domination, as well as dependency, subordination and obedience or second class citizenship.

Such kyriocentric ideology and the social-system of kyriarchy are characteristic not only of ancient but also of modern western societies. Long ago, Aristotle has argued that the freeborn, propertied, educated Greek man is the highest of moral beings and that all other members of the human race are defined by their functions in his service. Kyriarchal relations of domination and subordination are explicitly articulated in Western political philosophy in the context of both Greek democracy and Roman imperialism. They have been mediated by Christian scriptural-theological traditions such as the "household codes" and have decisively determined modern kyriarchal forms and ideologies of democracy.

Modern political philosophy continues to assume that propertied, educated elite Western man is defined by reason, self-determination, and full citizenship whereas wo/men and other subordinated peoples are characterized by emotion, service, and dependence. They are seen not as rational and responsible adult subjects but as emotional, helpless, and child-like. In short, kyriarchal societies and cultures need for their functioning a "servant class," a "servant race," or a "servant people," be they slaves, serfs, house servants, kulis, or mammies. The existence of such a "servant class" is maintained through law, education, socialization, and brute violence. It is sustained by the belief that members of a "servant class" of people are by nature or by divine decree inferior to those whom they are destined to serve.

This kyriarchal system is structured in modernity by race, gender, class, ethnicity, hetero-sexuality and imperialism. Genevieve Lloyd[27] among others

---

But She Said: Feminist Practices of Biblical Interpretation (Boston: Beacon, 1992); *Discipleship of Equals: A Critical Feminist Ekklēsia-Logy of Liberation* (New York: Crossroad 1993); *Jesus: Miriam's Child, Sophia's Prophet: Critical Issues in Feminist Christology* (New York: Continuum, 1994); *Sharing Her Word: Feminist Biblical Interpretation in Context* (Boston, Mass.: Beacon, 1998); *Wisdom Ways: Introducing Feminist Biblical Interpretation* (Maryknoll, N.Y.: Orbis, 2001).

27. Genevieve Lloyd, *The Man of Reason: "Male" and "Female" in Western Philosophy*

has argued that modern understandings of rationality and of the world have been articulated by white European American elite educated man, the "Man of Reason." He has not only defined white wo/men as "others," but also all the "others" as non-persons who lack human, i.e., masculine, qualities.

As a socio-political and psychological practice of domination and subordination, gender is only one of several social ascriptions that promote the exploitation and second class citizenship of wo/men. Since gender is always inflected by race, class, age, religion, sexual preference, culture, and ethnicity, "naturalized" gender can be demystified and so too, race, class, or ethnic oppositions; one sees then that actual wo/men and men are not defined exclusively by gender. As a socio-political-religious discursive practice, kyriocentrism produces not only sex differences but also those of race, class, sexual preference, culture, religion, age, and nationality.

Feminist theorists have elaborated that gender, like race, is not a natural "given" but rather a kyriarchal societal construct, a socio-cultural principle of classification that imposes psychological, social, cultural, religious, and political meaning upon biological sexual aspects. If one sees both sex and gender, together with race, ethnicity, or class as socio-cultural constructions, one can analyze the Western kyriarchal ideological system as a cultural symbolic structure of representation that has become naturalized and become "common sense." As an ideological structure, gender, race, class, ethnicity, and imperialism are active through grammar, language, biology, and culture, and function to naturalize, and to represent as "common sense," kyriarchal construction of difference. Nineteenth-century scientists, in one way or another, constructed the so-called lower races, wo/men, the sexually deviant, the criminal, the urban poor, and the insane as biological "races apart." Their differences from the white male, and their likeness to each other, "explained" their different and lower position in the social hierarchy, i.e., kyriarchy. In this scheme, the lower races represent the feminine aspect of the human species, and wo/men the "lower race" of gender.[28]

(Minneapolis, Minn.: University of Minnesota Press, 1984). See also Linda J. Nicholson, *Feminism/ Postmodernism* (New York: Routledge, 1990).

28. See Ronald T. Takaki, "Aesclepius Was a White Man: Race and the Cult of True Womanhood," in *The Racial Economy of Science: Toward a Democratic Future*, ed. Sandra Harding (Indianapolis, Ind.: Indiana University Press, 1993), 201–9; Nancy Leys Stepan and Sander L. Gilman, "Appropriating the Idioms of Science: The Rejection of Scientific Racism," Ibid., 170–93; and Nancy Leys Stepan, "Race and Gender: The Role of Analogy in Science," Ibid., 369–76.

This definition of other races and peoples—as the "feminine Other," for instance—has enabled colonial Western powers to exploit and use religion in the expansive capitalist quest for identity and property. The reality of wo/men may be conceptualized not in terms of gender dualism, but rather in terms of a socially constructed web of interactive systems of power structured as pyramids of domination and subordination. Societal oppression is engendered, then, by variegated social, interactive, and multiplicative structures of exploitation and dehumanization. In modernity as in antiquity, the heterosexual family is a key institution for sustaining such kyriarchal structures of domination.

Intersectionality does not denote an actual pattern of social organization but serves as an interpretive framework for comprehending how the interlocking structures of race, gender, class, sexuality, and ethnicity shape any group's experiences across specific social contexts.[29] Different groups will experience such structures of domination differently depending on their social location within the kyriarchal pyramid of economic, political, and ideological power relations. These power relations are kept in place by institutional mechanisms, such as separation and exclusion and/or family affiliation and inclusion. For instance, elite white wo/men have been excluded from the public realm and restricted to the private sphere, whereas black and working wo/men never had the luxury to stay at home. Thus, kyriarchal group power works through being hailed into the segregated spaces of subject positions as well as through emotional and practical identification.[30]

Wo/men are slotted by birth into the group categories "feminine" or "masculine," "black" or "white," "American" or another nationality, belonging to the "upper crust" of society or to the "serving poor." These categories assign us identity slots according to group membership. We find ourselves to be members of a gender group, which we experiences as a natural "given," rather than as historically and socially constructed. Individuals cannot simply opt out of group identities because social constructs such as sex, gender,

29. For the notion of intersectionality and interlocking systems of oppression, see the works of Patricia Hill Collins, *Black Feminist Thought: Knowledge, Consciousness and the Politics of Empowerment* (Boston, Mass.: Unwin Hyman, 1990); and *Fighting Words: Black Women and the Search for Justice* (Minneapolis, Minn.: University of Minnesota Press, 1998).

30. See Rosemary Hennessy, *Materialist Feminism and the Politics of Discourse* (New York: Routledge, 1993); Anne Marie Smith, *Laclau and Mouffe: The Radical Democratic Imaginary* (New York: Routledge, 1998).

race, class, or ethnicity are "common sense," "naturalized," and inscribed on the body.

Whether we understand ourselves primarily as wo/men, or as black, or as foreigners, or as working class depends on which group status functions as the nodal point for the structural subject positions into which we are born and in which everyone is implicated. For instance, if we are upper-middle class, white wo/men in a kyriarchal society, we are socialized to understand ourselves primarily in gender terms; if we are black or Asian in such a society, we might define ourselves primarily in racial terms rather than in gender or class terms; if we are Indian or African wo/men, we will tend to see ourselves first in co-lonialist terms as colonized peoples rather than in race or gender terms. Our individual identities, thus, are always constructed and pressures are exerted on us to identify with such social markers. If we refuse to do so, social censure and punishment will follow.

Kyriocentric scripts prescribe behavior and grant prerogatives to the members of the dominant groups, whereas subordinate groups may be exploited. Kyriarchal social controls entail rewards for conforming behavior and stigmatization and isolation for aberrant conduct. These disciplinary controls produce personalities that conform to hegemonic kyriarchal standards. Kyriarchal ideology and imagery, the cultural representations of kyriarchal power in symbolic language and artistic production, legitimate and support dominant statuses. In other words, the world is determined by relations of domination which have become naturalized and common sense. Sex/gender is a part of such relations of ruling, which also ground other divisions such as class, colonialism, heterosexuality, or race.

Chela Sandoval, among others, has pointed out that in the age of postmodernity and trans-national capitalism, power no longer gets generated out of a single source. A vertical pyramid positions at the top level the dominant master, king, class, race, sexual orientation, or gender, such that the white male, heterosexual, and capitalists form the top of the pyramid (Foucault has called this structure the "sovereign model" of power). Sandoval suggests, however, that power circulates not by a vertical pyramid structure but rather horizontally on a flattened plane.

As in the previous, sovereign, pyramidal model of power, the location of every citizen-subject can be distinctly mapped on this postmodern flattened, horizontal power grid according to such attributes as race, class, gender, age, or sexual orientation, but this re-territorialized circulation of power re-differentiates groups and sorts identities differently. . . . This late-capitalist retranslation of difference allows hierarchical and material differences in power between people to be erased from consciousness, even while these same economic and social privileges are bolstered. The growing metaphoric dominance of this newly conceived horizontal grid networking the globe generates a kind of double-reality and double-consciousness of power with new and old formations at work all at once.[31]

The horizontal grid of power, according to this formulation, occludes the workings of the "sovereign" or kyriarchal model of power and erases it from consciousness. If that is so, then it is important to read the kyriarchal inscriptions of power in scripture in order to bring into consciousness the workings of "sovereign power" in and through the pseudo-egalitarian circulation of globalizing power today. Since kyriarchal biblical values have shaped wo/men's self-understanding and socio-cultural political discourses in Western culture, it is necessary to deploy hermeneutical strategies that can focus, in the process of reading, on inscriptions of kyriarchal power in biblical texts in order to decolonize contemporary consciousness.

A Detoxifying/Decolonizing Reading of I Peter

The feminist hermeneutical method of consciousness-detoxification or conscientization (Paolo Freire) which I have developed in my work seeks to make conscious, and lift into critical reflection, the cultural and religious values and imperial frameworks, which wo/men internalize in and through a reading/hearing of biblical texts. At the same time, such a method creates a critical space for transforming wo/men's self-understanding, self-perception, and self-alienation. By analyzing the scriptural text's power of persuasion, this method intends to engender biblical interpretation as a critical feminist decolonizing practice against all forms of domination.

---

31. Sandoval, *Methodology of the Oppressed*, 74.

Such a hermeneutical process of decolonizing cultural-political consciousness and religious imagination cannot be done once and for all. Rather, it has to be repeated again and again, because in every new reading a different set of internalized imperial inscriptions emerges, which works hand in glove with cultural-religious "common sense" assumptions. By deconstructing the rhetoric and politics of imperial inequality and subordination inscribed in and through the reading of scripture, we are able to move towards ever fresh articulations of radical democratic religious possibilities and emancipatory practices of becoming conscious.

Whether one thinks of the interpretive process as detoxifying or decolonizing, as emancipative technique or conscientizing strategy, crucial hermeneutical moves are:

- A *hermeneutics of experience* reflects on socially located experience and lifts into consciousness how much experience is shaped by the inscriptions of dominance and submission.
- A *hermeneutics of domination* deploys a critical analytic of the systemic inscriptions of empire and domination (kyriarchy) in socio-political-religious consciousness and everyday life. It seeks to name the globalization of inequality and poverty as the context of biblical interpretation.
- A *hermeneutics of suspicion* analyzes the mechanisms of kyriocentric texts and ideologies that "naturalize" the systems of domination by making the ethos of empire "common sense" and, in the case of sacred scriptures, which sacralizes such kyriarchal worldviews and self-understandings.
- A *hermeneutics of evaluation* critically assesses biblical texts and their contemporary inscriptions in terms of the feminist the*logical norm "wo/men's salvation," i.e., well-being.
- A *hermeneutics of imagination* creatively envisions a world that is different from the world determined by empire and domination and seeks to identify visions of hope and transformation also inscribed in biblical texts.
- A *hermeneutics of remembrance* engages rhetorical analysis and historical re-construction for rewriting biblical history in terms of wo/men's struggles against empire and for well-being. It thereby reconstructs a different context for biblical texts and interpretations.[32]

---

32. See Elisabeth Schüssler Fiorenza, "Re-Visioning Christian Origins: *In Memory of Her* Revisited," in *Christian Beginnings: Worship, Belief and Society,* ed. Kieran O'Mahony (London:

- A *hermeneutics of transformation*[33] is at work in the hermeneutical process of de-toxification and has as its goal transformative action for changing the internalized ethos of empire and its structures of domination as well as for empowering wo/men's agency and commitment to alter relations of domination.

These interpretive practices are not to be construed simply as successive, independent methodological steps of inquiry. Rather, they are best understood as intersecting interpretive moves and movements; as detoxifying hermeneutical methods that interact with each other simultaneously in the process of deconstructing the inscriptions of empire, in particular biblical or cultural texts, in the context of the globalization of inequality and poverty. While the classic "hermeneutical circle" seems to be closed, a critical feminist hermeneutics moves in spiraling movements and circling spirals. Moving in spirals, feminist biblical interpretation is ongoing; it cannot be done once and for all, but must be repeated differently in different situations and from different perspectives. This hermeneutical process is exciting because in every new reading of biblical texts, a different meaning emerges. Such a detoxifying process of biblical interpretation has, as its "doubled" reference point, our contemporary present and the biblical past.

These seven hermeneutical strategies of critical feminist interpretation for reading the bible in the context of empire are guided by *democratics* in Sandoval's "methodology of the oppressed," which proposes

> a set of technologies for decolonizing the social [and religious] imagination. These technologies . . . are all guided by democratics, the practitioners' commitment to the equal distribution of power. They are technologies that seek to fashion the "dissident consciousness" of a revolutionary, mobile, and global coalitions of citizen-activists who are allied through the apparatus of emancipation.[34]

Continuum International, 2003), 225–50.

33. See the methodological reflections by Elaine Wainwright "Where Theory and Practice Meet: A Way Toward Transformation," in her book *Women Healing/Healing Women* (London: Equinox Publ., 2006).

34. Sandoval, *Methodology of the Oppressed*, 183.

If the tendency of texts and ideologies is to "naturalize" structures of domination by eliminating their socio-historical genealogy from consciousness, then it is important, in a process of conscientization, to lift into awareness such historical constructions of kyriarchal difference and ideologies of domination. My rhetorical reading of 1 Peter, therefore, will make use of these seven hermeneutical strategies albeit in an indirect fashion. I will first engage in a rhetorical analysis of the whole letter of 1 Peter, then focus on the kyriarchal rhetoric of subordination inscribed in it, in order to try to reconstruct the voices of the subordinates. In a last step, I will explicitly reflect on the hermeneutical moves that I have made and suggest questions for the process of decolonizing consciousness, which has been shaped by the inscriptions of empire in and through the process of reading/hearing this scriptural text.

A Feminist Rhetorical Analysis of 1 Peter

The Christian Testament writing called 1 Peter is addressed to "resident aliens" who live in the Roman Province of Asia Minor. It represents them as a marginalized group that experiences harassment and suffering. This pseudonymous epistle—which claims to be an authoritative letter of the apostle Peter—was sent from the imperial center Rome as a letter of advice and admonition to "good conduct and sub-ordination" in the colonial public of the provinces.[35] As a circular letter, 1 Peter is a rhetorical communication between those who live in the metropolitan center of imperial Rome, which is the*logically camouflaged as Babylon,[36] and those who live in Asia Minor as colonial subjects. Asia Minor had been for centuries colonized and had absorbed Hellenistic language and culture as well as Roman imperial commerce and religion.[37]

35. The opening greeting does not characterize the recipients in communal-democratic terms as ekklēsia but in social-individual terms as "transients" or "migrants" who have become "elect" through "the foreknowledge of G*d the Father," the "sanctification of the Spirit for obedience," and the "sprinkling of the blood of Christ." The letter's address also uses an elaborate, uniquely Pauline form of greeting ("may grace and peace be with you in abundance"). With the phrase "sanctification of the Spirit for obedience," the central topic of the letter is mentioned.

36. First Peter thus shares the language of the book of Revelation for the imperial power, Rome. The letter is probably written around the same time and to the same communities in Asia Minor. However, its politics are radically different from those of Revelation.

37. This section has been written in interaction with the following commentaries: Paul J. Achtemeier, *1 Peter: A Commentary*, Hermeneia (Minneapolis, Minn.: Fortress Press, 1996); Eugene M. Boring, *1 Peter*, Abingdon New Testament Commentaries (Nashville, Tenn: Abingdon,

The community, to which the first letter ascribed to the apostle Peter is addressed, is not called ekklēsia (which means the democratic assembly of the people) but *adelphōtēs* ("brotherhood"). Since in 4:17 it is understood as "the household of G*d" (*oikos tou theou*), the "brotherhood" is conceived, at least by the author, as the household of G*d, whose *pater familias* is G*d, the father (1:2, 3) and whose members are "obedient children" (1:14). The members of the "brotherhood" have been "set free" (ransomed like slave wo/men) from "the traditions of their fathers" (1:18) and are invoking now "the father who judges all people impartially" (1:17). Although they are like "newborn infants longing for the pure spiritual mother-milk" (2:2), no mother of the family is mentioned.[38] Finally, their characterization as resident aliens and transients of the Dispersion[39] characterizes them as Jewish exiles who no longer have a homeland and often were considered as second-class citizens in their host countries.

Key to understanding who the recipients are is their characterization as transients, migrants, or foreigners (*parepidēmoi* and *paroikoi*), which can be translated as non-citizens, resident aliens, settlers, or colonials. The *paroikos* lacked local citizenship and belonged to an institutionalized group ranked socially between the citizen population and above freed persons. According to Elliott,[40] such "by-dwellers" were excluded from major civic offices and honors, had only limited legal protection, and were restricted in commerce, intermarriage, and land tenure; they were allowed limited participation in cultic rites but excluded from the priesthood. Despite their lack of civic standing, they were like the citizenry in that they were responsible for taxes, financial civic support,

---

1999); John H. Elliott, *1 Peter: A New Translation with Introduction and Commentary*, Anchor Bible (New York: Doubleday, 2000). See also the feminist commentaries, Katherine E. Corley, "1 Peter," in *Searching the Scriptures*, in ed. Elisabeth Schüssler Fiorenza (New York: Crossroad, 1994), v. II, 349–60; Sharyn Dowd, "1 Peter," in *Women's Bible Commentary*, in eds. Carol A Newsom and Sharon H. Ringe, expanded edition (Louisville, Ky.: Westminster: John Knox, 1998), 462–64; Irene Foulkes, "Der erste Brief des Petrus," in Luise Schottroff and Marie-Theres Wacker, *Feministische Bibelauslegung*, 2nd. ed. (Gütersloh: Chr. Kaiser Gütersloher Verlagshaus, 1999), 701–7.

38. However, it is debated whether the final greeting, "the co-elect in Babylon sends you greetings," because of the substantive feminine form, refers to a wo/man (*hē en Babylōni syneklektē*) or to the ekklēsia in Rome. See Judith K. Applegate, "The Coelect Woman of 1 Peter," *NTS* 32 (1992): 587–604.

39. Paul J. Achtemeier, *1 Peter*, 82 ff., 174 ff., reads the terms "diaspora" (1:1), "aliens and exiles" (2:11) not in sociological but in metaphorical-spiritual terms.

40. Elliott, *1Peter*, 94, referring to Rostovtzeff.

tribute, and military service. Their status therefore was not very different from foreigners, visiting trades people, missionaries, and migrants (*parepidēmoi*) and they were exposed to suspicion and hostility. In short, the condition of the addressees of 1 Peter as *paroikoi* accounts for much of their suffering. Finally, their characterization as transients of the Dispersion characterizes them as Jewish exiles who no longer had a homeland and were often considered as second-class citizens in their host countries.

Taking the context of Roman colonialism into account, Prostmeier[41] has argued that some members of the community might have belonged to the imperial administration. Centuries of Hellenistic colonization of the kingdoms of Asia Minor had produced a deep social rift between the indigenous peoples of Asia Minor and the Greek settlers. In the Roman Empire this Hellenistic "middle class" took over the Imperial administration, commerce, and civic institutions. Hence, Rome did not change the basically Hellenistic culture of the cities which consisted of a rich aristocratic "upper-class," the new colonial "middle class," and the group of workers and slaves.[42] While the natives were the majority of the working and "lower class" people, the colonial settlers and Hellenized natives formed the cultured "middle class" who were most loyal to the Empire.

This new "middle class" of "diaspora-Greeks" imported their own standards of family and civic life and their cultural and political institutions, although they were not an independent political entity. Hellenistic settlers were a privileged class. Their language, knowledge, and financial and cultural capital enabled them to take over leading functions in the kingdom-states, although indigenous monarchs tried to prevent the co-habitation and social mixing of colonials and natives. Hellenistic "diaspora Jews" would have qualified for such colonial "middle class" status, although they were regarded with suspicion because of their different customs and perceived religious exclusiveness, on the one hand, and their history of militant struggle against Roman imperial occupation, on the other hand.

41. Ferdinand-Rupert Prostmeier, *Handlungsmodelle im 1. Petrusbrief,* Forschungen zur Bible, 63 (Würzburg: Echter Verlag, 1990).

42. I use the category of "class" not in the technical sense and place it in quotation marks because I realize that it is problematic to use the term for status relations in antiquity. However, it seems to serve best to express the difference in status. See Valerie Hope, "Status and Identity in the Roman World," in *Experiencing Rome: Culture, Identity and Power in the Roman Empire*, ed. Janet Huskinson (New York: Routledge, 2000), 125–82.

Hellenistic culture, religions, life style, and education were the *sine qua non* for social mobility. This new educated propertied "middle class," consisting of colonizing settlers, such as former military and merchants, and of the indigenous elite, had the function of assuring the stability of imperial colonial society for which the stability of the household was crucial. In the course of Hellenistic as well as Roman imperial colonization of Asia Minor and the Mediterranean, the discourse on household management (*peri oikonomias*) became an important ideological tool for preserving the stability and unity of the imperial order. Both the interpretations of Elliott and Prostmeier are important, since some in the community like the author(s) might have belonged to the colonizing settler class whereas others were suffering from the hardship of being resident aliens and foreigners.

It is not clear, moreover, whether the recipients who were Gentile converts understood themselves still as Jews[43] with a messianic bent,—*Christianoi*, as they are labeled by outsiders—or whether they saw themselves as the "new" people of G*d. The first interpretation is suggested by the rich Jewish language of the document, whereas the second is held by most modern Christian exegetes. First Peter's inscribed symbolic universe, expressed and modulated in the language of the Hellenistic Jewish bible, the Septuagint (LXX), is that of Israel. The letter's language is saturated with Scriptural allusions, quotations, and images. The language of 1 Peter remains the*-centric; the title *kyrios* fluctuates between G*d and Christ, whose vindication, resurrection, and glorification exhibits G*d's ultimate power for salvation/well-being. G*d is the father who has chosen them and whose mercy has given them a new birth and "living hope." G*d is called the faithful creator and impartial judge of all people who brings the ages to a close. G*d is the one who calls and whose will and "living word" have saving power.

Jesus has been manifested by G*d as the Christ, the Messiah and inaugurator of the end of the ages. Through his suffering and through his resurrection, he "has gone into heaven and is at the right hand of G*d with angels, authorities, and powers made subject to him" (3:22 NRSV). This the*-centricity of 1 Peter's symbolic universe is completely expressed in the language and conceptuality of Israel. Jesus is understood as the Messiah who inaugurates the end of the ages and who functions as mediator of G*d's saving plan and actions.

43. For the strength of Jewish communities in Asia Minor, see Paul Treblico, *Jewish Communtiies in Asia Minor* (Cambridge: Cambridge University Press, 1991).

Although a plethora of metaphors and titles portray the recipients of the letter in terms of the covenant people of Israel, the letter neither mentions Israel directly nor does it describe the "Christian" community as the "new Israel." Israel is not yet seen as the "other" of the community but as its constitutive identity.[44] This is programmatically expressed, for instance, in 1:15-16: "As the One who called you is holy, even you yourself must become holy in every respect of your lives, because scripture says, 'You shall be holy because I am holy.'" Those who have been born anew are elect and holy, which according to Lev 20:26 means that they are set apart from all other peoples.

This Jewish self-identity of the community comes to the fore especially in 1 Pet 2:4-10 which uses a plethora of traditional images to characterize the elect and holy ones as the covenant people of G*d (Exod 19:6). This section is steeped in the language of the scriptures and the traditions of Israel and Judaism. It not only echoes themes which have been already introduced previously but also integrates older traditions, which are similar to those found in Qumran, rabbinic Judaism, and the Pauline letters.

The following images characterize the dignity and lofty status of the recipients in terms of the traditional attributes of Israel: they are "living stones," being built into a temple of the Spirit or spiritual house. They are a "holy and royal priesthood," a "chosen race," a "holy nation," G*d's very own people who have been summoned to tell forth the great deeds of the one who has called them from darkness to light. They who were once a non-people are now the people of G*d, who have been graced with mercy.

Despite the Jewish characterization of the recipients, the abundant use of the scriptural language of Israel and the the*-centricity of the letter, most exegetes maintain that the letter is written to gentile Christians and that the author has appropriated the language and elect status of Israel for the audience.[45]

---

44. Scholars have pointed out that until late antiquity Jewish and Christian communities had so many close affinities that it was difficult to draw clear boundaries between them. This is why it is often difficult to explain which inscriptions come from which communities. See Paul Trebilco, "The Jewish and Christian Eumeneia Formula," in John M. G. Barclay, ed., *Negotiating Diaspora: Jewish Strategies in the Roman Empire* (London: T. & T. International, 2004), 66–88, esp., 81.

45. Horst Goldstein, "Das heilige Volk, das zuvor kein Volk war. Christengemeinde ohne Judenpolemik: 1 Petr 2, 4-10," in *Gottesverächter und Menschenfeinde? Juden zwischen Jesus und frühchistlicher Kirche*, ed. Horst Goldstein (Düsseldorf: Patmos Verlag, 1979), 279–303, sees clearly that the words "people" and "mercy" have lost their character as "anti-jüdische Kampfparolen"

Rather than considering that the community could have still understood itself as a Jewish messianic community, living in the dispersion, whose self-identity was determined by the large number of converts in their midst, commentators insist on reading the letter in a supersessionist way, assuming that it is Christianity and not Judaism that has inherited G*d's promises to the covenant people Israel.

The arguments of the letter are fashioned in traditional Jewish the*logical language in terms of authority (pseudepigraphy; references to scripture [LXX]), analogy (Christ's suffering), example (Sarah), comparison (like newborn babes), and vivid apocalyptic imagery (fiery ordeal; the adversary as a roaring lion). The overarching image of the letter is that of "election" and "chosenness" of those belonging to the "brotherhood." This image is elaborated in three strings of argument clusters (argumentation) pertaining to the notion of "good citizenship."

The first argument cluster describes, in the language of scripture, the recipients' "high" status as the people of G*d, "house (oikos) of the Spirit" and "royal priesthood" (1:15—2:10); the second argument cluster spells out the "good" behavior demanded especially from the subordinate members of the household (oikos). It uses the socio-political form of the colonial oikos-discourse,[46] which exegetes usually call "Household Codes." This argument, however, does not begin by addressing behavior in the household but by prescribing behavior toward the authorities of the empire. Thus the oikos-discourse is clearly intertwined with the imperial discourse and forms the central part of the overall letter. It is not just a paraenetic strategy among many (2:11—3:12) but is at the heart of 1 Peter's rhetoric. The third argument cluster speaks about the necessity of suffering (pathēmata) and explains what "doing good" means for the "stewards" (oikonomoi) of G*d's manifold grace, who are publicly put down, harassed, and defamed as Christians, i.e., as Messianists (3:13—4:11).

---

in 1 Peter but then goes on to surmise that the letter reflects a situation where the confrontation with Judaism is a thing of the past (297). Despite his explicit criticism of the anti-Jewish misreading of the letter in Lutheran theology and scholarship, he obviously is not able to imagine a time and place where the opposition Judaism-Christianity did not yet exist.

46. For an excellent discussion and analysis of the oikos discourse, see the works of Laura Beth Bugg, Baptism, Bodies, and Bonds: The Rhetoric of Empire in Colossians (Th.D. dissertation, Harvard University, 2006) for Colossians; and that of Yuko Taniguchi, To Lead Quiet and Peaceable Lives: A Rhetorical Analysis of the First Letter of Timothy (Th.D. dissertation, Harvard University, 2002) for 1 Timothy.

These three argumentative moves are summed up and amplified in 4:12—5:11 (*peroratio*), which continues to tell the readers to expect difficulties as "Christians" and to undergo "honorable suffering" because the end is in view. The "fiery ordeal" is upon them and the time has come for judgment to begin with the household (*oikos*)[47] of G*d. (4:12-19). These admonitions are followed by an address to elder and younger members of the community, which spell out the right order of the household of G*d and are reinforced by a vivid description of the adversary, the disorder creating *diabolos* who is compared to a roaring lion seeking to devour everyone (5:1-9). The whole summation ends with a doxology to "the G*d of all grace," who has called the addressees to "eternal glory in Christ" and will "restore, support, and strengthen" them in their troubles (5:10-11).

Thus, the argument of 1 Peter moves from an elaboration of the theoretically high but socio-politically precarious status of the recipients to the central part of the letter, addressing the problem as to how to behave in a politically correct manner (doing good) with regard to the imperial-colonial authorities. These admonitions are especially addressed to the subordinate members of the *oikos*. The rhetorical strategy then shifts to a more general argument, addressing all the intended recipients about "good" behavior in public and the "honorable sufferings" to be expected. Finally, it climaxes with admonitions regarding the exercise of leadership in the "household (*oikos*) of G*d."

The Rhetoric of Sub-Ordination and the Arguments of the Subalterns

Central to the rhetoric of the letter is the image of the household, *oikos*. Its inscribed argument engages the hegemonic socio-political and cultural discourses about household management (*peri oikonomias*) and about politics (*peri politeias*), which were intertwined in Greco-Roman political theory. Over and against more "liberalizing," emancipatory, and egalitarian tendencies in Greco-Roman culture and philosophy, a rich variety of household-literature (*peri oikonomias*) appeared that sought to mitigate ethically the rigorist exercise of domination on the part of the *pater familias*, through a combination of the motives of fear and love in the sense of fidelity, cooperation, and proper relations of domination.

---

47. Because of the understanding of *oikos* as temple in 2:5, exegetes argue that the term has this meaning here too. However, the context is different here. Only a positivist reading needs to reduce multivalent metaphorical language to a one-to-one meaning.

This literature which speaks about household management[48] seeks to mediate between the urban "middle class" colonial *oikos*-society and its ideals and virtues, on the one hand, and the axioms of equality of Stoic philosophy, on the other hand, which jeopardize the fundamental principles of the order of household and state. This emancipatory trend in Greco-Roman society resulted in a limited legal equality of freeborn wo/men, and some slaves and freed persons, in the household, in commerce, and in the wider society. In short, the discourse on household management was not just a moral discourse on how the members of the household (*oikos*) should behave but was also a part of imperial discourse and political theory.

As we have seen in 1 Peter, the Christian community soon comes to be called "the household of G*d," and G*d is understood as its Father (*pater familias*) with absolute power over his realm by analogy to the Roman emperor. Since from the time of Augustus the emperor was understood as the *pater patriae*, exegetes have long recognized that the household code trajectory Christianizes imperial social and ecclesial structures. Especially David Balch's research has documented a growing interest, among diverse philosophical directions and schools in the first century, to reassert the political ethos of subordination in the household in support of Roman imperial politics.[49]

Recognizing the significant role of the house-church for early Christian life, some studies of the social world of early Christianity have suggested that the kyriarchal emperor, lord, slave master, father, elite male-defined ethos of the household also expresses the ethos of early Christian mission. For instance Gerd Theissen has had great influence with his proposal that the radical ethos of the Jesus movement was ascetic, whereas the communities of the Christian missionary movement, in the upcoming Greco-Roman urban centers, were characterized by a softened form of patriarchalism, which with Troeltsch he terms *Liebespatriarchalismus*.[50]

48. See David L. Balch, "Household Codes," in *Greco-Roman Literature and the New Testament: Selected Forms and Genres*, ed. David E. Aune (Atlanta, Ga.: Scholars, 1988), 25–50.

49. See Klaus Thraede, "Zum historischen Hintergrund der 'Haustafeln' des NT," *Jahrbuch für Antike und Christentum, Ergänzungsband* 8 (1981), 359–68; Kathleen O'Brien Wicker, "First Century Marriage Ethics: A Comparative Study of the Household Codes and Plutarch's Conjugal Precepts," in *No Famine in the Land*, eds. James Flanagan and Anita W. Robinson (Missoula, Mo.: Scholars, 1975), 141–53; David Balch, "Household Ethical Codes in Peripatetic, Neopythagorean, and Early Christian Moralists," in *Society of Biblical Literature Seminar Papers II*, ed. Paul J. Achtemeier (Missoula, Mo.: Scholars, 1977), 397–404.

50. See the following by Gerd Theissen: "Itinerant Radicalism: The Tradition of Jesus

Oikos in 1 Peter does not mean "home"[51] but designates the household (*oikos*) as a social institution, which was fundamental to the stability of the Roman Empire. Within the context of the *oikos*-discourse, the designation "brotherhood" (*adelphōtēs*)[52] for the Christian community in 1 Peter 2:17 and 5:9 also is shaped by the author in terms of the imperial pattern of submission, but could have been understood differently by the recipients. This term was generally used as self-designation for political alliances, such as collegia and mystery cult groups, such as the Isis cult. Unlike the private sphere of the household, such religious and political associations[53] were not based on blood-lines and economic interests but on collegiality, solidarity, and mutual support, which fulfilled many of the emotional needs that we associate with family.

The proliferation of collegia and political associations[54] presented a constant problem for the imperial administration. Hence, steps were frequently taken to control such groups.[55] It was the fear that such secret organizations

---

Sayings from the Perspective of the Sociology of Literature," in *The Bible and Liberation: Political and Social Hermeneutics* (Berkeley, Calif.: Radical Religion Reader, 1976), 84–93; *Sociology of Early Palestinian Christianity* (Philadelphia, Pa.: Fortress Press, 1978); and *The Social Setting of Pauline Christianity: Essays on Corinth* (Philadelphia, Pa.: Fortress Press, 1982).

51. See Elliott, *A Home for the Homeless.*

52. For Paul see Reidar Aasgard, *"My Beloved Brothers and Sisters!": Christian Siblingship in Paul* (London: T. & T. Clark, 2004).

53. See, e.g., John Kloppenborg, "Collegia and Thiasoi: Issues in Function, Taxonomy, and Membership," in *Voluntary Associations in the Graeco-Roman World*, eds. John S. Kloppenborg and Stephen G. Wilson (London: Routledge, 1996), 16–30; idem, "Edwin Hatch, Churches, and Collegia," *Origins and Method: Towards a New Understanding of Judaism and Christianity*, ed. Bradley H. McLean (Sheffield: JSOT, 1993), 212–38; Philip A. Harland, *Associations, Synagogues, and Congregations: Claiming a Place in Ancient Mediterranean Society* (Minneapolis, Minn.: Fortress Press, 2003); idem, "Honouring the Emperor or Assailing the Beast: Participation in Civic Life among Associations (Jewish, Christian and Other) in Asia Minor and the Apocalypse of John," *JSNT* 77 (2000): 99–121; Peter Maser, "Synagoge und Ekklesia: Erwägungen zur Frühgeschichte des Kirchenbaus," in *Begegnungen zwischen Christentum und Judentum in Antike und Mittelalter: Festschrift für Heinz Schreckenberg* (Göttingen: Vandenhoeck & Ruprecht, 1993), 271–92; Steve Mason, "PHILOSOPHIAI: Graeco-Roman, Judean, and Christian," in *Voluntary Associations in the Graeco-Roman World*, 31–58; Wayne O McCready, "EKKLESIA and Voluntary Associations," in *Voluntary Associations in the Graeco-Roman World*, 59–73; Sandra Walker-Ramisch, "Graeco-Roman Voluntary Associations and the Damascus Document: A Sociological Analysis," in *Voluntary Associations in the Graeco-Roman World*, 128–45; S. G. Wilson, "Voluntary Associations: An Overview," in *Voluntary Associations in the Graeco-Roman World*, 1–15.

54. See also Philip A. Harland, *Associations, Synagogues, and Congregations: Claiming a Place in Ancient Mediterranean Society* (Minneapolis, Minn.: Fortress Press), 2003.

55. Wendy Cotter, "The Collegia and Roman Law: State Restrictions on Voluntary Associations 64 BCE-200 CE," in *Voluntary Associations in the Graeco-Roman World*, 74–89.

would pursue seditious political interests that led the authorities to forbid them. For the recipients of 1 Peter, who were probably known to outsiders as a type of Jewish association, to be labeled in the aftermath of the Jewish war as Messianists (*Christianoi*) could be very difficult and provoke harassment, loss of civic standing, suffering,[56] and even pogroms and lynchings. Hence, the rhetoric of 1 Peter counsels adaptation to the imperial ethos.

The injunction to sub-ordination (*hypotassein*) is used five times in 1 Peter. Four times it addresses a group of people: everyone in 2:13, household slaves in 2:18, wives in 3:1, and both elders (5:1) and younger people or neophytes in 5:5. Only once is it used in a descriptive praise statement in 3:22, which says that angels, authorities, and powers were made subject to Jesus Christ who "has gone into heaven and is at the right hand of G*d." This last statement makes it clear that *hypotassein* expresses a relation of ruling and power. Apocalyptic language and universe meta-mythologizes the kyriarchal order of the Empire. Like Caesar, Jesus Christ is Lord (*kyrios*) who is at the "right hand" of G*d, the Almighty. However, whereas later times understand church ministry by analogy to Christ's power of ruling, 1 Peter admonishes the elders of the community not to lord (*katekyrieuontes*) it over those in their charge.

In a classical-rhetorical analysis, the submission-code section 2:11—3:12 "emerges as the core of the letter"[57] and could be entitled: *Become Colonial Subjects/Subalterns*. In order to underscore the need for the subaltern behavior of household slaves and wives towards the imperial authorities, which is the *topos* of the central *argument* of the letter, the author(s) first combines and advocates here the imperial ethos spelled out in the discourses about politics (*peri politeias* [2:13]) and about household management (*peri oikonomias* [2:18—3:7]), then establishes it, with reference to the example of the suffering Christ and the matriarch Sarah, and finally moralizes such colonial submission as righteousness and as "doing good" (3:8-12).

---

56. Steven Richter Bechtler, *Following in His Steps: Suffering, Community, and Christology in 1 Peter*, SBL Diss. Series 162 (Atlanta, Ga: Scholars, 1998), 207, has focused on the rhetoric of suffering and interpreted it in terms of the honor-shame dualistic framework. Although Richter Bechtler recognizes that "most of what has been said . . . concerning honor and shame in Mediterranean societies actually applies predominantly to adult males," he does not recognize that by using it as an interpretive framework he masculinizes and kyriarchalizes the symbolic universe inscribed in the letter.

57. Barth L. Campbell, *Honor, Shame, and the Rhetoric of 1 Peter*, SBL Diss. Ser. 160 (Atlanta, Ga.: Scholars, 1998), 231.

The whole section is introduced with an appeal to "honorable conduct," addressed to the "non-citizens and transients," who are hailed as "beloved"(*agapētoi*). At this point it becomes obvious that the sender the*logizes and moralizes the dominant kyriarchal ethos of the Roman Empire and requests that the subordinates realize and live it in their practices of sub-ordination. The *ratio* and motivation given is missionary: they should conduct themselves "honorably" so that the Gentiles glorify G*d on the day of "visitation" (*episcopēs*) (2:12).

The summons to abstain from human desires (*sarkikōn epithymiōn*) that endanger their lives (*psychē*) is elaborated and elucidated in verses 11-17 with the admonition to subject themselves to the emperor, as the supreme one, and to the governors who are sent by him, i.e., to the imperial administration so that these recognize them as doing what is right, honorable, or good. The the*logical justification given here is that such submission, understood as "doing the honorable," is "the will of G*d." Here, the elite masculine ethos of "honorableness"[58] has become "Christianized." The overall rhetorical strategy of the letter is summed up in 2:17: Honor everyone, love the "brotherhood," fear G*d, honor the emperor!

Unlike in 2:13 the injunction to household-slaves (2:18) is not stated in an imperative but in a circumstantial participle grammatical form and indicates that the whole continues the imperatives of 2:11 and 13; the circumstantial participle is also used in 3:1, 7, 9 (in the injunctions to wives/husbands). The "doing good" of slave wo/men consists in their subjecting themselves even to harsh and unjust masters so that if unjustly beaten and suffering[59]—if that is

---

58. See John H. Elliott, "Disgraced Yet Graced: The Gospel According to 1 Peter in the Key of Honor and Shame," *Biblical Theology Bulletin* 24 (1994): 166–78. However, this dualistic construction is ideological. Whereas the sect model could engage in egalitarian reconstructions because "sect" was seen as over and against "church," the honor-shame model is constructed over and against American society which is assumed to be egalitarian. Operating within the antiquarian historical assumption that ancient culture is totally different from contemporary one, it cannot conceive of egalitarian relations in antiquity.

59. On slavery, see Carolyn Osiek, "Female Slaves, *Porneia*, and the Limits of Obedience," in *Early Christian Families in Context*, 255–74; Jennifer A. Glancy, *Slavery in Early Christianity* (New York: Oxford University Press, 2002); Moses Finley, *Ancient Slavery and Modern Ideology* (Princeton, N.J.: Markus Wiener, 1998); Keith R. Bradley, *Slavery and Rebellion in the Roman World* (Bloomington, Ind.: Indiana University Press, 1989). Idem, *Slaves and Masters in the Roman Empire* (New York: Oxford University Press, 1987); Allen Callahan, Richard Horsley and Abraham Smith, *Slavery in Text and Interpretation*, Semeia 83/84 (Atlanta, Ga.: Society of Biblical Literature, 1998); Marleen Boudreau Flory, "Family in *familia*: Kinship and Community in Slavery," *American Journal of Ancient History* 3 (1978): 78–95; Elisabeth Herrmann-Otto, *Ex Ancilla*

"G*d's will," they do so for "doing right." Christ's innocent suffering is then elaborated as an example for such honorable behavior in suffering. However, it is rarely noticed that here no reference to Christ's resurrection and glory is made.[60] In a similar fashion, freeborn wo/men are told to subject themselves to their husbands, even to those who are not believers. The goal here is the conversion of the husbands, which will be brought about not by their "preaching" to them but by their proper "lady-like" conduct of purity and sub-ordination, which is exemplified by the matriarch Sarah, the prime example for female converts to Judaism.[61]

Finally, the "brotherhood" is not only to be governed by mutual love and support but also by subordination. In 5:5 the "younger" members of the "brotherhood," who are either younger in age or converts, are told to subject themselves to the older, the presbyters. Although the presbyters are admonished at the same time not to exercise kyriarchal leadership, this injunction still indicates that the inscribed argument seeks to fashion the order of the community as one of sub-ordination. In sum, the letter's Roman colonial rhetoric of subjection advocates the submission of the subaltern migrants and non-citizens in Asia Minor. As problem cases, the rhetoric specifies unjust suffering of household slave women and the marriage–relationship between Christian wo/men and Gentile men. Contemporary exegetes are generally embarrassed by this rhetoric of subjection, which has been indicted by feminist biblical studies. Hence, they seek to eliminate or mitigate the problem for modern hearers/readers by translating *hypotassein*[62] with "accept the authority," "defer to," "show respect for,"

Natus: Untersuchungen zu den "hausgeborenen" Sklavinnen im Westen des Römischen Kaiserreiches (Stuttgart: F. Steiner, 1993); Dale B. Martin, "Slave Families and Slaves in Families," in *Early Christian Families in Context*, 207–30.

60. Yet, it is important to note that the admonition to the slave master is missing here.

61. While the husbands are addressed in 3:8, the pair "father/mother–children" is missing here.

62. Eugene A. Nida and Johannes Louw, *A Greek-English Lexicon of the New Testament: Based on Semantic Domains* (New York: United Bible Societies, 1989), 466, place the Greek verb *hypotassesthai* = to submit, subject oneself (middle and passive) to be in the same "semantic domain" as *hypakouein* (to be obedient) stating that these denote "guide, discipline, follow," while they put the active form of *hypotassein* in the separate semantic domain of "control, rule." Cynthia Briggs Kittredge, *Community and Authority: The Rhetoric of Obedience in the Pauline Tradition* (Harrisburg, Pa.: Trinity International, 1998), 50–51, has discussed the semantic field of "obedience/subordination" and concludes that both "occur in the context of military, political, and domestic subjection," and further "do not have substantively different meanings."

"recognize the proper social order," or with phrases such as "participate in," "be involved with," "be committed to."[63] Although such an apologetic translation is primarily concerned to avoid offending "wo/men" and "liberal" readers/hearers, it conceals the elite male character of *hypotassein* and its colonizing function, which in 1 Peter has become "the*logized." Such an apologetic reading takes the side of the authors rather than that of those whose subjection they advocate in the*logical terms.

Because of feminist work, however, most recent scholarship on 1 Peter is aware that the ethical-political meaning and socio-historical effects of the letter's subordination discourse is problematic for contemporary society and church. Hence, commentators tend to focus very little upon hermeneutical problems, such as those posed by the Jewish language of the letter, by the injunction to political subjection or by the use of the example of Christ, to pacify suffering slave wo/men. Instead, commentators tend to focus on the demand in 1 Peter for the subordination of wo/men. In response to feminist interpretation, malestream exegetes feel compelled to write a special hermeneutical excursus[64] or to articulate special hermeneutical rules for reading these texts today. One's hermeneutical stance decisively determines one's overall interpretation of the letter: whether one assumes a stable identity and rhetorical position or rather constructs differences and tensions between the recipients' and the senders' rhetoric. It is this focus—on this "different ethos" of the recipients—that is at issue in the contest between a critical feminist emancipatory and malestream colonizing interpretation of 1 Peter.

Whereas the author's rhetoric takes center stage in exegetical readings, it is more difficult to reconstruct the counter-arguments, which a rhetorical communication needs to address in order to develop a successful power of persuasion. Conceptualizing the argumentative strategies of slave, freeborn, and Jewish-Christian or Christian-Jewish wo/men, i.e., Messianists, requires a reading of 1 Peter "against the grain" of its kyriarchal argumentative strategies. If the center of 1 Peter's argument is the discourse of "*hypotassein*," i.e., subjection or sub-ordination, then a critical feminist postcolonial interpretation cannot uncritically repeat the rhetoric of the authors, but must first of all attempt in

63. Donald Senior, "The Conduct of Christians in the World (1 Pet. 2:11—3:12)," *RevExp* 79 (1982): 427–38, esp., 430.
64. See Elliott, *1 Peter*, 585–600.

Nelle Morton's words to "hear into speech" the submerged arguments of those whom the subordination discourse seeks to subject. Such a critical approach, which focuses on the subjugated knowledges inscribed in the letter, runs counter to malestream exegesis, which insists on valorizing the hegemonic rhetoric of the author.

Commentators agree that the context of the letter is one in which Jews and *Christianoi* were seen as seditious and as threats to colonial religious, cultural, and political Roman imperial "customs." The conversion of slave wo/men, freeborn ladies, and younger people, in which the master of the house did not convert already, constituted an offence against the "ancestral" laws and customs. According to these laws and customs the *pater familias*, like the emperor who was called the supreme Father of the empire (*pater patriae*), had absolute power over his subordinates in the household and determined the religion of its members. Hence, it was generally accepted as a matter of good civil order that slave wo/men, freeborn wo/men, and all other members of the household, practiced the religion of the master and lord of the house.

Since the letter writer is concerned with "honor," construes the "house of G*d" not as temple but as "household," advocates submission and the hegemonic ethos of "doing good," so that the recipients will not be attacked as wrong-doers, he advocates *accommodation* to the kyriarchal order of the household and empire for missionary purposes as long as it does not interfere with "Christian" calling. One could argue that the author understands the function of "Christian" calling as preserving messianic self-identity and praxis. However, such an interpretation does not square with his rhetoric of submission to the authorities and institutions of the empire.

Rather, this messianic ethos of the holy people of G*d stands in tension with the imperial ethos of submission and the socio-cultural hegemonic ethos of "honor and shame." This tension between the messianic ethos and the ethos of submission, which is inscribed in the letter, seems to have provoked a "rhetorical debate" in the community about what the "will of G*d" demands from them living under Roman rule. Slave wo/men for instance could have argued that it was "G*d's will" to be treated justly as members of G*d's elect people, rather than to suffer patiently the sexual abuse and mistreatment at the hands of their masters. Hence, it was justified to run away, if their masters treated them harshly. Freeborn well-to-do wives could have argued that it was their Christian calling to proclaim the "good news" to their Gentile husbands. If they could not convert them to the lifestyle of the elect people of G*d, it was the "will of G*d" to separate from them by divorcing them. They could have bolstered their argument with reference to Paul who supported the "marriage free" state of wo/men.

All of the members of the community could have argued that the covenant of G*d demanded that they separate from Gentile society, and resist Roman imperial culture, because their "low class" status, as non-citizens and migrants, had been changed in and through their conversion. They now were bound together in love and respect and formed a royal priesthood and holy nation, a temple of the Spirit. In consequence, they could not possibly pay obeisance to the Emperor, his governors, and other cultural institutional authorities—a political strategy also espoused by the book of Revelation.[65] Thus they could have advocated a separatist stance which would not totally avoid but might reduce harassment and suffering, since they would not have to mix daily with their Gentile neighbors. Such an interpretation is possible if one reads the arguments of 1 Peter as part of a broad-based debate in early Christian communities. To reconstruct the possible reactions of the recipients to the letter's arguments requires that one move from the level of text to that of the early Christian communities and their struggles with empire.

A reconstruction of these arguments is assisted by the recognition that the house-church was not congruent with the existing household. Since the conversion of entire households was not the norm in early Christianity, the Christian missionary movement potentially ran into conflicts with the existing order of the empire, because it converted *individuals* independently of their social status and function in the kyriarchal household. Christian mission might have caused social unrest because it admitted wives and slaves as well as daughters and sons into the house-church, even when the *pater familias* was still pagan and had not converted to Christianity. The pagan accusation that Christian mission was subversive, and destroyed kyriarchal household structures, was still being made in the second century.[66] This accusation was not a misunderstanding or slander but an accurate perception of the social implications of conversion to Christianity. The discourses of submission are therefore best understood as an attempt to mitigate the subversive impact that religious conversion may have had upon the kyriarchal order of household and society.

---

65. See Chapter 3 for this discussion.

66. See Margaret Y. MacDonald, "Early Christian Women Married to Unbelievers," in *A Feminist Companion to the Deutero-Pauline Epistles*, 14–28.

Independently of their fathers, husbands and masters, freeborn and slave wo/men held membership and gained leadership positions in the Christian = messianic movement. Even in the beginning of the second century, female and male slaves still expected their freedom to be purchased by the Christian community, as the letters of Ignatius and the Shepherd of Hermas document. Paul's letter to Philemon, which is the only Christian Testament writing addressed to a house-church, mentions a wo/man among the leadership of the church in Philemon's house.[67] In this letter Paul insists, employing all the means of ancient rhetoric, that Onesimus must be accepted into the house-church as a "beloved sibling," both as a Christian and as a human being.

The conversion of wo/men, slaves, and young people who belonged to the household of an unconverted *pater familias* constituted an infringement of the political order, for the kyriarchal order of the house was considered paradigmatic for the order of the empire. Since the kyriarchal *familia/domus* was the nucleus of the empire, conversion of the subordinated members of the house, who were supposed to share in the religion of the *pater familias*, constituted a subversive act.

The prescriptive household code trajectory attempted to ameliorate this subversion by asserting the congruence of the Christian ethos with that of kyriarchal house and state. This trajectory did not continue the ethos of the house-church, with its voluntary and collegial structures, but sought to modify it and bring it into line with the structures of kyriarchal family and imperial society. In doing so, the household code trajectory sought to kyriarchalize not only the early Christian ethos of "brotherhood," or better "siblinghood," of co-equality in community, but also the structures of the Christian community. However, the prescriptive character of the text, advocating the ethos of submission, indicates that such a process of kyriarchalization had not yet been accomplished by the beginning of the second century.

Now that historical-critical scholarship has exposed that the Christian Testament texts of submission exhibit a form of the Greco-Roman imperial ethos, and feminist post-colonial critical analyses have shown their destructive impact on wo/men and all subordinates, the challenge for the*logy and church is to articulate anew the early Christian vision and praxis of coequality in community and to incarnate it in Christian communities around the globe. In order to do

---

67. Later exegetes understood her to be Philemon's wife although she is not so designated by Paul.

so, we have to learn how to read the signs of "power over" and to deconstruct the inscriptions of empire in biblical texts, so that we are able to recognize how they are re-inscribed in the process of interpretation and proclamation. Listening to the lost voices of the recipients and hearing them into speech enables us to name the toxic substance of empire and begin the process of becoming conscious of empire, rather than internalizing the ethos of submission as advocated by 1 Peter. However, we can only do so in and through the hermeneutical process of detoxification and conscientization.

Decolonizing Practices of Conscientization—The "Dance" of Interpretation

In my rhetorical analysis of 1 Peter, I have underscored the kyriarchal inscriptions of empire and thus focused on the discourse of subordination and submission to the *kyrios*: the emperor, the slave master, and the husband. Those who are asked to submit—the whole community of resident aliens, slave wo/men, and elite wives—are told that they need to do so in order that they not give the impression of being subversive of the kyriarchal order of the Roman Empire. They must accept suffering only because they are accused of being Christians, i.e., belonging to the messianic community—but not because they may have threatened the kyriarchal order of empire and household. A hermeneutic of appreciation and consent will justify this scriptural rhetoric rather than critically investigating it. Critical investigation, in contrast, would dislodge its inscriptions of empire in and through the process of reading and proclamation.

In contrast to such a the*logical hermeneutics of appreciation and consent, a feminist spiraling process of decolonizing interpretation has as its goal to engender a critical process of detoxification and conscientization. For this reason, it does not approach the text with a hermeneutics of acceptance but rather with the critical feminist hermeneutical process of decolonizing the text and its the*logical rhetoric, through our experience, memory, and imagination.

A *hermeneutics of experience* begins not simply with individualized and privatized experience. Rather it starts with a critical reflection on how experience with a biblical text, such as 1 Peter, is shaped by the socio-political location of the interpreter. Hence, a hermeneutics of experience critically renders problematic the social-religious and intellectual locations not only of biblical interpreters but also those of biblical texts, and it does so in relation to global struggles for survival and well-being.

A hermeneutics of experience approaches a text by reflecting on readers' experience in relation to a text such as 1 Peter. It asks questions with respect to the experience inscribed in 1 Peter and that of those reading/hearing this text. What kinds of experiences does 1 Peter evoke? Does the experience inscribed in 1 Peter "resonate" with our own experiences? What kinds of experiences are inscribed in its arguments? What kinds of emotions and sentiments are engendered by the text? Whose experience stands in the center and whose experience is ruled out, silenced, or marginalized?

Further, it may be helpful to ask, does the letter's rhetoric of subordination resonate with our personal experiences? Are the arguments of the letter, which are such as to inculcate such subordination, familiar or are they alien to us? Which statements make us angry and which encourage us to struggle against injustice? Is 1 Peter preached or emphasized at certain occasions? How does its rhetoric of submission reinforce feminine behavior today? How does it re-inscribe prejudices of race and class which we have experienced? Are the statements of submission appealing to our imagination and why? Which statements have perpetrated the violence of empire in our experience?

In short, a hermeneutics of experience compels us to look at our own experience and reactions when reading 1 Peter. For example, post-biblical feminists engage in a purely deconstructive reading of such a scriptural text because their experiences with religion and the bible have been oppressive and self-alienating, whereas Jewish or Christian feminists have sought to develop a critique but also an appreciation of the bible because their experiences of biblical reading have not just been negative but have also inspired their self-affirmation and struggles for liberation.

To give another example: while, for instance, the oppressive social system of overt slavery seems no longer to exist today, covert slavery and international sex-trade are increasing and lucrative. Thousands of wo/men and children are forced or duped into it. Many will feel guilty fearing the wrath of G*d because of their sinfulness. Christian wo/men who have been socialized into a literalist understanding of the bible, as the word of G*d, will interpret 1 Peter as telling them that they should accept abuse, suffering, and beatings from their husbands as the will of G*d. When they experience domestic violence and abuse, they blame themselves and accept it as their fault. Many ministers when preaching this text underscore that we should suffer just as Christ has suffered.

These and similar questions seek to identify and name both our experiences when reading 1 Peter and those inscribed in the biblical text itself. Hence, it is important that a decolonizing reading help us to get in touch with such experiences—experiences of being silenced or asked to accept second-class citizenship, experiences of suffering and abuse—and help us critically to reflect on them in terms of a hermeneutics of domination.

A *hermeneutics of domination* investigates how the ethos and structures of empire are inscribed in the text by the author and how contemporary interpretations re-inscribe them. How are the experiences of wo/men mentioned in 1 Peter textualized, not only in terms of gender but also of race, class, ethnicity and religion? Such a hermeneutics does not only ask for the experiences of wo/men with a particular text such as 1 Peter and its interpretations. It also reflects on how our social, cultural, and religious location has shaped our experience with and our reaction to a particular biblical text such as 1 Peter. To that end, this hermeneutics engages the critical *analytics of domination* which I have discussed in the first part of this chapter. The kind of systemic analysis that we adopt will crucially determine our interpretation.

A hermeneutics of kyriarchal domination makes it possible for us to reflect critically on how relations of domination are operative, as socially-assigned categories and identity slots, which delimit the range of options within these group identity slots—options that we as individual wo/men can choose in constructing our unique identities as individuals. This hermeneutics also makes it possible to examine how we access cultural knowledges such as the bible. It helps us to explore how these different expressions of self- and group-identity are at work in the process of interpretation of a text such as 1 Peter. It also inspires us to seek for ways and possibilities inscribed in biblical and other cultural texts, so that we may transform identities that are articulated in terms of socially defined categories of domination.

For instance, we will read 1 Peter differently depending on whether we engage a Thomistic, Aristotelian, Freudian, capitalist, anarchist, postcolonial, womanist, gender, or critical feminist systemic analysis of domination. A feminist liberationist approach, however, prioritizes wo/men's struggles against multiplicative structures of oppression as hermeneutical frames and spaces from where to read. A systemic analysis of the socio-cultural and political-religious structures of domination seeks to identify not only contemporary situations of domination but also those inscribed in biblical texts. A critical feminist analytics of kyriarchy is particularly well placed to do this since it has been formulated precisely to investigate modern political structures of domination as well as the kyriarchal structures of antiquity inscribed in biblical texts.

With the help of such a critical feminist analytic, we first explore and articulate our own social location and participation in kyriarchal power relations. In so doing, we become conscious of how our experiences of reading biblical texts are constructed by kyriarchal relations of domination and how these relations of domination construct our self-identity, in terms of aspects that define our social locations, such as gender, race, class, religion, or nationalism. However, social location must not be mistaken for an identity category but rather is to be understood as a category that articulates our differential embeddedness in systems of domination.

Engaging this detoxifying strategy, one would ask questions on the level of the text such as: which Roman imperial socio-political and religious values does the rhetoric of 1 Peter articulate? Does its call to suffering as Christ has suffered, and to subordination as the foremothers have done, or to reflect imperial values that reinforce domination and exploitation? Does its rhetoric do so for all members of the community or does its meaning depend on the social location of those to whom it is addressed?

This hermeneutical strategy explores these historical-the*logical questions in the interest of contemporary meaning making and asks: into what kind of practices of empire and identity slots of domination and subordination are we socialized today? Did they provide the lenses with which we read the rhetoric of 1 Peter? How is the reading of 1 Peter shaped by kyriarchal socializations, privileges, and prejudices that inscribe systemic racism, hetero-sexism, class discrimination, and nationalism? How does this text function as ideological legitimization of the ethos of subordination? How do both legitimizations of kyriarchal domination—the christological legitimization of suffering and the ethical appeal to subordination—inculcate and legitimate collaboration in globalized oppression today? Hence a hermeneutics of suspicion is called for.

A *hermeneutics of suspicion*: As biblical readers, we are taught to approach the bible with a hermeneutics of respect, acceptance, consent, and obedience.[68] Instead of cultivating a hermeneutics of appreciation and consent, I have argued, a critical feminist interpretation for liberation must develop a

68. For instance, Elliott, 1 *Peter*, 599, insists that "we *must* [emphasis added] explore the Bible in its cultural context with an openness to the way that the good news of the past may continue to animate the good news in the present."

hermeneutics of suspicion that places on all biblical texts the warning, "Caution: could be dangerous to your health and survival." Texts such as "If a man lies with a male as with a woman, both of them have committed an abomination; they shall be put to death" (Lev 20:13) or "It was one of them, their very own prophet who said: 'Cretans are always liars, vicious brutes, lazy gluttons.' That testimony is true . . ." (Titus 1:12) cannot be approached with a hermeneutics of empathy, appreciation, and consent but must be approached with a hermeneutics of suspicion.

The primary task of a hermeneutics of suspicion is to disentangle the ideological functions of kyriocentric text and commentary. Yet, it must not be misunderstood as peeling away layers of debris in order to recover a pre-given ontological reality, which is understood in essentialist terms. Kyriocentric language, I have argued, does not cover up but constructs reality in a certain way and then mystifies its own constructions by naturalizing them. Hence, a hermeneutics of suspicion is concerned with the distorted ways of how wo/men's actual presences and practices are constructed and represented in and through kyriocentric language and media.

For that reason, a hermeneutics of suspicion problematizes kyriocentric language on both the level of text, and on the level of contemporary meaning making, because such language makes marginalized wo/men doubly invisible. For instance, today affirmative action job advertisements will invite "African Americans, Native Americans, Asian Americans and women to apply," language that suggests that the groups, "African Americans," "Native Americans," "Asian Americans" are only men and not also wo/men. How one understands kyriocentric language determines one's understanding of early Christianity and of our world today.

Since readers align themselves with the dominant voice represented by the kyriocentric text, a hermeneutics of suspicion critically analyzes such dominant strategies of meaning making. In addition, it draws out and makes manifest "masculine/feminine," "superior/inferior," "we/others" roles and values, which are inscribed in the text. Moreover, it engages in a conscious articulation of the ideological strategies of a text such as 1 Peter and makes apparent the text's interaction and resonance with our experience and cultural value-system. Finally, it seeks to determine and circumscribe the rhetorical situation and context in which the letter was formulated and in which it operates today.

For example, studies about "women in the Bible," often understand 1 Peter's admonitions to wives as the only ones that speak about wo/men because they take the kyriocentric text at face value. For this reason, they overlook that the admonitions to slaves are addressed also to wo/men. Hence, this reference must be read as addressed to slave wo/men since the generic masculine is usually used as inclusive. Thus, in a "normal" reading of the text that is not aware of kyriocentric language but unconsciously "naturalizes" grammatical gender, slave wo/men are erased from historical and contemporary consciousness. Or to give another example, 1 Peter names the community with the grammatically masculine term "brotherhood," although the admonition to freeborn wives indicates that wo/men were active members of the community.

A hermeneutics of suspicion does not only scrutinize the language of the text but also lays open the kyriarchal, the*logical tendencies inscribed in it and those re-inscribed by contemporary interpretations. For instance, it opens up to critical scrutiny the Christological legitimization of suffering, in the admonition to slave wo/men, or it points to the scriptural legitimization of the imperative, that wives be subordinate, even to unbelieving husbands.

A *hermeneutics of evaluation* presupposes and completes a hermeneutics of suspicion. It is necessary because texts always mean *in context*; they have a multiplicity of meanings. For this reason, this hermeneutic strategy seeks to assess the inscriptions of empire, in texts and traditions, as well as in contemporary discourses, in terms of a feminist liberationist scale of values. Just as a hermeneutics of suspicion, so also a hermeneutics of critical evaluation is difficult to practice for those interpreters who have been socialized into a hermeneutics of trust and/or obedience toward the texts of scripture.

Such a hermeneutics of evaluation does not take at face value the kyriocentric text and its claim to divine authority but rather evaluates it as to its ideological functions in the interest of domination. Emotionally, it might be difficult to engage in such a hermeneutics of evaluation, either because we have internalized biblical authority as unquestionable taboo or because our experiences with the bible have been positive and edifying. Hence, we need to work through our emotions, anxieties, and fears and to ask about what stake we have in upholding a hermeneutics of appreciation and consent before we can fruitfully engage in a hermeneutics of critical evaluation.

Accordingly, a hermeneutics of evaluation seeks to adjudicate the oppressive tendencies, as well as the liberatory possibilities, inscribed in biblical texts, their function in contemporary struggles for liberation, and their "resonance" with wo/men's experience. It does so not once and for all but has to do so again and again in particular social locations and situations.

A hermeneutics of evaluation has a double reference point. The first is *cultural-ideological*. Language and texts are not self-enclosed systems of signs but have performative power: either they legitimize or challenge power structures, serve to "naturalize" or to interrupt hegemonic world-views, or inculcate dominant or emancipatory values. For instance, Sheila Redmond has pointed out that such biblical values as suffering, forgiveness, purity, need for redemption, and obedience to authority figures, prevent recovery from child sexual abuse and continue to dis-empower their victims.[69] If such values which prevent recovery are espoused by a biblical text, they must be named and made conscious as kyriocentric values that perpetuate suffering and abuse. Consequently they must be judged for their possibly debilitating effects in particular situations where such abuse exists or is remembered. The key question of a hermeneutics of evaluation is: What does a text *do* to those who submit to its world of vision and values?

The second reference point for a hermeneutics of evaluation is *religious-the*logical*. As I have pointed out in the Introduction, in a Christian context biblical texts are understood and proclaimed as the Word of G*d. Canonization compels us to make sense out of scriptural texts in such a way that we can accept, consent, and submit to them. A hermeneutics of submission and consent understands canonical authority as kyriarchal authority that requires subordination. Such an understanding of canonical authority, in terms of the logic of kyriarchal identity, fosters exclusion and vilification of the other.

Yet, a hermeneutics of evaluation does not categorize biblical texts and traditions in a dualistic fashion either as oppressive or as emancipatory. Rather, it seeks to adjudicate again and again how biblical texts function in particular situations. Its criterion or standard of evaluation, the well-being of every wo/man (which includes the principle of human rights as wo/men's rights) must be established and reasoned out in terms of a systemic analysis of kyriarchal domination. For the*logical reasons, a hermeneutics of evaluation for proclamation insists that biblical religions must cease to preach kyriarchal texts as the "word of G*d," since by doing so we continue to proclaim G*d as legitimating kyriar-

---

69. Sheila Redmond, "Christian 'Virtues' and Recovery from Child Sexual Abuse," in *Christianity, Patriarchy and Abuse: A Feminist Critique*, eds. Joanne Carlson Brown and Carole R. Bohn (New York: Pilgrim, 1989), 70–88.

chal oppression. Instead, it argues, biblical religions must articulate visions of well-being that proclaim the Divine as a power for justice and well-being.

In order to adjudicate the ethical implications and impact of the rhetoric of subordination of 1 Peter and its effects in the past and in the present, we need a critical feminist scale of values and visions. Since such values are always context and theory dependent, they cannot be fixed once and for all but must be discussed and debated in each new situation. Therefore, biblical interpretation cannot do its work of detoxification without simultaneously engaging in a critical feminist the*logy and ethics. The academic disciplinary divisions between biblical studies, the*logy, ethics, and ritual, break down in emancipative practices of evaluation. Moreover, a hermeneutics of evaluation presupposes the vision of a world and church different from that of empire. We may not yet have experienced the realization of such a different world of well-being but it lives in our dreams and hopes that inspire us to continue the struggles for the well-being of all without exception. Consequently, we need not just detoxifying but also constructive practices that can envision alternatives to empire and domination.

A *hermeneutics of imagination*[70] searches for such egalitarian visions and seeks to "dream" a different world of justice and well-being. For the space of the imagination is that of freedom, a space in which boundaries are crossed, possibilities are explored, and time becomes relativized. What we cannot imagine, we will not have. As Toni Morrison so forcefully states in her novel, *Beloved*:

> She did not tell them to clean up their lives or to go and sin no more. She did not tell them they were the blessed of the earth, its inheriting meek or its glory bound pure. She told them that the only grace they could have was the grace they could imagine. That if they could not see it, they would not have it.[71]

The imagination is a space of memory and possibility where situations can be re-experienced and desires re-embodied. Because of our imaginative abilities, we can put ourselves into another person's position, relate to their feelings,

---

70. See David C. Robinson, ed., *God's Grandeur: The Arts and Imagination in Theology* (Maryknoll: Orbis, 2006).

71. Toni Morrison, *Beloved* (New York: Vintage, 2004), 88.

and participate in their deliberations and struggles. Because of the imagination we are able to conceive of change, of how situations can be altered. Historical imagination, like all other forms of imagination, is absolutely necessary for any knowledge of biblical texts and worlds.

A hermeneutics of imagination enables us to fill in the gaps and silences of the text. Reader-response criticism has pointed out that we "make meaning" in the process of reading by imaginatively filling in the gaps, fissures, and breaks in the text with reference to our experience and knowledge. Jewish hermeneutics, for instance, has imagined that the Shekhinah, the Divine Presence, dwells in the blank white spaces between the black letters. In the process of story telling or role playing, our imagination so-to-speak seeks to make present Divine Wisdom in the "blank spaces" between the slave wo/men in the community addressed by 1 Peter and our own lives. Retelling biblical stories and re-imagining biblical characters in creative imagination and play is a catalytic process that liberates us from the false images that we have made.

Such envisioning of an alternative reality is only possible if we have at least some experiences of it. Wo/men, who have experienced religion only as oppressive and discriminatory and not also as promoting justice and equality, cannot imagine its grace. This insight also applies to the level of text. If we do not discover visions of equality and well-being inscribed in biblical texts, we cannot imagine early Christian life and world differently. To discover the visions of justice, equality, dignity, love, community, and well-being that are also inscribed in biblical texts such as 1 Peter, one does not need to show that it is liberating, or to explain away or to deny the inscriptions of empire and domination in it.

Feminist interpretation might be able to imagine a different world to the imperial world advocated by 1 Peter if it focuses on those statements and visions that express a self-identity different from that of empire. Slave wo/men and wives who are told

> you are a chosen race, a royal priesthood, a holy nation, God's own people, in order that you may proclaim the mighty acts of God who called you out of darkness into his marvelous light. Once you were not a people, but now you are God's people. (2:9-10)

will have heard this message differently than elite propertied men, since kyriarchal culture told them that they were non-persons. Slave wo/men who understood themselves as a royal priesthood and chosen race might have claimed their new self-identity and argued that their conversion abolished their slave status. Freeborn wo/men, in turn, might have insisted on "proclaiming" in the community the great deeds of the One who had called them and therefore might have objected to living with husbands who did not heed the call. Thus, a hermeneutics of imagination results in a different historical memory and leads to a different historical reconstruction.

A *hermeneutics of re-membrance*[72] uses the tools of historiography to reconstruct the struggles of slave wo/men and freeborn wo/men, against kyriarchal domination and the violence of empire, which is inscribed in early Christian literature, in general, and 1 Peter in particular. It re-conceptualizes and rewrites early Christian history as feminist history and memory. It does so not from the perspective of the historical winners but from the perspective of those who struggled against the subjection of empire. By placing freeborn wo/men, slave wo/men, migrant wo/men, or sex workers at the center of its attention, our image of early Christianity changes, as well as our image of ourselves and of the church and world today.

Such a hermeneutics of remembrance uses constructive methods of re-visioning, insofar as it seeks not only for historical retrieval but also for a religious reconstitution of the world. It seeks these things in and through a recovery of the forgotten past both of wo/men's victimization and of our struggles for survival and well-being. With postmodern thinkers, this hermeneutics is fully conscious of the rhetoricity of its own re-constructions but nevertheless insists that such work of historical remembrance is necessary in support of wo/men's struggles for survival and transformation today. If it is a sign of oppression when a people does not have a written history, then feminists and other subaltern scholars cannot afford to eschew such rhetorical and historical re-constructive work.

In my own work, I have argued that a feminist historiography must replace the kyriocentric malestream models of world construction with a radical egalitarian model of re-membering. History writing can be likened to making a

---

72. See now also Alan Kirk and Tom Satcher, eds., *Memory, Tradition, and Text: Uses of the Past in Early Christianity* (Semeia 52; Atlanta: SBL, 2005) who seem not to know my book *In Memory of Her* and its theory of memory.

quilt, fitting all the bits and pieces of information into a new design and model. Thereby I have sought to open up the possibilities of wo/men's historical presence and awaken the capacity to envision alternatives to the kyriarchal past and its struggles. This requires new hermeneutical assumptions that can correct the kyriocentric tendencies of our historical sources.

- First, we cannot take the kyriocentric text at face value but must assume that wo/men were present and active in history until proven otherwise. In order to displace the kyriocentric dynamic of the biblical text in its literary and historical contexts, we need to read the text against the grain. For instance, since the grammatical form of "slave" is masculine, it is usually assumed that 1 Peter speaks only of slave men. Hence, we have to read the kyriocentric text of 1 Peter in an inclusive fashion unless it is explicitly stated that slave wo/men were not present.
- Texts and injunctions such as 1 Peter 3:1-6, which seek to censure or limit wo/men's behavior, must be read as prescriptive rather than as descriptive of reality. If wo/men are forbidden a certain activity, we can safely assume that they might actually have so much engaged in it that it became threatening to the kyriarchal order.
- Texts and information such as 1 Peter must be contextualized not only in their variegated cultural and religious environments but also in terms of the kyriarchal structures of domination. They must be reconstructed not only in terms of the dominant ethos of the Roman Empire but also in terms of alternative social movements for change, such as slave revolts, Jewish messianic movements, or the early Christian movements.
- In order to read the text against the grain, we need to re-contextualize kyriocentric texts and sources within a socio-political-religious historical model of reconstruction that aims at making the subordinated and marginalized "others" visible, and their repressed arguments and silences "audible" again. Hence, the "chasm" that historical positivism has constructed between contemporary readers and the biblical text needs to be overcome, if we seek to recover wo/men's religious history and the memory of their victimization, struggle, and accomplishments as wo/men's heritage for today.

In sum, to remember is to assert historical existence and to claim historical subjectivity. Such historical remembrance recaptures biblical traditions, such as 1 Peter, as wo/men's traditions of struggle, survival, and vision. It reclaims wo/men's historical heritage. History writing, envisioned as "quilting" feminist history, is best understood as a transformative praxis. Thus all seven detoxifying practices of interpretation have as their goal transformation and change.

A *hermeneutics of transformation* is at work in all the preceding hermeneutical moves and works as the driving force and power in a decolonizing process of interpretation. It compels us to read the inscriptions of empire and domination in biblical texts in order to change kyriarchal consciousness. To that end, it explores avenues and possibilities for changing and transforming relations of domination inscribed in texts, traditions, and everyday life. Such work stands accountable to those wo/men who struggle at the bottom of the kyriarchal pyramid of discriminations and dominations. It thereby seeks to articulate religious and biblical studies as a site of social, political, and religious transformation.

When seeking future visions and transformations of empire, we can only extrapolate from present experience, which is always already determined by past experience. Hence, we have to analyze the past and the present, biblical texts and our world, in order to articulate creative visions and transcending imaginations for a new humanity, global ecology, and religious community. Yet, only if we remain committed to work for a different, more just future will our imagination and our struggles be able to transform the past and present limitations of our vision. To deconstruct and re-imagine biblical visions is to reclaim the biblical power of transformation. Biblical texts have the power to evoke potent emotions and creative responses and thereby create a sense of community necessary to sustain contemporary visions and struggles for a different society, church, and world.

I have suggested in this chapter that a critical rhetorical feminist method and hermeneutical process is best understood as a process of detoxifying the inscriptions of empire in scripture and in our own consciousness. A detoxifying process of interpretation challenges us to become the*-ethically sophisticated readers by reflecting on our own socio-political locations and functions in global structures of empire. At the same time, it empowers us to struggle for a more just and radical-democratic society and religion. Such an interpretive process is not restricted to Christian canonical texts but can be and has been used successfully by scholars of other religious traditions and scriptures. Moreover, it is not restricted to the biblical scholar as expert reader. Rather, it calls all of us to become transformative and engaged biblical interpreters. It has been used in graduate education, in parish discussions, in college classes, and in work with illiterate wo/men.

In and through such a critical rhetorical process of interpretation and deliberation, biblical texts such as 1 Peter can be critically investigated and become sites of struggle and conscientization. Patricia Hill Collins has dubbed such a praxis of change and transformation *visionary pragmatism*.[73] Feminist visionary pragmatism points to an alternative vision of the world but does not prescribe a fixed goal and end-point for which it then claims universal truth.

In such a process of imaginative pragmatism, one never arrives but always struggles on the way. This process reveals how current actions are part of a larger, meaningful struggle. It demonstrates that ethical and truthful visions of self-affirmation and community cannot be separated from the struggles on their behalf. One takes a stand by constructing new knowledge and new interpretations. While vision can be conjured up in the historical imagination, pragmatic action requires that one remain responsive to the injustices of everyday life. If religion and biblical interpretation are worth anything, they must inspire such visionary pragmatism in the everyday struggles for justice and the well-being of all.

In the context of the exploitation and domination of today's global empire, Christians must reject the the*logical, scriptural claims of the imperial pattern of submission because of its oppressive effects on the life of wo/men and other subordinated peoples. A feminist Scriptural hermeneutics has as its canon the liberation of *all* wo/men from oppressive structures, kyriarchal institutions, and internalized imperial values. A feminist decolonizing critical interpretive practice that is committed to the emancipatory struggles of wo/men and the whole church, therefore, insists that the ethos and praxis of coequality in community must transform the kyriarchal inscriptions of empire in Christian scriptures, the*logies, and consciousness, if wo/men and the whole Christian community are to contribute to a radical democratic egalitarian future of well-being for all of creation.

73. Hill Collins, *Fighting Words*, 187–200.

Chapter 6

The Rhetoric of Empire and G*d[1] Talk: Decolonizing the Divine[2]

In the previous chapter, we have seen how the ethos of empire (kyriarchy) shapes the scriptural ethos of subordination. In this chapter, I will explore how this scriptural rhetoric of empire has determined our speaking about the Divine. It has not only been the Roman Empire but also successive empires of the Near East that have determined biblical G*d language and imagination. G*d is envisioned as a great King, heavenly Monarch, Lord of Lords, avenging Warrior and all-powerful Father who, in imperial splendor, is ruling heaven and earth and demanding absolute obedience and obeisance from His subjects. Whereas this imperial G*d language has been used in the past to legitimate monarchy and colonial expansion and to reject democracy as against G*d's will, today it is promulgated not so much in the political as in the religious-liturgical realm and thus functions as one of the "technologies of the self" that foster kyriarchal internalizations of empire. Consequently, how to imagine and speak about the Divine has become a central the*logical question in modernity and postmodernity.[3]

In their comprehensive article on "G*d," Gordon Kaufman and Francis Schüssler Fiorenza have traced the established white elite Western male G*d-discourse. Even though they do not explicitly define their approach as rhetorical, they are clearly concerned with the rhetoricity[4] of all discourses about G*d.

---

1. See footnote 6, Chapter 1: Introduction.
2. I draw here on my book, *The Open House of Wisdom: Critical Feminist Theological Explorations* (Tokyo: Shinkyo Shuppansha, 2005) which has appeared only in Japanese.
3. Unfortunately I received the uncorrected proof of Mayra Rivera, *The Touch of Transcendence: A Postcolonial Theology of God* (Louisville: Westminster John Knox, 2007) which will be published in October, too late to engage the book here.
4. This expression is derived from John Bender and David E. Wellbery, eds., *The Ends of*

They begin by analyzing the use of the word "G*d" in contemporary English and end by arguing that studies in religion ought to focus on the interaction of G*d-talk with its socio-political, historical locations. In this western kyriocentric, i.e., elite male-centered tradition, they single out four Christian discourses about G*d which can be distinguished by their different locations: the biblical-mythological, the philosophical-ontological, the modern-subjectivist, and the postmodern discourse of negative the*logy.

In postmodernity, we have become more and more conscious that all discourses about the Divine[5]—including those of the bible—are socially conditioned and politically interested. Critical feminist, black, latina, indigenous, or postcolonial studies have radically questioned the rhetoric of those white elite malestream the*logical discourses that have spoken about the Divine in masculinist terms as He or named G*d in the interest of empire and the powerful.[6] It is therefore necessary to investigate the practices of such G*d-talk as rhetorical practices and to inquire into the socio-political rules and contextualizations that have constructed G*d-talk, rather than approaching the*legein in abstract philosophical or the*logical terms.

The task of the*legein in the proper sense is therefore best positioned not in the sphere of metaphysics and ontology but in that of rhetorics, i.e., communicative practice. To say that all language about G*d and all knowledge of the world is rhetorical means to assert that all discourses about the Divine are articulated in specific socio-political situations, by particular people, with certain interests in mind, and for a certain audience with whom they share cultural codes and religious traditions. G*d-discourses are not just rhetorical in the sense of persuasive address, but they are also a form of ideological communication, which is always enmeshed in power relations.

Rhetoric: History, Theory, Practice (Stanford, Ca.: Stanford University Press, 1990), 25: "Rhetoric today is neither a unified doctrine nor a coherent set of discursive practices. Rather it is a trans-disciplinary field of practice and intellectual concern. . . . The classical rhetorical tradition rarified speech and fixed it within a gridwork of limitations: it was a rule-governed domain whose procedures themselves were delimited by the institutions that organized interaction and domination in traditional European society. Rhetoricality, by contrast, is bound to no specific set of institutions. . . . it allows for no explanatory meta-discourse that is not already itself rhetorical. Rhetoric is no longer the title of a doctrine and practice, nor a form of cultural memory; it becomes instead something like the condition of our existence."

5. For biblical studies see, e.g., Bernard J. Lee, S.M., *Jesus and the Metaphors of God: The Christs of the New Testament* (New York: Paulist, 1993).

6. See Karen M. Armstrong, *A History of God: The 4000-Year Quest of Judaism, Christianity, and Islam* (New York: Ballantine, 1993).

Accordingly, the*logy must focus on the rhetoricity of all language about the Divine, especially that of sacred scripture. In problematizing how G*d is named in the bible and in the*logy, feminist decolonizing inquiry therefore has to move from a philosophical-ontological to a socio-political rhetorical understanding and construction of G*d-discourse. It needs to uncover the hidden frames of meaning that determine malestream as well as feminist and postcolonial discourses about the Divine.

Rhetorical analysis assumes that language not only produces meaning but also affects reality.[7] Moreover, all communication circulates between a speaker and an audience who are both historically and socially located. Hence, a critical rhetorical analysis has to investigate the structures of domination that have produced the exclusion and marginalization of wo/men[8] from the Divine. With liberation the*logies, it insists that the central the*logical question today is not the modern question of whether G*d exists but the ethical-political question as to what kind of G*d religious communities and their scriptures proclaim. Is this kind of G*d one that legitimates empire, exploitation, injustice, and oppression or is it a G*d inspiring liberation and well-being?

Do scriptures proclaim an almighty ruler G*d of injustice and dehumanization or a G*d of liberation and well-being, a G*d of domination, or a G*d of salvation and flourishing? Do they speak about a G*d who sides with the poor, consisting of wo/men and children dependent on wo/men, or do they speak about the Almighty Lord who is aligned with those who wield the oppressive powers of empire? How is our language about the Divine shaped by and how, in turn, does it shape our social location? Who is the subject of G*d-talk and in whose interest does it take place? These questions are intensified in a global contemporary context by the experience of multiculturalism and by growing inter-religious awareness.

In short, the task of the*logy at large is a critical delineation, reflection, and evaluation of the "rhetoric of G*d," or of how scriptures, traditions, and believers speak about G*d and how our practices of *the*legein* shape our self-understanding, worldviews, and social-political relations.[9] Such a critical femi-

---

7. See Jane Tompkins, "The Reader in History: The Changing Shape of Literary Response," in *Reader-Response Criticism: From Formalism to Poststructuralism* (Baltimore, Md,: The Johns Hopkins University Press, 1980), 201–32.

8. See footnote 21, Chapter 1: Introduction.

9. See Terence E. Fretheim, "Is the Biblical Portrayal of God Always Trustworthy?" in

nist, decolonizing mapping and evaluation of biblical texts and their G*d-rhetoric with its the*logical values and visions, I have argued in the first chapter, does not presuppose that the bible is the unmediated word of G*d. Rather, it recognizes that G*d's revelation is mediated not only in and through human, mostly elite male, language but also through the political language of empire and domination. Such a process of critical the*-ethical reflection is engaging in a hermeneutical rhetoric of emancipation in an ongoing critical-constructive process of "doing" the*logy.[10]

If language and images for G*d say more about how those who use them envision the Divine than about Divinity itself, and about how their society and church do so, then biblical the*logy's proper task is to engage in a permanent critical analysis of all discourses about G*d inscribed in scripture. Whereas feminist the*logy has problematized androcentric—or better kyriocentric—language, postcolonial the*logy investigates the imperial structures inscribed in scripture and their Divine legitimizations.

To outline the work of such critical analysis, I will *first* sketch how feminists address the problem of androcentric or kyriocentric, i.e., male or lord centered G*d-language. While feminist analysis in general emphasizes the issue of gendered language and discusses the question of the Goddess, liberationist and postcolonial feminist studies, as I will show in a *second* step, underscore that G*d-language is not just androcentric but kyriocentric or elite male centered, and that in Revelation it functions as anti-language. In a *third* step I will approach the problem of masculine G*d language from a different angle and review the scholarly discussion on monotheism in order to show how this debate is determined by an ontological theoretical model that opposes the constructs *Monotheism-Polytheism* in a dualistic way. This dualistic model, which was constructed in the interests of colonialism, obscures the fact that both monotheism and polytheism have sanctioned imperial kyriarchal power. Finally, I will propose *three* strategies for a decolonizing feminist speaking about the divine. The *first* is to identify biblical G*d language that does not re-inscribe the kyriocentric language of empire whereas the *second strategy* engages the method of

---

Terence E. Fretheim and Karlfried Fröhlich, *The Bible As Word of God in a Postmodern Age* (Minneapolis, Minn.: Fortress Press, 1998), 97–112.

10. See my books *But She Said*; *Jesus: Miriam's Child and Sophia's Prophet*; and *Sharing Her Word*, for the elaboration of this approach.

reflective mythology[11] to open up the figure of Divine Wisdom as Kannon/Kuan Yin that draws on Asian traditions. Finally I introduce a differential movement engaging the four hermeneutic moves—the *via negativa, analogica, eminentia,* and *practica*—of traditional the*logy in order to destabilize and keep in motion any and all speech about the Divine.

Feminist Critique of Androcentric G*d Language

The feminist discussion of G*d language[12] has two focal points: One is the question of how to speak about the Divine in an andro-kyriocentric language system that uses masculine terms, such as "man" and "he," both in a gender specific and in a gender inclusive way. The other area of feminist the*logical inquiry is the rediscovery of the Goddess. Both areas of inquiry are controverted and their results are challenged not just by traditional the*logians but also by feminists themselves. I will focus here on these two areas of feminist attempts to reformulate G*d language in inclusive or feminine terms, because they are instructive for the methodological problems which "speaking about G*d" encounters, in general.

First: Androcentric—that is, male-centered—language has been a central problem not only for Western feminist the*logy but also for Asian feminist the*logy. Although Asian languages are more gender-inclusive or are "differently gendered" than Western languages, as Satoko Yamaguchi has pointed out, the question of

> truly inclusive language and imagination in our religious traditions is a
> crucial and urgent issue to which we cannot but give priority in an unjust
> world. It is because the kyriarchal religious imagination inscribes and nat-
> uralizes kyriarchal values into the deep subconscious levels of our minds.

11. For this concept see Hans Conzelmann, "The Mother of Wisdom," in *The Future of Our Religious Past*, Festschrift R. Bultmann, ed. James M. Robinson (London: SCM Press, 1971); and my article "Wisdom Mythology and the Christological Hymns of the New Testament" in *Aspects of Wisdom in Judaism and Early Christianity*, ed. Robert L. Wilken (Notre Dame, Ind.: Notre Dame University Press, 1975), 17–42, which introduced this notion into the feminist the*logical discussion.

12. See especially Rebecca Chopp, *The Power to Speak: Feminism, Language and God* (New York: Crossroad, 1989).

Thus it is influential not only on our relationship with other people as well as with G*d but also on the formation of our self-identities, our very being at the core.[13]

The often heated discussions and violent reactions[14] around inclusive language translations of the bible or the liturgy indicate how deeply ingrained is masculine G*d language and imagery in Christian self-understanding.[15] Although scripture seeks to avoid the essentialist reification of the Divine as male by prohibiting any image making of G*d, biblical and traditional G*d-language is predominantly masculine written in andro-kyriocentric language and addressed to and written, as well as interpreted, by people in kyriarchal cultures.

Even though the bible can speak of G*d in feminine terms and use female images, biblical G*d-language is overwhelmingly androcentric and its patriarchal bias is all pervasive. G*d acts like a typical Near Eastern potentate and Roman emperor who destroys not only Israel's enemies but also Israel, which like the church is figured as feminine although its leadership is traditionally masculine. This overlord is said to demand the wholesale destruction of cities and empires, which are figured in feminine language and imagery. In His wrath He sends deluges and hailstorms, draughts and pestilence in order to destroy the people and the earth. G*d also can be pictured as an abuser of children (cf. Gen 22) and as a sexual voyeur. For instance, in order to punish David, G*d is said to have given over the king's wo/men to another man for the explicit purpose of rape (2 Sam 12:11). Or, to give another example: G*d threatens "to lift up Israel's skirts for exposing her genitals." (Isa 3:17; Ezra 16: 35-43; 23:9-10, 28-30).[16] In the parables of Jesus G*d is envisioned as a harsh slave master who orders severe beatings and punishments.

13. Satoko Yamaguchi, "Father Image of G*d and Inclusive Language: A Reflection in Japan," in *Toward a New Heaven and a New Earth: Essays in Honor of Elisabeth Schüssler Fiorenza*, ed. Fernando Segovia (Maryknoll, N.Y.: Orbis, 2003), 219–24, esp., 223 ff., n.55.

14. See for instance, Susan Brooks Thistlethwaite, *Sex, Race, and God: Christian Feminism in Black and White* (New York: Crossroad, 1989), 109ff.

15. See for example, Donald Bloesch, *The Battle for the Trinity: The Debate Over Inclusive God Language* (Ann Arbor, Mich: Sevant, 1985); Alvin Kimel, ed., *Speaking the Christian God* (Grand Rapids, Mich.: Eerdmans, 1992); and Werner Neuer, *Man and Woman in Christian Perspective* (London: Hodder & Stoughton, 1990).

16. Fretheim, "Is the Biblical Portrayal of God Always Trustworthy?"

This biblical G*d-discourse[17] is cast in metaphorical, symbolic, mythological, analogical but not in philosophical-ontological language. The bible speaks
in a multiplicity of images that are not always gendered but draw on all kinds of
patri-kyriarchal experiences and cultural concepts. Moreover, the bible uses not
only human imagery for speaking about the Divine, but draws on the experience
of the whole creation. G*d is viewed as rock, light, roaring lion, water, love, as
acting and relating, threatening and consoling, as G*d "with us" and "over and
against us," as Elohim and Yahweh. Biblical the*logy insists on the holiness and
total otherness, as well as on the likeness and embeddedness, of the Divine in
human history. It uses the symbolic worlds and belief-systems of its surrounding cultures and at the same time insists that it is idolatry to make images of
G*d. It knows that human language and images are not able to comprehend
and express the Holy One, although believers are always tempted to reduce G*d
to limited and distorted human comprehension and conceptualization.

Despite these cautions, biblical discourses about G*d have not succeeded
in avoiding the danger of the*logically reifying biblical G*d-language, in terms
of the Western sex/gender system, because they have used predominantly masculine language, metaphors, and images in their G*d-talk. The*logy re-inscribes
such grammatically masculine biblical G*d-language when it understands, for
instance, the discourse about Divine Wisdom, or the Shekinah, in metaphorical
terms while at the same time it construes the masculine discourse about G*d,
the Father and Lord, as descriptive or ontological language that has a one-to-one
meaning which adequately expresses G*d's nature and being. Yet such reification
of masculine G*d-language obscures that biblical language is not descriptive but
symbolic-metaphoric. According to both Jewish and Christian tradition, human
language about G*d must always be understood as metaphorical or analogical
language. G*d-language is symbolic, metaphoric, and analogous because human
language never can comprehend and speak adequately about Divine reality.

Biblical translation,[18] therefore, has to adopt a theory of language that does
not subscribe to linguistic determinism and does not naturalize grammatical

---

17. However, one cannot solve the the*logical problem which such G*d discourse poses by
claiming in a supersessionist anti-Jewish fashion that the OT G*d is violent whereas the NT G*d
is love since both the OT/Hebrew Bible and the NT/Christian Testament constitute Christian
Sacred Scripture.

18. For the problem of translation see Randall C. Bailey and Tina Pippin, *Race, Class and
the Politics of Bible Translation*, Semeia 76, (Atlanta, Ga.: Scholars, 1996); Athalya Brenner and

gender by identifying it with actual wo/men or as referring to a male G*d. Androcentric language is not to be understood as "natural" propositional language which describes and reflects reality but rather as a grammatical classification system that constructs reality in kyriarchal terms. Conventional language is not only produced but also regulated and perpetrated in the interest of kyriarchal society and culture. If language is not a reflection of reality but rather a social cultural linguistic system, then the relationship between language and reality is not fixed as an essential "given." Rather it is always constructed anew in discourse.

This nature of language is especially true when language speaks about Divine reality since transcendent Divine reality cannot be adequately comprehended or expressed in human language. The inability to comprehend and express who G*d is prohibits any absolutizing of symbols, images, and names for G*d, be they grammatically masculine, feminine, or neuter. Such an absolute relativity of the*logical G*d language demands, on the contrary, a proliferation of symbols, images, and names in order to express Divine reality which is humanly incomprehensible and unspeakable.

If language is a social-cultural convention and a tool of power but not a reflection of reality,[19] then one must the*logically reject any essentialist identification not only of grammatical gender and Divine reality but also of grammatical gender and human reality. Not all languages have three grammatical genders or identify natural gender with grammatical gender. Masculine or feminine identity is not defined by biological gender but it is constructed in and through linguistic, social, cultural, religious, or ethnic conventions.[20] Biological wo/manhood and cultural femininity have had quite a different meaning, for instance, for a freeborn wo/man or a slave wo/man in Athens, for a queen and her serfs in medieval Europe or for the white lady of a plantation and her black slave wo/man in North America.[21] Hence, feminist the*logy must pay attention

---

Jan Willem van Henten, *Bible Translation on the Threshold of the Twenty-First Century* (Sheffield: Sheffield Academic, 2002).

19. On androcentric language, see the diverse contributions in Deborah Cameron, ed., *The Feminist Critique of Language: A Reader* (New York: Routledge, 1998).

20. See, e.g., Ean Beck, *The Cult of the Black Virgin* (Boston, Mass.: Arkana, 1985); Ivan Van Sertima, ed., *Black Women in Antiquity* (New Brunswick, N.J.: Transaction, 1988); Martin Bernal, *Black Athena: The Afroasiatic Roots of Classical Civilization* (New Brunswick, N.J.: Rutgers University Press, 1988); China Galland, *Longing for Darkness: Tara and the Black Madonna* (New York: Penguin, 1990).

21. Elizabeth V. Spelman, *Inessential Woman: Problems of Exclusion in Feminist Thought*

not only to gender but also to the ideology of the White Lady.[22] Wo/men are defined not just by gender but also by race, class, and other structures of domination that inflect gender.[23]

In short, the debate around inclusive biblical and liturgical translation requires that biblical interpretation and the*logy reflect on the inadequacy of andro-kyriocentric G*d language and problematize it. It compels us to continue the struggle not only with conventional masculine language for G*d but also with the exclusivist authoritarian functions and implications of such language. Feminist the*logy must be joined, I have argued, by malestream the*logy in re-articulating the symbols, images, and names of the biblical G*d and it must do so in light of the experiences of those wo/men who struggle at the bottom of the kyriarchal pyramid. Hence, not only must masculine ossified and absolutized language about G*d and Christ be radically questioned and undermined but the Western cultural sex/gender system needs also to be deconstructed. Only then will the*logy be able to open up biblical possibilities and visions of liberation and well-being[24] which have not yet been historically realized.

How is it possible at all to think of and to name the Divine differently in a male-dominated culture and society?[25] How can one speak of G*d in such a fashion that the biblical symbols for G*d no longer legitimate kyriarchal relations of domination nor continue to inculcate the cultural myth of the masculine and feminine in the*logical terms? How can one correct the masculine tradition of G*d language and ritual in such a way that wo/men can understand ourselves the*logically as paradigmatic manifestations of the Divine Image?

(Boston, Mass.: Beacon, 1988), has graphically depicted these relationships in antiquity and in the modern world.

22. For the elaboration of this expression, see H.V. Carby, "On the Threshold of Women's Era: Lynching, Empire and Sexuality," in *Race, Writing, and Difference*, ed. Henry L. Gates (Chicago, Ill.: University of Chicago Press, 1986), 301–28. See also the article by Kwok Pui-lan, "The Image of the White Lady: Gender and Race in Christian Mission," in *The Special Nature of Women*, eds. Anne Carr and Elisabeth Schüssler Fiorenza (Philadelphia, Pa.: Trinity International, 1991), 19–27.

23. See Susan Thistlethwaite, *Sex, Race, and God*.

24. See for instance, the practical exercises and liturgical rituals in Cady, Ronan and Taussig, eds., *Wisdom's Feast: Sophia in Study and Celebration* (New York: Harper & Row, 1989).

25. On this question, see the important work of Sallie McFague, *Models of God: Theology for an Ecological Age* (Philadelphia, Pa.: Fortress Press, 1987) and idem, *The Body of God: An Ecological Theology* (Minneapolis, Minn.: Fortress Press, 1993).

How can one undo the soteriological valorization of the cultural masculine and feminine constructs in Christian the*logy?

Second: Feminist the*logy has sought to address these questions by introducing female/feminine images into Christian G*d language.[26] It has done so both by re-valorizing traces of feminine imagery in the bible, such as those of Divine Wisdom, and by recovering lost Goddess traditions.[27] Jewish feminists in turn have re-claimed the female figure of the Shekinah particularly as She was elaborated in Kabbalah whereas Christian the*logians have focused on re-articulating the Trinity in terms of relationality[28] and female imagery. Feminists of various persuasions have begun to celebrate the female Divine in liturgy and art. They have sought to re-articulate traditional formulas and rituals not just in inclusive terms but in terms of wo/men's experience.

To that end, neo-pagan and post-biblical thealogians have revived Goddess cult and Goddess traditions.[29] They have postulated that patriarchal warrior societies have been preceded by peaceful matrilineal societies in which the Goddess was worshipped. They have rediscovered not only so-called prehistoric Goddesses but also sought to free those of classic Rome, Greece, and Egypt from their embeddedness in patriarchal myth. Feminists working in the area of comparative religion have made known to Western audiences the Goddesses of Asia, the Americas, Africa, and those of indigenous peoples around the world. In her by now classic essay "Why Women need the Goddess?" Carol Christ has summed up this quest for the Goddess as a quest for spiritual female power.[30]

---

26. See the overview by Linda A. Moody, *Women Encounter God: Theology Across the Boundaries of Difference* (Maryknoll, N.Y.: Orbis, 1996).

27. Silvia Schroer, "Die göttliche Weisheit und der nachexilische Monotheismus," in *Der eine Gott und die Göttin: Gottesvorstellung des biblischen Israel im Horizont feministischer Theologie*, eds. Marie-Theres Wacker und Erich Zenger (Freiburg: Herder, 1991), 151–83.

28. See Catherine Mowry LaCugna, "God in Communion With Us," in *Freeing Theology: The Essentials of Theology in Feminist Perspective*, ed. Catherine Mowry LaCugna (San Francisco: Harper San Francisco, 1993), 83–114; Elizabeth A. Johnson, *She Who Is: The Mystery of God in Feminist Theological Discourse* (New York: Crossroad, 1992) and Michelle A. Gonzales, *Created in God's Image: An Introduction to Feminist Theological Anthropology* (Maryknoll: Orbis, 2007).

29. See Carol P. Christ, *The Rebirth of the Goddess: Finding Meaning in Feminist Spirituality* (Reading, Mass.: Addison-Wesley, 1998), and among her other works, her very important book *She Who Changes: Re-Imagining the Divine in the World* (New York: Palgrave, 2003).

30. Carol P. Christ, "Why Women Need the Goddess: Phenomenological, Psychological, and Political Reflections," in *Women Spirit Rising: A Feminist Reader in Religion*, eds. Carol Christ & Judith Plaskow (San Francisco, Calif.: Harper & Row, 1979), 273–87.

My own work has introduced and elaborated the Wisdom-Sophia tradition as one but *not as the sole* early Christian discourse that might open up until now unfulfilled possibilities for feminist the*logical reflection.[31] Jewish sophialogy that is founded by the interactive meaning making of apocalyptic, prophetic and wisdom traditions, valorizes life, creativity, and well-being in the midst of injustice and struggle. The elements of the biblical Wisdom traditions—open-endedness, inclusivity, and cosmopolitan emphasis on creation spirituality as well as practical insight—have been especially attractive not only to feminists but also to Asian liberation the*logical reflections, as I will show in the last section of this chapter.

Yet, it also must be pointed out that feminist G*d-talk is always in danger of succumbing to "romantic" cultural notions of femininity.[32] Thereby it is in danger of re-inscribing the Western cultural androcentric gender binary, which either devalues wo/men and femininity or idealizes femininity as representing superior transcendent and salvific qualities. In extolling the femininity of Wisdom or of the Goddess, such a feminist binary-gender approach cannot but re-inscribe Western cultural systems of domination in the*logical terms, insofar as it divinizes the hegemonic gender ideology of cultural femininity that is shaped after the image and likeness of the [White] Lady. Whenever the*logy is positioned within a framework of essential gender dualism, it cannot but reproduce this ideological frame.[33]

In order to avoid this pitfall, I have argued, one must explicitly read against the grain of the cultural framework of the feminine[34] and shift the discussion of a Divine female figure from the ontological-metaphysical level to a linguistic symbolic rhetorical level of reflection. Such a shift is justified insofar as divine female as well as divine father language are not unified the*logical discourses about the essence and true being of G*d, but rather discourses embodying a variegated "reflective mythology."[35] The grammatically masculine language,

31. See my books, *Jesus: Miriam's Child and Sophia's Prophet*, 131–63; and *Sharing Her Word*, 137–60. Elizabeth A. Johnson, *She Who Is*, builds on this work and develops it in systematic the*logical terms.

32. See the roundtable discussion, Catherine Madsen et al., "If God is God, She Is Not Nice," *Journal of Feminist Studies in Religion* 5/1 (1989): 103–18.

33. As a case in point, see, e.g., Christa Mulack, *Jesus der Gesalbte der Frauen* (Stuttgart: Kreuz Verlag, 1987).

34. See the excellent dissertation of Linda Miller, *Divinity, Difference, and Democracy: A Critical Materialist Reading of Luce Irigaray's Politics of Incarnation* (Harvard Divinity School, 2006).

35. For this expression, see my article "Wisdom Mythology and the Christological Hymns

which determines ancient Wisdom discourses and modern biblical interpretation, the*logy as well as thealogy, has a difficult time speaking adequately of the Goddess or Divine Wisdom, considering the established "preconstructed" kyriocentric framework of Western language systems. For instance, biblical language about Divine Wisdom struggles to avoid turning Her into a second feminine deity who is subordinate to the masculine deity. In so doing it also struggles against the the*logical reification of monotheism in terms of western cultural elite male hegemony. When speaking about the biblical G*d, Christian liturgies and malestream the*logies have succumbed to this danger of reification, insofar as they have used predominantly masculine language, metaphors, and images for speaking of the Divine.

In short, it is neither patriarchal God nor matriarchal Goddess, neither the masculine nor the feminine, neither Divine Fatherhood nor complementary Motherhood that redeems and saves. Rather all kyriocentric symbols—masculinity and femininity, pale and dark skin, domination and subordination, relationality and vulnerability, wealth and exploitation, nationalism and colonialism—are to be carefully tested in an ongoing feminist ideology critique. Such a decolonizing feminist ideology critique may take its cues neither from established dogmatics nor from cultural constructs of the feminine. Instead it must attempt to name the negative as well as on the positive G*d experiences of wo/men under imperial conditions and critically reflect on them. For doing so, it needs to sustain a permanent critical self-reflexivity, which is able to reject not only male language about G*d that inculcates dominant masculinity, or the ideal feminine, but also the language of imperial domination that projects not only the Western cultural sex-gender system but also the mentality and imagination of empire into heaven.

---

of the New Testament" in *Aspects of Wisdom in Judaism and Early Christianity*, 17–42. I became intellectually fascinated with the Wisdom tradition in the Christian Testament, in the context of the 1973 Rosenstil seminar on Wisdom in Early Judaism and Christianity sponsored by the Department of Theology at the University of Notre Dame. Experientially, I had encountered the Wisdom tradition in the image of Mary as the "seat of Wisdom" (*sedes Sapientiae*) in Trier and elsewhere.

Kyriocentric G*d Language: The Language of Empire

While feminist studies have predominantly focused on androcentric language, postcolonial studies have centered on colonial situations and political ideologies but have not paid much attention to the mechanisms of kyriocentric language and imagery. As Kwok Pui-lan points out, many Asian the*logians are primarily concerned with issues of neocolonialism, militarism, or sex-tourism rather than with biblical or liturgical sexist language.[36] Yet, such a privileging of neocolonialist issues overlooks the intertwinement of androcentric and imperialist language, both of which together constitute kyriocentric God-language that functions as ideological legitimation of kyriarchal societies and cultures. Since the problem of androcentric and imperial language are like the two sides of the same coin, we have to pay attention to how the intersections of androcentric with imperial language shape the texts of scripture and our speaking about the Divine.

Scriptural and the*logical discourses about G*d have named the Divine in interaction with the political structures of their respective societies. The writings of the Hebrew Bible[37] use the imperial languages of Near Eastern empires, whereas those of the Christian Testament are imbued with Roman imperial language. In the context of medieval feudal society, Christian the*logy celebrated G*d the Father as an all-powerful king and omniscient ruler of the universe.[38] The absolute power of G*d has legitimated the power of princes and overlords, of bishops and popes, of fathers and husbands, of Christian mission and colonization. According to Jürgen Moltmann, monotheistic monarchism not only justified the power of a few over the many but also provided a unifying ideology for such imperial power.

36. Kwok Pui-lan, *Introducing Asian Feminist Theology* (Cleveland, Ohio: Pilgrim, 2000, 65–78).

37. I use "Hebrew Bible" instead of "Old Testament," and "Christian Testament" instead of "New Testament" because Old and New Testament are Christian expressions that announce the superiority of Christianity over Judaism.

38. Brian Wren, *What Language Shall I Borrow? God-Talk in Worship: A Male Response to Feminist Theology* (New York: Crossroad, 1989), 119, has aptly characterized the metaphorical system which undergirds Christian imagination, worship, prayer, and the*logy as that of "KINGAFAPP—the King-God-Almighty-Father-All Powerful-Protector." In this frame of reference, G*d is worshipped as a powerful king enthroned in splendor who receives homage and atonement for offences against His majesty, rules by word of command, and legitimates the cosmic kyriarchal order.

One God—one Logos—one humanity, and in the Roman Empire it was bound to be seen as a persuasive solution for any problems of a multinational, multi-religious society. The universal ruler in Rome had only to be the image and correspondence of the universal ruler in heaven.[39]

The language of scripture is greatly shaped by such imperial language. If I single out, here again, the book of Revelation or the Apocalypse of John as a paradigm of such language, I do so because it most clearly shows how Christian imagination is shaped by the bible in imperial terms, although Revelation's intention is anti-empire. With the imagery and language of Hebrew-Jewish, Hellenistic, and Roman imperial traditions Revelation proclaims Christ as conqueror who shares in the throne and power of G*d. Enthroned in eternal majesty and power with G*d, the victorious Christ exercises lordship over the world. The image of the throne occurs again and again like a keynote symbol throughout the whole book.[40]

In Revelation 4-5, Revelation describes heaven not so much as a temple but as a Roman emperor's throne hall. G*d reigns like a Hellenistic ruler in the splendor of unapproachable light, surrounded by the highest beings of the celestial court. The polished pavement of the royal hall stretches out before the throne like a sea of crystal-clear glass mirroring the resplendent majesty of the One on the throne. Lightning, thunder, and voices—the traditional signs of the*phany—emanate from the throne. As befits the "King of Kings," twenty-four vassal kings seated on thrones and wearing crowns of gold, as well as four living creatures, the representatives of all creation, attend to the one on the throne and give homage to the all-powerful ruler of the universe.

Just as the Roman emperor was depicted as surrounded by his friends and advisors when dispensing justice, so is G*d here seen in the role of judge. Just as the Roman emperor, surrounded by his court, was depicted as holding a petition letter in the form of an open scroll, so G*d is seen as holding a scroll with seven seals. The presentation of golden crowns before the emperor is part of the court ceremony taken over from Hellenistic kingship rituals. According

---

39. Jürgen Moltmann, *The Trinity and the Kingdom* (San Francisco, Calif.: Harper & Row, 1981), 129ff.

40. (Rev 1:4; 2:13; 3:21; 4:2-6, 9-10; 5:1, 6–7, 11, 13; 6:16; 7:9-11, 15,17; 8:3; 11:16; 12:5; 13:2; 14:3; 16:10, 17; 19:4-5; 20:4, 11–12; 21:5; 22:1-3).

to the Roman writer Tacitus, the Parthian King Tiridates placed his diadem before the image of the emperor Nero in order to give homage to the Roman emperor. In Revelation the twenty-four angelic vassal kings cast their crown before the One on the throne, acknowledging the almighty Creator with the political-religious language of the day. The Roman emperor is said to have been acclaimed as "Lord and God." Moreover, the acclamation formula, "Worthy are you!" greeted the triumphal entrance of the emperor. Like the Roman emperors, in Revelation G*d is envisioned as the almighty ruler of this world and receives unceasing honor and homage. Just as this vision, so the whole book is permeated by the language and imagery of domination and empire.

Yet unlike 1 Peter, Revelation does not preach that Christians should honor the emperor but uses imperial language as anti-language which nevertheless inscribes the imagery and the social imaginary that it opposes. In the genre of the prophetic apocalypse, Revelation both co-opts and re-inscribes the language of the Roman imperial cult for G*d and Christ in order to demystify the destructive imperial powers of Rome. The question of power and justice constitutes Revelation's central rhetorical problem.[41] Its key the*logical question is: To whom does the earth belong? Who is the ruler of this world? Taking the standpoint of those who are poor and have little power, John answers this question by constructing an alternative world of vision and symbolic universe in socio-economic language and political-mythological imagery.[42]

Christian belief in G*d is here expressed in terms of imperial lordship. Such proclamation of G*d, as the Lord of the world, had by definition run into conflict with the proclamation of Roman civil religion and imperial cult which

41. Leonard Thompson, *The Book of Revelation: Apocalypse and Empire* (Oxford: Oxford University Press, 1990), 185–95, argues that John's dualistic rhetoric is not primarily directed against Rome but seeks to establish "binary opposition and boundary formation—to distinguish insiders from outsiders." His work is part of a depoliticizing trend in Revelation research that has gained widespread acceptance. In a similar fashion, Stephen L. Cook, *Prophecy and Apocalypticism: The Postexilic Social Setting* (Minneapolis, Minn.: Fortress Press, 1995), challenges the conventional "conventicle" approach pioneered by Otto Plöger and Paul Hanson, which assumes that apocalyptic writings stem from the losers in political power struggles, and instead argues that apocalyptic texts "are *not* products of groups that are alienated, marginalized, or even relatively deprived" (2). This depoliticizing trend in apocalyptic research needs to be problematized and discussed critically in light of the conservative political use of Revelation in particular and of apocalyptic symbolism in general.

42. See J. Nelson Kraybill, *Imperial Cult and Commerce in John's Apocalypse* (Sheffield: Sheffield Academic, 1996).

proclaimed: "Caesar is Lord!" Revelation maintains that the one who "makes all things new," and the one who is "Lord of Lords and King of Kings," are one and the same. G*d's and Christ's coming and reign bring total salvation not only for Christians but also for all those now oppressed and slaughtered by the political powers of Rome. Conversely, Revelation maintains that G*d's and Christ's judgment brings about the destruction of all those "who corrupt the earth." The agent behind the political domination of the imperial world power, which "corrupts the earth," is not merely human. It is Satan, the anti-divine power par excellence who is behind the Roman Empire on earth. The dragon-devil has given to the beast from the sea, the Roman emperor, "his power and his throne, and his great authority" (Rev 13:12). This power appears to be absolute and universal. It affects Christians and non-Christians alike.

Since Roman political power was understood in cultic terms, the symbolic universe of Revelation appeals to cultic-religious symbols in order to draw its audience away from the magnificent symbols and cultic drama of the imperial cult.[43] Yet such an appeal was difficult, since Christians at the end of the first century had no cultic institutions, priests, sacrifices, or temples. John, therefore, had to derive his cultic language and symbolism not only from the traditional temple cult of Israel but also from the cultic celebrations of the emperor popular in Asia Minor.

By taking over traditional Jewish and imperial cultic symbols such as temple, altar priests, sacrifice, vestments, hymns, incense, and cultic purity, John attempts to construct not only an anti-universe but also a symbolic alternative to the splendor of the imperial cult. In so doing, he seeks to appeal especially to Jews and Jewish Christians who "own" the tradition in order to persuade them to accept his vision of the world. Revelation's appropriation of the cultic symbols and institutions of Israel serves rhetorical purposes.[44] Its cultic symbols do not describe or refer to actual cultic practices of Jews and Christians in Asia Minor, as some scholars have argued, but rather the author uses cultic symbolism as "evocative language" to construct G*d's empire as anti-image to Rome.

43. David Aune, "The Influence of Roman Imperial Court Ceremonial on the Apocalypse of John," *Biblical Research* 28 (1983): 5–26.
44. David Barr, *Tales of the End* (Santa Rosa, Calif.: Polebridge, 1998) has consistently pointed to the oral and narrative character of the book.

As we have seen, Revelation's engagement of cultic language is not restricted to the appropriation of Jewish religious symbols. The heavenly liturgy celebrated in the throne room of G*d (Revelation 4–5) bears striking resemblance not only to Near Eastern court ceremonial but also to that of the imperial cult. The hymns of Revelation allude to the hymns of praise mentioned in the court ceremonial. Hymnic acclamations and signs of obeisance were not reserved for the emperor but were also paid to his representatives in the provincial celebrations of the imperial cult.[45] Finally, the visions of the New Jerusalem fulfill the ideals of the Hellenistic cosmopolitan city and the idyllic projections of the Pax Romana.

In short, Revelation re-inscribes the symbolic discourse of Rome's hegemonic colonizing power. It does so by co-opting Roman imperial language for constructing a rival symbolic universe that seeks to unmask the evil power behind Rome in order to alienate its audience from the persuasive power of the empire's hegemonic discourses.[46] At the same time, Revelation's symbolic universe and persuasive world of vision seeks to motivate the audience to pay obeisance only to G*d rather than to the Roman state, religion, and cult even if such a decision should threaten their livelihood and well-being. It seeks to encourage Christians to participate actively in a struggle, the outcome of which is already known. The situation of discrimination and exploitation will be abolished, it promises, and a qualitatively different earth will be the outcome of this struggle, a world that is freed from all dehumanizing oppressive powers of empire. Revelation's rhetoric is cosmopolitan and not sectarian.

Revelation's world of vision thus is best understood as a rhetorical response to its political historical and religious communicative situation.[47] Nevertheless, its co-optation of Roman imperial language and imagery re-inscribes them and thereby shapes Christian imagination in terms of empire.[48] While it is important

45. See Steven Friesen, *Imperial Cult and The Apocalypse of John: Reading Revelation in the Ruins* (New York: Oxford University Press, 2001).

46. Allen Dwight Callahan, "The Language of Apocalypse," *Harvard Theological Review* 88/4 (1995): 453–70.

47. See Brian K. Blount, *Can I get a Witness? Reading Revelation through African American Culture* (Louisville, Ky.: Westminster John Knox, 2005), 88, argues that even if there was only sporadic persecution, Revelation talks about a spiritual crisis which resulted in a social crisis when the churches started to resist the imperial cult.

48. Harry O. Maier, *Apocalypse Recalled: The Book of Revelation after Christendom* (Minneapolis, Minn.: Fortress Press, 2002), recognizes that Revelation is an in-version of the militaristic

to recognize that Revelation's dualistic worldview is rooted in a socio-economic political situation of discrimination and oppression, we also must pay attention to how its imperial language functions in situations where Christians are in power. Both liberationist and decolonizing readings help us to do so whereas imperializing readings uncritically re-inscribe such imperial power and violence.

A *liberationist* reading of Revelation's rhetoric, which is not at the same time critical and feminist, subordinates the book's depiction of cosmic destruction and holy war to its desire for justice, valorizing symbols, and language of equity and well-being. It foregrounds those rhetorical features of the text that aim at moving the audience to practical engagement in the struggle for G*d's qualitatively new world of salvation—a world also at home in the imperial cult, whose key word was *sōtēria*, i.e., salvation.

Imperializing readings focus, for instance, on the destructive power and violence of the plague visions, or stress the mythological features of holy war and the outcries of revenge, or the misogynist depiction of Babylon-Rome. These imperializing readings lead to a quite different perception of G*d and a quite different evaluation of Revelation's world of vision. Such interpretations that attribute the destruction of the world to G*d and to Christ are very dangerous today at a time in history when members of the global empire have the technological means to stage the annihilation of all living beings and to bring about the cosmic cataclysms of total atomic destruction and deadly plagues of biological warfare.[49]

Both the liberationist and the imperializing reading are possible. Since they cannot be adjudicated simply on grounds of the text, the liberationist approach must be supplemented with a *decolonizing*, ideology-critical method of interpretation which I will elaborate in section two of this chapter. A critical feminist decolonizing reading is called for. Such a reading does not seek to correct just the androcentric but also the kyriocentric inscriptions of empire in G*d-talk. Critics of religion have rightly pointed out that all text-based religions promote violence and destruction in the name of G*d. They continue to do so because

---

and violent ideals of the first-century Roman Empire, which insists that true power belongs to the slain Lamb, but he does not consider the negative implications of such an inscription of empire.

49. See the critique of the popular, best-selling *Left Behind* series by Barbara Rossing, *The Rapture Exposed: The Message of Hope in the Book of Revelation* (Boulder, Colo.: Westview, 2004).

they were formulated and interpreted in historical contexts of imperial domination. The lively academic debate about biblical monotheism, which I will sketch out in the next section, for the most part circles around the problem of violence and exclusiveness in biblical G*d–language.

The Debate on Monotheism

The problem of domination, and the question of violence, require that we critically place into question the dualistic oppositional construct *Monotheism-Polytheism*, which is undergirded by onto-the*logy. In order to deconstruct the rhetoric of domination that is inscribed in this dualistic pattern *Monotheism-Polytheism*, one needs to examine its conceptualization rather than just its symptoms.

In 1997 two important books appeared in English, which have been discussed extensively in biblical studies and the*logy in the last decades.[50] One was the much debated book of Jan Assmann, *Moses the Egyptian: The Memory of Egypt in Western Monotheism*,[51] and the other was that of Regina M. Schwartz, *The Curse of Cain: The Violent Legacy of Monotheism*. Both books refer to the Hebrew Bible, the "First" or the "Old Testament." According to Assmann, the "either/ or" of monotheism (something is either true or false) engenders situations of violence and practices of domination; according to Regina Schwartz,

---

50. See, e.g., Ernst Haag, ed., *Gott, der Einzige. Zur Entstehung des Monotheismus in Israel*, QD 104 (Freiburg: Herder, 1985); Tilde Binger, *Asherah: Goddess in Ugarit, Israel and the Old Testament* (Sheffield: Sheffield University Press, 1994); Judith M. Hadley, *The Cult of Asherah in Ancient Israel and Judah: Evidence for an Ancient Goddess* (Cambridge: Cambridge University Press, 2000); Mark S. Smith, *The Origins of Biblical Monotheism: Israel's Polytheistic Background and the Ugaritic Texts* (New York: Oxford University Press, 2001); Bob Becking, et al., *Only One God? Monotheism in Ancient Israel and the Veneration of the Goddess Asherah* (London: Sheffield Academic, 2001); J. Manfred Oeming, und Konrad Schmid, eds., *Der eine Gott und die Götter. Polytheismus und Monotheismus im antiken Israel* (Zürich: Theologischer Verlag, 2003); Markus Witte, Hg., *Der eine Gott und die Welt der Religionen. Beiträge zu einer Theologie der Religionen und zum interreligiösen Dialog* (Würzburg: Religion & Kultur-Verlag, 2003); John Day, *Jahweh and the Gods and Goddesses Of Kannaan* (Sheffield: Sheffield Academic, 2004); Magnus Striet, ed., *Monotheismus Israels und christlicher Trinitätsglaube* (Freiburg im Breisgau: Herder, 2004); Hermann Düringer, Hg., *Monotheismus—eine Quelle der Gewalt?* (Frankfurt am Main: Haag + Herchen, 2004); Mark S. Smith, *The Memoirs of God: History, Memory, and the Experience of the Divine in Ancient Israel* (Minneapolis, Minn.: Fortress Press, 2004); Wiard Popkes und Ralph Brucker, eds., *Ein Gott und ein Herr. Zum Kontext des Monotheismus im Neuen Testament* (Neukirchen-Vluyn: Neukirchener Verlag, 2004); Reinhard Gregor Kratz und Hermann Spiekermann, eds., *Götterbilder-Gottesbilder-Weltbilder. Polytheismus und Monotheismus in der Welt der Antike* (Tübingen: Mohr Siebeck, 2006).

51. Jan Assmann, *Moses der Äypter. Entzifferung einer Gedächtnisspur* (München: Carl Hanser

214 / THE POWER OF THE WORD

the principle of scarcity as the principle of the One (one G*d, one country, one people, one nation) calls forth violence by dividing humans into Israelites and Non-Israelites, Insiders and Outsiders, and thereby defining religious identity as exclusive identity. Monotheism, as well as its the*logy, must therefore be critically questioned for its practices of domination.

However, the debate about biblical monotheism is much older than one or two decades. Celsus had already criticized Christian monotheism in 178 CE likening the refusal of Christians to venerate any other G*d except their own to a revolt by people who distance and separate themselves from all other people.[52] By portraying monotheism as a threat to the order of the Roman Empire, Celsus associates Christian monotheism with violence and contempt for humanity.

In various writings, Marie-Theres Wacker has sifted through and brought into conversation with each other feminist and the interdisciplinary discussions on the monotheism of the First or Old Testament. According to her, the critique of monotheism is crystallized around three dualistic contrasts: *first*, totalitarian unity versus differences in power and pluralism; *second*, dualistic worldview versus divinization of the cosmos, and *third*, violence versus tolerance.[53] She points to the anti-Jewish aspect of the critique of monotheism which comes to the fore again and again"[54] in dominant as well as in feminist scholarship.

For the feminist discourse in search of the Goddess it is important, she notes, that "one cannot yet characterize Israel's pre-exilic faith in God as monotheistic, insofar as the power of the surrounding Gods and the fascination they had for Israel is still very alive and effective."[55] Wacker asks further whether the figure of Divine Wisdom can interrupt the rigidly held exegetical opinion of "definitely achieved postexilic monotheism" and whether or how an inclusive monotheism could be formulated with reference to Divine Wisdom. In light of this discussion she concludes:

Verlag, 1998); Idem, *Herr-schaft und Heil. Politische Theologie in Altägypten, Israel, und Europa* (München: Carl Hanser Verlag, 2000); Idem, *Religion und kulturelles Gedächtnis* (München: C.H. Beck, 2000); Idem, *Die Mosaische Unterscheidung oder der Preis des Monotheismus* (München: Carl Hanser Verlag, 2003).

52. Origen, *Contra Celsum*, VIII, 2.

53. Marie-Theres Wacker, *Von Göttinnen, Göttern und dem einzigen Gott. Studien zum biblischen Monotheismus aus feministisch-theologischer Sicht* (Münster: LIT Verlag, 2004), 80–87.

54. Wacker, *Von Göttinnen*, 87.

55. Wacker, *Von Göttinnen*, 91.

The alternative of a women-friendly Goddess religion must be kept in mind whenever the biblical tradition of monotheism is claimed in the interests of what is dominant at the time, perhaps Euro-centrism in politics and economics, as racism, as androcentrism. . . . However, if the demand for universal justice is permanently connected with this God of the Hebrew Bible, then we must speak of this God today and witness actively to his name in such a way that it becomes apparent in what ways his justice also pertains to women.[56]

Such a domination-critical moment is also necessary for the interpretation of the New Testament—or better, the Christian Testament—and the history of early Christianity, because it was articulated in the context of the Roman Empire. Erik Peterson's essay "Der Monotheismus als politisches Problem," which appeared in 1935 and revived political the*logy in the 1960s[57] is important for this discussion. The philosophic principle of *monarchia*, first documented by Aristotle, Peterson argues was identified by Philo of Alexandria with the G*d of the Jews and is then confronted with a pagan political the*logy. According to this the*logy, "the Divine monarchy rules in analogy to the Roman Empire whereas the national Gods must reign." Hence, the Pax Augustana[58] can be understood by Christians as the fulfillment of the promises of the Hebrew Bible. In this Peterson recognizes the intertwinement of monarchic monotheism and political-imperial rhetoric which legitimated the Roman *imperium*. However, he weakens this insight when at the same time he asserts that, on the one hand, the doctrine of the Divine monarchy did not prevail because of the Trinitarian dogma and that, on the other, the reception of the Pax Augustana did not succeed because of Christian eschatology. Jürgen Moltmann, who positively takes up Peterson's thesis, argues in a similar fashion but elaborates Peterson's thesis in a patriarchy-critical way.[59] A the*logical apologetics is not able to answer the

56. Ibid., 102–3 (my translation).
57. Erik Peterson, *Theologische Traktate* (1. Aufl. München: Kösel Verlag, 1951; Würzburg: Echter Verlag, 1994), 23–82; see also Alfred Schindler, ed., *Monotheismus als politisches Problem? Erik Peterson und die Kritik der politischen Theologie* (Gütersloh: Gütersloher Verlagshaus, 1978).
58. See Lorna Hardwick, "Concept of Peace," in Janet Huskinson, ed., *Experiencing Rome: Culture, Identity and Power in the Roman Empire* (New York: Routledge, 2000), 335–68.
59. Jürgen Moltmann, "Kein Monotheismus gleicht dem anderen. Destruktion eines untauglichen Begriffs," *Evangelische Theologie* 62/2 (2002): 112–22.

question as to why, despite its Trinitarian ethos and eschatology, Christianity exercised imperial domination and violence, especially in those times when it had direct access to political power. On the one hand, the proponents of Christian-Trinitarian monotheism don't pose this question. In light of the postmodern critique of monotheism, on the other hand, these proponents formulate apologetic arguments according to which Christian monotheism is preferable to Jewish or Islamic monotheism because it is allegedly less violent. However, this argument overlooks that, without question, Christianity has historically exercised force in the name of the Trinity whenever it had the political power to do so. Today, it still legitimizes domination either biblically or the*logically, with reference to G*d or scripture, whenever it seeks to enforce a particular conservative morality and religious vision.[60]

However, the scholarly discussion of monotheism in the past decades, which has been predominantly Christian, did not critically focus on the problem that the early Christian rhetoric of monotheism has been determined by Roman imperialism. Rather, scholarship concentrated its work on the problem of monotheism in the Hebrew Bible. It has argued that biblical monotheism goes hand in hand with violence and exclusivism because of the biblical commandment, "You shall not have other Gods beside me."[61]

For instance, Regina Schwartz emphasizes that her book was inspired by the question of a college student. After a lecture in which Schwartz emphasized that Israel's G*d is a G*d of justice and liberation, this student raised the question: "What about the Canaanites?" Yes, she thought, what about the Canaanites, the Amorites, the Moabites, the Hittites and all the other peoples against whom the biblical G*d exercised violence? It is this question

60. See, e.g., Erin Runions, "Biblical Promise and Threat in U.S. Imperialist Rhetoric, Before and After 9/11," in *Interventions: Activists and Academics Respond to Violence*, eds. Elizabeth A. Castelli and Janet R. Jacobsen (New York: Palgrave, 2004), 71–88.

61. In his newest book *Monotheismus und die Sprache der Gewalt* (Wien: Picus Verlag 2006), Assmann emphasizes, "that violence is not inscribed into monotheism necessarily as an intrinsic consequence" ("dass die Gewalt dem Monotheismus nicht als eine notwendige Konsequenz eingeschrieben ist" [56]) and sees the problem much more in the fact "that the language of violence is inscribed in the sacred Scriptures of Jews, Christians, Muslims and of many other religions that are based on an exclusivist notion of truth" ("die Sprache der Gewalt in den heiligen Schriften der Juden, Christen, Muslime und vieler anderer auf einem exklusiven Wahrheitsbegriff gegründeter Religionen" [20]). This is a problem which has been intensively discussed in feminist and postcolonial hermeneutics, which Assmann seems not to know or want to acknowledge.

of violence against the others and the identity formation engendered by it that inspires her book.

Although Schwartz had long before realized that the bible was often used to engender hatred toward blacks, Jews, gays, wo/men and the poor, she only now began to understand that the bible is implicated in generating these prejudices, "for over and over again the Bible tells the story of a people who inherit at someone else's expense." Thus she became "keenly aware that our deepest cultural assumptions are biblical and not always attractive."[62] Hence, she started to inquire into the problem of collective identity and monotheism. She was not only interested in analyzing the biblical narratives that speak of liberation and justice, in conjunction with the extinction of the Canaanites, but she also sought to understand how the bible has negatively determined Western culture and defined ethnic, religious, and national identity as violent opposition to the other. In investigating the problem of "monotheism and identity," Schwartz is not so much concerned with the question of "the one G*d in distinction to the many Gods," as with the price that is to be paid when collective identity is imagined under a single principle, be it G*d or nationalism which necessitates violence against others and defines religious identity as exclusive identity.

As a Jew, Regina Schwartz is very conscious of the fact that her interpretation could be understood as anti-Jewish. Hence, she stresses, again and again, that the biblical texts of violence and conquest are not historical descriptions of events but are written only later, many years after the Exile, at a time when Israel had no ruling power. The victory over the Canaanites was the "fantasy of a people in Exile," who were powerless. This rhetoric could only engender social-political violence after it was adopted by groups who had ruling power in Christianity.

Furthermore, Schwartz stresses repeatedly that the bible has also inscribed glimpses of monotheistic plenitude and of G*d's unending gifts of well-being for all. But these moments of abundance did not have the same cultural-religious impact on politics, culture, and religion as did the stress on scarcity, which engendered monotheism. Jan Assmann is equally careful not to make the Jews responsible for the atrocities of monotheism. According to him, Judaism separated itself from others, whereas Christianity and Islam often excluded others with the

---

62. Regina Schwartz, *The Curse of Cain: the Violent Legacy of Monotheism* (Chicago, Ill.: University of Chicago Press, 1997), 2.

help of state power. Their violence is directed toward insiders, the heretics, and toward those outside through the process of evangelizing other people for the sake of mission.

In sum, the debate on violence and monotheism has stressed the violence inscribed in the bible, in order to show that violence and monotheism go hand in hand. As a consequence, Christian identity is articulated in violent opposition to the Other and Christian politics cannot but exercise force because violence is intrinsic to monotheistic religions. In short, the debate on monotheism argues that violence is inscribed in the ontology of Christian faith. Hence a hermeneutics of suspicion is called for.

A hermeneutics of suspicion requires an ideology-critical analysis of the theoretical frameworks and models that organize and determine biblical interpretation and knowledge. To investigate ideologies critically means to investigate ways of interpretation which either serve to strengthen the violence of domination or to undermine it. Such a critical analysis can show that the discussion of biblical monotheism is framed by the dualistic pattern *Monotheism-Polytheism* or *Monotheism-Cosmotheism/Pantheism*, articulated by the philosophy of religions in ontological terms. Hence in a rhetorical approach, it is necessary critically to contextualize and deconstruct this dualistic-oppositional model *Monotheism-Polytheism* in order not to conceptualize monotheism in terms of philosophical ontology but rather to understand it in rhetorical terms.

It is generally acknowledged that the contrasting pattern *Monotheism-Polytheism* is not a biblical-the*logical concept but a concept of modernity which we use as a lens with which to read biblical texts. This pattern *Monotheism-Polytheism* was introduced as a heuristic concept by the philosophy of religions in order to classify religions according to their ideas about G*d. The notion of polytheism goes back to Philo of Alexandria and was rediscovered in 1580 by Jean Bodin. This concept was then introduced by Henry Moore in 1660 as a contrasting concept to that of monotheism. Monotheism is thus a dualistic concept which cannot function without its contrary notion, polytheism.

This dualistic philosophical model re-inscribes the classic Neoplatonic-Pythagorean dualism of a sequence of binary dualisms, such as unity and plurality or limit and unlimitedness.[63] According to Erik Peterson, Philo of Alexandria

---

63. Grace M. Jantzen, *Becoming Divine: Towards a Feminist Philosophy of Religion* (Bloomington, Ind.: Indiana University Press, 1999), 265–75, esp., 266f: "In his *Metaphysics* Aristotle

has taken over this dualistic Neoplatonic-Pythagorean scheme and associated its onto-the*logy with the notion of *monarchia*, whereas Roman legal philosophy elaborated the dualistic thought pattern unity (monarchy, peace, empire) and plurality (chaos, war, violence). The One is the symbol of the Pax Romana whereas the Two is that of *discordia* (discord and strife). If one outlines this philosophical-the*logical dualistic construct in two parallel columns, *monotheism* equals the positive left-hand sequence whereas *polytheism* equals the right-hand negative sequence of the Neoplatonic-Pythagorean pattern. In contrast to polytheism, monotheism is understood as a positive, genuinely Christian category which maintains the superiority of the Christian notion of G*d.[64] Biblical G*d-talk and imagery have become ontologized.

In modernity and during colonialism, this philosophically constructed dualistic pattern was used by Christian the*logians for asserting that Christianity is the only true religion (*vera religio*) and for disqualifying polytheistic religions as pagan.[65] However, in the last century, a reassessment of this pattern has taken place that has shifted the evaluation of the two terms. Now monotheism is seen as negative and polytheism/cosmotheism, with its emphasis on religious multiplicity and cultural variety, is seen as the positive term.

This postmodern negative evaluation of monotheism maintains that it is monotheism, with its insistence on the one transcendent G*d, that has resulted in the impoverishment of religion, the repression of the human spirit and the sanctioning of all freedoms and independencies.[66] At the beginning of the twenty-first century, monotheism with its denial of all other Gods is no longer a matter of course in a pluralistic society in which many religions live together. The logic of monotheism goes against the principles of pluralist

---

ascribed to Pythagoras a 'table of opposites' which has had pernicious effects on Western thought. The left-hand column (limit, odd, one, right, male, resting, straight, light, good, square) was orderly, good and masculine, while the right hand column (unlimited, even, plurality, left, female, moving curved, darkness, bad) was chaotic, bad and feminine."

64. See the review of the application of the concept of Monotheism: C. Schwöbel, "Überblick zur Verwendung des Monotheismusbegriffes in der Theologiegeschichte der Neuzeit," in "*Monotheismus IV*," *TRE* 23 (1994): 256–62.

65. Gregor Ahn, "Monotheismus und Polytheismus als religionswissenschaftliche Kategorien?" in *Der eine Gott und die Götter. Polytheismus und Monotheismus im antiken Israel*, AThANT 82, Hg. M. Oeming/ K Schmidt (Zürich: Theologischer Verlag, 2003), 1–10.

66. Friedrich Nietzsche, "Der Antichrist," in Friedrich Nietzsche, *Sämtliche Werke. Kritische Studienausgabe in 15 Bänden, hg. Von C. Colliund M. Montinari,Bd 6* (Berlin/New York, 1980), 185.

Western societies that insist on respect for human dignity and freedom of religion insofar as it tends to deny the truth of other religions.[67]

In response, Christian the*logians often seek positively to defend monotheism over and against its cultural critics. Often they do so in order to prove that their own particular monotheism is superior to other forms of monotheism. Postmodern cultural critics, in turn, are eager to praise the merits of polytheism, its pluriformity and rich differences in contrast to the totalizing concept of the One as the Same.

However, the present debate on monotheism is not so much about philosophical ontology as about the problem of exclusive claims to truth, exclusive identity formations and the exclusion of the feminine, questions which point to the unavoidable problem of domination and violence. Violence and domination are, however, not just a problem of monotheistic religions, but also the problem of polytheistic, pantheistic, or cosmotheistic religions. Not monotheism but access to the power of domination produces violence and force, as the example of Roman imperialism graphically documents.

The problem of domination, and the question of violence, require that we critically place into question the dualistic oppositional construct *Monotheism-Polytheism*, together with the onto-the*logy which undergirds it, in order to deconstruct the rhetoric of domination that is inscribed in this dualistic pattern. For that reason, we have to move away from the assertion of onto-the*logy that claims to know and adequately express Divine Being. We need to develop a critical-the*logical rhetoric that is concerned with how we speak of the Divine in the context of globalizing empire. We also have to relinquish the colonialist theoretical model that constructs the relation between *Monotheism* and *Polytheism* in oppositional dualistic terms, valorizing either *Monotheism* as was done in the colonial period or *Polytheism* as is the case in post-modernism.

Decolonizing Strategies for Speaking about the Divine

In the preceding sections, I have shown that Christian language for G*d is tainted by masculinism, empire, and ontological dualism. In this last section, I would like to move to a constructive approach that is able to negotiate androcentric language, the rhetoric of empire and dualistic ontological conceptualizations. I begin with the biblical discourse on Divine Wisdom, as a biblical space

---

67. Wolf Krötke, "Der Glaube an den einen Gott. Zur christlichen Prägung des 'Monotheismus,' *Berliner Theologische Zeitschrift* 22 (2005), 70–85, esp., 74.

where these concerns can be addressed. By resorting to another religious tradition, I seek to broaden and deepen this discursive space in order to negotiate the question of how to speak about the infinite and unspeakable. In this discursive space, the female, hybrid figure of Wisdom emerges in Jewish and Christian tradition as an image that is neither defined in masculinist terms nor by the inscriptions of empire. The practice of reflective mythology, at work in the biblical Wisdom tradition, can find her in other religious traditions not only in ancient but also in contemporary ones, such as in, for example, the shape-shifting figure of Kuan Yin. However, as I conclude in my argument, even the Divine appearing in this biblical Wisdom space needs to be rearticulated, again and again, in and through the traditional the*logical process of decolonizing deconstruction and imaginative reconstruction.

Wisdom-Sophia: An Other Name for G*d

In the past two decades, feminists have rediscovered and recreated the submerged traditions of Divine Wisdom in all their splendor and possibilities. Feminist the*logians have discovered anew the creativity of wisdom and have searched for Her presence in the spaces "in-between," the blank spaces between the words of the bible. They have sought "to hear Wisdom into speech," to use the expression coined by Nelle Morton, one of the first feminist the*logians and teachers of Wisdom, who recognized that "Wisdom is feminist and suggests an existence earlier than Word."[68]

In the Hebrew Bible, Spirit (*Ruach*), Presence (*Shekhinah*), and Wisdom (*Chokmah*) are all three grammatically feminine terms. They refer to very similar female figurations who express G*d's saving presence in the world. They signify that aspect of the Divine which is involved in the affairs of humanity and creation. Christian feminist the*logy, especially Catholic feminist reflection, has elaborated the female figure of divine Wisdom (which in Greek is called *Sophia* and in Latin *Sapientia*). Jewish feminist the*logy, in turn, has rediscovered a spirituality of Shekhinah because this figure plays a significant part in some Jewish traditions. Several books of the bible speak about Wisdom-Sophia; however, some of these are not found at all in Protestant versions of the bible or only in an appendix.[69] Divine Wisdom-Sophia-Sapientia plays a

68. Nelle Morton, *The Journey is Home* (Boston, Mass.: Beacon, 1985), 175.
69. The following books that are called by Protestants "apocryphal" or "deuterocanonical"

significant role in Greek Orthodox but less so in modern Western Protestant the*logy.

In biblical as well as in contemporary religious discourses, the word "wisdom" has a double meaning: it can either refer to a quality of life and of a people and/or it can refer to a figuration of the Divine. Wisdom, in both senses of the word, is not just a characteristic of the biblical traditions but it is found in the imagination and writings of all known religions. It is trans-cultural, international, and inter-religious. It is practical knowledge gained through experience and daily living as well as the contemplation of creation and human nature. Both word meanings, that of capability (wisdom) and that of female personification (Wisdom), are crucial for articulating a feminist Christian the*logy and global spirituality.

Wisdom-Sophia is most fascinating to feminist the*logians as a representation of the Divine in female *Gestalt* or form. Her ways are ways of justice and well-being.[70] She is a Divine female figure who in extra-biblical traditions is represented by a variety of Goddesses and Goddess traditions. The biblical discourse about Divine Wisdom-Chokmah-Sophia-Sapientia is reflective mythology that retains the subjugated knowledges and the submerged language of the Goddess within Christian tradition, just as the figure of the Divine Shekhinah-Presence does so within Judaism.

Although the feminist scholarly search for the footprints of Divine Wisdom-Sophia in biblical writings encounters a host of historical-the*logical problems, it is nevertheless commonly accepted that the biblical image of Wisdom-Chokmah-Sophia-Sapientia has integrated Goddess language and traditions. In the mode of reflective mythology, post-exilic wo/men in Israel and Jewish wo/men in

---

are usually printed in Protestant bible editions in an appendix and placed after the Christian Testament; they are found in the Roman Catholic, Greek, and Slavonic canon: Tobit, Judith, Wisdom of Solomon, Ecclesiasticus, also called the Wisdom of Jesu Ben Sirach, Baruch, 1 and 2 Maccabees, 3 Maccabees (only in Greek and Slavonic bibles), 4 Maccabees (only in an Appendix to the Greek bible), 1 Esdras (in the Greek bible; = 2 Esdras in the Slavonic bible), Prayer of Manasseh (in Greek and Slavonic bibles; as appendix in the Vulgate, the Latin translation of the Catholic bible), Psalm 151 (following Psalm 150 in the Greek bible), and additions to the books of Daniel and Esther.

70. For the most recent discussion and literature, see the contributions of Marie-Theres Wacker, "Von Göttinnen, Müttern, und dem einzigen Gott. Zum Stand der feministisch-exegetischen Diskussion um die Göttin/nen im Alten Israel," and Angelika Strotmann, "Die Entdeckung der personifizierten Weisheit im Ersten Testament durch die feministische Theologie," in *Die Tochter Gottes ist die Weisheit. Bibelauslegung durch Frauen*, eds. Andreas Hölscher and Rainer Kampling (Münster: LIT Verlag, 2003), 7–34, 34–68.

Egypt have conceived of Divine Wisdom as prefigured in the language and image of Egyptian (Maat, Isis) or Greek Goddesses (Athena or Dike).

According to a very well-known prayer, all the different nations and people use divine titles derived from their own local mythologies when they call on the Goddess, Isis. They do so in the full knowledge that Isis is one, but encompasses all. Like the Goddess Isis, so Divine Wisdom is using the "I am" proclamation style for announcing her universal message of salvation. In the same way as the widespread Isis cult and mythology, so also the variegated Wisdom discourses of post-exilic Palestinian sages elaborate the image and figure of Divine Chokmah-Sophia-Wisdom as the "other name" of G*d. In the figure of Chokmah-Sophia-Wisdom, ancient Jewish scriptures seek to hold together belief in the "one" G*d of Israel and the language and metaphors of a female Divine being. Hence the texts struggle both to subordinate Wisdom to YHWH and at the same time to portray her as Divine by establishing the functional equivalence between the deeds of Wisdom-Sophia and those of YHWH.

Some feminist the*logians have raised serious historical and the*logical objections against attempts at recovering the Wisdom-Sophia discourses in order to valorize "Lady Wisdom."[71] They have argued that feminists must reject the figure of Divine Lady Wisdom as an elite male creation that serves both misogynist and elitist interests. Feminist objections to the feminine valorization of the biblical Wisdom tradition also point out that this tradition is permanently suspect not only as an elite male tradition but also as one that, in a dualistic fashion, plays the "good" woman against the "evil" woman.[72] Such a misogynist tradition cannot be concerned with justice at all.

The fascination of feminist theologians with Wisdom-Sophia is misplaced, they insist further. Wisdom speculation is at home in Israel's elite male circles and bespeaks their interests. They also point to the possible the*logical dangers inherent in such biblical language and imagination. The spirituality of the Divine Feminine that extols the romantic ideal of the "Lady" and the "Eternal Feminine" has a long ideological tradition in biblical religions and is still pervasive in malestream and even some feminist spirituality.

---

71. For this discussion and extensive documentation, see my book *Jesus: Miriam's Child and Sophia's Prophet.*

72. However, in fairness to the Wisdom traditions, let us note that the prophetic or apocalyptic traditions are equally suspect because they are also permeated by kyriocentric bias.

The Eternal Feminine or the *Cult of True Womanhood*, which I have dubbed the discourse of the "White Lady," was developed in tandem with Western colonization and romanticism that celebrated Christian white elite European-American women/ladies as paradigms of civilized motherhood and cultured womanhood. This ideology has the function of legitimating the exclusion of elite wo/men from positions of power in society and church while at the same time it makes them colonial representatives who mediate Euro-American culture and civilization to the so-called "savages."

A similar ideal for Asian Christian wo/men is, for example, articulated by the Japanese writer Junichi Natori:

> Mrs. Hosokawa was a self-sacrificing woman whose chastity and affection for her husband was really unique. Her life was one of suffering but she lived solely for the faith. . . . When I read about her life, I was struck by admiration for her chastity, her self-sacrifice, her gentleness and her strong faith which was felt by anyone who came in contact with her. . . . Her obedience to her husband's wishes are still remembered in the nation's memory as a perfect example of a model Japanese woman.[73]

This image of genteel femininity and self-sacrificing motherhood is a projection of elite, Western, educated gentlemen and clerics who stress the complementary nature of wo/men to that of men, in order to maintain a special sphere and place for upper-class "cultured" *ladies*. This construct of Christian femininity does not have the liberation of every wo/man as its goal but seeks to release the repressed feminine in order to make men whole. Associated with this cult of the *White Lady* was and is a feminine spirituality of self-alienation, submission, service, self-abnegation, sentimentality, dependence, manipulating power, backbiting, powerlessness, beauty, body regimen, duplicity, and helplessness—"feminine" behaviors which are inculcated in and through cultural socialization, spiritual direction, and secular "ascetic" disciplines such as dieting and cosmetic surgery.

In and through traditional biblical spirituality, wo/men either internalize that they are not made in the Divine image because G*d is not She but He,

---

73. Junichi Natori, *The Life of Gracia Tama Hosokawa* (Tokyo: Hokuseido Press, 1955), 35. I owe this quotation to Elisabeth Gössmann, "Gracia Hosokawa Tama (1563–1600)," in *Japan—Ein Land der Frauen?*, ed. Elisabeth Gössmann, 56–80, see 62, n. 12.

Emperor/Lord/Slave-Master/Father/Male (Greek *kyrios*), or wo/men are told that if they fulfill their religious and cultural calling to supplement and complement the Divine Other, they will embody the Divine Feminine. In both cases, cultural and religious structures of self-alienation and domination are kept in place in and through biblical Wisdom spirituality and the the*logical articulation of the Divine as Father-Lord.

Other scholars specializing in Wisdom literature have rightly objected to such a negative evaluation of the Wisdom traditions.[74] They have pointed out not only that Wisdom discourses are permeated with the teachings of justice[75] but also that in the first century, prophetic-apocalyptic and sapiential (Wisdom) traditions were intertwined, integrated, and changed. They espouse a cosmopolitan ethos that can respect local particularities without giving up claims to universality.

In addition, the advocates of Divine Wisdom-Sophia argue that the wisdom traditions had long been democratized and that much of the sapiential traditions of the gospels reflect folk wisdom which very well could have been articulated by and for wo/men. Finally, they point out that feminist exegetical-historical objections against the feminist regeneration of Divine Chokmah-Sophia-Wisdom may also be due to different confessional locations and indebtedness of some feminist the*logy to neo-orthodox the*logy.[76]

Furthermore, the earliest Sophia-traditions that still can be traced in the margins of early Christian works intimate a perspective that combines Jewish prophetic, Wisdom, and *basileia* (which means the political realm of G*d or G*d's vision of a transformed creation and world) traditions as central to a political, open-ended, and cosmopolitan religious vision of struggle and well-being for everyone. In short, biblical Wisdom spirituality is a spirituality of

---

74. See especially, Silvia Schroer, "Weise Frauen und Ratgeberinnen in Israel: Vorbilder der personifizierten Chokma," in *Auf den Spuren der Weisheit: Sophia—Wegweiserin für ein neues Gottesbild*, ed. Verena Wodtke (Freiburg: Herder, 1991), 9–23. See also Silvia Schroer, "Die göttliche Weisheit und der nachexilische Monotheismus," in *Der eine Gott und die Göttin: Gottesvorstellungen des biblischen Israel im Horizont feministischer Theologie*, eds. Marie-Theres Wacker and Erich Zenger (Freiburg Herder, 1991), 151–83.

75. See also Claudia V. Camp, *Wisdom and the Feminine in the Book of Proverbs*, BLS 14, (Sheffield: Almond, 1985).

76. See Silvia Schroer, "The Justice of Sophia: Biblical Wisdom Traditions and Feminist Discourses," in María Pilar Aquino and Elisabeth Schüssler Fiorenza, *In the Power of Wisdom* (London: SCM, 2000), 67–77.

roads and journeys, public places and open borders, nourishment, and celebration. It seeks for sustenance in the struggles for justice and cultivates creation and life in fullness.

Mayra Rivera's excellent postcolonial discussion of Sophia-Wisdom very helpfully illuminates this debate by suggesting that Divine Wisdom-Sophia is best characterized as a hybrid figure.

> Socially, religiously and even cosmologically, Sophia occupies the space of the hybrid. In her manifold in-betweenness she "intervenes in the exercise of authority not merely to indicate the impossibility of its identity but to represent the unpredictability of its presence."[77] Out in the street . . . . in the squares . . . at the busiest corner (Prov 1:20-21)—literally and symbolically, Sophia stands at the crossroads. . . . She is where the text locates honorable men and "loose women" (Prov 7:12)—thus resisting any simple opposition to the Strange Woman. She is at the crossroads of "proper" gender roles. Depicted as mother, lover, and wife, Sophia is not a stable sign of any of these categories.[78]

A closer look at the biblical Wisdom-Sophia traditions thus reveals that these traditions do not so much portray Divine Wisdom in terms of the Lady and the cultural Feminine. Rather, Wisdom is a cosmic figure delighting in the dance of creation, a "master" craftswo/man and teacher of justice. She is a leader of Her people and accompanies them on their way through history. Very unladylike, she raises her voice in public places and calls everyone who would hear her. She transgresses boundaries, celebrates life, and nourishes those who will become her friends. Her cosmic house is without walls and her table is set for all. Nevertheless she remains an oscillating figure. To quote Rivera again:

> For despite persistent attempts to locate, to define, to fix and to grasp Sophia's identity, her location at the crossroads, her puzzling foreign accent, her undecidable ontological position will not be resolved. Her identity

---

77. Gloria Anzaldúa, *Borderlands/La Frontera: The New Mestiza* (San Francisco, Calif.: Aunt Lute, 1999), 216.

78. Mayra Rivera, "God at the Crossroads: A Postcolonial Reading of Sophia," in *Postcolonial Theologies: Divinity and Empire*, eds. Catherine Keller, Michael Nausner and Mayra Rivera (St. Louis, Mo.: Chalice, 2004), 186–203, esp., 192 ff.

remains indefinable and, for that matter, open. . . . What Bhabha says of the hybrid is also true of Sophia: Her hybridity is "not a third term that resolves the tension between two cultures" [or two religions, or two ontological poles]. . . . [It] creates a crisis for "authority" based on a system of recognition.[79]

This threat to authority comes to the fore in the practical consequences of the rediscovery of Wisdom-Sophia. Feminists in the churches have translated the results of biblical scholarship on early Jewish and Christian Wisdom discourses into the idiom of song, poem, story, art, and ritual.[80] This practical and creative feminist attention to the divine female figure of Wisdom has brought the results of scholarship on biblical wisdom literature to public attention and has raised public objections. While in its worship practices, the Eastern Orthodox Christian tradition has always retained the memory of Her as Hagia Sophia, she has been virtually forgotten in Western christocentric the*logy. In Catholicism, traces of her splendor have been reflected in Mary, but mariology has relegated Divine Wisdom-Sophia to a subordinated feminine figure or completely erased her from the religious consciousness of the people. At the same time, it has made her a "second-class citizen" in the symbolic space of the Divine.

Hence, reclaiming the submerged knowledge of the Divine in female *Gestalt* has run into trouble especially in Protestantism. For instance, in 1993 Protestant feminists sponsored a conference in Minneapolis that not only featured lectures on Divine Wisdom-Sophia but also invoked and celebrated her in prayer and liturgy. This Re-Imagining Conference was allegedly the most controversial ecumenical event in decades. Conservatives claimed that it challenged the very foundations of mainline Protestantism in the USA. The reaction of the Christian Right to this conference was so violent that one high-ranking woman lost her church job and others have run into grave difficulties.[81] This struggle indicates the significance and power of Divine Chokhmah-Sophia-Sapientia-Wisdom for contemporary Christian self-understanding.

79. Ibid., 201, with reference to Homi K. Bhabha, *The Location of Culture* (New York: Routledge, 1994), 114.
80. See, e.g., Susan Cady, Marian Ronan, and Hal Taussig, *Sophia: the Future of Feminist Spirituality* (San Francisco, Calif.: Harper & Row, 1986).
81. See Nancy J. Berneking and Pamela Carter Joern, eds., *Re-Membering and Re-Imagining* (Cleveland, Ohio: Pilgrim, 1995).

This reading indicates that Divine Wisdom-Sophia, the Presence of G*d the Creator and Liberator, is not only controversial because she is a female figure of the Divine but also because she is not exclusive of other religious traditions but is at work among all peoples, cultures, and religions. She teaches justice, prudence, and well-being. She is present as the guide of the people and the wise wo/man of the ancients and indigenous peoples. She embraces creation in its living beauty and manifold variety and delights in its wonders. Divine Wisdom encompasses and sustains everything and everyone.

The biblical discourses on Divine Wisdom are most significant today not only because they are a rich resource of female language for G*d but also because they provide a framework for developing a feminist ecological Christian the*logy of creation and an inter-religious ethos and identity that is not exclusive of other religious visions but can be understood as a part of them, since wisdom/Wisdom is celebrated in all of them. If Christian anti-Judaism is replaced by anti-Paganism in the efforts of scholars to overcome the "othering" functions of imperial discourse, as we saw in chapter 2, then it becomes even more important to resort to the discourses on Divine Wisdom for naming G*d in a non-exclusivist way.

Kannon/Kuan Yin: An Other Name for G*d

Two images stand out in my mind when I reflect on my visit and conversations in Japan in 2004. These are the image of Divine Wisdom and that of Divine Kannon[82] or more formally Kanzeon.[83] They concern the central the*logical problem as to how to speak about G*d and how to image the Divine. Both the shape-shifting figure of Kannon/Kuan Yin, which means "S/he who hears/sees all," and the oscillating biblical figure of Wisdom-Sophia, I suggest, provide religious resources for the refashioning of Christian the*logy which calls for intercultural and inter-religious collaboration.

I was delighted to discover in Japan again the manifold images and worship of the Buddhist Bodhisattva, "Goddess of Mercy" or "Goddess of Compassion

---

82. For the following, I draw on my book *The Open House of Wisdom* (which appeared only in Japanese).

83. See Martin Palmer and Jay Ramsay with Man-Ho Kwok, *Kun Yin: Myth and Prophecies of the Chinese Goddess of Compassion* (San Francisco, Calif.: Thorsons, 1995). See also Ulrich Pauly, *Kannon: Wandel einer Mittlergestalt* (München: Iudicium, 2003).

and Wisdom"[84] whom I had already previously encountered as Kuan Yin[85] during my visits to Hong Kong and Korea. She had become for me the manifestation of Divine Wisdom in Asia. Since Kannon/Kuan Yin is ubiquitous in Asia, celebrated in many different images, and has numerous places of worship, it is safe to assume that this divine-like figure must also have great impact on the subconscious of Asian Christians. The lively interest of diverse audiences in the figure of Divine Wisdom-Sophia, I reasoned, therefore might be due to the cultural-religious context of Japan, Korea, and China that knows of and celebrates divine female figures.[86] The hesitancy directly to engage the divine figure of Kannon/Kuan Yin might be due to the status of Japanese Christians as a tiny minority within a minority (not quite 1 percent) and to the fear of possibly being accused of syncretism and heresy.[87]

Yet, as Judith Plaskow has demanded for Jewish the*logy quite some time ago, so Christian feminists must also insist that the*logy overcome its "fear of the Goddess."[88] The threat to Jewish and Christian monotheism consists not in Goddess worship[89] but rather in the misuse of monotheism for religiously legitimating kyriarchal domination. This domination has sanctified not only the exploitation of wo/men, but also that of the poor, subjected races, other

84. I want to thank Rev. Claudia Genung-Yamamoto who went out of her way to find more information for me about Divine Kannon.

85. Other forms of her name are Guan Yin, Kwan-yin, Kun lam Kwun Yam or Avalokiteshvara. Kwok Pui-lan, *Introducing Asian Feminist Theology*, 72 ff., writes Guanyin.

86. Like that of Kannon, so also the gender of the archaic Divinity Amaterasu, whose name is gender neutral, is debated. However, Amaterasu is mostly understood as Goddess. For literature and discussion see Thomas Immoos, "Das Land der mächtigen Frauen. Archaisches im Gegenwärtigen—Frauen in schamanistisch-kultischen Funktionen," in *Japan—ein Land der Frauen?*, ed. Elisabeth Gössmann (München: Iudicium Verlag, 1991), 13–33. For Japanese as a much less gendered language than English, and the significance of this observation for feminist Christian G*d-language, see Yamaguchi, "Father Image for G*d and Inclusive Language," 199–224.

87. In the article cited above, Satoko Yamaguchi points, on the one hand, to the fear of syncretism instilled by white elite Western male the*logy and, on the other hand, to the oppressive history of political intentional syncretism in Japan. See also her article "The Invention of Traditions: The Case of Shintoism," *In God's Image* 18 (1998): 40–46.

88. Judith Plaskow, *Standing Again at Sinai: Judaism from a Feminist Perspective* (San Francisco, Calif.: Harper & Row, 1990), 121–69.

89. For an extensive annotated bibliography, see Anne Carson, *Goddesses & Wise Women: The Literature of Feminist Spirituality 1980–1992* (Freedom, Calif.: Crossing, 1992); for an interreligious discussion, see Carl Olsen, ed., *The Book of the Goddess: Past and Present* (New York: Crossroad, 1983); for a personal thealogical account, see especially Carol P. Christ, *Laughter of Aphrodite: Reflections on a Journey to the Goddess* (San Francisco, Calif.: Harper & Row, 1987).

religions, and the whole earth. The salvific power of the biblical G*d of justice and love is not endangered by G*ddess language but by the (ab)use of Her/Him as an idol for inculcating kyriarchal interests.[90]

The question of how to speak about the Divine is a problem that is common to all Christian feminists around the world. We all have to face, on the one hand, the problem of deeply ingrained and internalized kyriarchal language about G*d and, on the other, a symbolically and socially entrenched dualistic gender system in which the feminine always is supportive of and supplementary to the masculine. Although issues such as neocolonialism, militarism, and sex-tourism[91] are important feminist challenges, the issue of G*d-language and imagination is equally important, according to Satoko Yamaguchi, for decolonizing our religious traditions. This crucial and urgent issue is one to which we cannot but give priority in this unjust world. The kyriarchal religious imagination inscribes and naturalizes kyriarchal values into the deep subconscious levels of our minds.[92]

Consequently, the problem of how to speak about G*d in female language and imagery, without re-inscribing the cultural feminine as divine, is a problem that is common to all religious feminists around the globe.[93] Kuan Yin or Kannon at first glance seems to subvert cultural gender inscriptions. Nevertheless, an uncritical appropriation of the feminine Bodhisattva figure—like that of Wisdom-Sophia—could result in a strengthening of the internalized structures of gender domination. For as Haruko Okano has argued, the Bodhisattva figure, in its amalgamation of Japanese Buddhism with Shinto, is seen as the embodiment of the feminine principle of motherhood, because one of the most important attributes of the Bodhisattva figure is wisdom and compassion which is envisioned as motherly embrace.[94]

Both the ubiquitous figure of Divine Kannon in Asia as well as the vacillating hybrid figure of biblical Wisdom-Sophia, I suggest, at one and the same time

90. For the interconnection of G*d language and self-esteem, see Carol Saussy, *God Images and Self Esteem: Empowering Women in a Patriarchal Society* (Louisville, Ky.: Westminster John Knox, 1991).

91. In response to Kwok Pui-lan, *Introducing Asian Feminist Theology*, 69, who argues that concern for inclusive language is a preoccupation of Western but not of Asian women.

92. Satoko Yamaguchi, "Father Image of G*d and Inclusive Language," 224.

93. For Asia, see Abraham Dulcie et al., eds., *Asian Women Doing Theology: Report from Singapore Conference, November 20-29, 1987* (Hong Kong: Asian Women's Resource Center for Culture and Theology, 1989); *Faith Renewed: A Report on the First Asian Women's Consultation on Interfaith Dialogue* (Hong Kong: Asian Women's Resource Center for Culture and Theology, 1989).

94. Haruko K. Okano, *Christliche Theologie im japanischen Kontext* (Frankfurt: IKO Verlag, 2002), 168.

display the possibilities as well as the problematics of using cultural-religious resources for Christian G*d-talk. On the one hand, both seem to be figures that transcend and destabilize the dualistic kyriarchal, naturalized sex-gender system. On the other hand, both seem also to embody typically feminine features and the virtues of the Lady such as mercy, beauty, self-sacrifice, and motherliness. Like Mary they therefore can be easily (mis)used to re-inscribe the oppressive cultural gender image of the Lady that inculcates decorum, docility, self-sacrifice, humility, subordination, or wifely devotion as attributes of the Divine Feminine.

Kannon/Kuan Yin is first mentioned in chapter 25 of the Lotus Sutra, a Sanskrit writing dated around the first century CE in India. S/he is pictured as the Bodhisattva Avalokitesvara, a male figure, who postponed his/her final release into Nirvana in order to hear the cries of the suffering world and to pour out his/her compassion over all those in need of salvation. However, it would be wrong to "naturalize" this gender ascription because according to the text this Bodhisattva can take any form, be it male or female, monk or nun, animal or human in response to the needs of the suffering person, the time, and the place. To ask for her/his gender is like asking for the gender of wind or water. Kannon is envisioned in this chapter of the Lotus Sutra as

> Wisdom's sun, destroying darkness,
> Subduer of woes, of storm, of fire,
> Illuminator of the world!
> Law of pity, thunder quivering,
> Compassion wondrous as a great cloud,
> Pouring spiritual rain like nectar
> Quenching all the flames of distress.[95]

Beginning in the fifth century CE in China, and with the seventh/eighth century in Japan, one can find statues of Avalokitesvara, whose name was translated into Chinese as Kuan Shih Yin and into Japanese as Kannon. In his/her earliest forms the Bodhisattva of Mercy is depicted as male. Yet, by the end of the eighth century, Kuan Yin was portrayed as female and by the late ninth

95. Palmer and Ramsay with Man-Ho Kwok, *Kun Yin*, 5.

century her cult was established. Yet the cult of Kuan Yin grew not in the heartland of historic China but on the northwest borders from where it spread across China and to Japan. It is theorized that Kannon's cult grew out of the ensuing rivalry between Taoism and Buddhism:

> Buddhism is a male-dominated faith. At this time it lacked a divine feminine aspect. In the wider world of Chinese belief devotion to the Queen Mother of the West and other powerful creator or local female deities had been taken over by the resurgent forms of shamanism, namely popular Taoism and especially the Mao Shan sect of Taoism, whose central scriptures were, interestingly enough, revealed to them by the spirit of a woman shaman, who it was believed had become an immortal.[96]

Around the same time, Christianity in its Nestorian form arrived on the scene in China (635 CE) and brought with it the figure of the Madonna with child whose image in turn was patterned after that of the Egyptian Goddess Isis and her divine child Horus. Hence, it is safe to assume that the figure of Kuan Yin and her cult probably was engendered by the conflation of the traditions of Mary/Isis, the Great Mother of the West, and other female deities of old China with the predominantly male-defined Avalokitesvara who was able to manifest her/himself in different forms.

Bodhisattva Avalokitesvara-Kannon Boatsu also first arrived as a male figure within Buddhism in Japan. However, in the ninth and tenth centuries, Japanese travelers probably brought from China female Kuan Yin statues. In Japan, Kannon, as in China, Kuan Yin, crosses religious boundaries since she is found in both Buddhist and Shinto temples. Most characteristic of Kannon in Japan is the tradition that she has had 33 major manifestations of whom the majority are female while some are in the form of creatures such as a snake, a winged bird, a horse, or a dragon. Whereas in China these manifestations are seen as more symbolic, in Japan they are understood to be incarnational.

Kuan Yin has many manifestations and names. The most widespread image is that of the *White Clad Kuan Yin/Kannon*, the image of serene beauty, purity and compassion. A variation of it is *Kuan Yin as a Child-Bearer*, which

96. Ibid., 17.

resembles the figure of the Madonna. The *Willow Branch Kuan Yin/Kannon* is characterized by the willow, known for its ability to bend without breaking, and its magical powers to cast out demons and to make contact with the spirit world. Kuan Yin/Kannon is also pictured as the protector of all creatures and of all life and her devotees are often practicing vegetarians. The Kuan Yin/Kannon of the Southern Ocean has absorbed all the ancient sea goddesses and is the protector of fisher folk.

The *Warrior* or *Armed Kuan Yin* is the protector in the struggle against evil demons and the forces of ignorance. Finally, the *Thousand-Armed, Thousand-Eyed Kuan Yin/Kannon* embodies the all-embracing compassion and ability of Kannon to see the suffering of all. Whereas in China there is a three-headed Kuan Yin, in Japan Kannon is often eleven-headed symbolizing her ability to look both stern and gentle over all parts and regions of the world simultaneously.

In short, the "Goddess" Kannon has the ability to reveal herself in different manifestations and to be symbolized as both male and female as well as at one and the same time as neither male nor female. I suggest that her tradition provides language and imagery that can be used by Christian the*logy to express that G*d transcends gender, race, and class, that s/he is neither male nor female, as well as both male and female, and much more. The figure of Kannon with her many different, often grotesque manifestations and alternating gender incarnation thus fashions a discourse that does not define identity in essentialist feminine or masculine terms and at the same time sees the female body and feminine values as divine. A similar dynamics can be detected in the biblical Divine Wisdom figure.

It is clear that in all cultures and religions the desire and longing for a female deity is strong and has found many different expressions. I have focused here on two such Divine female figures: Kuan Yin/Kannon and Wisdom-Sophia. However, I have also argued that a feminist decolonizing the*logy cannot simply and uncritically take over these female figurations of the Divine because they also work in the interest of cultural gender stereotypes. If Christian the*logy is not to perpetuate the inscriptions of empire, it has to develop a G*d-rhetoric that is not only hybrid, fluid, and ever–changing, but also critically aware of its embeddedness in the structures of domination. At the same time, Christian the*logy and spirituality may not go on to name the heavenly world and the Divine in purely masculine terms and imperial language and images that are exclusive of wo/men. Hence, it needs to adopt feminist, liberationist, and postcolonial methods not only of deconstruction but also of re-visioning.

Naming G*d Again and Again Anew[97]

In order to sustain a persistent critical and constructive impetus for biblical the*logical reflection, I have argued, G*d-talk must transform the traditional rules and ontological-metaphysical terms for speaking about G*d, instead of simply complementing or replacing male G*d language with female/feminine language. For so doing, it has available a critical method of traditional the*logy which has developed four rhetorical strategies or ways for speaking about the Divine: the *via affirmative*, the *via negativa*, the *via eminentiae*, and the *via practica*. The rhetoric of the Divine entails affirmative analogy, critical negation, enriching proliferation, and the praxis of transformation.

I suggest that only a the*logical strategy that approaches classic discourses about G*d with a mobile method of deconstruction and proliferation, of symbolic critique and amplification, of construction and imagination[98] is able to develop a decolonizing and liberating feminist way for engaging and transforming G*d-language, symbols, and images. For its inquiry into the rhetoricity of G*d-language, a critical feminist rhetorics of transformation can use and combine the four ways of speaking about G*d developed in the Christian the*logical tradition.

First, in a decolonizing feminist paradigm, inquiry begins with the assumption that G*d is not a G*d of oppression but of liberation and seeks to articulate this conviction in a multiplicity of ways. Since G*d is a G*d of liberation and well-being, an affirmative the*logical strategy (*via affirmativa* or *analogica*) ascribes to G*d positively all the utopian desires of liberation and well-being of which countless people dream and for which they hope. Such an affirmative analogical discourse about G*d may, however, not restrict itself to anthropological individualism but must remain oriented toward the reality and vision of creation. Moreover, affirmative discourses about G*d always need to be conscious that their language is only analogical because G*d transcends human desires for liberation and our images of salvation.

97. Based on the insight that G*d is essentially incomprehensible and all language is analogical, Thomas of Aquinas concluded: "From this we see the necessity of giving to God many names" (*Summa Contra Gentiles* 1, 31:4). See Elizabeth A. Johnson, *She Who Is*, 117.

98. See Susan Heckman, *Gender and Knowledge: Elements of Postmodern Feminism* (Boston, Mass.: Northeastern Univ. Press, 1990), 152–90.

Since the Christian G*d has been understood mostly in masculine terms as father and son, this affirmative strategy of speaking about the Divine has the special task of introducing new symbols, and images of differently colored wo/men, into language about G*d so that the fact becomes conscious that wo/men as well as men, blacks as well as whites, young as well as old, poor as well as rich, Asians as well as Europeans, Christians as well as Jews, Hindus as well as Muslims are all the images of G*d. As long as the*logy remains conscious of the analogical character of G*d-language and the apophatic character of the Divine, it will be able critically to introduce into Christian G*d-language the images and names of the G*ddess which have been transmitted in Catholicism and the Eastern Churches in and through mariology[99] and Hagia Sophia.

However, such female Divine images and G*d-language must not be reduced to abstract principles or used to inculcate the eternal feminine. They must not be seen as feminine aspects or attributes of a masculine God or applied to only one person of the Trinity. Instead, many different images of different wo/men, and variegated symbols of the Goddess, must be applied to G*d generally as well as to all three persons of the Trinity equally. Just as language about Jesus Christ does not introduce a masculine element into the Trinity, female symbolic language must not be used to ascribe femininity or motherhood to a G*d whose essence is defined as masculine. Just as references to the lamb of G*d do not introduce animalistic features, or speaking of G*d as light does not suggest a Divine astral element, so also anthropomorphic G*d-language must not be misunderstood in ontological terms as maintaining femininity or masculinity as a quality and attribute of the Divine. Finally, such a critical-affirmative integration of female symbols and G*ddess-images into Christian discourses about G*d would make it possible for thea/*logy to make clear that wo/men as well as men are images and representatives of G*d.

---

99. Such a mode of multifaceted the*logical association and imaginative amplification comes to the fore, for instance, in *Akathistos*, a Marian hymn of the Eastern church. It can serve to show how such biblical language can be appropriated in feminine form: "Gegrüßt, du Meer, das verschlungen den heiligen Pharao; gegrüßt, du Fels, der getränket, die nach Leben dürsten; gegrüßt du, Feuersäule, die jene im Dunkeln geführt; . . . Gegrüßt, o Land der Verheißungen; gegrüßt, du, aus der Honig und Milch fließt. Gegrüßt, du unversehrte Mutter. . . ." See Gerhard G. Meersemann, ed., *Der Hymnos Akathistos im Abendland. Die älteste Andacht zur Gottesmutter* (Freiburg: Herder, 1958).

Second, since G*d radically transcends human experience, because She/He/It is the X beyond Beyond-Being, no human language, not even that of the bible, is able adequately to speak about the Divine. Hence the *via negativa* of classic the*logy underscores that we are not able to say properly who G*d is, but must emphasize again and again who G*d is *not*. God is *not* like man, *not* like white, *not* like father, *not* like king, *not* like ruler, *not* like lord. She is also *not* like wo/man, *not* like mother, *not* like queen, *not* like lady. It is also *not* like fire, *not* like womb, *not* like wind, *not* like eagle, *not* like burning bush.

Because Christian tradition and the*logy, for the most part, have used masculine language for the Divine, the*logy today must especially focus on and elaborate the inadequacy of such masculine language, imagery, and titles for the Unnamable and reject their sole and often exclusive use for speaking about G*d. The same applies to symbolic language and images which identify Divinity with the eternal feminine or with eternal otherness. Such a critical rejection and deconstruction of kyriocentric masculinity and femininity, ruling and subjection, orthodoxy and heresy, as determinative for the language about G*d, is one of the most important tasks not only of feminist but of all the*logy.

The *third* strategy of classic the*logical reflection, the *via eminentia,* presupposes the first two strategies but stresses that both the rejection of masculine G*d language and the mode of speaking about G*d positively as Goddess does not suffice. Divinity is always greater and always more than human language and experience can express. This "excess" of the Divine calls for a conscious proliferation and amplification of images and symbols for G*d which are to be derived not only from human life but also from nature and cosmological realities. Such a creational experience of Her is expressed by the great medieval mystic Hildegard of Bingen in the following "I am" statements which are reminiscent of the "I am" statements of the Goddess Isis and of Divine Wisdom.

> I, the highest and fiery power, have kindled every living spark and
> I have breathed out nothing that can die. . . .
> I flame above the beauty of the fields,
> I shine in the waters; the sun, the moon and the stars,
> I burn and by means of the airy wind

I stir everything into quickness with a certain invisible life which sustains all. . . .

I, the fiery power, lie hidden in these things and they blaze from me.[100]

The *via eminentiae* is able to retrieve a rich treasure of symbols and metaphors not only from nature but also from the manifold Goddess images and traditions for the*logical discourse about the Divine. One cannot object to such a method of proliferating and amplifying Goddess images that this would mean a remythologization of the Divine. Such an objection overlooks that all language about the Divine uses mythic images and symbols. A strategy of mythologization leads of necessity into the multiplicity of myths and mythologies, but does not result in polytheism as long as it is not construed in ontological terms and remains within the rhetorical boundaries set by the *via negativa* and *via analogica*. Such a strategy of both retrieving the cultural-religious images of the Goddess from different social and religious locations, and reconstructing or re-integrating them into Christian G*d language would lead to an articulation of the Divine that is no longer conceptualized as masculinist exclusive or as agent of domination.

Fourth, the last traditional the*logical strategy, the *via practica*, is usually associated with liturgy and spirituality. Yet, a critical feminist the*logy seeks to locate G*d-language[101] in the praxis and solidarity of anti-kyriarchal, transnational, societal, and ecclesial liberation movements. The creativity and emotionality of Goddess spirituality must be positioned and integrated within these liberation discourses in order not to be misused in a kyriarchal reactionary way. Although G*d is "beyond" oppression, Her revelatory presence can be experienced in the midst of the struggles against dehumanization and injustice. Hence, the Divine must be re-named, again and again, in such experiences of struggling for the change and transformation of oppressive structures and dehumanizing ideologies. G*d is to be named as active power of justice and well-being in our midst. It is S/he who accompanies us in our struggles against injustice and for liberation, just as S/he has accompanied the Israelites on their desert journey from slavery to freedom.[102]

---

100. Hildegard von Bingen, *Mystical Writings*, trans. Robert Carver, ed. Fiona Bowie and Oliver Davies (New York: Crossroads, 1990), 93 ff.

101. See Ruth C. Duck, *Gender and the Name of God: The Trinitarian Baptismal Formula* (New York: Pilgrim, 1991).

102. See *Wisdom of Solomon*, 10:1-21.

Chapter 7

Transforming Biblical Studies[1]

In the chapters of this book, I have argued that the task of biblical studies is to research both the inscriptions of empire, on the one hand, and to trace alternative radical democratic visions in biblical language and texts that function as "scripture" in Christianity and Western culture, on the other. Biblical interpretation, in the horizon of the ekklēsia of wo/men,[2] takes place in a radical democratic space; it is the space of Divine Wisdom, we have seen in chapter 5, not the space of the "Lord of Lords and Kings of Kings." Chapter 4 in turn dealt with the power of empire, the power of domination and subordination, and has in a critical reading put into practice the seven critical interpretive strategies of the feminist hermeneutical "dance."

In this concluding chapter, I will explore what it would take to transform the discipline of biblical studies and its practices of Christian the*logical apologetics, of antiquarian historical science, and totalizing ideology critical deconstruction. For thinking about such a transformation of biblical studies in the open house of Wisdom, I have found it helpful to construct disciplinary paradigms. Such a typological construction can serve as an analytic instrument to assess the ethos and location of graduate biblical studies.

1. This is a revision of my article "Rethinking the Educational Practices of Biblical Doctoral Studies," *Teaching Theology and Religion* 6 (April 2003): 65–75. I want to thank the Wabash Center for Teaching and Learning and its former director, Lucinda Huffaker, for a research grant in 2002–2003 that enabled me to research and develop the arguments of this chapter. Subsequently, Kent H. Richards, Executive Secretary of SBL and I initiated an ongoing SBL seminar on *Graduate Biblical Education: Ethos and Discipline* which has used this article for framing its discussions at the international and annual meetings of the Society of Biblical Literature since 2003.

2. *ekklēsia* (Gr. "assembly") is usually translated as a religious term, "church," but is primarily a political term of ancient democracy—see the discussion in Chapter 1: Introduction and Chapter 2. In order to lift into consciousness the linguistic violence of so-called generic male-centered language, I write the term "wo/men" with a slash—see footnote 21, Chapter 1: Introduction.

A transformation of biblical studies requires the articulation of a theoretical and practical framework for overcoming the division between scholars and church leaders, between "expert" readers and the "common" reader, between scholarly interpretation and popular application. The once reigning hermeneutical division of labor between the exegete, who says what the text meant, and the pastor/theologian, who articulates what the text means, has been seriously challenged in the past two decades and been proven to be epistemologically inadequate.

Although it was Krister Stendahl who advocated this division of labor between biblical scholar and theologian/pastor in his famous article on biblical the*logy,[3] he did so not in order to immunize historical-critical scholarship from critical the*logical reflection. Rather he wanted—as he puts it—to liberate the the*logical enterprise from what he perceived as "the imperialism of biblical scholars" in the field of the*logy.[4] However, twenty years later Stendahl saw the problem somewhat differently when he called for scholarly attention to the public health aspect of biblical interpretation. Reflecting on the fact that his own exegetical-the*logical thinking has circled around two Christian Testament issues—Jews and women—he points to the clearly detrimental and dangerous effects that the bible and Christian tradition have had as a major problem for scriptural interpretation.[5]

Stendahl's call for a public-ethical-political self-understanding of biblical studies has become even more pressing today because of the continuing impact of the Moral Majority in the 1970s, the influence of the Christian New Right in the 1980s, the resurgence of religious fundamentalism in all major religions in the 1990s, and the biblical rhetoric in the interest of war by the President of the United States in the beginning of this century. In a "public health" self-understanding of biblical studies, graduate studies would need to be transformed in such a way that they can design research and teach how to analyze the imperial power relations that are inscribed in past and present biblical texts and discourses.

---

3. Krister Stendahl, "Biblical Theology, Contemporary," in *The Interpreter's Dictionary of the Bible*, v. 1, ed. Keith Crim (Nashville, Tenn.: Abingdon, 1962), 418–32.

4. Krister Stendahl, *Meanings: the Bible as Document and as Guide* (Philadelphia, Pa.: Fortress Press, 1984), 1.

5. Krister Stendahl, "Ancient Scripture in the Modern World," in *Scripture in the Jewish and Christian Traditions: Antiquity, Interpretation, Relevance*, ed. Frederick Greenspahn (Nashville, Tenn.: Abingdon, 1982), 201–14, esp., 204.

Hence the crucial question today is: How can the discipline of biblical studies be changed into a field of study committed to a comprehensive approach that is able to integrate the*logy, history, and ideology critique in the interest of articulating a radical democratic religious imaginary and pedagogical praxis of transformation? To explore this question, I will again proceed in two steps. First, I will sketch the present formation of the discipline, and in a second step, explore developments that call for the transformation of biblical studies into the "open house of Wisdom" appearing in the horizon of the ekklēsia of wo/men.

The Discipline of Biblical Studies

Considering the array of critical questions that face biblical studies today, it is surprising how little substantive work has been done either on its disciplinary practices or on graduate education in order to address these questions. This is especially true for doctoral education in biblical studies. While there has been some creative thinking and educational transformation happening at the Masters and College levels, this seems with one or two exceptions not to be the case for doctoral education.

Emancipatory approaches such as feminist[6] or postcolonial critical studies[7] have brought about some change in the curriculum and education of ministerial and undergraduate students. However, doctoral studies—as a quick Internet search of departments can show—are still mostly devoted to the philological-historical or exegetical-doctrinal disciplinary paradigm.[8] Although the annual meetings of the Society of Biblical Literature (SBL) display a great variety of

6. The Cornwall Collective, *Your Daughters Shall Prophesy: Feminist Alternatives in Theological Education* (New York: Pilgrim, 1980), Katie G. Cannon et al., *God's Fierce Whimsy: Christian Feminism and Theological Education* (New York: Pilgrim, 1985). See especially also Rebecca S. Chopp, *Saving Work: Feminist Practices of Theological Education* (Louisville, Ky.: Westminster John Knox, 1995).

7. See Fernando Segovia and Mary Ann Tolbert, eds., *Teaching the Bible: The Discourses and Politics of Biblical Pedagogy* (Maryknoll, N.Y.: Orbis, 1988); William H. Myers, "The Hermeneutical Dilemma of the African American Biblical Student," in *Stony The Road We Trod: African American Biblical Interpretation*, ed. Cain Hope Felder (Minneapolis, Minn.: Fortress Press, 1991); and R. S. Sugirtharajah, *Voices from the Margin: Interpreting the Bible in the Third World*, Revised and Expanded Edition (Maryknoll, N.Y.: Orbis, 2006).

8. Our seminar panel on doctoral education in leading U.S. NT/Early Christian departments, at the annual meeting 2006 in Washington, D.C., confirmed this impression.

methodological approaches and intellectual voices, which increasingly are no longer able to talk to one another, the central paradigm for doctoral studies seems still to be either the philological-historical, the literary-cultural or the biblical-the*logical paradigms depending on institutional location. Prospective students are generally told that the central requirement is the acquisition of several languages and that the goal of their training is the control of factual and disciplinary knowledge which is tested in qualifying exams.

In short, it seems that the self-understanding of the discipline is still that of antiquarian "hard science" or confessional the*logy which stresses the necessary language skills for professional education and subscribes to the positivist scientist or the*logical paradigms—with their banking and master models of education. Hence a broad based study not only of the populations in but also of the theoretical production of biblical studies is called for.[9] However, as a check with the SBL indicates, such a critical study is not yet possible because we do not have sufficient quantitative research "data" on populations of doctoral programs, the experience of participating students and faculty, as well as critical analyses of dissertations, or annual meetings.

In addition, I have found only a very few critical pedagogical studies that challenge the discipline to a comprehensive articulation of its ethos and identity, in such a way that it could pioneer a radical democratic emancipatory form of pedagogy.[10] As in other areas of positivist scientific studies, pedagogy seems not to be a concern of research at all. Hence, it is necessary to engender a critical investigation and debate on doctoral studies because they are the professional space where future scholars and religious leaders are socialized. To start the debate, one needs to focus on the theoretical issues raised by professionalization and turn attention to the genealogy of modern scientific biblical studies since disciplinary genealogy shapes disciplinary identity.

9. For German speaking countries, see the very important study by Oda Wischmeyer et al., "Das Selbstverständnis der neutestamentlichen Wissenschaft in Deutschland. Bestandaufnahme. Kritik, Perpsektives. Ein Bericht auf der Grundlage eines neutestamentlichen Oberseminars," *Zeitschrift für Neues Testament* 5 (2002): 13–36 which gives a critical review of graduate biblical education in Germany.
10. See, e.g., the important work of Fernando F. Segovia, *Decolonizing Biblical Studies: A View from the Margin* (Maryknoll, N.Y.: Orbis, 2000).

Professionalization of Biblical Studies

Central to the self-understanding of biblical studies, whether practiced in the academy, in public discourses, or religiously affiliated institutions, is its insistence on the scientific character and/or historical or the*logical truth of its research. Whereas it seeks to establish scientific positivism in terms of quantitative methods, refinement of the technology of exegesis, archeological research, production of factual knowledge, anti-the*logical rhetoric, and the deployment of social-scientific models which are derived from cultural anthropology or quantitative sociology for authorizing its scientific character, it advocates the*logical positivism when claiming that scientific exegesis hands down the word of G*d as revealed truth rather than explicates the words of "men." Both discourses insist on such positivist knowledge in order to maintain their public credibility.

The discipline continues to socialize future scholars into methodological positivism and future ministers/the*logians into the*logical positivism. Biblical discourses are advocating either literalist biblicism or academic scientism. As long as this is the case, discourses and struggles for justice, radical equality, and the well-being of all will remain marginal to biblical scholarship. By identifying itself as a scientific positivist practice, biblical studies are formed by the theoretical assumptions that have shaped and governed scientific discourse.

Students tend to enter biblical studies for the most part either because they highly value the bible and its history or because, as future ministers or professors, they want to preach or teach regularly on biblical texts. In any case, their intellectual frame of reference accords the bible intrinsic canonical authority or significant cultural value as an esteemed classic. Critical biblical scholarship, in contrast, is dedicated to the critical study of biblical texts to which it denies religious authority or contemporary significance.

To enroll for graduate biblical studies then means to undertake a double agenda of professionalization. This entails a change of discursive frameworks from a discourse of acceptance of the bible as a cultural icon, or from a discourse of obedience to it as the word of God, to a critical academic discourse that assumes the authority of inquiry and scholarship as a site from which to challenge the cultural and doctrinal authority of the bible.

Like white male students, wo/men and other outsiders who enter graduate programs have to undertake a double agenda of professionalization: they are to be socialized both into "scientific" the*logical thinking and into professional training at once. Like male students, wo/men female students must undergo a process of transformation from a "lay" person in the religious and educational sense to a scholarly professional one. Such a transformation requires not only that students become familiar with the methods, literature, and technical procedures of biblical disciplines but also that they transform their intellectual the*logical frameworks.

Professionalization then means for all students first of all to become socialized into the ethos of biblical studies as a scientific academic discipline. Florence Howe has pointed to the crucial shift in the ethos of American higher education after the Civil War.[11] For almost two hundred and fifty years, college education in the United States was understood as a discipline for the training of elite white men in "religious and moral piety." After the Civil War, the new model for the production of knowledge and higher education became that of German scientific research. This transformation of the curriculum after the Civil War replaced religion with science as a rational philosophy that claimed to account for the entire universe. This change resulted in a galaxy of separate "disciplines" and "departments" that accredit persons for a particular kind of professional work. The unifying ethos of objective method, scientific value-neutrality and disinterested research, in the emerging scientific academy, unseated the centrality of the bible and religion.

Despite claims to professional objectivity, virtually every academic discipline operates on the unarticulated common sense assumption of academic discourse that equates elite male reality with human reality. Intellectual histories and other canonized cultural and academic texts have generally assumed that natural differences exist between all wo/men and elite men and have defined wo/men and colonized men as rationally inferior, marginal, subsidiary, or derivative. Wo/men and other subaltern intellectuals who have shown leadership and claimed independence have been judged as unnatural, aggressive, and disruptive figures.

As Adrienne Rich has eloquently stated, "There is no discipline that does not obscure and devalue the history and experience of women as a group."[12] A similar statement could be made about working class-wo/men, people of color,

---

11. Florence Howe, *Myth of Coeducation: Selected Essays 1964–1983* (Bloomington, Ind.: University of Indiana Press, 1984), 221–30.
12. Adrienne Rich, "Toward a Woman Centered University," in *On Lies, Secrets and Silence: Selected Prose 1966–1978* (New York: W.W. Norton, 1979), 134.

or colonized peoples. The recourse of "scientific" arguments to biological determinism and gender differences is still frequent today in scientific debates that
seek to defend the kyriocentric framework of academic disciplines as "objective
and scholarly."[13]

The Genealogy of Scientific Biblical Studies

It is well known that biblical studies emerged on the scene together with other
disciplines in the humanities that sought to articulate their discourses as scientific
practices in analogy to the natural sciences. The feminist theorist Sandra Harding
has pointed to a three-stage process of modern science shaping and determining
scholarly discourses, their presuppositions, and intellectual frameworks.

The first stage, according to Harding, consisted in the breakdown of feudal
labor divisions and slave relations and the emergence of a new class of inventors
of modern technology.[14] The second stage is exemplified in the New Science
Movement of the seventeenth century that flourished in Puritan England and
brought forth a new political self-consciousness with radical social goals. To
quote Harding, "Science's progressiveness was perceived to lie not in method
alone but in its mutually supportive relationship to progressive tendencies in
the larger society."[15] Scientific knowledge was to serve the people and to be used
for redistributing knowledge and wealth. It is this notion of science that needs
to be recaptured by graduate biblical education.

The third stage of professionalization produced the notion of purely technical and value-neutral science. The progress which science represents is based
entirely on scientific method. The emergence of this third stage, in the development of science, also spelled the end of the collaboration between science
and social, political, or educational reform—a price paid for institutionaliza-
tion and political protection. "Pure" science, according to Harding, goes hand
in hand with value neutrality, which captures what is real through impersonal,

---

13. See the critical reflections on the Arizona project for curriculum integration by S. Har-
dy Aiken, K. Anderson, M. Dinnerstein, J. Nolte Lensinck, P. MacCorquodale, eds., *Changing
Our Minds: Feminist Transformations of Knowledge* (Albany, N.Y.: State University of New York,
1988), 134–63.

14. Sandra Harding, *The Science Question in Feminism* (Ithaca, N.Y.: Cornell University
Press, 1986), 218, with reference to Edgar Zilsel, "The Sociological Roots of Science," *American
Journal of Sociology* 47 (1942).

15. Harding, *The Science Question*, 219.

246 of THE POWER OF THE WORD

quantitative language; and method, understood as norms, rules, procedures, and scientific technologies. Historically and culturally specific values, emotions, and interests must be kept separate from de-politicized transcendental scientific practices. Abstract thinking, mathematical intelligibility, and mechanistic meta-phors become the hallmarks of true science.

The discipline of biblical studies is located at this third scientific stage which constructs a sharp dualism between science and the*logy, or scientific discourse and ideology, in order to prove itself as scientific. Disciplinary discourses re-in-scribe such structuring dualisms as a series of methodological dichotomies and oppositions. Thus, as a scientific discourse, biblical studies participates in the discourses of domination which were produced by science.

For it is also at this third stage of the development of academic scientific disciplines that the discourses of domination—racism, heterosexism, colonial-ism, class privilege, ageism—were articulated as "scientific" discourses.[16] While previously discourses of colonization were developed on the grounds of Chris-tian the*logy, now science takes the place of religion and continues its work of hegemonic legitimization. The discourses of domination were formed as elite discourses that justified relations of ruling. Hence, "soft" academic disciplines, such as history, sociology, and anthropology, in their formative stage, developed as discourses of domination in order to prove that they also belonged to the "hard" sciences. Thereby academic social-science disciplines supported Euro-pean colonialism and capitalist industrial development.

For instance, the nineteenth-century professionalization of history fostered scientific practices advocating commitment to an objectivity above the critical scrutiny of such categories as class and gender, along with strict use of evidence, less rhetorical style, the development of archives, libraries, peer reviews, and professional education. Scientific historical discourses created an intellectual space inhabited by an "invisible and neutered I" which was considered as a "gender-and race-free" community of scholars.[17]

16. See Ronald T. Takaki, "Aesclepius Was a White Man: Race and the Cult of True Woman-hood," in *The Racial Economy of Science: Toward a Democratic Future*, ed. Sandra Harding (India-napolis, Ind.: Indiana University Press, 1993), 201–9; Nancy Leys Stepan and Sander L. Gilman, "Appropriating the Idioms of Science: The Rejection of Scientific Racism," Ibid., 170–93, and Nancy Leys Stepan, "Race and Gender: The Role of Analogy in Science," Ibid., 369–76.

17. Bonnie G. Smith, "Gender, Objectivity, and the Rise of Scientific History," in *Objectiv-ity and its Other*, eds. Wolfgang Natter, Theodore R. Schatzki, and John Paul Jones III (New York: Guilford, 1995), 59.

American sociology, in its formative years, exhibits the same symptoms as scientific historiography. It was influenced by European anthropological discourses that emerged with imperialism, and understood colonized peoples as "primitives" who were considered to be more natural, sexual, untouched by civilization, and inferior because of their innate biological differences—for instance, their allegedly smaller brains. In the United States, Indian Americans and African Americans were those who represented the "primitive" in sociological and anthropological scientific discourses. They were construed to be either violent or childlike or both. People who were Not-white and Not-male were praised as "noble savages" or feared as "bloodthirsty cannibals" on biological and cultural grounds. Asians, Africans, Native peoples, and White wo/men were viewed as childlike, a factor used to explain their supposedly inferior intelligence.[18]

To give an example from the area of biblical studies: In an article entitled "The Use of the New Testament in the American Slave Controversy: A Case History in the Hermeneutical Tension between Biblical Criticism and Christian Moral Debate," J. Albert Harrill[19] has convincingly shown that the discourse on slavery has decisively shaped the development of historical-critical biblical studies. He argues that the abolitionist arguments during the American slave controversy pushed the field toward a critical hermeneutics and a more critical reading of the text in terms of an ethics of interpretation.

The pro-slavery arguments in contrast "fostered a move to literalism emboldened by the findings of biblical criticism that the New Testament writers did not condemn slavery."[20] According to the plain literal sense of the biblical text, Jesus and Paul did not attack slavery but only its abuse. Hence, the pro-slavery argument required a positivist literal reading of the bible which was done in the name of biblical science. In sum, in the nineteenth and beginning twentieth century the scientific ethos of value-free scholarship, which was presumed to be untainted by social relations and political interest, has been institutionalized in the professions that assure the continuation of the dominant disciplinary ethos.[21]

18. Hill Collins, *Fighting Words*, 100–1.
19. J. Albert Harrill, "The Use of the New Testament in the American Slave Controversy: A Case History in the Hermeneutical Tension between Biblical Criticism and Christian Moral Debate," *Religion and American Culture* 10/2 (2000): 149–86.
20. Ibid., 174.
21. Nancy Leys Stepan and Sander L. Gilman, "Appropriating the Idioms of Science: The

This professionalization of the academic disciplines engendered theoretical dichotomies such as pure and impure, theoretical or applied science. Dualistic opposites such as rational and irrational, objective and subjective, hard and soft, male and female, Europeans and colonials, secular and religious were given material form not only in professional disciplines but also in their discursive practices. For instance, the methodologically dense, scientific, depersonalized, empirical-factual text of the research paper emerged as a new standardized academic genre. This genre replaced the more metaphorically porous, literary varied, clearly comprehensible forms of writing that were accessible also to the non-scientific popular reader. The development of biblical studies as a scientific discipline adopted a similar scientific professional elite male ethos.[22]

The Disciplinary Formation of Biblical Studies

The Society of Biblical Literature (SBL) was founded in 1880,[23] around the same time that the American Philological Association (1869), the American Social Science Association (1869), the Archeological Institute of America (1879), the Modern Language Association (1883), and the American Historical Society (1884) were initiated. The feminist historian Bonnie G. Smith has argued, for instance, that the ethos of the American Historical Association cultivated a value-detached, "gender-neutral" community of scholars and developed an "objective" narrative in the course of professionalization as "a modern scientific profession."

> Its ethos and practices demanded "the strict use of evidence, the taming of historical narrative to a less rhetorical style, the development of archives

---

Rejection of Scientific Racism," in *The "Racial" Economy of Science: Toward a Democratic Future*, ed. Sandra Harding (Bloomington, Ind.: Indiana University Press, 1993), 170–93, esp., 173. See also Londa Schiebinger, *The Mind Has No Sex? Women in the Origins of Modern Science* (Oxford: Oxford University Press, 1981).

22. See Anne Witz, *Professions and Patriarchy* (New York: Routledge, 1992), for the medical profession. For the notion of professional authority, see the sociological study by Terrence J. Johnson, *Professions and Power* (London: MacMillan, 1972).

23. For the history of biblical studies, see the forthcoming book by Thomas Olbricht and his various published contributions, e.g., Thomas Olbricht, "Alexander Campbell in the Context of American Biblical Studies," *Restoration Quarterly* 33 (1991): 13–28; idem, "Biblical Interpretation in North America in the 20th Century," in *Historical Handbook of Major Biblical Interpreters*, ed. Donald K. McKim (Downers Grove, Ill.: Inter Varsity, 1998), 541–57; and idem, "Histories of North American Biblical Scholarship," *Current Research in Biblical Studies* 7 (1999): 237–56.

and professional libraries, the organization of university training in semi-
nars and tutorials, and in the case of the United States, a commitment to
democratic access to the profession based on ability." In addition, pro-
fessionalizing historians attempted to eliminate all personal or subjective
meaning from their work. Thus, historians "created a space inhabited by
an invisible 'I,' one without politics, without an ego or persona, and certainly ungendered."[24]

Like its brother-profession, the American Historical Society, the SBL was
founded according to Saunders, by Protestant "gentlemen,"[25] who were for the
most part "European trained in such universities as Berlin, Heidelberg, Halle,
and Tübingen."[26] The professional scientific stance was complicated in biblical
studies by the struggle of the discipline not only to prove its scientific "value-
neutral" character within the Enlightenment University, which had only very
recently more or less successfully thrown off the shackles of religion. It also was
marked, for instance, by the struggle to free itself from the dogmatic fetters of
the Protestant and Roman Catholic[27] churches. This conflict emerged between
the advocates of scientific higher criticism and those interested in safeguarding
the the*logical purity of the bible in the heresy trials at the turn of the twentieth
century.

The same rhetorical tension remains inscribed in professional biblical studies still today. Emblazoned in the professional ethos of biblical criticism is the
conflict of how to study the bible. Should it be viewed as a collection of ancient
texts or as a normative document of biblical religions? Is the critical study of the
the*logical meaning and normativity of traditions and scriptures part of the research program of biblical studies or must it be left to confessional the*logy? Is

24. Bonnie G. Smith, "Gender, Objectivity, and the Rise of Scientific History," in *Objectivity and Its Other*, 52.

25. *JBL* 9 (1890): vi.

26. See J. W. Brown, *The Rise of Biblical Criticism in America 1858–1870: The New England
Scholars* (Middleton, Conn: Wesleyan University Press, 1988), the above references to Thomas
Olbricht's work, and Ernest W. Saunders, *Searching the Scriptures: A History of the Society of Bibli-
cal Literature 1880–1980* (Chico, Calif.: Scholars, 1982), 6.

27. For the history of Roman Catholic scholarship, see Gerald P. Fogarty, S.J., *American
Catholic Biblical Scholarship: A History from the Early Republic to Vatican II* (San Francisco: Harper
& Row, 1989); for Jewish scholarship see S. D. Sperling, ed., *Students of the Covenant: A History
of Jewish Biblical Scholarship in North America* (Atlanta, Ga.: Scholars, 1992).

it part of the professional program of "higher criticism" to study the communities of discourse that have produced and sustained scriptural texts and readings in the past and still do so in the present? Finally, does competence in biblical criticism entail the ability to engage in a critical theoretical interdisciplinary meta-reflection on the work of biblical studies? Would this require that students of the bible be trained not only in textual-historical-literary analysis but also in the ideological analysis of the social and political discursive positioning and social religious-political relations of the discipline and its practitioners?

The scientific academic ethos of the discipline also governs its pedagogical and credentialing practices. It reproduces the professional "club culture" that has engendered modern detached and value-free science. In Saunders' judgment, after 100 years the Society becomes (some would say has become) an antiquarian association more closely resembling an English gentleman's club than a laboratory. "Do the Cabots speak only to the Lodges and the Lodges speak only to God? Some think so."[28]

If professionalization seeks to discipline its practitioners, because it has the "making of professionals" as its goal, doctoral education becomes central to maintaining such a positivist elite masculine ethos. Hence, one must problematize the discipline not only in theoretical terms but also with respect to its educational practices.[29] Rather than reproducing, e.g., in dissertation after dissertation on Paul or John, the scientist-positivist approach that restricts biblical studies to ascertaining the single true meaning of the text, research could focus both on the rhetorical function of biblical and other ancient texts in their past and present historical and literary contexts and on the ideological justifications presented by their ever more technically refined interpretations. In short, professional ethos determines disciplinary discourses by establishing what can be said and what is *a priori* ruled out of court.

Transforming Biblical Studies

To change the educational practices of the discipline, I argue, would mean to change its ethos and vice versa. This ethos is institutionalized in disciplinary

28. E. Saunders, *Searching the Scriptures*, 101.
29. See Mark Roncace and Patrick Gray, eds., *Teaching the Bible: Practical Strategies for*

paradigms. Thomas Kuhn's categories of "scientific paradigm" and "heuristic model" provide a theoretical framework[30] for comprehending theoretical and practical shifts in the self-understanding of biblical studies. A paradigm articulates a common ethos and constitutes a community of scholars formed by its institutions and systems of knowledge. However, a shift in scientific paradigm can only take place if and when the institutional conditions of knowledge production change. Moreover, in contrast to Kuhn I would stress that paradigms are not necessarily exclusive of each other but they can exist alongside each other and are best understood as working in corrective interaction with each other.

Toward a New Paradigm of Biblical Studies

It has now been more than twenty years that a paradigm shift is underway in biblical studies, indicating a shift in disciplinary ethos, so that one can now speak of four paradigms: the Scriptural-the*logical, the philological-historical, the hermeneutical-postmodern, and the rhetorical-emancipatory paradigms.[31] However, these paradigms do not describe successive stages but are to be understood as dynamically interacting with and correcting each other. Consequently, my understanding of paradigm research differs from the conceptualization of Kuhn, who stresses the struggle of paradigms for hegemony and the power of exclusion and replacement. While I recognize the impact of such struggles for power and hegemony especially on the institutional level, I nevertheless want also to draw attention to the possibility of constructing paradigm research in terms of dynamic intellectual collaboration.

In addition, paradigms are not just theoretical but also institutional formations that develop both distinct methodological approaches and disciplinary languages and cultures. Practitioners are judged by professional criteria of excellence maintained by the reigning paradigm of biblical studies and students are socialized into its disciplinary practices. Within the *doctrinal paradigm*, for instance, they learn to understand biblical authority in terms of kyriarchal obedience, often without knowing that this paradigm also has understood biblical authority in terms of salvation. Or, within the historical and literary

---

Classroom Instruction (Atlanta: SBL, 2005).

30. Thomas S. Kuhn, *The Structure of Scientific Revolutions* (Chicago, Ill: University of Chicago Press, 1962).

31. Schüssler Fiorenza, *Rhetoric and Ethic*.

paradigms, students are socialized into accepting scientific "facticity" and disinterestedness as authoritative, without ever reflecting on the kyriarchal tendencies of the scientific ethos to marginalize and objectify the "others" of elite white Western men.

Today, the traditional scriptural-doctrinal and the *modern scientific paradigms* seem to be in the process of being decentered and replaced by a *(post) modern hermeneutical or cultural paradigm*. Whereas a decade ago the historical-positivist and literary-structuralist paradigms of interpretation were still in ascendancy, today postmodern[32] epistemological and hermeneutical discussions abound which are critical of both the religious truth claim and the positivist scientific ethos of biblical studies. Their theoretical and practical force has destabilized the foundations of the field. Even the critical theory of the Frankfurt school, and ideological criticism, have arrived on the program of biblical congresses. Critical theory, semiotics, ideology critique, reader response criticism, social world studies, and poststructuralist literary analyses, among others, have engendered the recognition of the linguisticality of all interpretation and historiography and have generated postmodern elaborations of the undecidability of meaning and the pluralism of interpretive approaches.[33]

Such a (post)modern disciplinary paradigm does not assume that the text represents a given Divine revelation or a window to historical reality, nor does it operate with a correspondence theory of truth. It does not understand historical sources as data and evidence but sees them as perspectival discourses constructing a range of symbolic universes.[34] Since alternative symbolic universes engender competing definitions of the world, they cannot be reduced to one single, definitive meaning. Therefore competing interpretations are not simply either right or wrong,[35] but they constitute different ways of reading and constructing historical and religious meaning. Texts have a surplus of meaning that can never be fully mined.

---

32. See, e.g., David Jobling, Tina Pippin, Ronald Schleifer, eds., *The Postmodern Bible Reader* (Oxford: Blackwell Publ., 2001).

33. Amos N. Wilder articulated this literary-aesthetic paradigm as rhetorical. See his SBL presidential address, "Scholar, Theologians, and Ancient Rhetoric," *JBL* 75 (1956): 1–11; and his book *Early Christian Rhetoric: The Language of the Gospel* (Cambridge, Mass.: Harvard University Press, 1971).

34. See the discussion of scientific theory choice by Linda Alcoff, "Justifying Feminist Social Science," *Hypatia* 2 (1987): 10–27.

35. Maurice Mandelbaum, *The Anatomy of Historical Knowledge* (Baltimore, Md: Johns Hopkins University Press, 1977), 150.

Feminist and liberation the*logical interpretation have played a great part in the (post)modern hermeneutical transformation of academic biblical scholarship. Nevertheless, even a cursory glance at the literature can show that the hermeneutical contributions of critical feminist scholarship are rarely recognized, and much less acknowledged, by malestream biblical studies, except to be co-opted or re-defined. While the postmodern hermeneutical paradigm has successfully destabilized the certitude of the scientific objectivist paradigm in biblical studies, it still asserts its own scientific value-neutral and a-the*logical character. Consequently, it tends to result in a playful proliferation of textual readings and to reject any attempt to move from kyriocentric text to the socio-historical situation of struggle that either has generated the text or determines its function today.

Thus, this third hermeneutical-postmodern paradigm of biblical studies also cannot address the increasing insecurities of globalized inequality nor accept the constraints that the ethical imperative of emancipatory movements places on proliferations of meaning that serve to relativize truth. Therefore, a *fourth rhetorical-political paradigm* needs to be acknowledged, one that inaugurates not just a hermeneutic-scientific but an ethical-political turn.

This fourth paradigm understands biblical texts as rhetorical discourses that must be investigated as to their persuasive power and argumentative functions in particular historical and cultural situations. It rejects the Enlightenment typecasting of rhetoric as stylistic ornament, technical skill, linguistic manipulation, or "mere words," and maintains not only "that rhetoric is epistemic but also that epistemology and ontology are themselves rhetorical."[36] At the heart of rhetoric are both the ethical and the political. In this paradigm, biblical studies are not understood as doctrinal, scientific-positivist, or relativist but rather seen in rhetorical-ethical terms.

Such a critical-rhetorical understanding of interpretation investigates and reconstructs the discursive arguments of a text, its socio-religious location, and its diverse interpretations in order to underscore the text's possible oppressive as

---

36. Richard Harvey Brown, *Society as Text: Essays on Rhetoric, Reason, and Reality* (Chicago, Ill.: University of Chicago Press, 1987), 85. See also, for example, John S. Nelson, Allan Megill, Donald McCloskey, eds., *The Rhetoric of the Human Sciences: Language and Argument in Scholarship and Public Affairs* (Madison, Wis.: University of Wisconsin Press, 1987); Hayden White, *Topics of Discourse: Essays in Cultural Criticism* (Baltimore, MD: Johns Hopkins University Press, 1978); John S. Nelson, "Political Theory as Political Rhetoric" in *What Should Political Theory Be Now?*, ed. John S. Nelson (Albany, N.Y.: State University of New York Press, 1983), 169–240.

well as liberative performative actions, values, and possibilities in ever-changing historical-cultural situations. This approach understands the bible and biblical interpretation as a site of struggle[37] over authority, values, and meaning. Since the socio-historical location of rhetoric is the public of the polis, the rhetorical-emancipatory paradigm shift seeks to situate biblical scholarship in such a way that its public character and political responsibility become an integral part of its contemporary readings and historical reconstructions. It insists on an ethical radical democratic imperative that compels biblical scholarship to contribute to the advent of a society and religion that are free from all forms of kyriarchal inequality and oppression.

Changing Biblical Studies

The current crisis and paradigm shift in critical scriptural-the*logical and religious-historical/literary biblical studies, I suggest, is not only engendered by a dramatic change both in disciplinary methods and in social location. It is also required because biblical, like the*logical and religious, studies have to face four changes and developments that stand in tension with each other and need to be dynamically integrated.

First, *Diverse Populations*: In the last two decades the population of divinity schools and religion departments and therefore the character of the*logical education in the United States have radically changed. Non-denominational university divinity schools such as Harvard Divinity School have granted full citizenship to populations previously not included, such as Catholics, Evangelicals, or Jews as well as beginning to attract Buddhist, Confucian, and Muslim students. Populations from different socio-cultural locations and traditions have also been admitted but have not really been granted full academic citizenship: such as, white wo/men, African American, Native American, Asian, Latina/os, gay, lesbian, and transgendered people, who have traditionally been excluded from the*logical discourse or from elite religious educational institutions. In addition, second-career students seek the rich intellectual inquiry offered by the*logical and religious studies.

37. John Louis Lucaites, Celeste Michelle Condit, "Introduction," in John Louis Lucaites, Celeste Michelle Condit, Sally Caudill, eds., *Contemporary Rhetorical Theory: A Reader* (New York: Guilford, 1999), 11: "Disagreement is thus considered a rather 'natural' result of different social, political, and ethnic groups, with different resources. On this view, struggle, not consensus, is the defining characteristic of social life; accordingly, social discord is not a pathology to be cured but a condition to be productively managed."

This change in populations requires a change in the kind of knowledge taught and the pedagogy used to communicate it. It requires a complete re-conception of academic disciplinary culture that has been defined not only by false claims to value-neutrality but also by the exclusion of the Other. The change is usually realized more completely by the student body than by the faculty who understandably show some resistance, since it throws into question professional expertise and traditional academic standards of excellence. This change in population and the resistance to it on the faculty level pose a serious problem for achieving diversity in faculty hiring and promotion.

Furthermore, student-participants from many different Christian denominations and different religious persuasions, cultural contexts, social locations, and international areas seek to be equipped for religious leadership both in religious communities (churches, mosques, synagogues, and temples) and in the academy, society, and culture (communications, law, medicine, and the arts) at large. Hence, it is not only impossible but also not advisable to devise a set curriculum in terms of traditional ecclesiastical or academic requirements and Eurocentric elite male modes of certification. Rather then spend faculty time on developing fixed curricula, I argue, graduate biblical education needs to focus on evolving educational democratic processes of communication for different religious and cultural communities,[38] processes that are intellectually challenging while at the same time enabling students to qualify for academic and professional leadership, irrespective of whether they intend or not to be ordained or to join the clergy.

Additionally, schools also have to provide the intellectual resources for those students who want to go on for doctoral work in the study of diverse religious/the*logical disciplines or to get a degree in religion for leadership in other professions, such as for instance medicine, business, law, social work, public health, politics, journalism, or education. Finally, the life-experiences and the professional know-how of second career students and life-long learners must be allowed to fructify their doctoral studies. Rather than neglect such rich diversity as irrelevant for academic studies, we need to find educational models that insist not only on difference and diversity as *sine qua non* of academic excellence but

---

38. For international feminist democratic citizen education see Madeleine Arnot and Jo-Anne Dillabough, eds., *Challenging Democracy: International Perspectives on Gender, Education and Citizenship* (New York: Routledge, 2000).

also on collaboration rather than competition, paradigms which would allow for the intellectual fruition of such a rich diversity.

Such appreciation of social, cultural, intellectual, and religious diversity requires a reframing of biblical studies and the construction of an alternative theoretical model and epistemological framework that allows one to move toward the articulation of a critical pedagogy in graduate biblical education. Such a critical pedagogy aims for the self-understanding of the biblical scholar as a public, transformative, connected, or integrated intellectual[39] who is able to communicate with a variegated public with the goal of personal, social, and religious transformation for justice and well-being for all.

Second, *Globalization of Knowledge*: In the past two decades, knowledge— the intellectual capital of religious and academic institutions—has become *globalized*, or as I would prefer, internationalized and democratized. This change has two implications for biblical graduate education and religious leadership: on the one hand, knowledge is no longer the preserve of male clergy but has become accessible through the communications revolution to anyone who seeks it. International inter-religious dialogue and collaboration has not only become a possibility but a necessity.

On the other hand, the flood of knowledge available requires that students learn how to develop intellectual skills of investigation, ethical criteria of evaluation, and hermeneutical frameworks. Not knowledge accumulation but critical evaluation of knowledge is called for. Hence, the*logical disciplines and religious studies no longer can prove their excellence simply by understanding themselves as depositories and repositories of scholarship rather than creators of knowledge. Today the computer is a site of knowledge storage and access. It can provide, within seconds, knowledge of historical sources, literary parallels, philological data, or foreign language translations—knowledge that our predecessors in biblical studies have spent years or a lifetime to find, record, and learn.

It has become increasingly important that students learn to discriminate between different kinds of knowledge, work collaboratively, recognize intellectual problems, and debate them with others who have different experiences,

---

39. For the expression "transformative intellectual," see "Teaching and the Role of the Transformative Intellectual," in Stanley Aronowitz and Henry A. Giroux, *Education Still under Siege*, 2nd ed. (Westport, Conn. and London: Bergin & Garvey, 1993).

standpoints, and belief-systems. They need to learn to interpret and critically evaluate not only the rhetoric of biblical texts but also that of biblical interpreters. A collaborative model of education is called for, a model that is greatly facilitated by the Internet. Students learn from each other in team work, write critical evaluation and integration papers, explore different hermeneutical perspectives, lead discussions, explore different ways of communication, and learn to understand the field and its sub-fields, such as New Testament Ethics, as rhetorical constructions depending on the scholar's social location and systematic framework, rather than as an area of scientific data and the*logical givens. The intellectual acuity and excellence of inquiry required today is much harder to achieve, to teach, and to certify than the traditional curriculum of packaged knowledge, competitive standards of evaluation, and skills acquisition that relies on memorization, repetition, and imitation of the great masters.

As a result, academic excellence cannot be judged in light of past models of scholarship but must come under critical scrutiny. Moreover, the stress on skills acquisition, training, and practical know-how, rather than theory, buys into the mentality of what Stanley Aronowitz calls the "knowledge factory" that turns teachers and professors into technicians of social control. Because of the university's close ties to business, what was once the hidden curriculum—the subordination of higher education to the needs of capital—has become an open, frank policy of public and private institutions. At the turn of the century, critic Thorstein Veblen had to adduce strenuous arguments that, far from engaging in disinterested "higher learning," American universities were constituted to serve corporations and other vested interests. Today, however, leaders of higher education "wear the badge of corporate servants proudly."[40]

This market mentality is fed by the articulation of excellence in terms of technical skills rather than critical pedagogy—technical skills, such as, data accumulation, quantitative publishing, and market-research type evaluations as producing consumer satisfaction. Furthermore, the stress on products rather than critical thinking still determines curricular offerings and examinations. For instance, departments have to offer "bread and butter courses" such as Paul, Synoptic Gospels, etc., which are taught in terms of the banking model rather than in terms of critical knowledge and hermeneutical ability. Moreover,

---

40. Stanley Aronowitz, *The Knowledge Factory: Dismantling the Corporate University and Creating Higher Learning* (Boston, Mass.: Beacon, 2000), 81.

ordination boards still tend to test their candidates not on whether they can critically interpret and hermeneutically work with a text or a complex of problems but rather on whether they are able to reproduce packaged scientific theories such as, e.g., the Two Source theory.

Third, *Religion and The*logy*: The academy has not yet been successful in overcoming the artificial disciplinary dichotomy between religious and the*logical studies, a dichotomy which has been institutionalized in departments of allegedly value-neutral studies of religion, on the one hand, and religiously committed denominational the*logical schools, on the other. This split goes very deep as the AAR Hart Report indicates.[41]

This split, however, obfuscates the fact that both religious and the*logical studies are not value-detached disciplines but speak from a particular socio-religious location and position. To avoid this disciplinary split one has to both re-conceptualize religious academic studies and ministerial the*logical studies as situated knowledges and textualities. In the past, Christian divinity schools and denominational seminaries had the function to educate future ministers and priests. Such seminaries were denominational (Protestant, Catholic, or Jewish) and followed a required curriculum that led to ordination. Because of the restriction of the*logical studies to the education of the clergy, religious studies has developed as a discipline that supposedly investigates biblical and other religions from a value neutral, phenomenological academic standpoint. However, hermeneutics, the sociology of knowledge, ideology critique, critical theory, and especially critical feminist and postcolonial studies have questioned this reifying conceptualization of religious studies.

Moreover, in the last decade or so, the Western (Christian) study of other "alien" religions is slowly being transformed. The hegemony of the traditionally Protestant Christian curriculum has been broken and religious or the*logical studies more and more feel the need for inter-religious and interdisciplinary inquiry. Scholars of other religions (Jews, Muslims, Buddhists, or Hindus), who study Christianity and the bible, articulate knowledge about their own religions and scriptures that is different from that of colonial Western religious studies and somewhat similar to a the*logical studies approach. Such non-Western scholars of the bible and Christianity usually do not call their work "the*logy," however, because the*logy is a Christian-typed term.

41. Ray L. Hart, "Religious and Theological Studies in American Higher Education: A Pilot Study," *Journal of the American Academy of Religion* LIX/4 (1991): 715–82.

Diana Eck's book, *A New Religious America: How a "Christian Country" Has Become the World's Most Religious Nation*[42] elucidates that this dialogue between religions has a socio-political location. It does not only take place in the academy but also on the local level. Hence, future ministers and religious leaders need to be schooled in both ecumenical and inter-religious scripture knowledge and communication. Future biblical scholars or professionals need to acquire the ability of the*logical, religious, and ethical reasoning, as well as a critical analysis of power relations, in the interest of justice for all. The question is how doctoral studies can be so designed that it fosters and ascertains such intellectual capabilities. How can it be shifted from an objectivist study of religions and scriptural or traditional texts to a study of the power of religion, in general, and scriptures, in particular, for fostering violence or justice and well-being.

One possibility would be, for instance, to replace the traditional segregated departments in the*logical and religious studies with trans-disciplinary research teams that focus on problem areas, rather than on disciplinary matters, in order to destabilize exclusive disciplinary boundaries in doctoral education and research. Interdisciplinary faculty and students would be involved in exploring a research problem, such as "religion and violence," a research area that could study the inscriptions of empire in bible, tradition, church, liturgy, Christology, ethics, and other areas. Such a research project would not only address questions of academic and religious communities but would also be of interest to the public at large.

Such a problem-oriented research focus would not replace instruction in the traditional biblical disciplines but would organize their knowledges and methods to different ends. It would use the tools of research made available by the disciplines but use them to produce trans-disciplinary knowledge that could be drawn upon both by communities of faith and the public at large. It would require therefore not only interdisciplinary but transdisciplinary work, a reorientation of the disciplines and a re-tooling of the faculty. At the same time, it would foster team-work, the spirit of collaboration, and communication skills, abilities that are highly desirable for future teachers, researchers, pastors, and community leaders.

Fourth, *Religious Fundamentalist Movements*: We have seen that in the past twenty years or more, virulent forms of—explicitly political—fundamentalism

---

42. Diana L. Eck, *A New Religious America: How a "Christian Country" Has Become the World's Most Religious Nation* (New York: HarperSanFrancisco, 2001).

and religious extremism have emerged in all major religions and in all societies around the globe. Studies of such fundamentalisms have shown that the term can be applied cross-culturally and cross-religiously. They have argued that the common denominator of such fundamentalisms is the opposition to modernism and secularism, Enlightenment values and institutions, and the contempt for all outsiders or others within and outside their community.

In his book *Defenders of God: The Fundamentalist Revolt Against the Modern Age*, Bruce Lawrence, for instance, has pointed to several characteristics which fundamentalist movements have in common: (1) They are comprised of secondary level male elites; (2) They utilize a technical vocabulary or discourse; (3) They profess totalistic and unquestioning allegiance to sacred scriptures or religious authority; and (4) they privilege the authority of their own leaders and subordinate democratic values and processes to this authority. Since traditional institutions of higher education often subscribe to the same positivist—albeit more academic rather than religious—values and discourses, they are not able to articulate discourses and practices that would foster a different radical democratic mentality and religious leadership. Research is necessary into the procedures and elements that reproduce such fundamentalist thinking in biblical studies. Doctoral dissertations should include this aspect of inquiry.

Most important, much more attention needs to be paid to religious identity formation that is not exclusive and anti-democratic. Kurt Salamun argues that education in a democratic society would need to enable as many people as possible: *first,* to prize democratic values, such as, pluralism, freedom, tolerance, equality, justice, human rights; *second,* to recognize and resist anti-democratic tendencies; and *third,* to criticize worldviews and thought patterns that are totalitarian.[43] Such education for democracy would enable biblical readers

- To identify biblical categorizations and value judgments that are determined by dichotomies and bi-polar labels for the interpretation of political, social, cultural, and religious reality.
- To recognize highly emotional biblical stereotypes, scapegoat strategies, negative othering strategies and demands for subordination.

43. Kurt Salamun, "Liberal Education in the Face of Anti-democracy," in Alan M. Olson, M. Steiner, and Irina S. Tuuli, eds., *Educating for Democracy: Paideia in an Age of Uncertainty* (Lanham, Md.: Rowman & Littlefield, 2004), 71–178.

- To problematize assertions that biblical statements and principles are infallible and true once and for all.
- To inquire whether leading biblical figures articulate authoritarian and exclusivist knowledges and demand unquestioning obedience to an absolute leader.
- To detect the strategies of colonizing statements and immunizing belief-systems.

To learn how to critically read the inscription of empire would become the basic grammar of biblical education for democracy if we were to change the theoretical underpinnings of the discipline. Radical democratic rather than positivist or fundamentalist teaching-learning experiences, however, are generally not part and parcel of graduate education in general and doctoral education in particular. While much creative teaching is done on the undergraduate and M. Div. levels, doctoral education is still very Eurocentric,[44] insofar as it is mostly focused on Germanic or British scientific research and the "master-disciple" model of the graduate seminar. Moreover the dominant ethos of graduate schools often does not appreciate the change in knowledge production and populations but operates out of an outdated model of top-down education.

Biblicist fundamentalism not only reads the bible through the the*logical lenses of individualized and privatized bourgeois religion, but also asserts militantly that its approach is the only legitimate Christian one. It thereby obscures the fact that different Christian communities and biblical religions use the bible differently; it ignores that throughout the centuries different models of biblical interpretation have been and still are being developed. Although such dogmatic biblicism berates mainline religious groups for succumbing to modernity and secularization, it itself has adopted a particular modern rationalist understanding of religion and the bible as the only approach that is truly Christian. In spite of the fact that fundamentalism combats modern liberal religion and biblical criticism, it is itself a thoroughly modern mode of interpretation. Its ethos has been shaped in confrontation with modern science and critical thinking. Conversely, graduate biblical studies is shaped by the same modern scientific ethos

44. For the imbrication of Eurocentric American biblical scholarship with racism, see the book by Shawn Kelly, *Racializing Jesus: Race, Ideology and the Formation of Modern Biblical Scholarship* (New York: Routledge, 2002).

but it does not derive its positivist certainty from the bible; rather this certainty is derived from a positivist scientific understanding of language and method.

In the scientific-positivist paradigm that still dominates the self-understanding of the discipline, graduate studies often compel religious students to become in a certain sense "schizophrenic," that is, having, for instance, to write a critical exegesis for a qualifying paper and to preach biblicist literalism in their church. They are not encouraged to bring into the critical learning process their own faith based questions, religious experiences, and fundamental convictions and therefore do not have the possibility to work through them critically in dialogue with the hegemonic discourses of the field. Instead they are told that they need to reproduce as accurately as possible the standard knowledge of the field and remove their own preconception or prejudices from inquiry, rather than being enabled to work through them.

Yet, such a positivist disciplinary stance overlooks that the field of biblical studies presently cultivates a great variety of methods, sub-fields, and theoretical perspectives. It also overlooks that the*logical and religious studies can be scientifically responsible today only if they become interdisciplinary and inter-religious. Instead of seeking to give the power of interpretation to so-called popular audiences or students, scholarship often denies them the tools for investigating the ideologies, discourses, and knowledges that shape their religious self-identity and determine their lives. Instead of empowering students/readers as critical thinkers, education/publication in general and biblical education in particular often contributes to their self-alienation and adaptation to the values and mores of hegemonic kyriarchal societies and religions.

The Radical Democratic Learning Space of Wisdom[45]

Such a scientific disciplinary ethos neglects the spiritual desire for the Sacred that has brought many students to the study of the bible. bell hooks reflects on this ethos saying that she knew when she went to Stanford University from her small town that there would be no "discussion of divine spirit." Her years of teaching at elite universities confirmed the knowledge "that it was only the mind that mattered, that any care of our souls—our spirits—had to take place in

45. For a fuller development see my book *Wisdom Ways* and its discussion in "Pedagogy and Practice: Using Wisdom Ways in the Classroom," *Teaching Theology and Religion* 6 (2003): 208–210, 225–226.

private." However, as a student and later as a faculty member, she continued to "reclaim the sacred at the heart of knowing, teaching, and learning." Hence she asserts: "It is essential that we build into our teaching vision a place where spirit matters, a place where our spirits can be renewed and our souls be restored."[46]

A feminist, emancipatory, radical, democratic model of education in the open house of Wisdom lives in this visionary space "where spirit matters," a space that I have called the "open house of Wisdom." In this space, graduate biblical education can no longer serve to internalize kyriarchal biblical teachings and malestream scientific knowledges but it rather seeks to foster critical thinking, ethical accountability, and intellectual self-esteem. Its basic assumption is that knowledge is publicly available to all who can think and that everyone has something to contribute to knowledge. It seeks to engender radical democratic thinking, which requires a particular quality of vision and civic imagination.

One of the most important contributions of sixteenth-century Reformation the*logy was its insistence on a radical democratization of bible reading. The Reformers gave the bible into the hands of everyone and insisted that one does not need advanced training to understand it. Equally, biblical studies in the horizon of the ekklēsia of wo/men are best understood in a radical democratic Wisdom key, insisting that all wo/men are competent biblical interpreters. It seeks to facilitate wo/men's critical readings by fostering examination of our own presuppositions and social locations. Feminist bible study searches for freedom from cultural bias and religious prejudice and seeks to replace them with critical arguments that appeal to reason and the emotions. It wants to foster self-scrutiny and the ability to think what it would be like to be in the shoes of someone different from oneself and to see the world from the point of view of an Other who is not like oneself, but still much like oneself. It requires us to make sure that books—even bibles—and authors/teachers do not become unquestioned "authorities."

Instead of looking to "great books" and "great men," a radical democratic model of biblical reading/learning, in the open house of Wisdom, engages in critical questioning and debate in order to be able to arrive at a deliberative judgment about the bible's contributions to the "good life," to democratic self-determination and self-esteem. It is about choice and deliberation and the

46. bell hooks, *Teaching Community: A Pedagogy of Hope* (New York: Routledge, 2003), 183.

power to take charge of our own life and thought, rather than about control, dependence, obedience, and passive reception. Its style of reasoning is not combative-competitive but deliberative, engaging in conversations about values and beliefs that are most important to us rather than retreating into positivism, dogmatism, or relativism that avoids engagement with differences.

In this Wisdom model of learning, thought and study are problem oriented rather than positivistic or dogmatic; perspectival rather than relativistic; they are contextual-collaborative, recognizing that our own perspective and knowledge are limited by our social-religious location and that differences enrich our thought and life. Truth and meaning are not a given fact or hidden revelation but are achieved in critical practices of deliberation.

To achieve a constructive engagement with difference and diversity inscribed in the bible and in our own reading contexts, we need to become aware of the pitfalls of one-dimensional thinking that strives to find in the bible definite answers and final solutions. A hermeneutics of indeterminacy, which fosters plural readings, will be most significant in this Wisdom paradigm of biblical studies. As Alicia Suskin Ostriker so succinctly puts it:

> Human civilization has a stake in plural readings. We've seen this at least since the eighteenth century when the notion of religious tolerance was invented to keep the Christian sects from killing each other. The notion of racial tolerance came later. . . . Most people need "right" answers, just as they need "superior" races. . . . At this particular moment it happens to be feminists and other socially marginal types who are battling for cultural pluralism. Still, this is an activity we're undertaking on behalf of humanity, all of whom would be the happier, I believe, were they to give up their addiction to final solutions.[47]

Because of the all-too-human need to use the bible in an imperialistic way for bolstering our identity over and against that of others, because of our need for using the bible as a security-blanket, as an avenue for controlling the divine, or as a means for possessing revelatory knowledge as an exclusive privilege, we are ever tempted to build up securing walls and to keep out those who are not

---

47. Alicia Suskin Ostriker, *Feminist Revision and the Bible* (Cambridge, Mass.: Blackwell, 1993), 122–23.

like us. Instead, we need to tear down the disciplinary walls erected by dogmatic, scientific, and cultural interpretive paradigms so that the enlivening breath of Spirit-Wisdom can blow through it.

Understanding the bible in the paradigms of the open cosmopolitan house and of the spiraling dance of Divine Wisdom allows one to conceptualize scripture as an open-ended prototype rather than as an archetype that has to be repeated in every generation. It enables us to understand the bible as a site of struggle over meaning and biblical interpretation as debate and argument rather than as transcript of the unchanging, inerrant Word of G*d. It requires that we rethink the notion of struggle, debate, and argument that is usually understood in terms of battle, combat, and competition. Within the radical democratic space of Wisdom-Spirit, struggle can be recognized as turning conflict into opportunity, and debate and argument as fostering difference and respect for a multiplicity of voices. If we do not understand debate and argument as an antagonistic-bellicose form of communication, we can practice it as the rhetorical means to clarify practical and theoretical differences and to respect different voices and perspectives as strengthening, rather than weakening, diverse struggles against kyriarchal relations of domination.

The goal of Wisdom education is to enable one to cope with life and to impose a kind of order on the myriad experiences that determine a person. Wisdom teaching is an orientation to proper action, to knowing when to do what. It means to engage in value judgments that urge a certain course of action. Truthfulness, fidelity, kindness, honesty, independence, self-control, and doing justice means to walk in the way of Wisdom.

In short, Wisdom holds out as a promise the fullness and possibility of the "good life"; it is a search for justice and order in the world that can be discerned by experience. Wisdom teaching does not keep faith and knowledge apart, nor does it divide the world into religious and secular, but rather provides a model for living a "mysticism of everyday things." In short, the educational space of Wisdom consists of roads and journeys, public places and open borders, nourishment and celebration. Divine Wisdom provides sustenance in the struggles for justice and cultivates creation and life in fullness.

The open cosmic (school) house of Divine Wisdom needs no exclusive walls or boundaries, no fortifications and barricades to shut out and separate the insiders from the outsiders, the bible from its surrounding world. Wisdom imagination engenders a different understanding of the bible. To approach the bible as Wisdom's dwelling of cosmic dimensions means to acknowledge its multi-valence and its openness to change. It means to give up using it as a "security blanket" and to recognize that the free spaces between the letters and words of the bible invite the Spirit to blow where it wills.

Wisdom's inviting biblical table with the bread of sustenance and the wine of celebration is imagined in Proverbs 9:1-6 as set in a temple with seven pillars that allow the spirit of fresh air to blow through it. This image seeks to replace the understanding of canonical and scholarly authority as limiting, controlling, and exclusive authority and "power over" which demands subordination. Instead it understands the power of the bible in the original Latin meaning of authority (*augere/auctoritas*), as enhancing, nurturing, and enriching creativity. Biblical studies and graduate education, renewed in the paradigm of Divine Wisdom, will be able to foster such creativity, strength, self-affirmation, and freedom in the Wisdom space of the sacred.

Selected Bibliography

Alcock, Susan E., ed. *The Early Roman Empire in the East*. Oxford: Oxbow Monograph 95, 1997.

An, Choi Hee, and Katheryn Pfisterer Darr, eds. *Engaging the Bible: Critical Readings from Contemporary Women*. Minneapolis, Minn.: Fortress Press, 2006.

Anderson, Janice Capel. "Mapping Feminist Biblical Criticism." *Critical Review of Books in Religion* 2 (1991): 21–44.

Ando, Clifford. *Imperial Ideology and Provincial Loyalty in the Roman Empire*. Berkeley, Calif.: University of California Press, 2000.

Ania, Loomba. *Colonialism/Post-colonialism*. London: Routledge, 1997.

Anzaldúa, Gloria. *Borderlands/La Frontera: The New Mestiza*. San Francisco, Calif.: Aunt Lute, 1999.

Appiah, Kwame Anthony. *Cosmopolitanism: Ethics in a World of Strangers*. New York: W.W. Norton & Co, 2006.

———. "Is the 'Post' in 'Postcolonial' the 'Post' in 'Postmodern'?" In *Dangerous Liaisons: Gender, Nation, & Postcolonial Perspectives*, edited by Anne McClintock, Aamir Mufti, & Ella Shohat, 420–44. Minneapolis, Minn.: University of Minnesota Press, 1997.

Aquino, María Pilar, Daisy L. Machado, and Jeanette Rodríguez, eds. *A Reader in Latina Feminist Theology: Religion and Justice*. Austin, Tex.: University of Texas Press, 2002.

———. "The Dynamics of Globalization and the University: Toward a Radical Democratic-Emancipatory Transformation." In *Toward a New Heaven and a New Earth: Essays in Honor of Elisabeth Schüssler Fiorenza*, edited by Fernando F. Segovia, 385–406. Maryknoll, N.Y.: Orbis, 2003.

Arnot, Madeleine, and Jo-Anne Dillabough, eds. *Challenging Democracy: International Perspectives on Gender, Education and Citizenship*. New York: Routledge, 2000.

Aronowitz, Stanley. *The Knowledge Factory: Dismantling the Corporate University and Creating Higher Learning*. Boston, Mass.: Beacon, 2000.

Ashcroft, Bill, Gareth Griffin, and Helen Tiffin, eds. *The Empire Writes Back: Theory and Practice in Post-colonial Literatures*. New York: Routledge, 1989.

———, eds. *Key Concepts in Post-colonial Studies*. New York: Routledge, 1998.

———, eds. *The Post-colonial Studies Reader*. New York: Routledge, 1995.

Assmann, Jan. *Monotheismus und die Sprache der Gewalt*. Vienna: Picus Verlag, 2006.

———. *Religion und kulturelles Gedächtnis*. Munich: C.H. Beck, 2000.

Avram, Wes, ed. *Anxious About Empire: Theological Essays About the New Global Realities*. Grand Rapids, Mich.: Brazos, 2004.

Bacevich, Andrew J. *American Empire: The Realities & Consequences of American Diplomacy*. Cambridge, Mass.: Harvard University Press, 2002.

Bail, Ulrike, et al., eds. *Die Bibel in gerechter Sprache*. Gütersloh, Ger.: Gütersloher Verlagshaus, 2006.

Balakrishnan, Gopal, ed. *Debating Empire*. London: Verso, 2003.

Balch, David L. "Household Codes." In *Greco-Roman Literature and the New Testament: Selected Forms and Genres*, edited by David E. Aune, 25–50. Atlanta, Ga.: Scholars, 1988.

Balch, David, and Carolyn Osiek, eds. *Early Christian Families in Context: An Interdisciplinary Dialogue*. Grand Rapids, Mich: Eerdmans, 2003.

Barkun, Michael. *Religion and the Racist Right: The Origins of the Christian Identity Movement*. Chapel Hill: University of North Carolina Press, 1994.

Barr, David L. *The Reality of Apocalypse: Rhetoric and Politics in the Book of Revelation*. Atlanta, Ga.: Scholars, 2006.

Beavis, Mary Ann. "Christian Origins, Egalitarianism and Utopia." *The Journal of Feminist Studies in Religion* 23/2 (2007), forthcoming.

———. *Jesus & Utopia: Looking for the Kingdom of God in the Roman World*. Minneapolis, Minn.: Fortress Press, 2006.

Bender, John, and David E. Wellbery, eds. *The Ends of Rhetoric: History Theory, Practice*. Stanford, Ca.: Stanford University Press, 1990.

Bendroth, Margaret Lamberts. *Fundamentalism and Gender: 1875 to the Present*. New Haven, Conn.: Yale University Press, 1993.

Benhabib, Seyla, ed. *Democracy and Difference: Contesting the Boundaries of the Political*. Princeton, N.J.: Princeton University Press, 1996.

Blount, Brian K. *Can I get a Witness? Reading Revelation through African American Culture*. Louisville, Ky.: Westminster John Knox, 2005.

———. *Cultural Interpretation: Reorienting New Testament Criticism*. Minneapolis, Minn.: Fortress Press, 1995.

———. *True to Our Native Land: An African American New Testament Commentary*. Minneapolis, Minn.: Fortress Press, 2007.

Bradley, Keith R. *Discovering the Roman Family: Studies in Roman Social History*. New York: Oxford University Press, 1991.

———. *Slavery and Rebellion in the Roman World*. Bloomington: Indiana University Press, 1989.

Brenner, Athalya and Jan Willem van Henten. *Bible Translation on the Threshold of the Twenty-First Century*. Sheffield, UK: Sheffield Academic, 2002.

Breytenbach, Cilliers, and Jörg Frey, eds. *Aufgabe und Durchführung einer Theologie des Neuen Testaments*. Tübingen, Ger.: Mohr Siebeck, 2007.

Brown, Joanne Carlson, and Carole R. Bohn, eds. *Christianity, Patriarchy and Abuse: A Feminist Critique*. New York: Pilgrim, 1989.

Bryan, Christopher. *Render to Caesar: Jesus, the Early Church, and the Roman Superpower*. Oxford: Oxford University Press, 2005.

Buell, Denise Kimber. *Why This New Race: Ethnic Reasoning in Early Christianity*. New York: Columbia University Press, 2005.

Bugg, Laura Beth. *Baptism, Bodies, and Bonds: The Rhetoric of Empire in Colossians*. Th.D. dissertation. Harvard University, 2006.

Bussman, Hadumond, and Renate Hof. *Genus. Geschlecherforschung/Gender Studies in den Kultur und Sozialwissenschaften*. Stuttgart, Ger.: Kröner, 2005.

Callahan, Allen, Richard Horsley and Abraham Smith, eds. *Slavery in Text and Interpretation*. Semeia 83/84. Atlanta, Ga.: Society of Biblical Literature, 1998.

Cameron, Averil. *Christianity and the Rhetoric of Empire: The Development of Christian Discourse*. Berkeley: University of California Press, 1991.

Capps, Walter H. *The New Religious Right: Piety, Patriotism and Politics*. Columbia: University of South Carolina Press, 1990.

Carter, Warren. *Matthew and Empire: Initial Explorations*. Harrisburg, Pa.: Trinity International, 2001.

Castelli, Elizabeth A. "Globalization, Transnational Feminisms and the Future of Biblical Critique." In *Feminist New Testament Studies: Global and Future Perspectives*, edited by Kathleen O'Brien Wicker, Althea Spencer Miller, Musa W. Dube, 63–78. New York: Palgrave, 2005.

———. "The Ekklesia of Women and/as Utopian Space: Locating the Work of Elisabeth Schüssler Fiorenza in Feminist Utopian Thought." In *On The Cutting Edge: The Study of Women in Biblical Worlds*, edited by Jane Schaberg, et al., 36–52. New York: Continuum, 2004.

———. *Martyrdom and Memory: Early Christian Culture Making*. New York: Columbia University Press, 2004.

Castelli, Elizabeth A., and Janet R. Jakobsen, eds. *Interventions: Activists and Academics Respond to Violence*. New York: Palgrave, 2004.

Chakravorty Spivak, Gayatri. "Can the Subaltern Speak?" In *Marxism and the Interpretation of Culture*, edited by Cary Nelson and Lawrence Grossberg. Urbana: University of Illinois Press, 1988.

———. *A Critique of Postcolonial Reason: Toward a History of the Vanishing Present*. Cambridge, Mass: Harvard University Press, 1999.

Champion, Craige B., ed. *Roman Imperialism: Readings and Sources*. Malden, Mass.: Blackwell, 2004.

Clark, Elizabeth A. *History, Theory, Text: Historians and the Linguistic Turn*. Cambridge, Mass.: Harvard University Press, 2004.

———. "The Lady Vanishes: Dilemmas of a Feminist Historian after the Linguistic Turn." *Church History* 67/1 (1998): 1–31.

Cohen, Shaye. *The Jewish Family in Antiquity.* Atlanta, Ga.: Scholars, 1993.

Collins, John J. *The Bible after Babel: Historical Criticism in a Postmodern Age.* Grand Rapids, Mich.: Eerdmans, 2005.

Cooper, Anna Julia. *A Voice from the South.* 1892. Reprint, New York: Oxford University Press, 1988.

Crossan, John Dominic, and Jonathan L. Reed. *In Search of Paul: How Jesus' Apostle Opposed Rome's Empire with God's Kingdom: A New Vision of Paul's Words & World.* New York: HarperSanFrancisco, 2005.

D'Angelo, Mary Rose. "Veils, Virgins, and the Tongues of Men and Angels: Women's Heads in early Christianity." In *Off With Her Head! The Denial of Women's Identity in Myth, Religion and Culture,* edited by Howard Eilberg-Schwartz and Wendy Doniger, 131–64. Berkeley, Calif.: University of California Press, 1994.

De Gruchy, John W. *Christianity and Democracy.* Cambridge: Cambridge University Press, 1995.

Diamond, Larry, Marc F. Plattner, and Philip J Costopoulos. *World Religions and Democracy.* Baltimore, Md.: The Johns Hopkins University Press, 2005.

Diamond, Sara. *Spiritual Warfare: The Politics of the Christian Right.* Boston, Mass.: South End Press, 1989.

Dixon, Suzanne. *The Roman Family.* Baltimore: Johns Hopkins University Press, 1992.

———. *Reading Roman Women.* London: Duckworth, 2001.

Donaldson, Laura E., *Decolonizing Feminisms: Race, Gender & Empire Building.* Chapel Hill: University of North Carolina Press, 1992.

———, ed. *Postcolonialism and Scriptural Reading.* Semeia 75. Atlanta, Ga.: Scholars, 1996.

Donaldson, Laura E., and Kwok Pui-lan, eds. *Postcolonialism, Feminism, & Religious Discourse.* New York: Routledge, 2002.

Dube, Musa W. "Postcolonial Biblical Interpretation." In *Dictionary of Biblical Interpretation,* edited by John H. Hayes, 299–303. Nashville, Tenn.: Abingdon, 1999.

———. *Postcolonial Feminist Interpretation of the Bible.* St. Louis, Mo.: Chalice, 2000.

———. "Villagizing, Globalizing and Biblical Studies." In *Reading the Bible in the Global Village: Cape Town,* edited by Justin S. Upkong, et al., 41–63. Atlanta, Ga: Scholars, 2002.

———, ed. *Other Ways of Reading: African Women and the Bible.* Atlanta, Ga.: SBL, 2001.

Dube, Musa W., and Musimbi Kanyoro. *Grant me Justice: HIV/AIDS & Gender Readings of the Bible.* Maryknoll, N.Y.: Orbis, 2004.

Dube, Musa W., and J.L. Staley, eds. *John and Postcolonialism: Travel, Space and Power.* London: Sheffield Academic, 2002.

DuBois, Page. *Centaurs and Amazons: Women and the Pre-History of the Great Chain of Being.* Ann Arbor: The University of Michigan Press, 1982.

———. *Torture and Truth.* New York: Routledge, 1990.

Eck, Diana L. *A New Religious America: How a "Christian Country" Has Become the World's Most Religious Nation*. New York: HarperSanFrancisco, 2001.

Ehrensperger, Kathy. *That We May be Mutually Encouraged: Feminism and the New Perspective in Pauline Studies*. New York: T. & T. Clark, 2004.

Elliott, John H. "The Jesus Movement was not Egalitarian but Family-Oriented." *Biblical Interpretation* 11 (2003): 173–210.

Elliott, Neil. *Liberating Paul: The Justice of God and the Politics of The Apostle*. Maryknoll, N.Y.: Orbis, 1994.

Fanon, Franz. *Black Skin, White Masks*. New York: Grove, 1967.

———. *The Wretched of the Earth*. New York: Grove, 1963.

Fischler, Susan. "Imperial Cult: Engendering the Cosmos." In *When Men were Men: Masculinity, Power and Identity in Classical Antiquity*, edited by Lin Foxhall and John Salmon. New York: Routledge, 1998.

Fraser, Nancy. "Mapping the Feminist Imagination: From Redistribution to Recognition to Representation." *Constellations* 12/3 (2005): 295–307.

———. "Identity, Exclusion, and Critique: A Response to Four Critics." *European Journal of Political Theory* 6/3 (2007): 305–338.

Freire, Paulo. *Education for Critical Consciousness*. New York: Seabury, 1973.

———. *Pedagogy of the Oppressed*. New York: Harper & Row, 1971.

Friesen, Steven J. *Imperial Cults and the Apocalypse of John: Reading Revelation in the Ruins*. Oxford: Oxford University Press, 2001.

Gallagher, Sally. *Evangelical Identity and Gendered Family Life*. New Brunswick, N.J.: Rutgers University Press, 2003.

Gandhi, Leela. *Postcolonial Theory: A Critical Introduction*. New York: Columbia University Press, 1998.

Georgi, Dieter. *Theocracy in Paul's Praxis and Theology*. Minneapolis, Minn.: Fortress Press, 1991.

Giesen, Heinz. "Das Römische Reich im Spiegel der Johannes-Apokalypse." ANRW II/26 (1996): 2501–2614.

Glancy, Jennifer A. *Slavery in Early Christianity*. New York: Oxford University Press, 2002.

Gordon, Lewis R. T., Deneon Sharpley-Whiting, and Renee T. White, eds. *Fanon Critical Reader*. Oxford: Blackwell, 1996.

Griffin, David Ray, John B. Cobb, Richard A. Falk, and Catherine Keller. *The American Empire and the Commonwealth of God*. Louisville, Ky.: Westminster John Knox, 2006.

Grubbs, Judith Evans. *Women and the Law in the Roman Empire: A Sourcebook on Marriage, Divorce and Widowhood*. New York: Routledge, 2002.

Halliday, Michael A. K. *Language as Social Semiotic: The Social Interpretation of Language and Meaning*. Baltimore, Md.: University Park Press, 1978.

Harding, Sandra, ed. *The "Racial" Economy of Science: Toward a Democratic Future*. Bloomington: Indiana University Press, 1993.

Hardt, Michael, and Antonio Negri. *Empire: A New Vision of Social Order*. Cambridge, Mass.: Harvard University Press, 2000.

Harland, Philip A. *Associations, Synagogues, and Congregations: Claiming a Place in Ancient Mediterranean Society*. Minneapolis, Minn.: Fortress Press, 2003.

Harrill, J. Albert. "The Use of the New Testament in the American Slave Controversy: A Case History in the Hermeneutical Tension between Biblical Criticism and Christian Moral Debate." *Religion and American Culture* 10/2 (2000): 149–86.

Hatch, Nathan O. *The Democratization of American Christianity*. New Haven, Conn.: Yale University Press, 1989.

Hennessy, Rosemary. *Materialist Feminism and the Politics of Discourse*. New York: Routledge, 1993.

Hernández, Adriana. *Pedagogy, Democracy, and Feminism: Rethinking the Public Sphere*. New York: SUNY Press, 1997.

Hill Collins, Patricia. *Fighting Words: Black Women and the Search For Justice*. Minneapolis: University of Minnesota Press, 1998.

Hölscher, Andreas, and Rainer Kampling, eds. *Die Tochter Gottes ist die Weisheit. Bibelauslegung durch Frauen*. Munich: LIT Verlag, 2003.

Horsley, Richard A. *Jesus and Empire: The Kingdom of God and the New World Disorder*. Mineapolis, Minn.: Fortress Press, 2002.

———. *Religion and Empire: People, Power and the Life of the Spirit*. Minneapolis, Minn.: Fortress Press, 2003.

———, ed. *Paul and Empire: Religion and Power in Roman Imperial Society*. Harrisburg, Pa.: Trinity International, 1997.

Howland, W., ed. *Religious Fundamentalisms and the Human Rights of Women*. New York: Palgrave, 1999.

Huskinson, Janet, ed. *Experience in Rome: Culture, Identity and Power in the Roman Empire*. New York: Routledge, 2000.

Ingersoll, Julie. *Evangelical Christian Women: War Stories in the Gender Battles*. New York: NYU Press, 2003.

Janssen, Claudia, Luise Schottroff, and Beate When, eds. *Paulus. Umstrittene Traditionen—lebendige Theologie. Eine feministische Lektüre*. Gütersloh, Ger.: Chr. Kaiser Gütersloher Verlagshaus, 2001.

Jantzen, Grace M. *Becoming Divine: Towards a Feminist Philosophy of Religion*. Bloomington: Indiana University Press, 1999.

Jobling, David, Tina Pippin, Ronald Schleifer, eds., *The Postmodern Bible Reader*. Oxford: Blackwell, 2001.

Jobling, J'annine. *Feminist Biblical Interpretation in Theological Context: Restless Readings*. Burlington, Vt.: Ashgate, 2002.

Johnson-DeBaufre, Melanie. *Jesus Among Her Children: Q, Eschatology and the Construction of Christian Origins*. Cambridge, Mass.: Harvard University Press, 2005.

Johnson-DeBaufre, Melanie and Laura Nasrallah. "The Pauline Correspondence: Struggling Subjectivities under Empire." In the "Paul and Politics" Section. SBL annual meeting, 2006.

Keller, Catherine, Michael Nausner, and Myra Rivera, eds., *Postcolonial Theologies: Divinity and Empire*. St. Louis, Mo.: Chalice, 2004.

Kelly, Michael, ed. *Critique and Power: Recasting the Foucault/Habermas Debate*. Cambridge, Mass.: MIT Press, 1995.

Kelly, Shawn. *Racializing Jesus: Race, Ideology and the Formation of Modern Biblical Scholarship*. New York: Routledge, 2002.

Kirk, Alan and Tom Satcher, eds. *Memory, Tradition, and Text: Uses of the Past in Early Christianity*. Semeia 52. Atlanta: SBL, 2005.

Kittredge, Cynthia Briggs. *Community and Authority: The Rhetoric of Obedience in the Pauline Tradition*. Harvard Theological Studies. Harrisburg, Pa.: Trinity International, 1998.

———. "Corinthian Women Prophets and Paul's Argumentation in 1 Corinthians." In *Paul and Politics: Ekklesia, Israel, Imperium, Interpretation: Essays in Honor of Krister Stendahl*, edited by Richard A. Horsley, 103–109. Harrisburg, Pa.: Trinity International, 2000.

———. "Rethinking Authorship in the Letters of Paul: Elisabeth Schüssler Fiorenza's Model of Pauline The*logy." In *Walk in the Ways of Wisdom*, edited by Shelly Matthews, et al., 318–33. Harrisburg, Pa.: Trinity International, 2003.

Kloppenborg, John S. and Stephen G. Wilson, eds. *Voluntary Associations in the Greco-Roman World*. New York: Routledge, 1996.

Kraybill, Nelson. *Imperial Cult and Commerce in John's Apocalypse*. Sheffield, UK: Sheffield Academic, 1996.

Kwok Pui-lan, "The Image of the White Lady: Gender and Race in Christian Mission." In *The Special Nature of Women*, edited by Anne Carr and Elisabeth Schüssler Fiorenza. Philadelphia, Pa.: Trinity International, 1991.

———. *Discovering the Bible in the Non-Biblical World*. Maryknoll, N.Y. Orbis, 1995.

———. *Introducing Asian Feminist Theology*. Sheffield, UK: Sheffield Academic, 2000.

———. *Postcolonial Imagination and Feminist Theology*. Louisville, KY: Westminster John Knox Press, 2005.

Laqueur, Thomas. *Making Sex: Body and Gender from the Greeks to Freud*. Cambridge: Harvard University Press, 1990.

Levine, Amy-Jill, ed. *A Feminist Companion to the Deutero-Pauline Epistles*. New York: Continuum International, 2003.

Lieu, Judith, M. *Christian Identity in the Jewish and Greco-Roman World*. New York: Oxford University Press, 2004.

Lucaites, John Louis, Celeste Michelle Condit, Sally Caudill, eds. *Contemporary Rhetorical Theory: A Reader*. New York: Guilford, 1999.

Lukes, Steven, ed. *Power: Readings in Social and Political Theory*. New York: New York University Press, 1986.

Maier, Harry O. *Apocalypse Recalled: The Book of Revelation after Christendom*. Minneapolis, Minn.: Fortress Press, 2002.

Marchal, Joseph A. *Hierarchy, Unity, and Imitation: A Feminist Rhetorical Analysis of Power Dynamics in Paul's Letter to the Philippians*. Atlanta: SBL, 2005.

———. "Imperial Intersections and Initial Inquiries: Toward a Feminist, Postcolonial Analysis of Philippians." *JFSR* 22:2 (Fall 2006): 5–32.

Martin, Clarice. "The Haustafeln (Household Codes) in African American Biblical Interpretation: 'Free Slaves' and 'Subordinate Women.'" In *Stony the Road We Trod: African American Biblical Interpretation*, edited by Cain Hope Felder, 206–31. Minneapolis, Minn.: Fortress Press, 1991.

———. "Polishing the Unclouded Mirror: A Womanist Reading of Revelation 18:13." In *From Every People and Nation: A Biblical Theology of Race*, edited by Daniel J. Hay, 82–109. Downers Grove, IL: InterVarsity Press, 2003.

Martin, Dale B. *The Corinthian Body*. New Haven, Conn.: Yale University Press, 1995.

Mason, Carol. *Killing for Life: The Apocalyptic Narrative of Pro-Life Politics*. New York: Cornell University Press, 2002.

Matera, Frank. "New Testament Theology: History, Method and Identity." *Catholic Biblical Quarterly* 67/1 (2005): 1–21.

Matthews, Shelly, and E. Leigh Gibson, eds. *Violence in the New Testament*. NY: T&T Clark, 2005.

Matthews, Shelly, Cynthia Briggs Kittredge, and Melanie Johnson-DeBaufre, eds. *Walk in the Ways of Wisdom: Essays in Honor of Elisabeth Schüssler Fiorenza*. Harrisburg, PA: Trinity International Press, 2003.

Mattingly, D. J., ed. *Dialogues in Roman Imperialism: Power, Discourse and Discrepant Experience in the Roman Empire*. Portsmouth, R.I.: Oxbow, 1997.

McClintock, Anne. *Imperial Leather: Race, Gender and Sexuality in the Colonial Contest*. London and New York: Routledge, 1995.

McClintock, A., Aamir Mufti, and Ella Shohat, eds. *Dangerous Liaisons: Gender, Nation & Postcolonial Perspectives.* Minneapolis: University of Minnesota Press, 1997.

McHoul, Alec, and Wendy Grace. *A Foucault Primer: Discourse, Power and the Subject.* New York: NYU Press, 1997.

McKinley, Judith. *Reframing Her: Biblical Women in Postcolonial Focus.* Sheffield, UK: Sheffield Phoenix, 2004.

McLean, Bradley, ed. *Origins and Method: Toward a New Understanding of Judaism and Christianity.* Sheffield, UK: Sheffield Academic, 1993.

McLeod, John. *Beginning Post-colonialism.* Manchester: Manchester University Press, 2000.

Meeks, Wayne. "The Bible Teaches . . . Through a Glass Darkly." In *Christ is the Question.* Louisville, Ky.: Westminster John Knox, 2006.

Mellor, Ronald. *Thea Roma: The Worship of the Goddess Roma in the Greek World.* Göttingen, Ger.: Vandenhoeck & Ruprecht, 1975.

Miller, Linda Jean. *Divinity, Difference and Democracy: A Critical Materialist Reading of Luce Irigaray's Politics of Incarnation.* Harvard Divinity School, Th.D. thesis, 2006.

Moller Okin, Susan. *Women in Western Political Thought.* Princeton, N.J.: Princeton University Press, 1979.

Moore, Stephen D. *Empire and Apocalypse: Postcolonialism and the New Testament.* Sheffield, UK: Sheffield Phoenix, 2006.

Moore, Stephen D., and Fernando F. Segovia, eds. *Postcolonial Biblical Criticism: Interdisciplinary Intersections.* New York: T. & T. Clark International, 2005.

Mouffé, Chantal, ed. *Dimensions of Radical Democracy.* London: Verso, 1992.

Moxnes, Halvor. *Constructing Early Christian Families: Family as Social Reality and Metaphor.* London: Routledge, 1997.

Narayan, Uma, and Sandra Harding, eds. *Decentering the Center: Philosophy for a Multicultural, Postcolonial, and Feminist World.* Bloomington: Indiana University Press, 2000.

Nelson, John S., Allan Megill, Donald McCloskey, eds. *The Rhetoric of the Human Sciences: Language and Argument in Scholarship and Public Affairs.* Madison: University of Wisconsin Press, 1987.

Newsome, Carol and Sharon Ringe, eds. *The Women's Bible Commentary.* Louisville, Ky.: Westminster John Knox, 1998.

Olbricht, Thomas. "Histories of North American Biblical Scholarship." *Current Research in Biblical Studies* 7 (1999): 237–56.

Olson, Alan M., M. Steiner, and Irina S. Tuuli, eds. *Educating for Democracy: Paideia in an Age of Uncertainty.* Lanham, Md.: Rowman & Littlefield, 2004.

Økland, Jorunn. *Women in Their Place: Paul and the Corinthian Discourse of Gender and Sanctuary Space.* London: T. & T. Clark, 2005.

Palmer, Martin, and Jay Ramsay with Man-Ho Kwok. *Kun Yin: Myth and Prophecies of the Chinese Goddess of Compassion.* San Francisco, Calif.: Thorsons, 1995.

Pauly, Ulrich. *Kannon: Wandel einer Mittlergestalt.* Munich: Iudicium, 2003.

Petersen, Norman R. *Rediscovering Paul: Philemon and the Sociology of Paul's Narrative World.* Philadelphia, Pa.: Fortress Press, 1985.

Pharr, Suzanne. *In the Time of the Right: Reflections on Liberation.* Berkeley, Calif.: Chardon, 2001.

Pieterse, Jan Nederveen, ed. *Christianity and Hegemony.* Oxford: Berg, 1992.

Pieterse, Jan Nederveen, and Bhikhu Parekh, eds. *The Decolonization of Imagination: Culture, Knowledge and Power.* London: Zed, 1995.

Pippin, Tina. "Wisdom and Apocalyptic in the Apocalypse of John: Desiring Sophia." In *In Search of Wisdom*, edited by Leo Purdue, 285–95. Louisville, Ky.: Westminster John Knox, 1993.

————. "The Heroine and the Whore: The Apocalypse of John in Feminist Perspective." In *From Every People and Nation: The Book of Revelation in Intercultural Perspective*, edited by David Rhoads. Minneapolis, Minn.: Fortress Press, 2005.

Popkes, Wiard and Ralph Brucker, eds. *Ein Gott und ein Herr. Zum Kontext des Monotheismus im Neuen Testament.* Neukirchen-Vluyn, Ger.: Neukirchener Verlag, 2004.

Porter, Stanley E., ed. *Paul and His Opponents.* Boston: Brill, 2005.

Price, S. R. F. *Rituals and Power: the Roman Imperial Cult in Asia Minor.* Cambridge: Cambridge University Press, 1984.

Prior, Michael. *The Bible and Colonialism: A Moral Critique.* Sheffield, UK: Sheffield Academic, 1997.

Quayson, Ato. *Postcolonialism: Theory, Practice or Process?* Oxford: Polity in Association with Blackwell, 2000.

Radford Ruether, Rosemary, ed. *Feminist Theologies: Legacy and Prospect.* Minneapolis, Minn.: Fortress Press, 2007.

Radl, Shirley Rogers. *The Invisible Woman: Target of the Religious New Right.* New York: Dell, 1981.

Ramsay, W. M. *The Letters to the Seven Churches.* First edition 1904. Updated edition by Mark W. Wilson. Peabody, Mass.: Hendrickson, 2001.

Reck, Reinhold. *Kommunikation und Gemeindeaufbau. Eine Studie zur Entstehung, Leben und Wachstum paulinischer Gemeinden in den Konmmunikationsstrukturen der Antike.* Stuttgart: Katholisches Bibelwerk, 1991.

Ring, Jennifer. *The Political Consequences of Thinking: Gender and Judaism in the Work of Hannah Arendt.* New York: NYU Press, 1997.

Rivera, Mayra. "God at the Crossroads: A Postcolonial Reading of Sophia." In *Postcolonial Theologies: Divinity and Empire*, edited by Catherine Keller, Michael Nausner, and Mayra Rivera. St. Louis, Mo.: Chalice, 2004.

Roncace, Mark, and Patrick Gray, eds. *Teaching the Bible: Practical Strategies for Classroom Instruction*. Atlanta: SBL, 2005.

Rossing, Barbara. *The Choice Between Two Cities: Whore, Bride, and Empire in the Apocalypse*. Harrisburg, Pa.: Trinity International, 1999.

———. *The Rapture Exposed: The Message of Hope in the Book of Revelation*. Boulder, Colo.: Westview, 2004.

Roy, Arundhati. *An Ordinary Person's Guide to Empire*. Cambridge: South End, 2004.

Royalty, Robert M., Jr. "The Rhetoric of Revelation." *SBL 1997 Seminar Papers*. Atlanta, Ga.: Scholars, 1997.

Runions, Erin. "Biblical Promise and Threat in U.S. Imperialist Rhetoric, Before and After 9/11." In *Interventions: Activists and Academics Respond to Violence*, edited by Elizabeth A. Castelli and Janet R. Jacobsen. New York: Palgrave, 2004.

Said, Edward. *Culture and Imperialism*. London: Chatto & Windus, 1993.

———. *Orientalism*. Hammondsworth: Penguin, 1978.

———. *The World, The Text, The Critic*. London: Vintage, 1993.

Saller, Richard. *Patriarchy, Property, and Death in the Roman Family*. Cambridge: Cambridge University Press, 1994.

Sandoval, Chela. *Methodology of the Oppressed*. Minneapolis: University of Minnesota Press, 2000.

Schaberg, Jane, Alice Bach, and Esther Fuchs, eds. *On the Cutting Edge: the Study of Women in Biblical Worlds: Essays in Honor of Elisabeth Schüssler Fiorenza*. New York: Continuum, 2004.

Schroer, Silvia, and Sophia Bietenhard, eds. *Feminist Interpretation of the Bible and the Hermeneutics of Liberation*. Sheffield, UK: Sheffield Academic, 2003.

Schüssler Fiorenza, Elisabeth. *In Memory of Her: A Feminist Theological Reconstruction of Christian Origins*. Originally published 1983. Tenth Anniversary Edition. New York: Crossroad, 1994.

———. *But She Said: Feminist Practices of Biblical Interpretation*. Boston, Mass.: Beacon, 1992.

———. *Discipleship of Equals: A Critical Feminist Ekklesia-logy of Liberation*. New York: Crossroad, 1993.

———, ed. *Searching the Scriptures*. 2 vols. New York: Crossroad, 1993 and 1994.

———. *Jesus, Miriam's Child, Sophia's Prophet: Critical Issues in Feminist Christology*. New York: Continuum, 1994.

———. *The Book of Revelation: Justice and Judgment*. Second edition with a new epilogue. Minneapolis, Minn.: Fortress Press, 1998.

———. *Rhetoric and Ethic: The Politics of Biblical Studies*. Minneapolis, Minn.: Fortress Press, 1999.

———. *Jesus and the Politics of Interpretation*. New York: Continuum, 2000.

———. *Wisdom Ways: Introducing Feminist Biblical Interpretation*. Maryknoll, N.Y.: Orbis, 2001.

————— et al., "Pedagogy and Practice: Using Wisdom Ways in the Classroom." *Teaching Theology and Religion* 6 (2003): 208–210, 225–226.

—————. "Rethinking the Educational Practices of Biblical Doctoral Studies." *Teaching Theology and Religion* 6 (April 2003): 65–75.

—————. *Grenzen überschreiten. Der theoretische Anspruch feministischer Theologie. Ausgewählte Aufsätze*. Munich: LIT Verlag, 2003.

—————. "The Power of the Word: Charting Critical Global Feminist Biblical Studies." In *Feminist New Testament Studies: Global and Future Perspectives*, edited by Kathleen O'Brien Wicker, Althea Spencer Miller, and Musa W. Dube. New York: Palgrave MacMillan, 2005.

—————. "The First Letter of Peter." In *A Postcolonial Commentary of the New Testament Writings*, edited by Fernando F. Segovia and R. S. Sugirtharajah. London and New York: T. & T. Clark International, 2007.

Schwartz, Regina. *The Curse of Cain: the Violent Legacy of Monotheism*. Chicago, Ill.: University of Chicago Press, 1997.

Segovia, Fernando F. *Decolonizing Biblical Studies: A View from the Margins*. Maryknoll, N.Y.: Orbis Press, 2000.

—————, ed. *Toward a New Heaven and a New Earth: Essays in Honor of Elisabeth Schüssler Fiorenza*. Maryknoll, N.Y.: Orbis, 2003.

Segovia, Fernando F. and Mary Ann Tolbert, eds. *Teaching the Bible: The Discourses and Politics of Biblical Pedagogy*. Maryknoll, N.Y.: Orbis, 1998.

Smith, Andrea. *Conquest: Sexual Violence and American Indian Genocide*. Cambridge: South End Press, 2005.

—————. *Native Americans and the Christian Right: The Gendered Politics of Unlikely Alliances*. Duke University Press, forthcoming 2008.

Smith, Anne Marie. *Laclau and Mouffe: The Radical Democratic Imaginary*. New York: Routledge, 1998.

Stendahl, Krister. "Ancient Scripture in the Modern World." In *Scripture in the Jewish and Christian Traditions: Antiquity, Interpretation, Relevance*, edited by Frederick Greenspahn, 201–14. Nashville, Tenn.: Abingdon, 1982.

Stichele, Caroline Vander, and Todd Penner. *Her Master's Tools? Feminist and Postcolonial Engagements of Historical-Critical Discourse*. Atlanta, Ga.: Society of Biblical Literature, 2005.

Sugirtharajah, R. S. *Asian Biblical Hermeneutics and Postcolonialism, Bible and Liberation*. Maryknoll, N.Y.: Orbis, 1998.

—————. *Postcolonial Criticism and Biblical Interpretation*. Oxford: Oxford University Press, 2002.

—————. *Voices from the Margin: Interpreting the Bible in the Third World*. Revised and Expanded Edition. Maryknoll, N.Y.: Orbis, 2006.

————, ed. *The Postcolonial Bible*. Sheffield, UK: Sheffield Academic, 1998.

————, ed. *The Postcolonial Biblical Reader*. Oxford: Blackwell, 2006.

Talpade Mohanti, Chandra. *Feminism Without Borders: Decolonizing Theory, Practicing Solidarity*. Durham: Duke University Press, 2003.

Talpade Mohanti, Chandra, Ann Russo, and Lourdes Torres, eds., *Third World Women and the Politics of Feminism*. Bloomington: Indiana University Press, 1991.

Tamez, Elsa. *Struggles for Power in Early Christianity*. Maryknoll: Orbis 2007.

Taniguchi, Yuko. *To Lead Quiet and Peaceable Lives: A Rhetorical Analysis of the First Letter of Timothy*. Th.D. dissertation. Harvard University, 2002.

Tannehill, Robert C. "Paul as Liberator and Oppressor: How Should We Evaluate Diverse Views of First Corinthians?" In *The Meaning We Choose: Hermeneutical Ethics, Indeterminacy and the Conflict of Interpretations*, Charles H. Cosgrove. London: T. & T. Clark International, 2004.

Taubes, Jacob, ed. *Religionstheorie und politische Theologie. Vol 3: Theokratie*. Paderborn, Ger.: Ferdinand Schöningh, 1987.

Theissen, Gerd. *The Bible and Contemporary Culture*. Minneapolis, Minn.: Fortress Press, 2007.

Tibi, Bassam. *The Challenge of Fundamentalism: Political Islam and the New World Disorder*. Berkeley: University of California Press, 1998.

Treblico, Paul. *Jewish Communtiies in Asia Minor*. Cambridge: Cambridge University Press, 1991.

Veyne, Paul. *The Roman Empire*. Cambridge, Mass.: Harvard University Press, 1987.

Wacker, Marie-Theres. *Von Göttinnen, Göttern und dem einzigen Gott. Studien zum biblischen Monotheismus aus feministisch-theologischer Sicht*. Munich: LIT Verlag, 2004.

Wald, Kenneth D. and Allison Calhoun-Brown. *Religion and Politics in the United States*. Lanham, Md.: Rowman and Littlefield, 2007.

Weems, Renita. *Battered Love: Marriage, Sex and Violence in the Hebrew Prophets*. Minneapolis, Minn.: Fortress Press, 1995.

Welch, Sharon D. *After Empire: The Art and Ethos of Enduring Peace*. Minneapolis, Minn.: Fortress Press, 2004.

Wengst, Klaus. *Pax Romana and the Peace of Jesus Christ*. Philadelphia, Pa.: Fortress Press, 1987.

West, Cornel. *Democracy Matters*. New York: Penguin, 2004.

Wicker, Kathleen O'Brien, Althea Spencer Miller, Musa W. Dube, eds. *Feminist New Testament Studies: Global and Future Perspectives*. New York: Palgrave, 2005.

Wiley, Tatha. *Paul and the Gentile Wo/men: Reframing Galatians*. New York: Continuum, 2005.

Wimbush, Vincent, ed. *African Americans and the Bible: Sacred Texts and Social Textures*. New York: Continuum, 2000.

————, ed. *The Bible and the American Myth: A Symposium on the Bible and Constructions of Meaning*. Macon. Ga.: Mercer University Press, 1999.

Clark Wire, Antoinette. *The Corinthian Women Prophets: A Reconstruction through Paul's Rhetoric.* Minneapolis, Minn.: Fortress Press, 1990.

Wischmeyer, Oda, et al. "Das Selbstverständnis der neutestamentlichen Wissenschaft in Deutschland. Bestandaufnahme. Kritik, Perpsektives. Ein Bericht auf der Grundlage eines neutestamentlichen Oberseminars." *Zeitschrift für Neues Testament* 5 (2002): 13–36.

Witte, John, Jr., ed. *Christianity and Democracy in Global Context.* Boulder, Colo.: Westview, 1993.

Wolin, Sheldon S. "Transgression, Equality and Voice." In *Demokratia: A Conversation on Democracies, Ancient and Modern*, edited by Josiah Ober and Charles Hedrick, 63–90. Princeton, N.J.: Princeton University Press, 1996.

Yamaguchi, Satoko. "The Invention of Traditions: The Case of Shintoism." *In God's Image* 18 (1998): 40–46.

Young, Robert. *Postcolonialism: An Historical Introduction.* Oxford: Blackwell, 2001.

CPSIA information can be obtained at www.ICGtesting.com
Printed in the USA
BVOW04s1940080415

395355BV00003B/13/P